The Prisoners' World

Issues in Crime & Justice

Series Editor
Gregg Barak, Eastern Michigan University

As we embark upon the twentieth-first century, the meanings of crime continue to evolve and our approaches to justice are in flux. The contributions to this series focus their attention on crime and justice as well as on crime control and prevention in the context of a dynamically changing legal order. Across the series, there are books that consider the full range of crime and criminality and that engage a diverse set of topics related to the formal and informal workings of the administration of criminal justice. In an age of globalization, crime and criminality are no longer confined, if they ever were, to the boundaries of single nation-states. As a consequence, while many books in the series will address crime and justice in the United States, the scope of these books will accommodate a global perspective and they will consider such eminently global issues such as slavery, terrorism, or punishment. Books in the series are written to be used as supplements in standard undergraduate and graduate courses in criminology and criminal justice and related courses in sociology. Some of the standard courses in these areas include: introduction to criminal justice, introduction to law enforcement, introduction to corrections, juvenile justice, crime and delinquency, criminal law, white collar, corporate, and organized crime.

TITLES IN SERIES:

Effigy, By Allison Cotton

Perverts and Predators, By Laura J. Zilney and Lisa A. Zilney

The Prisoners' World, By William Tregea and Marjorie Larmour

The Prisoners' World

Portraits of Convicts Caught in the Incarceration Binge

William Tregea and Marjorie Larmour

LEXINGTON BOOKS

A division of
ROWMAN & LITTLEFIELD PUBLISHERS, INC.
Lanham • Boulder • New York • Toronto • Plymouth, UK

LEXINGTON BOOKS

A division of Rowman & Littlefield Publishers, Inc.
A wholly owned subsidiary of The Rowman & Littlefield Publishing Group, Inc.
4501 Forbes Boulevard, Suite 200
Lanham, MD 20706

Estover Road
Plymouth PL6 7PY
United Kingdom

British Library Cataloguing in Publication Information Available

Library of Congress Cataloging-in-Publication Data
Tregea, William, 1944–
  The prisoners' world : portraits of convicts caught in the incarceration binge /
William Tregea and Marjorie Larmour.
    p. cm. — (Issues in crime & justice)
  Includes bibliographical references and index.
  ISBN 978-0-7391-2915-9 (cloth : alk. paper) — ISBN 978-0-7391-2916-6 (pbk. :
alk. paper) — ISBN 978-0-7391-3255-5 (electronic)
  1. Prisoners—California—Social conditions. 2. Prisoners—California—
Biography. 3. Prisoners—Michigan—Social conditions. 4. Prisoners—
Michigan—Biography. I. Larmour, Marjorie, 1920– II. Title.
  HV9475.C2T74 2009
  365'.609774—dc22   2008047176

Printed in the United States of America

♾ ™ The paper used in this publication meets the minimum requirements of
American National Standard for Information Sciences—Permanence of Paper
for Printed Library Materials, ANSI/NISO Z39.48-1992.

Contents

Preface

The United States' prison and jail system, the world's largest, housed 2.2 million prisoners in 2008 and is still growing. Who are these people in prison? This book presents eighty short prisoner essays on "the prisoners' world": their life before prison, their experiences upon coming to prison, their experience within "the system" of the expanding prison world, and their view of the American inner city where many of them came from.

Why do we have the world's largest, and still expanding, prison system, even though crime rates have been falling since 1991 (Zimring 2007)?

We live in an increasingly risk-conscious society. Until recently we have seldom questioned the overuse of confinement characteristic of the last twenty-five years. The causes for the massive expansion of this prison system seem distant from us, buried in the details of politics and policies. And, after all, isn't it right to "lock them up and throw away the key?"

But the proximate answer for the massive prison growth lies in the harsh drug laws established in 1986 during a media-driven moral panic over drug-related crime. Often reflecting punitive values and linked-up with political expediency, since 1986 we've had a rush to more laws, more crackdowns, and more convictions at the "front end," along with excessively long sentences with fewer paroles. The prison system has become a "growth machine" characterized by an "incarceration binge" subculture. And, there has also been a worrisome "revolving door" of re-admission to prison off the "back-end" from a high rate of failure on parole. This book presents "the prisoners' world" amidst the "incarceration binge culture."

THE AUTHORS

William Tregea, who holds a Ph.D. from Michigan State University, is director of the bachelor of criminal justice program at Adrian College, Michigan, and has taught criminology and sociology for over thirty-four years. He has taught many hundreds of prisoners over twenty-five years in prison college programs and volunteer classes in eleven prisons in Michigan and California. He founded the *Michigan STEPP Consortium* (Skills Training and Education for Prisoners and Prevention), and is a founding member and board member of the Michigan *Citizens Alliance on Prisons and Public Spending* (www.capps-mi.org).

Marjorie Larmour (died August 2007) held a masters degree (M.A.) in journalism and a B.A. in psychology, both from the University of California, Berkeley, and had been a journalist, writer and editor for many years. She had completed sixty credits of doctoral work in Adult Education and Sociology at Michigan State University. For twenty years she taught college in prisons in Michigan. Minimum, medium, maximum prisons, twelve of them, including two of the oldest prisons in the state—Jackson State Prison (maximum) (SPSM), and also Michigan Reformatory (MR) for prisoners under twenty-five years of age, most from Detroit's tough inner city. During this time she wrote stories about her prison experiences.

WHY AND HOW THIS BOOK CAME ABOUT

Over a twenty-five year period of prison college teaching starting in 1981, teaching during the Incarceration Binge (1986–2008 to the present), both teachers have seen the nation's massive prison growth. Michigan's prison system swelled from eight prisons and 14,000 prisoners in 1983, to forty-two prisons and six camps with 52,000 prisoners in 2008. The same spectacular growth occurred nationwide.

Why have the nation's prisons grown so much? As mentioned, the short answer is an increase since 1986 in the criminal penalties for drug-defined and drug-related crime (see Figure 2.2). The result: longer sentences, fewer paroles, more parole violations, creating an "incarceration binge" swelling U.S. prisoner population up to a world-record 2 million prisoners between 1986 and 2001 (Austin & Irwin 1997/2001).

As teachers, our experience of this war-on-drugs prison buildup was an *in-the-classroom experience*. We walked into prisons (with the same type of Prison IDs as used by correctional officers) and into prison classrooms several times a week, each week, for over twenty years. Our many hours interacting with, and listening to, prisoners give us some unusual access to prisoners' views. We saw the impact of the "war on drugs" from the changing prisoner/student-body. The prisoner/students from 1981 to 1986 were still the more "traditional" criminals, whereas from 1986 the sudden influx of prisoners were more drug-related, younger, more directly off-the-streets of Detroit's inner city, marking the beginning increase in incarceration resulting from the new 1986 drug laws into the 1990s; there were many more African-American prisoners, with some whites from suburbia and rural towns—pretty much all in for drugs. As the old prison cons were saying, "These new young convicts are not real prisoners, they're just druggies."

Students majoring in criminal justice today know little of the history of this drug-law prison build-up.

Like any retired teacher might do, Larmour had collected favorite prisoner/student essays—in a big box—to remember the years of prison teaching. Tregea meanwhile, studying the reentry issue, was collecting prisoner opinions at Michigan's Gus Harrison prison (2003–2008) and from San Quentin Prison, California (2004).

This book is the result of the collaboration of the two authors.

THE PRISONERS

The prison populations from which permission to publish essays were obtained included two separate categories of prisoners.

One category of prisoner writing focused on the experiential world of prisoners—their lives in prison, their former lives, their life stories and ideas about criminology theories, their hobbies, poetry, diaries, dreams and nightmares. These prisoner essays are culled from Larmour's big box of teaching memories. Faces of prisoner writers, all in prison college classes, march back in time over a twenty-year period from the recent college classes that ended in 2000, to classes in the early 1980s. Many prisoner/students have been released, paroled and left the system. Some are assigned to a parole officer. Some are still in prison with outdates in the near or distant future. For a few, the outdate will never come; they will die in prison.

Another category of prisoners was sampled more recently: Six volunteer classes offered 2003 to 2008, included three "advanced skills reentry workshops" classes, and three "social science and personal writing" classes, given by Tregea as a volunteer teacher at Gus Harrison prison (1,500 population, level two and four) near the City of Adrian, Michigan. The workshops explored the article "Perpetual Incarceration

Machine: Overcoming Obstacles to Reentry," by "Convict Criminology" authors (Richards & Jones 1996). The prisoners also studied reentry recommendations from Joan Petersilia's (2003) book, *When Prisoners Come Home,* combined with class discussion.

The workshops had guest speakers on jobs and skill training and trade school. The workshops also had information on community college facilities and programs available to prisoners and Pell grant (FAFSA) application procedural information. The "social science and personal writing" classes included textbook assignments "like a 1-credit college course." In both workshops and classes, prisoners wrote short essays on home, family, drugs, high school, prison workday, cells, daily work routine, personal growth, free time, contraband and guns.

WHAT THE BOOK COVERS

This book presents portraits of convicts experiencing the incarceration binge through an array of thoughts, impressions, reflections and opinions from state prisoners in Michigan who showed up in the described prison college classes, reentry workshops, and volunteer classes over a twenty-seven-year period from 1981 to 2008. The book presents the typical individual passage through prison as a journey commonly experienced by most state prisoners. We hope the prisoner voices we present in the eighty prisoner essays will be meaningful to the reader.

Chronologically, such a typical passage is presented as life before prison, pathways to prison, and entering prison and orientation, daily routines and work life in prison during incarceration, personal lives or "free time" in prison, personal reflections on past life such as in the inner city and criticisms of the prison system. The collective portrait of this experiential journal through "the system" of the prison world is often captured in poignant individual snapshots from specific, and memorable, prisoner essays. The reader can learn and recall what the prisoner experience is like by *listening* to the prisoner voices.

Part I of *The Prisoners' World* explores alternative views on why the United States has witnessed a massive growth in the prison system. Part II describes typical prisoner life before prison (homes, family) and introduces pathways to prison (learning drugs, dropping out of school). Part III describes how the formal criminal justice system works and adult experiences of "getting into the system," with a description of prison reception and guidance centers, presenting prisoner essays about coming to prison, their first days in prison and experiencing orientation, thoughts on their cell, their prison work, their daily routine. Part IV describes the prison self (free time, personal growth and self-concept and prison issues such as homosexuality, drugs and contraband). Part V explores the inner city background of many Michigan prisoners with a focus on the expanding African American prison world, it includes both young and older black prisoner's critique of their inner city backgrounds and experiences with cocaine, crack and guns. Part VI presents the prisoner as citizen, with their criticisms and analyses of why the prison system grows. This section also offers the coauthors' reflections on the future of the incarceration binge: hope on the future of the inner city, outlines the context of state budget crises, legislative ideas for safely capping prison growth and shifting resources to prevention, a brief review of the progress being made on better prisoner reentry programs and, finally, reflections on whether—and when—the incarceration binge might end.

Many prisoners, over 80 percent of whom are high school dropouts, gradually experience a reversal of opinion on education, going from "hating school," right-off-the-street at the entry to prison, to actively seeking a college degree and job preparations. They look back on their "crappy" days in a high school, which they almost universally hated, and how time spent reflecting on their lives in a prison cell changed the attitude of many. They now want to pursue more education in prison by completing a GED (high school equivalency). And some—when prison college was available—embarked on and often completed a two-year college degree which gave them increased self-assurance, more sense of responsibility and, especially, a halfway decent shot at a job on the outside. As prison college teachers from 1981 to 2000 we were a part of this personal awakening.

We hope that from behind the veil of prison bureaucracy our prisoner voices can help readers grapple with and understand that those among us who have "crossed the line" are human beings. These "prisoner voices" help educate, not only about criminology theories, but also about the need for better, more just and more sensible criminal justice system policies.

HOW READERS CAN USE THIS BOOK

What do contemporary students know about the U.S. prison system? *The Prisoners' World* takes the reader from the streets, into the prison world. Chapter after chapter of prisoner essays detail prison life. The book presents prison realities such as overcrowding. Prisoner essays reveal their life before prison, and their life as a prisoner. The expanding prison world of the African American, in particular, is explored through student essays and prison teacher accounts.

This book—through the witness of *prisoner essays*—opens the door to this prison world. Why should we go there? For many decades, prior to the incarceration binge, American prisons were hidden bureaucratic posts in rural towns and valleys, far removed from everyday U.S. life. Then, especially since the 1986 anti-drug laws, convicts became politicized. A public, seemingly fed-up with crime and druggies, led to a politician's vote-getting strategy of "politics of tough."

The public responded, in turn, to a demonizing of criminals by politicians and the media became more fearful. It's a "chicken and the egg" question: what comes first? An increasing punitiveness, driven by the public's pragmatic desire to punish crime (Useem & Piehl 2008), or a politician's strategy or media hype (Beckett & Sasson 2000; Pratt, et al. 2005)? Either way, the politicians have seemed ready to get votes by "fanning the embers of fear and offering incarceration solutions" (Tonry 1999).

Crime has sold newspapers and television shows, padlocks and security systems. Politicians, in a series of legislation that could be seen as pandering to public fear, established sentencing guideline laws that took away decisions by judges and created, instead, legislation such as "mandatory minimums," and "three strikes" laws, that have led to much longer time behind bars. Then again, prosecutors and judges, who are often elected in U.S. jurisdictions, can find themselves pandering to public fears and become painted into a corner of "tough on crime" (Tonry 2007).

For politicians—cynical and sincere, alike—a handy politicized "war" metaphor emerged. A shift occurred. The U.S. moved away from a rehabilitative approach and attempting to solve underlying problems characteristic of the 1960s. An underfunded "war on poverty" in the mid-1960s (Berger 1985) gave way to a symbolic use of politics by the 1970s and 1980s. We moved toward a "war on crime" and a "war on drugs," with a punitive emphasis on incarceration (Berger 1985).

"Crime" had developed a particular salience for the American public (Zimring 2006). In our political system, being "tough" and not "soft" on crime became a wedge issue and got votes and re-election (Tonry 1999). In this shift of perspective, prisoners were no longer expected to be rehabilitated, but became "dangerous categories" of people (Feely & Simon 1992). As demonized "person categories" the solution for the convicted is to "lock them up and throw away the key." The U.S. prison system more than *quadrupled* during the last twenty-five years up to 2.2 million incarcerated by 2008. *Rates* of incarceration per 100,000 population have skyrocketed in the United States from just over 100 in 1980 to nearly 500 by 2007 (Zimring 2007; Useem & Piehl 2008).

Readers of this book can get a grasp of the prisoners' experiential world during this incarceration boom period.

A NEW ERA BEYOND THE INCARCERATION BINGE?

Are prisons a form of "hyperincarceration" used to manage jobless ghetto residents living in America's throwaway inner cities, or "hyperghettos?" Is the story here that, instead of essential social justice, we have been "looking the other way," and should be asking ourselves: "Have we no sense of decency?" (Tonry 2007:28). But now—in our states plagued by budget deficits and recession—we have pragmatic concerns: it is necessary to address our bloated prison bureaucracies because we need the money tied up in them for other priorities, like public education. Also, how do we shift precious state budget resources to invest now in better evidence-based crime prevention (Farrington & Welsh 2006)?

We cannot possibly create longer sentencing and we cannot possibly keep building ever more prisons. State budget problems in several states require that we examine how to downsize our prisons (Tregea 2002). By "locking them up and throwing away the key" we have not thought about what to do afterward, for instance, how to absorb the masses of convicts transitioning back to society. As the prison wardens note: "The doors to the prison swing both ways."

But in all of these matters, the voice of the prisoner is never heard. Who is the prisoner? And what does he or she think? How do American university and college students learn about the U.S. prison world? Most students learn through textbooks and readers. Seldom, however, are ordinary prisoner voices heard.

Why should we—faculty, students, and the taxpaying public—be concerned with what prisoners think?

Faculty members need to know if their research and policy analyses are being applied. The taxpayer, aware of budget crises and spending restrictions, asks if we can safely cut corrections budgets so there is more state money for other priorities—like higher education for their children. The criminal justice student might well wonder what a prison is really like. What do prisoners think?

This book describes all this and presents the prisoner's own thoughts and words, putting a human face on prisoners.

Will such unprecedented high rates of incarceration ever come back down again? Today's student is beginning to enter a different era of prison issues and political realities. Change is in the wind. For several years people have become increasingly interested in crime prevention. Also, persistent state budget crises have developed to plague several state Governors and legislators. A new *pragmatic* concern for the cost of overuse of prison confinement, and a search for ways to cut costs, has emerged (Jacobsen 2005). In a related trend, more emphasis is beginning to be put on enhancing the success of prisoners as they reenter society. Can we safely downsize our prisons? Can we improve success on parole and reduce return to prison once released? Can we enhance crime prevention in our communities? A better understanding of prisoners can help in answers to all of these questions.

The Prisoners' World leads the reader into the realities of prison. So, why should the reader enter this prison world? Because prisoners can describe many parts of the criminal justice system for us—cops, courts, corrections; life on the streets; family backgrounds; prison life—and help us in our understanding as a professional considering going into criminal justice work. Today's students want "the real thing." And the prisoners in *The Prisoners' World* are the real thing, *and* they were also prisoner/ students, connecting you—the main campus student—to the prison campus student.

To understand the policy world of the prison world, main campus students need to learn the pragmatic world of state budget crises—through what policies can we safely downsize prisons? Coauthor Bill Tregea, a founding member and board member of the Michigan *Citizen Alliance on Prisons and Public Safety* (www.capps-mi.org), has been associated with practical efforts to safely downsize Michigan prisons. After nine years of research by consultants, and the help of professional lobbyists forming draft legislation, CAPPS, since its founding in 1998, had, by 2007—in the context of a severe budget crisis—some influence on Michigan's Governor Jennifer Granholm, the Michigan Department of Corrections (MDOC) under the leadership of MDOC Director, Pat Caruso, and the Michigan Legislature, who have all "seen the handwriting on the wall" to become more and more interested in these policy ideas to downsize prisons, which are presented more fully in the final chapter of this book.

The United States can no longer afford to ignore the prisoner voice. Who are these prisoners? Many have served their minimum sentence and need to be released. But we are conditioned to worry about public safety, to be fearful of these "animals." Yet, as John Irwin and may other scholars of the prison world remind us, almost half of today's criminals are nonviolent, (no crimes against persons, no gun or other violence), most charged with drug-defined or drug-related crimes. Over 600,000 prisoners reenter society each year, and in Michigan 11,000 prisoners reenter each year. Convict (and ex-convict) voices can contribute to our understanding about problems and issues of sentencing, prison programming, parole issues and success in reentry.

Where do they come from? Prisoner voices can alert us to the deviant world experiences they've lived through. For example, studies show that over 80 percent of state prisoners have a history of child abuse and neglect. Criminogenic "variables" such as family, community characteristics, anonymity (lack of home ownership, poverty) and peers—and the criminal street culture of the impoverished jobless ghetto—show up in these prisoners' stories.

The prisoners' voice, "looking backward" from the prison, helps us understand how these family- and community-level variables work to produce the kind of strain that leads toward criminality (Merton 1938; Agnew 1999). Prisoner voices help us to connect criminology to people's lives, and to understand prevention and corrections work with early childhood development, families, peers, neighborhoods and schools and in our communities.

We are at a turning point. We need the prisoners' voices. We need their voice to help understand how to work at better crime prevention (Farrington & Welsh 2006; Agnew 1999; Newbold 2003; Rosenbaum & Lurigo 1998; Berger 1985), and to downsize prisons, improve success on parole, and close down the revolving door (Jacobson 2005; Petersilia 2003; Richards & Jones 1996).

This is, above all, a fun book where the reader meets prisoner/students who—though not boy scouts and, for some, recovering from being messed up (as well as messing others over)—are, in their humanity, very much like ourselves.

We need more sensible sentencing, parole, and reentry policies (Austin and Irwin 2001; Tonry 1995; CAPPS 2008). Truly, to be a criminal justice practitioner or criminologist is to be a social reformer. In becoming aware of issues and making efforts to reform, however, people often come to the realization that things are the way they are because of certain power arrangements. How did the "power world" in our society contribute to making the massive "prison world" we have arrived at? We will address this question in chapter 1, "Historical Periods of Prisoners' Worlds," chapter 2, "Premises of the Incarceration Binge Culture," and chapter 3, "Prison Binge Growth Theory."

Acknowledgments

B ooks are the outcome of many hours of work from authors and from a network of individuals who have contributed to the writing process. William Tregea would like to acknowledge now deceased coauthor Marjorie Larmour for her inspiration in designing this book and for her wonderful ideas in the collaborative writing process. He acknowledges the many hours that Michigan prisoner/students put into studying and preparing, and in writing, their essays, including prisoner/students at: Jackson Prison (central complex, SHU); Egeler Facility; Cotton Facility, Trusty-SPSM/Parnall; Michigan Reformatory (MR); MR-Dorm; Riverside Correctional Facility; Ionia Temporary Facility (ITF); Carson City Correctional Facility; Scott Correctional Facility (for women); and Gus Harrison Correctional Facility.

Bill Tregea extends gratitude to his criminal justice classes at Adrian College for reviewing chapters in, and assessing the usefulness of, this book. Thanks to Adrian College students Brian Boyer and Erin Bulgrien for typing up the many original handwritten prisoner essays.

Special thanks to Michael McGandy of Rowman & Littlefield and Gregg Barak of Eastern Michigan University, both of whom have helped substantially with revising and editing suggestions, and to acquisition editors and support help at Rowman & Littlefield/Lexington Books. Thanks also to Michael Braswell and Leanne Anderson for publishing and revision ideas.

Bill Tregea wants to thank Stephen Richards and Ian Jeffrey Ross, editors of *Convict Criminology* (Wadsworth 2003), for their help in the writing and editing of his chapter 15, "Twenty Years Teaching Prison College," in that book; and thanks to Stephen Richards for his encouragement to continue to give voice to prisoners' views. Appreciation is given to John Irwin for his leadership in convict criminology.

For the many directors of prison college programs over the last twenty-five years who have encouraged us to become good prison teachers, we give our appreciation, including Paul Wreford, former director of the Jackson Community College Jackson "North Campus" Prison community college degree program, and Danny Herman, former director of the Montcalm Community College "College Opportunity Prison Education" (COPE) program at Ionia, Michigan.

Special thanks to Steve Steurer, director, International Correctional Education Association (CEA), for his assistance and consulting help in the coauthors' efforts to reinstate prison college programming in Michigan. Also, special appreciation to Barbara Levine for her support of prison educational programs as part of her leadership of Michigan's Citizen Alliance on Prisons and Public Spending (www.capps-mi.org), an organization that has forged many policy ideas and legislation (such as parole guidelines) to downsize Michigan's prisons.

The prisoner voices in this book will not be wasted if the public can move away from the expanding prison world and overuse of confinement (especially for drug crimes) that makes prisons the revolving door for the young men of our throw-away cities. Overuse of warehouse incarceration locks up our tax dollars as social resources (Jacobsen 2005), and neglects the development of social skills and human capital of prisoners (Useem & Piehl 2008). Let's hope that prisoner voices can help in the effort to move toward a set of more sensible laws, prison programming, and parole policies—and a new harm reduction and community-justice approach for Americans to address the problems of our cities.

I

—⚏—

EMERGENCE OF THE PRISONERS' WORLD

INTRODUCTION

One of the easiest things to do is to take the context of your life for granted: your current and most recent past historical context can be unquestioned as "the way it is." Yet, when you look more broadly at social change over many decades, even centuries, you see drastically different historical periods. Think about your grandparents and all the social changes they lived through in their lifetime. People living through one historical period in the past may have very different experiential worlds than those living in the present. And, the present historical period can be transformed into a different social, political and cultural situation in the future (Mannheim 1938). This is the lesson of studying history and social change.

In chapter 1, "Historical Periods of Prisoners' Worlds," five distinct periods in American social history are reviewed: the period of debtor's prisons, the slavery era and runaway slave law, the Prohibition of alcohol era, the transition from a nation of tobacco smokers to a non-smoking culture and the recent "war on drugs" incarceration binge era.

We review how different historical eras have the same commonly agreed-upon behavior as criminal—murder, rape, assault, types of theft—but also how some behaviors are crimes in one historical era but not crimes in another historical era. For example, in past eras, debtor prisoners, runaway slaves and alcohol production and distribution were all crimes. We highlight how the approach to street drugs changed, from the rehabilitative ideal to putting many people from inner cities in prison in a "war" on drugs approach. We focus on how each of these historical

1

eras was related to the power world: who made laws and how laws were made. We explain how the power world makes the prison world.

Reflecting on the historical period of the "getting tough on crime" contemporary incarceration explosion as it has played out in Michigan, the highly respected *Citizens Research Council of Michigan* noted on June 12, 2008:

> With an incarceration rate of 489 persons per 100,000 residents, Michigan far exceeds the average incarceration rates for the surrounding Great Lakes states (338 per 100,000) and the U.S. as a whole (401 per 100,000).
>
> The single most important contributing factor to the growth of Michigan's incarceration rate has been average prisoner length of stay, which lengthened from 28.4 months in prison in 1981 to 43.5 months by 2005.
>
> Average length of stay, in turn, grew as a result of various public policy changes aimed at "getting tough on crime" including mandatory sentences, lower rates of parole and probation, and harsher sentences. These policy changes were made at many different times, by many different people and generally with little or no reference to their likely fiscal consequences.
>
> Because of the states' high incarceration rate, Michigan's spending on Corrections has grown to the point that Corrections is now:
>
> - The largest program operated directly by Michigan State Government.
> - The employer of ¹/₃ of the state government's classified work force.
> - Responsible for $2 billion in annual expenditures or roughly 20 percent of the General Fund budget.
> - Account for 5.2 percent of total Michigan state expenditures compared to a national average spending on Corrections of 3.4 percent of total stated expenditures.
> - Likely to grow to $2.6 billion/year or more by 2012.
>
> This seemingly uncontrollable growth in Michigan's Corrections spending has been a major contributor to Michigan's structural deficit which is discussed at length in CRC's recent publication, "Michigan's Fiscal Future." (CRC Report No. 349, June 2008; CRC 2008)

Instead of a long-sentence, low probation and parole rate, and "warrior" approach to drugs and drug-related crime, we recommend partial decriminalization, treatment-based sentencing, shorter sentences, prison-based drug treatment, and parole guidelines to result in a presumption of parole at the minimum sentence. We recommend the "harm reduction" approach, as practiced by the British government, in the example given in chapter 1 of white worker inner city drug use and drug-related crime among the unemployed of Liverpool, England.

In chapter 2, "Premises of the Incarceration Binge Culture," the question becomes: Why did America allow a panic over crack cocaine in 1986, with crime rates increasing from 1986 to 1991, to lead to a quadrupling of the U.S. prison population over a twenty-five-year incarceration binge, even though the crime rate had been falling since 1991? Not only did the "war on drugs" during this recent historical period (1986–2008) put more people in prison and increase sentence length to keep them there longer, but it was also disproportionately African Americans that went to prison. We argue that one premise of the incarceration binge is that it has served as a form of "convenient oppression"—another "in the series of social and legal institutions of racism in the United States."

From this view, it is drug laws and racism that fed the growth toward the world's largest prison system. We recommend sentencing reform, prison reform and a rethinking of the correctional project along the lines of community justice (Clear 2008), and to turn around the unemployment in the inner city—a $300 billion federal investment act enhancing "green jobs" (Apollo Alliance 2008).

In chapter 3, "Prison Binge Growth Theory," we explore other explanations for the world's large prison system, and what else in addition to, or in tandem with, harsh drug laws and racism, contributed to the growth of "the prison state" in the United States. First, we outline the view that a rational American public purposely chose more conservative values and supported policies that led to the massive prison system. Two scholars, who argue the public was rational to act against the 1986–1991 increase in crime, now suggest that this prison build-up movement "may have over done it." Second, we present a less "rational" view that cynical politics, sensationalist media and unwarranted fear *interacted* among the American voting public and political institutions, during the "drug crime era," accelerating an inherent bureaucratic tendency toward a self-interested "prison-industrial growth complex." And, third, we present a view that this extraordinary prison growth has served to function as a convenient oppression of black inner city residents—and that this is especially so for "high impact communities" (high incarceration, high probation and parole neighborhoods).

We hope to educate about the role of power and inequality in constructing the "drug crime era," and its tendency toward "convenient oppression." By focusing on how and why we have quadrupled our prison system we hope to highlight the need to now see a *competition* between overuse of confinement and other state priorities. This would represent a new rational public model: more rational sentencing and parole policies, and a pragmatic set of policies to safely downsize the prisons. This increasingly possible reversal of prison growth could shift significant resources to other state priorities, and some resources to evidence-based crime prevention. We hope—through such a new rational public model—that the American people could move beyond the "drug crime" era, explore and resolve the racism inherent in the incarceration binge culture and end the hyperghetto-hyperincarceration era of "the prisoners' world" as witnessed by the prisoner voices in this book.

1

—◊◊◊—

Historical Periods
of Prisoners' Worlds

The convicts writing essays in this book engaged in criminality. All convicts in prison have engaged in criminality. But the prisoners in this book were also swept up into prison during an unusual American incarceration binge. Their journeys through "the prisoners' world" are individual experiences that are also part of an historical period. The stable, backwater prison world was greatly expanded and politicized by a "war on drugs" approach that stems from an ever-changing political power world.

The sudden growth of the prison world since 1986 had happened, as it were, "behind the prisoners' back," as they entered the experiential world of the prison amidst a changing definition of the law. Any book on prisoners, thus, must look first at the historical context of the legal definition of the word "criminal." What were the specific relevant laws that were in effect during the period in which the book was written? For only then can the student understand that those in power at the time decide what may or may not be legal. It is this power world that also decides how severe the penalty for what is considered a crime should be, and who should or should not be labeled as a "criminal." As Randall Shelden says:

> The making of laws and the interpretation and application of these laws throughout the criminal justice system has, historically, been class, gender, and racially biased. More to the point, as Cole has noted, there are really two systems of justice: "one for the privileged and another for the less privileged" (Cole, 1999:9). Moreover, one of the major functions of the criminal justice system has been

5

largely to control and/or manage those from the most disadvantaged sectors
of the population, that is, the dangerous classes. . . . (Shelden 2008:17–18)

Laws do not just "manage those from the most disadvantaged sectors
of the population." Clearly there is, and always has been for many centuries, wide consensus that certain behaviors are crimes. For instance, most
people agree that the crimes reported by the FBI in the annual Uniform
Crime Reports (UCR) should be seen as crimes: murder, rape, robbery,
burglary, arson, larceny, auto theft, serious assaults. These laws are not
created for the powerful to "manage" the powerless. There are, however,
historical differences—changes in the law—around behaviors related to
vices such as alcohol and other drugs, gambling and prostitution. For
these "moral vices" the cultural capacity of one societal segment can
"power over" against another societal segment, to its' own cultural defini-
tions of what is "criminal."

The cultural power groupings can change from century to century or
decade to decade. Moreover, it is not just "moral vices" at stake here.
There are also historical eras which powerful social strata use the law to
enforce their political and economic interests. They define laws that keep
a social order that favors them the way it is. For instance, what would
happen to you if you could not pay your debts?

THE PRISONERS' WORLD OF DEBTOR PRISONS

Obviously a book about prisons written during the thirteenth to the
middle of the nineteenth century in England, when debtor's prisons were
common, would include "a debtor" as a category of criminal to be found
in prisons. If this seems unfamiliar we should note that it is a much different view than we have today (where debt issues are settled in civil
court). However, in the United States, in the late 1700s and early 1800s,
"the prisoners' world" would have included many people who were still
sentenced to prison for not paying (or not being able to pay) their debts.
Such a person sentenced to a term in debtor's prison would, upon sentencing and until release, be labeled and treated as a *criminal*. How did
this situation come to be?

After the establishment of the "Statute of Merchants" in 1285, debt
registration spread to many towns in England. Prior to this statute the
only recourse for a debt owed a creditor was for the creditor to ask the
sheriff to seize and sell the debtor's goods. Now, with the new statute,
instead of first trying to get the mayor and sheriff to seize and sell the
debtor's goods, the creditor could immediately have the debtor seized
and incarcerated. People could not get out of these prisons until their

debts were paid. Many people died in England's debtor's prisons (Shelden 2008:117).

Authors such as Charles Dickens, whose father had been incarcerated in a debtor's prison, wrote critical novels about debtor's prisons. England ended debtor's prisons in 1861.

During the early years of the United States, up to the mid 1800s, you could get tossed in prison for failing to pay back your debts (Shelden 2008:117). By the middle of the nineteenth century the practice of imprisonment for debts was eliminated in the United States at the federal level and most states followed suit.

The origin of the debtor's prison came from the rising political and economic interests of the people in power at that time, members of a rising business class able to define the law.

There are other examples of power social strata who define who is a "criminal" in ways that preserve their self-interest. Today's students on college campuses are familiar with injustices and fight against "trafficking in human slaves," but there was a time, of course, when slavery was an established practice, with "the law" on the slave owner's side.

Runaway Slaves as "Criminals"

A book in the 1700s or up to the end of the Civil War in 1865 in the United States, when slavery was legal and a slave was considered the property of the owner, would define a "criminal" in yet a different way. For example, if a slave ran away from the master, that was a crime—and harboring that "slave" was a crime too, as if "stealing property" from an owner. "The prisoners' world" of these times would include runaway slaves, and those convicted of harboring them, as a category of prisoner. Slavery was a function of ownership of property and richer property owners were landowners, slave owners, and comprised the power world of the day.

Shelden, describing the rise of early forms of stratified societies, empires and capitalism, draws an important generality for us:

> a centralized power base arose that began to compel or coerce a surplus from the work . . . once (the group that rises to power and has control over the means of production) occurs . . . there comes the threat of trouble in the form of "revolutions, peasant and slave uprisings, labor strife, and common crimes as groups or individuals seek to affect either a personal or more general redistribution of wealth and power" (Michalowski, 1985:74–75). Thus there arises the need for a formal system of "law" to respond to such threats to the prevailing order. (Shelden 2008:30)

This stark description of "the law" as an outcome of a power system may seem uncomfortable. Many textbooks read by young adults looking to go into jobs in the criminal justice area introduce the "criminal justice" field as *constituted* in work roles—cops, courts, corrections—enforcing commonly agreed-upon laws: murder, rape, assault.

But in the quote above, Shelden says, once a group rises to power, "there comes a threat of trouble" that includes not only the *form* of uprisings and labor strife, but also "common crimes as groups or individuals seek to affect either a personal or more general redistribution of wealth and power." This *tension* between the powerful who benefit from the existing structure and those who are disadvantaged by that existing social structure is built into highly unequal societies characterized by major injustices.

However, most introductory criminal justice texts do not highlight class conflict, but rather detail the major tension in the criminal justice world as that between "due process" and "crime control" values. These two values exist in a conflictual tension *within* a constitutional and essentially "consensual" society (Packer 1968). Criminal justice students familiar with sociology, because they have taken an introductory sociology course, will recall that a "consensual" view of society see's society as "glued together" through a set of norms held in common (Durkheim 1995). But a normatively consensual society does not accurately describe the *conflict* systems of past historical societies, such as feudal lord over peasant, or slaveholders over slaves in the slave society, or a rising business class over poor peasant and the emerging working class (Marx 1995).

The Prisoners' World raises the question of whether the last fifty years of uneven development in the growth of the suburbs leading to festering inner cities and the incarceration of their residents in the development of the world largest prison system can be seen as an outcome of each other: a structural conflict where a "formal system of 'law' respond(s) to" the "threat(s) to the prevailing order" in the form of young blacks "acting up" in the jobless ghettos (Eitzen & Baca Zinn 2000:139–73; Tonry 2007:23; Wacquant 2007; Irwin 2005:222–23). Several times before the United States needed a "formal system of law" to handle the tensions of a social setting with raw inequalities and social injustice: the debtor's prisons era laws, and the slavery era laws are examples. How did the slave laws work?

At the beginning of the United States, around the time of the first census, there were about 750,000 blacks, just under 20 percent of the total population. Less than one out of ten of these blacks were free at that time (Becker 1999).

Although enslavement in New Jersey was somewhat benign during the Dutch period, it changed during the British era into a more oppressive system. Slaves were not allowed to carry firearms, gather with other slaves, walk in the streets at night, or hunt unless accompanied by their masters.

Before the 1790s slavery had become a weakened institution. Years of over-planting of tobacco (worked by slaves) had left the land worn out. But the introduction of cotton increased the demand for slaves in the south. Eli Whitney's cotton gin made the production of the heartier short-staple cotton profitable. Cotton became the principal cash crop of the South and of the nation. The sale and transportation of Black people within the United States thus became big business (Becker 1999).

A runaway slave, considered legally as property, was treated as a wanted criminal, with posters advertising rewards for their return. And the "Fugitive Slave Law" (1793) would prosecute as a criminal anyone helping the slave escape. Thus laws in a book of the period might read, "That it shall be the duty of all marshals and deputy marshals to obey and execute all warrants and precepts issued under the provisions of this act." The marshals or his deputy must not let a fugitive escape from his custody or, himself, suffer the thousand-dollar fine. "Slave hunters" could also "summon and call to their aid bystanders, or posse comitatus of the proper county" and, furthermore, "all good citizens are hereby commanded to aid and assist in the prompt and efficient execution of this law" (Avalon Project at Yale Law School 1996).

The slavery system arose and continued in the United States (and Britain) because the ruling class wanted low-cost, manageable labor to work its profitable agricultural crops, like sugar cane in the then-British-owned Bermuda and other islands, and first tobacco in the upper South, then cotton in the American plantation South. As Shelden says,

The development of legal institutions in America corresponded to the development of racist ideologies and the oppression of Native Americans, African Americans, and other racial and ethnic minorities. The law, especially during the nineteenth century, was used to regulate and control the labor of minorities. (Shelden 2008:36)

LAWS INSTITUTED BY POWER CLASS

Thus, we see how laws are instituted and enforced by the class in power. So-called "criminals" are *created*. Now, of course, there are common crimes that everyone agrees on; but then there are these "peculiar institutions." In one year, debtors may be labeled as criminals, in another the same person may live as a free man. Events may cause one black man or woman living free in Africa, another, a slave in America and subject, as a fugitive slave, to being labeled a criminal. A civil war was fought, in part, to resolve the slavery issue.

Readers, perhaps, will agree that the examples we give—debtor prisons, runaway slave laws—are examples of social injustice, unjust situations caused by an unjust social order. Now think about the current United States prison system as, by far, the largest in the world. Think about how the development of this huge prison system is linked to jobless inner city areas. There are, for example, situations like 80 percent of New York's state prisoners that come from eight city boroughs of New York City (Jacobsen 2005; Clear 2007). As Michael Hallett writes in his Foreword to Randall Shelden's 2008 second edition of *Controlling the Dangerous Classes*:

> As part of a growing body of work bespeaking dissatisfaction with mainstream criminology's myopic focus on hot spots and statistical residues, this book gets to the heart of the matter of social justice versus criminal justice . . . a detailed accounting of the fundamental pattern of the history of criminal justice—the exploitation and suppression of the poor and marginal through legal means—is offered the students who are often encouraged to *ignore* questions of social justice entirely. (Shelden 2008:ix)

We see that the average "criminal" of today—a "drug crime era" inner city black caught in an incarceration binge—would be described differently than would a "criminal" in previous decades. The organization of who will be deviant, who will have a "person category" of criminal—like debtor in prison, or runaway slave—is socially constructed through the power world of the day (Best & Luckenbill 1994). For instance, if today you make alcohol in your own basement still, are you a "criminal?" No. But the United States did have a "war on alcohol" during a period in the past that would have put you in prison for "the production, distribution, and sale of intoxicating liquors."

Criminals in the Prohibition Era "War on Alcohol"

Clearly, as in the example of debtor's prison and runaway slave, the power world can change creating a situation where a lot of people are criminals. In the late nineteenth century a "bandwagon" push to outlaw alcohol was led at first by the Women's Christian Temperance Union (WCTU) as part of a set of social reform policies that included child labor, social welfare, and women's right to vote. The push to ban alcohol was then picked up by powerful political interests organized through the Anti-Saloon League, a professional lobbying organization that was supported by large and powerful manufacturers such as Henry Ford.

This political, cultural and economically powerful juggernaut led to a state-by-state campaign of legislation between 1880 and 1920 outlawing production, distribution and sale of alcohol that resulted in the "federalization" of alcohol laws. A new "criminality" surrounding alcohol was materializing through the power world of those days.

In 1920 the new law took effect—the U.S. Congress had passed, and two-thirds of the states had ratified, the Eighteenth Amendment making the manufacturing and distribution of alcohol illegal. This era from 1920 to 1933 became known as "Prohibition." How could this happen?

During the years just before and after 1900, twenty-five million immigrant workers came to the United States. Unlike the pious, Protestant, sober, rural, mostly farming and small town middle-class whites that had come earlier in the U.S. history of immigration from England and Northern Europe, the new immigrants during the period 1870–1920 came from Southern Europe, Eastern Europe, and Ireland. Streaming into the rapidly industrializing U.S. cities and mining camps, this was a new, white, Catholic, urban working class. And, they came from drinking cultures.

The consumption of alcohol, always popular in America with the workers, became increasingly heavy, especially in the expanding manufacturing and mining communities in the mid-Atlantic, and mid-West, as well as "out West" in mining towns of western states. Public drunkenness became conspicuous. Partly this was due to the difficult working conditions. Immigrants worked without rights in the raw, newly industrializing American factory cities and mines: long hours, no unions, little consideration for worker safety, for low pay. Not much time for recreation outside of work and family. Under this duress, many working-class males spent much of their available time and weekly paychecks in bars. Wives (represented by the WCTU), small farmers and politically powerful big factory owners who wanted efficient workers (represented by the Anti-Saloon League), began a sophisticated lobbying effort. This set of different social forces put enough pressure on lawmakers to make it almost impossible to resist the "bandwagon," despite the objections and resistance of working-class males.

Starting about 1870 the "dry movement" began, first in Kansas, and then spreading to other states. The fifty-year dry movement benefited from professional lobbying. By the turn of the century the result was a national campaign that led up to the approval of two-thirds of the state legislatures and the passage in Congress of a constitutional Prohibition Amendment. As Gusfield notes:

> Agents of government are the only persons in modern societies who can legitimately claim to represent the total society. . .their acts makes it possible for them not only to influence the allocation of resources but also to define the public norms of morality and to designate which acts violate them. (Gusfield 1967:228)

Was the passage of the Prohibition Amendment really a law "representing the total society?" No. Probably the majority of the American people did not support the law. As Gusfield continues:

> In a pluralistic society these defining and designating acts can become matters of political issue because they support or reject one or another of the competing and conflictual cultural groups in the society.

We have called attention to the fact that deviance designations have histories; the public definition of behavior as deviant is itself changeable. It is open to reversals of political power, twists of public opinion, and the development of social movements and moral crusades.

The "lifting" of a deviant activity to the level of a political, public issue is thus a sign that its moral status is at stake, that legitimacy is a possibility . . . The present debate over drug addiction laws in the United States, for example, is carried out between defenders and opposers of the norm. . . .

The threat to the legitimacy of the norm is a spur to the need for symbolic restatement in legal terms. In these instances of "crimes without victims" the legal norm is *not* the enunciator of a consensus within the community. On the contrary, it is when consensus is least attainable that the pressure to establish legal norms appears to be greatest. (Gusfield 1967:228–36)

The liberal and radical social movements of the 1960s and 1970s took drug use in their stride as part of a left libertarian philosophy of "if it doesn't hurt anybody its' ok," which included a tolerant view of drug use. Meanwhile a strong conservative counter-movement had been brewing since the Goldwater campaign of 1964. By the mid-1970s and especially in the early 1980s, this strong conservative counter-movement gained political power with the presidency of Ronald Reagan and redefined morality around drug use and drug trafficking as deeply immoral, deserving of strong "war on drugs" laws. As in the earlier case of the "war on alcohol," the new intolerant mood led to a new federalizing of law around street drugs.

Clearly the United States has a tendency to have "swings in the pendulum" around drugs. Prohibition, for example, would last for nearly fifteen years, until December of 1933, when the Act was repealed (Twenty-First Amendment).

What was this "war on alcohol" swing in the pendulum like? In January of 1919 the Eighteenth Amendment was passed, making the "manufacturing, sale, or transportation of intoxicating liquors" illegal (Cox & Wade 2002). Henceforth, after midnight of December 31, 1919, the manufacturing, sale or transporting of alcohol was a criminal offense punishable by incarceration.

Under the new Prohibition law, which was immediately an unpopular law, demand for "intoxicating liquors" continued—but now supply was illegal. People were making "bathtub gin" at home, local groups were conducting bootleg operations in whisky-making stills in the hills and running liquor in boats from Canada—and all the while they were now being "chased" by the agents of the newly formed Bureau of Prohibition.

Soon organized gangs conducted the import, distribution and sales of illegal liquor. Late night bars or clubs arose, dubbed speakeasies or "blind pigs" (in that the police would be "blind" to the activity in this establishment). There developed a significant amount of corruption in the new federal "Bureau of Prohibition," and in local police forces. The corruption also crept up into legislatures and Governors' offices, and all the way into the first Prohibition Presidential administration.

Increased competition between gangs in the Prohibition era soon resulted in use of guns. Heavily armed "gangsters," the like of the "Machine Gun Kellys," were needed to protect the bootleggers. In response to these highly publicized and shocking gang killings by and between these "mobs" of bootleggers and distributors, the enforcement laws became tougher, with more crackdowns, and incarcerations became more frequent. Now, more "war on alcohol" prisons were needed.

"WAR ON ALCOHOL" PRISON EXPANSION

The incarceration rate in the United States from 1860–1920 had stayed much the same, in a range of sixty to seventy-five Americans incarcerated for every 100,000 in the population. After the passage of Prohibition, the rate immediately went up to a range of 79 to 113 per 100,000 population (Austin & Irwin 2001:2). As the "war on alcohol" brought forth more "alcohol sweeps," arrests and convictions, "Big House" prisons like Jackson State Prison (built 1927) and New York's Attica (built 1930) immediately filled up with Prohibition gangsters. In the West, the walled Federal bastion of Alcatraz, San Francisco's "prison in the bay," also represented a final solution for many criminals of the Prohibition era. The Federal Bureau of Prisons took over Alcatraz Island in 1934, just after the end of Prohibition. The Alcatraz prison took over the site of an old army prison built on a rock in the middle of the bay, the nation's first super-max escape-proof prison for the really tough and incorrigible. Alcatraz's initial slate of desperate criminals included Al Capone and Machine Gun Kelly, and many other "alcohol gangsters" still serving Prohibition-era sentences.

San Quentin, another California state prison across the San Francisco Bay from Alcatraz—and the state's oldest and original prison, built in 1852—also held its share of gangsters and bootleggers during the 1920s and 1930s Prohibition years.

In 1933, Prohibition was repealed, largely because the American people had become appalled at the scandalous level of "street violence" in the form of Prohibition-era gangland violence. Once Prohibition ended, one could now produce, sell or buy and transport liquor without fear of being arrested, charged or labeled a criminal.

THE PRISONERS' WORLD IN THE DRUG CRIME ERA

What are now called street drugs have been a part of American life for a long time, especially since the middle of the late nineteenth century (Abadinsky 2008; Musto 1991). In the 1950s and 1960s the accepted approach to handling drug-defined crime was the "rehabilitative ideal," which defined drug possession or drug sales as a short-sentence felony, and, since a lot of drug-defined crimes are related to drug abuse and addiction, the emphasis was on a minimum time in prison with concurrent or alternative sentence of substance abuse treatment.

Even Republican president Richard Nixon reflected this outlook as he responded to increasing drug-related crime, and the return from war of addicted Vietnam veterans. President Nixon supported drug treatment for these social problems, rather than an overly punitive approach of prison time during the period 1968–1974. President Jimmy Carter continued the rehabilitative ideal and proposed decriminalizing marijuana. But, by Ronald Reagan's election in 1980, this was to change. A new, punitive cultural conservative outlook and a political shift occurred: a new "warrior ideal" was emerging for drug enforcement, as part of a larger "war on drugs." Was this just a change in Presidents? What was the context in U.S. life that helped this transformation happen? The answer lies in changes in the American city.

After World War II, suburbs were being built with malls. People who could afford to live in the growing suburbs—mostly European-American whites—were drawn to the new malls with lots of stores. They parked and shopped there instead of shopping downtown. In countless U.S. downtown business districts large manufacturing and warehouse corporations moved to suburban and small city industrial parks, giant office buildings grew up in business centers near highway exits and suburbs, drawing office workers away from downtown, and small retail goods and services firms were lured away from their central city location to the new suburban malls to serve the new suburban customers. U.S. inner cities suffered from both "white flight" and capital flight.

Since the industrial revolution (1870–1920) the United States had always had ghettos, but these early American ghettos were a place where people went off to work during the day and returned at night. With suburbanization, however, America's former central city ghettos, where blacks and other "minorities" could live and *work jobs* in the nearby city factories and warehouses, and "downtown" and local neighborhood businesses, now became lower-working-class neighborhoods without the "work"—that is, they became "job-less ghettos" where the truly disadvantaged gathered or remained (Wilson 1997; Agnew 1995; Wacquant 2007; Irwin 2005; Tonry 2007; Clear 2007; Western 2006:36–38).

The U.S. Civil Rights Movement (1954–1968) had lifted the hopes of tens of millions of African Americans. However, suburbanization and the flow of capital and investment to the suburbs by U.S. businesses were now devastating the inner cities. Black political administrations were voted into city government by the new black majority populations, but the city itself was an "empty shell" with few jobs and diminishing tax base. Now jobless, ghetto residents saw their youth, restless with despair, hopelessness and rage, beginning to make trouble as their neighborhoods were festering. Writing about the initial emergence of contemporary U.S. jobless ghettos in the mid-1960s, John Irwin notes:

> The ghetto youths of the late 1960s and early 1970s, excluded from conventional paths to fulfill their intense desires and needs, were available for any activity that promised profit, respect, and excitement.

> They formed neighborhood gangs and carried on wars with other gangs. They pimped or pretended to pimp, used and sold drugs; stole from each other, their neighbors. (Irwin 2005:222–23)

The South-Central Los Angeles area called Watts burned in a riot of disaffected black youth in 1965. Detroit, Michigan, burned along 12th street in a similar 1967 riot. The Republicans won the 1968 election. They had used a "Southern Strategy" and a "war on crime" approach to rally the conservative white vote and elected Richard Nixon in 1968. Then, into the jobless economic vacuum of the now increasingly abandoned and powerless jobless ghetto, the illegal street drug economy began to expand, to become a major "employer" of inner city high school drop-out youth. In subsequent elections throughout the 1970s and 1980s the Republican's played on a conservative reaction to the liberal 1960s. They reversed the left libertarian tolerance toward drugs into a moralistic and punitive zero tolerance toward drugs—and, they began to play the "race card." As Tonry notes:

> If crime and drugs are matters of good and evil, and criminals and drug users are evil, there is little reason to expect sympathy or empathy toward them from the holders of those views. . . . And Wacquant's analysis may help make it clear how and why the race card was played, as Hofstadter more than 40 years ago described. Although, he observed, Republicans historically had sympathy with the plight of U.S. Blacks in the South,

>> By adopting the 'southern strategy,' the Goldwater men abandoned this inheritance. They committed themselves not merely to a drive for a core of Southern states in the electoral college but to a strategic counterpart in the North which required a search for racist votes. They thought they saw a good mass issue in the white backlash which they could indirectly

exploit by talking of violence on the streets, crime, juvenile delinquency, and the dangers faced by our mothers and daughters (1965:99).

No informed person disagrees that the national Republican party from the late 1960s through our time pursued a "Southern strategy" of focusing on nominally nonracial issues—law and order, welfare reform, opposition to affirmative action on color-blindness grounds—to appeal to the racial fears and antipathies of white Southerners and working-class voters through the country. (Tonry 2007:26)

Meanwhile, the inner cities festered and drug sales drastically increased there, related drug-turf competition and gun homicides, particularly by juveniles, skyrocketed.

Spurred by an overall more general conservative reaction to the liberal 1960s and 1970s, and led by the continuing political vote-getting "Southern strategy," Americans elected conservative Republican leader Ronald Reagan in the 1980 Presidential election. The stage was set for President Reagan to respond to middle class and "Reagan Democrat" working-class voter anxieties with a new campaign carrying on Nixon's legacy of the "war on crime," but now adding a new "war on drugs" approach. He pressured the U.S. Congress in the summer of 1986 to federalize laws against street drugs—a national "prohibition" now emerged.

President Reagan proclaimed the new national "war on drugs" with the federal Anti-Drug Abuse Act of 1986. A new, white backlash, "Southern punitive" approach was to introduce a "mandatory sentence" to prison for various drug offenses that undercut the discretion of judges to consider mitigating or aggravating circumstances. And the national mood seemed to tilt strongly from "the rehabilitative ideal" outlook to the "lock them up and throw away the key" view. This new punitive national approach had been preceded by New York's state-level "Rockefeller Drug Laws" (1973) (A set of mandatory minimums). A drug offense was now more typically a major felony offense punishable with a "mandatory minimum" (long) prison term. These circumstances (more coming into prison, more staying longer) rapidly built up state prison populations.

The launching of this new era of "zero tolerance" (prohibition) was especially sparked by a new epidemic (1986–1993) of crack cocaine. Federal law enforcement agencies, and U.S. attorneys around the country, now began to play a major role in what had previously been a state and local drug enforcement effort (CFECP 1998; Obermaier 1996; Heyman & Moore 1996). Federal drug control budgets greatly increased (Diulio, Smith & Saiger 1995:456). Federal prisons shot up to 40 percent of their population incarcerated for drug-related federal sentence. State legislatures followed the federal mandatory sentence model with punitive mandatory state drug offense laws spread across the nation. *State prison populations shot up from 6 percent drug related to now house up to 30 percent of their prisoners solely from drug-related convictions or drug-related parole violations.*

These new "war on drugs" laws made production, distribution and sales of street drugs a new "bandwagon" of stiff sentences and enforcement, similar to how "intoxicating liquors" had been made over into a punitive emphasis sixty-five years earlier. But, while "possession" and use of alcohol was not illegal under Prohibition, possession and use of street drugs *is* illegal under the "war on drugs" with stiff penalties. "Felony drug possession" is one of the easier arrests a police officer can make. And especially long sentences ensue if the person is arrested with amounts of drugs sufficient to suggest "possession with intent to deliver."

These initial Antidrug Acts of 1986 and 1988 triggered immediate police sweeps of inner cities, with the arrest and imprisonment of a host of drug users, drug dealers and drug sellers. The cleanup action came down especially hard on young black drug sellers who had been hawking drugs openly along the inner city streets of New York, Baltimore, Los Angeles, Detroit and other U.S. cities. In Michigan these new young black drug sellers and other white, black and brown "druggies" began to populate Michigan prisons. The coauthors of this book lived through the very beginning of this historical period, witnessing in our prison college classrooms the change in racial composition and offense category as the classrooms filled up with the new "war on drugs" convicts.

Recall the story of the social context creating these "inner city street criminals." As we've mentioned, after World War II suburbs drew businesses and investment out of central city business districts and the result for central city ghetto residents was to create a set of American jobless ghettos that were so bad they were set afire by the frustrated residents in the mid-1960s riots. What was the national response? Starting in 1973 in New York and in 1986 across the nation, a set of punitive laws arose. As Hallet says, "while both crime and imprisonment rates fluctuate over historical periods, the continued pattern of operation in criminal justice over the centuries . . . is a targeted focus on the poor, the politically powerless, and the socially marginal" (Shelden 2008:ix).

It is hard to move out to the suburbs from the low-rent but jobless inner city if you have few job skills or educational credentials. Then again, there has been very little low-cost housing available in the suburbs. The typical low-cost housing that is available in suburban areas, such as mobile home parks, is often sold off to be converted to strip malls or condominiums. Abandoned low-skilled populations in American inner cities—far away from entry-level jobs, in a job-location mismatch—become a "problem population" requiring "management." Available to be designated as deviant and dangerous, the inner city residents, particularly young black males—now invoking middle class anxieties and fear of crime—become confined in probation, prison or parole in what becomes the worlds' largest prison system. Shelden continues:

> As Greenberg and West put it: "Sociological analysis of the history of penalty have *taken as their premise* that institutionalized punishment practices are not entirely determined by the functional necessity of preventing crimes" (2001:638). Many other things are going on in the operation and unfolding of punishment than crime control—such as political posturing by politicians and social entrepreneurs, confinement and demonization of the dangerous classes, artificial management of surplus labor and official unemployment, profit-taking, and not least, the assuaging of middle-class anxieties about crime and vulnerability. (Shelden 2008: ix–x)

THE CONTEMPORARY INCARCERATION EXPLOSION

Even with a small prison build-up spike during the alcohol prohibition of the 1920s, the U.S. prison population dynamics, for over 120 years, from 1860 to 1980, held stable, as mentioned, at a low incarceration rate of 75 to 125 per 100,000. Then we get a really rapidly expanded massive new "prison world." In this, what might be called "The Great American Drug Bust," ever more prisoners were charged with drugs or drug-related crimes. As mentioned, state prison admittance shot up from 6 percent to 30 percent drug convictions, federal prisons shot up to 40 percent drug convictions. Ultimately the nation went, in a brief twenty-five years, from 329,821 prisoners in 1980 to 2.2 million prisoners in 2007 (Austin & Irwin 1997/2001:1; Useem & Piehl 2008). The largest single cause of this massive prison expansion has been the "war on drugs." Shelden states:

> Convictions for drug law violations (mostly possession) accounted for more than *one-half* of the increase in state prison inmates during the 1980s and early 1990s. Between 1985 and 1995 the number of prisoners in state institutions who have been convicted of drug offenses went up by 478 percent. (Shelden 2008:56)

"Drug law violations" include both mere possession and "possession with intent to deliver." This second category of drug law violation is often spelled out in state sentencing guidelines with long sentences for people arrested with larger amounts of an illegal drug. An implicit consequence of these laws was that more people were going to go to prison, and more people were going to go to prison for longer sentences. This meant that existing prisons were going to become overcrowded.

The nation's states were thus forced (and, to some degree, encouraged by federal "truth in sentencing" prison building grants) to hurriedly build over 1,000 new prisons. Thirty-four new prisons were built in Michigan alone. In a state that had previously had only seven state prisons and some camps in 1983, there were now forty-one prisons and eight camps in 2008. Many of the prisoners' lives whose writings are presented in this book span this entire period. Coauthor Tregea reports that aging African Americans with long graying beards appear in his volunteer classes (2003–2008) and they "touch up old cuts" with instructor Tregea about "back when" they were in a prison college class he taught in the 1980s at some other Michigan prison. With the long mandatory sentences (twenty to life for first possession of crack cocaine with intent to deliver; or parolable life for committing a murder at seventeen as part of a gang war), prisoners entering prison in the mid-1980s have been in these prisons for the entire period described in this book—"caught in the incarceration binge."

THE PAST AND THE PRESENT—A SIMILARITY

In this recent massive incarceration binge the "abuse substances of choice" were street drugs. Sixty-five years earlier, in a very much smaller but equally violence-ridden "incarceration explosion," the "abuse substances of choice" were intoxicating liquors. Certainly, the few dozen "war on alcohol" prisons constructed during the Prohibition years of 1920–1933 were far fewer in number than the 1,000 new prisons hastily thrown up nationwide as "temporary facilities" during the 1986–2008 "war on drugs" incarceration binge.

Can you say that it's not fair to compare alcohol with street drugs because street drugs are much more dangerous? To the contrary, alcohol is responsible for more death and violence—and more health problems—*than all the street drugs combined*. Abadinsky notes:

> According to scientific and pharmacological data used to classify dangerous substances for the protection of society, *alcohol* should be a schedule II narcotic, a Drug Enforcement Administration (DEA) category referring to a substance that is highly addictive and available only with a government narcotic registry number. *The cost of alcohol is twice the social cost of all illegal drug abuse.* Alcohol is reputed to be the direct cause of 80,000 to 100,000 deaths annually and alcohol-related auto accidents are the leading cause of death for teenagers. (Wicker 1987; Li, Smith & Baker 1994; Abadinsky 2008:2–3; emphasis added)

But the consequence of criminalizing alcohol back in the 1920s was predictable. And the extreme criminalization of street drugs today has had a similar script. First there came the "underground" protest, culture conflict and resistance—in the working class, from well-off residents, and the poor neighborhoods alike—against an unpopular law. Because of law enforcement, demand was now claimed to have been reduced, but the continued visible demand by the public supported the continued production and import of the banned substance. This was followed by a "professionalization" of such importing, with added organizing of distribution and sales of the product also soon handled by organized gangs. You could get the banned substance "just around the corner," or through a friend.

Subsequent deadly in-fighting broke out between such "professional" law-breaking groups, resulting in increased violence—turf wars and killings leading to public alarm (bringing in the media and the politicians)—and consequent crackdowns, arrests and imprisonments. In the case of crack cocaine this "professionalization" of distribution broke down into youth dealers, with fifteen-year-olds leading street corner "crews" of crack dealers and even more wild "posse's" of rival drug-turf youth gangs fighting rival youth gangs with guns (National Geographic 1996). Out of this legacy, the United States has had 10,000 deaths a year by handguns, while Germany—without a "war on drugs"—has had an average of thirty-eight handgun deaths a year.

Finally, incarcerations in both punitive eras—the "war on alcohol" and the "war on drugs"—multiplied to the point where more prisons were needed to house the several hundreds of thousands entering "the system" in the aftermath of passage of (1) the initial punitive alcohol law (1919), and (2) a set of punitive street drug laws (1986–1988).

"UNDERWORLD" AND STREET
CULTURE LEGACY OF PROHIBITION

The legacy of Prohibition still lives on in the slang and popular music of urban culture today. This holds especially true within Detroit and its inner city, which saw so much of the beginnings of alcohol Prohibition and its gangster era.

Today, this ultra-tough Prohibition gangster period of rampant law breaking back in the 1920s is looked on almost as a matter of historic pride by contemporary poverty-stricken inner city young people who grow up with few role models and little sense of personal or community pride and accomplishment. Gangsters, who defy the police and all-powerful institutions of "the man," become folk heroes to be emulated.

So we see this throwback to the 1920s Prohibition days in the many common inner city expressions found in essays by black prisoners in this book. Expressions born of years of bootlegging like "the racket" or "the game" to denote today's different racket or game of drug dealing; the "mob," "mobsters" or "gang" to identify close associates in drug operations; a "player," i.e. player in the drug "game," to denote a finely-dressed free-spending member of a drug gang who can "play" several woman; "piece," a Prohibition term for gun; and "snitch," meaning someone who might inform on drug-dealing gang members.

Expressions in popular music like "gangsta rap" arising in the late 1980s continue to be heard still today. Much of black music has come out of Detroit. The hopeful and catchy Motown sound of the 1950s through the 1970s gave way to the angry "rap" which became big for teenagers in the 1980s and 1990s when many of the black prisoners, with writings in this book, were growing up.

Other music and dance crazes of the day are remembered by these black prisoners—the smooth cool "DJ," idol of the ladies, who spun records, tapes or CDs, and hosted the neighborhood dances; the contests in popular break dancing, which all teenage males practiced for hours to win.

For many of the black prisoners whose thoughts we present in this book, their ambition, like that of most young inner city kids in the "drug crime era," became to be a real life "gangster." And, one day, to be a real "player." A person who "has everything," as a teenager! Living life in the "fast lane," accumulating fast cash, fast cars and fast women through the game of selling drugs, just like they saw their big brothers, uncles or other teenagers they admired doing around them.

Meanwhile, they dreamed of snaring the beguiling female "whore" and outmaneuvering the poh-lice "pigs," just like their rap heroes did. But at the same time, there was a lot of harm going on. As in the "What's Going On" Marvin Gaye song, "too many brothers (were) dying," and too many inner city lives were ruined by drugs and revolving-door incarcerations.

REDUCING HARM OR CRACKING DOWN?

As we have seen, in the twentieth century the United States has passed two major federalizing laws—one criminalizing alcohol and the other vastly increasing the penalties for street drugs. Things were not good before passing the laws: there were health consequences, work consequences or family and community life consequences for both alcohol and street drugs. And, things were (are) not good *after* passing the law: too much violence in the community, kids growing up having to negotiate "the streets," too many in prison, families broken up, punishment not solving the problem with continued demand for drugs.

The first major law, Prohibition (1920–1933), made production, distribution, and sale of types of "intoxicating liquors" illegal. The second major law, the Anti-Drug Abuse Laws (1986–present), shifted types of street drugs from a medical problem with short incarceration as minor felonies, to the category of major felonies with long sentences. Hallet concludes:

> criminal justice activities have demonstrably not been about reducing crime or demand for drugs or curtailing addiction—but instead about cracking down on socially reviled groups that have not managed to become part of the mainstream, dominant culture. (Hallett in Shelden 2008:x)

Today we regulate and tax the alcohol industry, which has become a legitimate business in production, distribution and sales. We have adult criminal laws applying only to sale of alcohol to minors, or the juvenile law of "minor in possession."

Alcohol abuse is a major part of American life. There has been, however, a social movement to emphasize health and wellness dimensions of choices around alcohol use. While high school and college students still "binge-drink," many in the adult population have responded to social pressure and moderated their drinking. But there persists much alcohol abuse and addiction and many deaths and injuries due to drinking and driving.

Decriminalization of alcohol did not address the continuing problems of substance abuse and alcohol addiction such as consequences for health, families, domestic violence and negligent thinking—like driving drunk—in the United States.

Substance abuse is defined as taking alcohol or other drugs in a way that becomes dysfunctional: you lose your job, your marriage, your house, your health, or you harm somebody—or you get in trouble with the law through a substance-abuse-related offense (Abadinsky 2008:4–8). This behavioral definition is related to becoming addicted (a brain disease), but it is possible to be addicted and still be "functional." Someone may be able to drink every night and still hold his or her job. However, there can also be personal health problems such as life-threatening medical condition: damage to the heart or liver. Alcohol abuse and heavy drinking are also associated with an increase in irritability and violence.

Criminality and death are definitely associated with alcohol, such as alcohol-related crimes of assault, domestic violence, negligent homicide driving while drunk (Abadinsky 2008:116; Wanberg & Milkman 1998). On the other hand, the *criminalization* of alcohol, street drugs or tobacco adds the legal dimension of being arrested, charged, convicted in a court (or plea) and sentenced to probation, jail or prison time. There will often be surveillance while on parole. There may be impacts on your family, children and community, and restrictions on your employment, housing and ability to vote after release as a convicted felon (Petersilia 2003; Mauer & Chesney-Lind 2002). And then, after years in prison, there can be the problem of overcoming *both* addiction and prisonization (Terry 2003).

Could street drugs be reduced in their harmful effects to the individual and the community through a "health and wellness" social movement? This has happened before. The use of tobacco, another major addictive substance that qualifies as a medical problem to self and social problem to others, has, in the last fifty years, declined dramatically. This decline in smoking occurred solely through social pressure and social movements, (and some class action civil suits), without bringing any criminal punitive penalties to bear with the exception of sale to minors and restrictions on advertising. Tobacco is another "vice" industry, then, where it is legal to produce, distribute and sell; and where the industry is regulated and taxed, like today's approach to alcohol.

A CULTURAL CAMPAIGN SHIFTS
NATION AWAY FROM SMOKING

In 1950, smoking was socially accepted, promoted by a highly profitable cigarette industry and the Hollywood film industry, and, in part because of this, a vast majority of adult American men and many women smoked. Many people today will watch old "black and white" movies and television series from the 1950s and 1960s and will see many of the actors smoking; television depicted actors smoking and had cigarette ads; magazines and billboards advertised cigarettes. Smoking was "cool."

Then came the well-publicized 1964 U.S. Surgeon General's report on research findings that cigarettes were clearly linked to alarming health consequences. Cigarette smoking was now linked to about 90 percent of all lung cancer cases. Smoking also caused lung diseases like emphysema. Smoking is also associated with cancers of the mouth, tongue, pharynx, esophagus, stomach, pancreas, cervix, kidney, ureter and bladder (Abadinsky 2008:152–54).

By 1975, a wellness movement had started in the United States and with public education focused on the health hazards of smoking, an antismoking campaign began. Even though there was some public resistance, over time, smoking became "uncool." In 1964 cigarette smokers represented 44 percent of the American population. By 1987 that rate was down to 37 percent, and by 1991 only 27 percent of Americans were still smokers (Shubinski 2006).

By 2000, studies indicated 35,000 deaths a year occurred from second-hand smoke. Office workers, spouses and children were affected (Abadinsky 2008:153). With this news, another round of well-publicized antismoking campaigns revved up. States' Attorney Generals, and private lawyers, were winning substantial claims in public class action suits and private civil lawsuits filed against cigarette companies, and new laws banning smoking in many public and private buildings and places went into effect. Smoking in the United States had reached a new low, now down from 44 percent in 1964 to 24 percent of men and 19 percent of women continuing to smoke cigarettes in 2006 (American Heart Association 2008). The Michigan legislature, responding to continued concerns about second-hand smoke, passed a "no smoking in bars or restaurants" law in the Spring of 2008.

A much more smoke-free population has been reached simply through education, prevention, treatment and health norms and mild rules (no smoking in buildings). We did not need harsh punitive measures or criminalization, although there has been an increase of enforcement in sales to minors. An almost entirely smoke-free population is a goal for the next ten or twenty years. This is an example of a *harm reduction* approach.

Contrast this result. A virtual cost-free (no expensive prison expansion) and successful social method of controlling or eliminating what once was, not too long ago, a deadly nationwide habit of substance abuse—tobacco—versus two instances of failed and tremendously costly (massive prison expansion) punitive incarceration methods: the "war on intoxicating liquors" and the "war on drugs." Each of which has failed.

Ending Prohibition became a strong public demand by the early 1930s and the "war on alcohol" was ended in 1933 with yet another amendment to the Constitution to repeal the Prohibition Amendment.

Law enforcement officials often state that *street drugs* are dangerous and police crackdowns and incarceration reduce harm to victims, offenders and the community. To some extent this is true. But it is not the case that *alcohol* is not also harmful. Prohibition for the years 1920 to 1933 did reduce alcohol consumption. As we have mentioned, "intoxicating liquors" have proven to be twice the health, violence and addiction risk than all the street drugs combined. But the "cure" of attempting to reduce alcohol use by criminalizing alcohol had proved to be worse than the disease.

The "war on drugs" also was a failure almost immediately. Drug dealers sent to prison were replaced on the streets by other drug dealers. Demand and supply of illegal drugs has continued. Addiction itself, as a chronic relapse brain disease, is not reduced by incarceration alone, but requires lengthy drug treatment programs. Overcoming addiction *and* prisonization is not easy. Ten years after the 1986 Anti-Drug Abuse federal legislation, the United States still had drug dealers and drug addicts, and drug-related crime. And this is true today, nearly twenty-five years later.

In 1996 a coalition of libertarians, Democrats, Independents, some Republicans and the medical community in Arizona joined together and were able to produce enough political support to pass a "treatment not prison" referendum proposal for that state. Arizona now had a public health approach—or harm reduction involving treatment rather than prison approach—to street drugs for those with first or second offense drug possession or drug-related offense.

California passed a similar harm reduction law in 2000, and other states are exploring the harm reduction approach, and rescinding or moderating their drastically punitive mandatory drug laws. Michigan passed the McConico Bill in the Fall of 2002, scaling back the punitiveness of that state's drug laws. And New York in the early 2000s repealed parts of the 1970s Rockefeller laws (FAMM 2008).

The failed fight against street drugs has cost the United States a tremendous amount. What are the costs? Governmental expenditures on corrections, which includes the costs for prison, jail, probation and parole, grew from $14 billion in 1982 to $31 billion in 1992 (Blumstein 2002:451), and then further, by 2005, with 2.2 million now in state or federal prison, or jail, and with another 4.8 million on probation or parole, the national corrections costs had risen further to reach $60 billion.

Moreover, more than 1,000 prisons have needed to be built since 1982, at an average construction-cost rate of $100,000 per prison bed. Subtracting the jail population, there are 1.4 million prisoners incarcerated in state and federal prisons as of 2006. At an average rate over $20,000 per year for the costs of prison incarceration alone ($20,000 times 1.4 million prisoners), the total prison costs for housing prisoners alone in 2005 are close to $30 billion. (In Michigan in 2007 the average cost is $32,000 per year per bed space.) This does not include the costs of building and maintaining those extra 1,000 prisons. Nor do these figures include the extra time and resources used by police, prosecutors and judges in processing the large number of non-violent drug-defined or drug-related crimes. The decimation of black communities, and ruining of many lives, goes uncalculated (Lynch & Sabol 2001; Clear 2007, 1996).

There is a debate on whether the incarceration effect is "worth it" in terms of being cost-effective (Conklin 2003; Jacobson 2005; Useem & Piehl 2008). If we reduced our rate of incarceration we would have more money for other priorities in crime prevention—early childhood education, home visits, after school programs, substance abuse treatment programs, and including state revenue sharing money to hire more local Sheriff deputies and police.

On the other hand, there are all the costs to victims caused by criminality. There is, then, both an incarceration effect in lowering crime and a prevention effect in lowering crime. Obviously we need both. The "balancing act" of public safety through sending more to prison *versus* cost-effective and safe reduction of the prison population has heated up as more and more states encounter budget crises caused by unprecedentedly large corrections budgets (Council of State Governments 2008).

But where to set the balance between incarceration and prison downsizing, while important, often does not itself focus discussion on the idea of a fundamentally different blend of law enforcement and crime prevention: the harm reduction approach.

THE HARM REDUCTION MODEL

A *drug-defined crime* would be something like a felony drug arrest for "possession" or "possession with intent to deliver." A low-level *drug-related crime* typical of first or second offense would be something like home invasion or shoplifting. A high-level drug crime would be defined as major dealing, wholesaling or distribution operations, with ancillary violent "contract" enforcement and "management." In the United States, over the last twenty-five years, the sentencing for these drug-defined and lower-level drug-related crimes has typically involved several years of prison time. Some European nations have moved to a response to first- or second-offense drug-defined and drug-related crime with an approach called *harm reduction.* Abadinsky reports:

> Harm reduction is offered as an alternative to the *supply reduction* strategy—aggressive law enforcement and pressure on producer nations—and the *demand reduction* strategy—treatment and prevention. This alternative recognizes that while abstinence is desirable, it is not a realistic goal. Instead, this approach examines harm from two points of view: harm to the community and harm to the drug user. The focus, then, is on lowering the amount of harm to each. (Abadinsky 2008:408)

In the harm reduction approach, the use of drugs is accepted as a fact. Instead of a "warrior" approach of aggressive law enforcement on *all* drug behavior, as exampled by our current zero tolerance with mandatory sentences, the focus in harm reduction—for low-level offenders without prior criminal records—is placed on reducing harm while use continues. The characteristic principles of the harm reduction approach include: (1) pragmatism, (2) humanistic values, (3) focus on harms, (4) balancing costs and benefits, and (5) priority of immediate goals (Abadinsky 2008:409–10). In this approach the focus is on reducing the *risky consequences* of drug use rather than on reducing drug use per se. "In place of the 'war' analogy and 'total victory' rhetoric," researchers and practitioners of the harm reduction approach "support even small steps that reduce harm."

> For example, intravenous use would be made safer through needle-exchange programs. The next step would be to encourage safer methods of ingestion. Risk would be further reduced by substituting methadone for heroin or other legal substances for cocaine and then by moderating the use of drugs—including nicotine and alcohol—en route to abstinence when this is possible. (Abadinsky 2008:410)

The British, in the region of Merseyside, do not tackle the problems of economic decline and "inner city" drug-related crime with a massive incarceration binge, as in the United States. Instead, they offer a comprehensive harm reduction program. For instance, in this severely disadvantaged region of Merseyside, that includes the city of Liverpool, England, thousands of unemployed dockworkers are without work because their jobs were replaced by containerization. They have turned to drugs, and a nascent drug economy. The British criminal justice system (Home Office) supports a program that:

> involves needle exchange, counseling, prescription of drugs including heroin, and employment and housing services . . . services are integrated to provide drug users with help when they need it. Pharmacists . . . fill prescriptions for smokeable drugs . . . and other drugs.

> The police sit on health authority drug advisory committees . . . to refer arrested drug offenders to services. (Abadinsky 2008:412)

In this example of harm reduction the community is also protected. The Merseyside police use resources to deal with middle- and high-level drug traffickers "while operating a cautioning policy toward drug users." Cautioning involves "confiscating the drug," and the person is taken to a police station.

> The offender must also meet certain conditions, such as not having a previous drug conviction and not having an extensive criminal record. He or she is given information about treatment services in the area. . . . The overall effect of this policy is to steer users away from crime and possible imprisonment. (Abadinsky 2008:412)

Recall Hallett's view that in the U.S. "war" on drugs "criminal justice activities have demonstrably not been about reducing crime or demand for drugs or curtailing addiction—but instead about cracking down on socially reviled groups that have not managed to become part of the mainstream, dominant culture" (Hallett, in Shelden 2008:x). This example of how the British "handled" the white male "jobless ghetto" dockworkers in Liverpool certainly differs from the U.S. approach to its unemployed inner city black males.

DRUGS AND GROWING INEQUALITY

Everyone knows that drug abuse can happen anywhere in the social class structure. Yet significant drug abuse is not randomly dispersed over the population. Rather, research shows drug abuse tends to be concentrated in areas of poverty. Street drug addiction and related criminality is also often "part of a syndrome that includes family disintegration, child abuse and neglect, delinquency, and alcohol abuse" (Abadinsky 2008:419–20). As coauthors we endorse the approach taken by Britain in Liverpool and would wish that this harm reduction approach could be utilized in American inner cities. We also feel some drugs could be decriminalized. However, the harm reduction model itself does not address the creation of economically devastated regions or inner cities and does not, in itself, slow the growing inequality within nations.

> Successful treatment of individual drug abusers would not stem the tide of new entries generated by unchanged social conditions that serve as a fertile breeding ground. "Even the best, most comprehensive programs to help addicts transform their lives will inevitably be compromised if we do not simultaneously address the powerful social forces that are destroying the communities to which they must return." (Currie 1993:279; Abadinsky 2008:420)

Thus, we also feel that investment in "green jobs" related to alternative energy technology should be directed toward the U.S. inner cities (Apollo Alliance 2008). Abadinsky notes that "The United States has the widest gap between rich and poor in the industrialized world and that gap is growing." He emphasizes, in citing a research study, that this problem of widespread deprivation in the United States is relevant to the issue of drug abuse:

> We are far from suggesting that all types and levels of drug use are at all times and in all circumstances deprivation-related. What we do, however, feel confident in asserting is that deprivation relates statistically to types and intensities of drug use which are problematic." (Advisory Council on the Misuse of Drugs 1998:111, in Abadinsky 2008:420)

When we think of the harm reduction model efforts to reduce "harm to the community" and to reintegrate the drug abuse "offender," we have to ask: what kind of "community" are we reintegrating the offender to? When Currie states we need to "simultaneously address the powerful social forces that are destroying the communities to which they must return" (Currie 1993:279), he alerts us to a need for concern about justice, reparation and human well-being (Sullivan & Tifft 2001:143). For instance, we do not want to demonize all young men in the African American community. Yet politicians have played the "crime and race card" as we have mentioned. As Sullivan and Tifft observe:

> Indeed, this card and its demonization strategy, has been followed ever since the Reagan-Bush eras by policies such as the war-on-street-level-dealing-and-drug-use, especially in African-American neighborhoods, race-based profiling, race-based penal sanctions, and the heightened use of imprisonment for economic street crime. (Sullivan & Tifft 2001:144)

Reflect again, on the difference between the British response of *harm reduction* with minimal incarceration, for the devastated communities of unemployed white dock workers who get into drugs and street-crime in Liverpool, with the *massive imprisonment* of jobless ghetto blacks sucked into drug-related street-culture crime in the jobless ghettos of the U.S. cities.

CONCLUSION

The coauthors of this book lived for a couple of decades (1976–1995) in two somewhat rough neighborhoods. In the first neighborhood we were victims of two home invasions and a serious arson. In all three cases we gave statements to the police, which helped gain plea-bargained sentences. We were fed-up with being preyed upon. Drug abuse was involved in the arson and we hoped the individual involved could receive mandatory drug treatment and psychological counseling. In the second neighborhood we worked with the community policing officer, and the landlord involved, to get rid of a drug house on our block. Using the tools of self-protection, working with the police and being involved with community organizing to make a healthier neighborhood is not incompatible with thinking through the implications of the "war on drugs."

In 1981, when we started prison teaching, we did not, therefore, enter the Michigan prison system with any particular or special sympathy for convicted felons. As prison college teachers, we were tough and demanding teachers, but thoughtful of prisoners. Prisoners gave us respect. Prisoners would say, regarding Tregea, "Instructor Bill, he's all business." Entering prison teaching we *saw* the awful prison conditions in 1981 at Jackson Prison; over the period 1986–2008 we *learned* by experience and observation the effects of the "war on drugs" on the growth of the prison system.

The coauthors also knew enough about life, before teaching in prison, to appreciate the role of "corrections." Teaching became our informal connection to the formal, "official" world of corrections. Prison teaching was another teaching job, along with simultaneously teaching on community college main campuses. But it was a job in which we were learning a whole new world.

It is true that there are a lot of victims of street-drug-related crime. We had been victims. It is also true that there were a lot of victims of alcohol-related use and abuse before Prohibition. But Prohibition was repealed. In the end, we can reflect that laws are made by women and men and laws can, and are, repealed by women and men. Too often criminal justice students want to carry a "warrior" outlook of simplification with them into the quest to "become a cop." Abadinsky notes:

> Our current policy of "shared simplifications" (Gerstein and Harwood 1990) appears to reflect the popular will: allowing the majority of society to be against drug abuse while remaining free to abuse alcohol and tobacco. In other words, laws and law enforcement efforts against substances that are desired by a substantial minority of our citizenry provide symbolic opposition for the majority without actually impairing their own freedom to enjoy dangerous substances and activities—a policy that most Americans would be pleased to "drink to." (Abadinsky 2008:420–21)

As a criminal justice student, remember that in some cases today's "criminal" may be tomorrow's teacher, leader, neighbor or friend. Many prisoners need and want role models, not another judge. As you read this book of prisoner voices, be reminded of old sayings such as "Do unto others as you would have them do unto you," and "To understand another you must first walk a mile in that person's shoes."

This book will present eighty prisoner essays. We show how prisoners think and feel as they enter the prison system and how it constitutes an experiential world for them. But "behind the scenes" are social dynamics that have been shaping this prison system experiential world.

The massive growth of the U.S. prison world is mainly explained by the "war-like" criminalization of street drugs, and is also due to long sentences and fewer paroles. However, why does the United States take this "war" approach to drugs when Britain does not? There is an interrogation we must make. What features of the American context help explain *why* the United States has been particularly vulnerable to the "war on drugs" approach?

2

—ɯ—

Premises of the
Incarceration Binge Culture

As we have moved into the new constellation of 1,000 new prisons and imprisonment booms in each state, an "incarceration binge culture" within prisons has developed, and also in our society. The United States, before 1980, along with Great Britain and Europe had long been among nations with few prisons and low prisoner populations. The "prison culture" was not influential in our society. Countries like Russia, China and South Africa (under apartheid) were nations who imprisoned massive numbers of citizens. *They* had "prison-state" societies. The U.S. rate of incarceration had remained stable around 100 per 100,000. The national total prison population stayed in a range of from 200,000 to 400,000. Sentencing was fairly predictable, prisoners moved in and out of prison roughly on schedule, most leaving prison on or before their "minimum" release date (due to a good institutional record), or before their minimum sentence (because of earning "good time" or disciplinary credits). Parole served as a "safety valve"—if prisons get a little crowded, more were released on parole (Abadinsky 2006:1–2). So, as explained in earlier chapters, new prisons were not needed.

No more. Now, since 1986, not only were more prisons needed—*a thousand* new prisons were needed. And they were always overcrowded. Before the "war on drugs," the American prison had a distinctive "endogenous" prison subculture created by the interaction of prisoners, guards and prison administration; by the late 1960s, gang culture and other street culture influences were being "imported" into this endogenous prison subculture. After the 1986 drug laws, added to "the prisoners' experience" in the prison subculture, (endogenous and imported), was now the "incarceration binge subculture": many more druggies, many more blacks from specific inner city neighborhoods, overcrowding (double-bunking), longer sentences, more flops (denials of parole) and more visible "revolving door" of ex-cons returning to be "in the mix" in the prison yard.

THE RISE OF PRISON INCARCERATION BINGE CULTURE

For the entering convict "the prisoners' world" inside has its own values, norms, customs and rules—its own *subculture.* How did that distinctive prison subculture get there? One of the classic issues about the academic study of the prisoners' world centered around two models, both explaining the origins of prison culture: (1) the endogenous model, and (2) the importation model.

In the endogenous model the prison is seen as "a society of captives." The prison, as a *small society,* develops its own subculture. Gresham Sykes noted in his 1958 study that, if men were merely locked in their cell, the prison would be an "aggregate" of prisoners. But Sykes's research for the book *Society of Captives* found "the prisoners' world" emerges as a subculture through *interactions* at: mess hall, chores, exercise, work, recreation, school and religious activities (Sykes 1958:5).

Guards, because of their working conditions, tend to establish relationships with prisoners and cut them some slack. The slightly loose social order the prisoners establish through their interactions with each other and the guards must, however, be held in check by the prison administration that typically, for public relations reasons, holds the values of strict custody and order. And "the prior deviance of the prisoner is a rationalization for using . . . extreme measures (of deprivation) to avoid any events which would excite public indignation" (Sykes 1958:33).

The Gresham Sykes view that the prison culture came pretty much entirely out of the internal tension between prisoner interaction and the deprivations required by administration concern with custody and control (Sykes 1958:63–83) was challenged in the late 1960s by a view of the prison where prisoners *bring in* their values, norms and customs. That is, prison culture and life is best explained by the influence of imported subcultures, such as the growing American black Muslim religion entering the prison by 1957 (Haley & Malcolm X 1964), and gangs entering the prison in the 1960s (Jacobs 1977), and particular inner city neighborhood street cultures becoming imprisoned (Clear 2007). Clearly, both the endogenous deprivation model and the importation model can help in understanding the subculture of the prison.

As the incarceration binge built up, however, and certain inner city neighborhoods supplied the majority of prisoners in state prisons, a reciprocal reality emerged: the culture of the street enters the prison, and the culture of the prison is exported back out to the street. Both "prison yard" and "the streets in the hood" begin to look and feel similar: same razor wire on back fences of businesses in the neighborhoods as around the prison yard, same drug-user and drug-sales cultures, same drug-hawking gangs or crews, same relatives on the inside as on the street.

Because of the "war on drugs" there is a build-up of the "drug-related" prisoners—as we've emphasized, state prisons shot up in the last twenty-five years from 6 percent drug-related in 1980 to 30 percent drug-related by 2006. More "druggies" in prison alters the prison subculture—this is a premise of the "incarceration binge subculture." The incarceration binge culture, or more druggies, inside the prison interacts in the yard with the large sets of prisoner categories, including sharing yard time with convicts who manifest traditional opportunistic criminality and who show manipulative personality. For a non-violent prisoner serving ten years for a drug crime, trying to sustain an "I'm-not-coming-back-here" personal growth project has to hold up against the constant scheming in the yard on how-to-do-better-crimes-next-time. In other words, the yard is "the inner city streets."

Out in the "real world" the incarceration binge era *societal values*—a rational effort to reduce crime combined with a new Southern punitiveness—reinforced a set of increasingly harsh policies and long sentences. Amplified by middle-class anxiety and fear of crime, a convenient oppression of banishment arises: send more and more to prison (hyperincarceration) to "manage" the problems of the jobless ghetto (hyperghetto). Inside the prison, the incarceration binge era *prison values* become long sentences in overcrowded conditions with selected inner city neighborhoods cycling in and out, where, as mentioned, increasingly "the yard is the streets." However, recall the wardens' phrase: "The doors to the prisoner swing both ways."

There has been, inside the prison, in addition to more druggies and negotiating the yard, the fact of more African American's from specific neighborhoods, overcrowding, long sentences, more parole denials and more ex-cons coming back into prison. These factors combine to alter the prison subculture into an "incarceration binge subculture" where prisoners stay longer under conditions that are worse for success on reentry.

Over 600,000 prisoners return from U.S. prisons to society each year. The policies driving massive prison growth have set up the problem of planning for reentry. Imported from the policy world now grappling with success in reentry is a "binge culture hangover": the criminal justice network (community corrections probation, prison, parole) now has a set of issues and tensions related to a change in the organizational culture of the prison system that began about 2001 and had become very real by

2003—instead of "sending them back to prison through a revolving door of (necessary to be tough) parole enforcement," how do we now "increase the (necessary to save money) success in reentry?"

The new, emerging policies are focused on capping prison growth and, hopefully, downsizing the prison (Jacobson 2005; CAPPS 2008; MPRI 2008). However, this new "organizational culture of reentry success" must address the set of values, fears and oppressions that are representative of the "old organizational culture" of state departments of corrections—a culture that emphasized control and enforcement *more* than prison rehabilitation and reform (Sykes 1958).

Moreover, there is no sign that states are seriously addressing the "functional" premise of the incarceration binge: that prison growth plays a surrogate welfare system role for the inner city black males. That is, that hyperincarceration is another in a "series of American cultural practices and legal institutions (that) has operated in to maintain American patterns of racial dominance and hierarchy for two centuries" (Tonry 2007:23). It is this strong dose of racism that has helped to orchestrate the growth of the prison system (Wacquant 2007; Tonry 2007; Zimring 2006). Where is the drive—so far—to reduce this dose of racism in our prison system?

Exploring prisoner "complaints" about overly long sentences, lack of correctional programming, getting "flopped" too often for "no reason" and existing in a "system" that is interested in "keeping us in here and making sure we come back," reveals, in fact, the set of social dynamics and related social policy we've discussed.

It is not the prison society itself (Sykes 1958), so much, nor the importation of street culture, religion and gangs (Jacobs 1977) (although both still clearly have some importance), but rather the creation since 1986 of the "war on drugs" *as* a convenient oppression of and "solution" for the festering inner cities. The resulting long sentences, spurred by fear and racism, and "tough on crime" politics and policies reflect the norms and values of an overwrought "incarceration binge culture." Whether the prison build-up is, or remains, a rational response to crime is discussed in chapter 3, but it is important to grasp this "incarceration binge culture" in order to understand the last twenty-five years of experience within "the prisoners' world."

DRUGS AND RISE IN BLACK PRISONER POPULATION

The incarceration binge period saw the worsening of an already significant racial imbalance in prisoner population. Before the incarceration binge started in 1986, blacks were 30 percent of the prison population, whites 70 percent. After the imprisonment explosion, African Americans, who represent 12 percent of the population, were now 48 percent of the state prison population.

Michael Tonry, giving his Presidential Address to the American Society of Criminology in the Fall of 2007 notes:

> (In my 1995 book) *Malign Neglect,* I tried to unravel the reasons why black Americans were so much likelier than whites to be arrested, convicted, imprisoned and executed . . .
>
> Here is what I learned. First, although blacks had for a century been more likely to be held in prison than whites, racial disparities began to increase in the 1960 and then shot up to all-time highs in the 1980s: by then blacks were half of American prisoners, although only 12 percent of the U.S. population, and they had an imprisonment rate seven times higher than whites. Second, blacks were much more likely than whites to be arrested for the "imprisonable" offenses of robbery, rape, aggravated assault, and homicide. . . . Third, however, critically, no significant shifts had occurred in racial patterns in arrests for a quarter century, and involvement in serious violent crime could not explain why black imprisonment rates had increased so rapidly. Fourth, the principal driver of the increase was imprisonment for drug crimes, and policy makers knew or should have known that the enemy foot soldiers in the war on drugs would be young, disadvantaged, inner-city members of American minority groups. That seemed to me then and seems to me now a profoundly unwise and immoral exercise of governmental power. (Tonry 2007:21–22)

At the same time as these two changes were taking place—the fourfold increase in rate of incarceration and the "blackening" of our prisons—the prisoner profile was changing from the long-familiar violent white "bad guy" image to that of the drug-related crimes of black and white "druggie" prisoner. Unlike the traditional, violent criminal of the past—the robber, rapist or murderer—or the non-violent property criminal of the past—the burglar, thief, shoplifter, bad checks—today up to 30 percent of state prisoners and probably more than 40 percent of federal prisoners that enter prison are convicted of drug and drug-related crimes. According to the Michigan Department of Corrections (MDOC) 43 percent of prisoners in prison during the incarceration binge period were classified as non-assaultive (MDOC 1996).

In terms of the rate of incarceration, Blumstein notes:

> The growth in the incarceration rate has been far from uniform. . . .
>
> The most striking observation (is that) . . . In the 17 years from 1980 to 1996, drugs climbed from the single offense with *almost the fewest* prisoners *to* the one with by far *the largest number*. There were an estimated 23,900

state and federal prisoners for drug offenses in 1980, which represented an incarceration rate of less than 15 per 100,000 adults. By 1996, that incarceration rate had grown to 148 per 100,000, more than a nine-fold increase. The drug incarceration rate in 1996 was about equal to the (incarceration) rate that had prevailed for fifty years for the entire U.S. prison system. (Blumstein 2002:453; italics added)

Moreover, the amount of time served for drug offenses rose dramatically. There were now the long-sentence mandatory minimum drug laws (meaning no release for "good time"). There were now fewer paroles once the minimum sentence had been completed. And there were now more parole violations sending people back to prison—often for failure to pass drug tests while on parole (Blumstein 2002:461). As Blumstein observes:

> The intensity of the crackdown on drug offenders shows itself in prison populations. In 1998, 58 percent of the prisoners in federal prisons and 21 percent of those in state prisons were there on a drug charge. This contrasts sharply with the rates in 1986, twelve years earlier, when drug offenders accounted for only 8.6 percent of state prisoners. (Blumstein 2002:468)

How did all of this come about? (See Figures 2.1 and 2.2.) How did the United States, in a short twenty years, change from having a traditionally low prisoner population into becoming the world's prison and jail leader, with over 2.2 million prisoners and still growing?

Was this type of prison growth happening elsewhere in the Western industrialized world? In fact, the incarceration rate remained constant in the other Western nations. Between 1970 and 2000 Europe's custody rate per 1,000 stayed at less than 1, around 0.8 to 0.9, while the U.S. custody rate between 1970 and 2000 shot up from 1.8 to 8.4 individuals incarcerated per 1,000. Clearly huge prison growth has been a peculiarly American phenomenon.

Michael Tonry, in his 2007 "Presidential Address" to the American Society of Criminology, in reviewing the work of Loic Wacquant (2007; 2008) notes that his historical view can help explain *why* we had a "war on drugs." Tonry notes that Wacquant's "basic, functionalist argument is that a series of American cultural practices and legal institutions has operated to maintain American patterns of racial dominance and hierarchy for two centuries" (Tonry 2007:23).

Well, didn't we have a Civil Rights Movement? Both coauthors are old enough to have lived through, and participated in, the American Civil Rights Movement (1954–1972). That important movement resulted in considerable increased economic and social integration of blacks in American

Violent crime rates, 1973-95 (with adjustments based on the redesign of the National Crime Victimization Survey)

Victimization rate per 1,000 persons age 12 or older

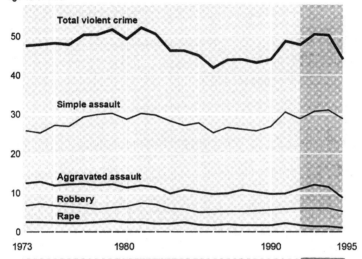

Collected under the National Crime Survey (NCS) and made comparable to data collected under the redesigned methods of the National Crime Victimization Survey (NCVS)

Collected under the redesigned NCVS

Violent crime includes murder, rape, robbery, and aggravated and simple assault. Murder is not shown separately. Sexual assault is excluded, as explained on page 3.

• A decline in the violent crime rate beginning in 1994 interrupted a rising trend that existed after the mid-1980's.

• In 1995 rape, robbery, and aggravated assault, measured by the National Crime Victimization Survey (NCVS), and murder, measured by the FBI's Uniform Crime Reports (UCR), were at or near a 23-year low.

• The rates of theft and household burglary have steadily declined since the late 1970's. In 1995 burglary was at about half the rate in 1973.

• The motor vehicle theft rate in 1995 was well below the highest rate of 1991.

• 1973-91 estimates were adjusted to reflect improved survey methodology put in place in 1992. The adjustments preserve the year-to-year changes in relationships for earlier estimates.

Figure 2.1.   "Trends in criminal victimization in United States, 1973–1995." (USDOJ)

Percent of new court commitments
to State prisons

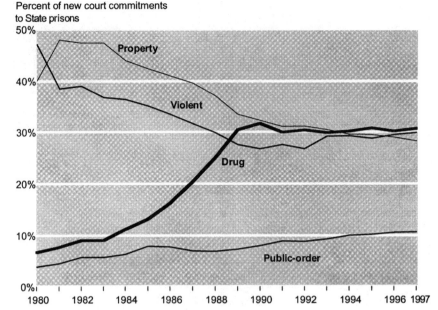

Figure 2.2. "Most serious offence of convicts admitted to state prisons, 1980–1997." (USDOJ)

society. However, *when you look at the criminal justice system*, there is a "7-to-1 racial difference in imprisonment rates."

Tonry notes: "The Bureau of Justice Statistics (BJS)(2003) has estimated that 32 percent of black males born in 2001 will spend some time confined in a state or federal prison. . . . BJS has also estimated that nearly a third of black men in their twenties on any given day are in prison or in jail, or on probation or parole" (Tonry 2007:23). While the Civil Rights Movement opened the job structure to African Americans to produce good working-class, middle-class and government jobs, and while school integration since 1971 produced a measure of equality between students, the criminal justice system produces devastatingly *reduced* life chances for poor black Americans (Western, 2006). The criminal justice system with "nearly of third of black men in their twenties . . . in prison or jail, or on probation or parole" reduces black men's chances for jobs, marriage, being a good father, or being socialized into prosocial values. "There has to be a reason why the criminal justice system treats American blacks so badly, why its foreseeable disparate impacts on blacks and whites are disregarded . . ." (Tonry 2007:23–24).

To answer this question requires a history of narcotics before the war on drugs and an analysis of the emergence of the war on drugs.

A SHORT HISTORY OF NARCOTICS
BEFORE THE WAR ON DRUGS

For years typical street drugs—heroin, marijuana, opium, cocaine, speed (meth)—had been arriving into large U.S. cities: Los Angeles, San Francisco, New York, Chicago, Miami, New Orleans, Detroit and Dallas.

The narcotics would arrive at these cities and filter through the inner city neighborhoods by all possible routes. Some, like cocaine, perhaps marijuana, would go overland by truck, car and human carrier ("mules") through Central America and Mexico into Florida and north into Texas and California. Almost all could go by sea, unloaded in large ports or small marinas disguised as cargo or hidden in the hulls of motor launches or sailing ships. Quantities of all drugs would be smuggled into the country by personnel on airline and ships or by passengers crossing the borders in cars, trains or buses. Marijuana could also come from Northern California where it has been the largest single agricultural crop (in an agricultural state noted for "specialty crops") since the 1970s. Or, from British Columbia, another specialty-crop area marijuana producer.

Once in the inner cities, regular distribution sources were familiar. Unadvertised "dope houses" were common. Drug dealers maintained lists of regular clients for certain drugs. And a few street peddlers—mainly young jobless African American men—sold drugs on the street. In the case of marijuana and other drugs, most got their drug of choice from friends connected to friends who were connected to dealers selling to friends and "checked out" acquaintances.

In the twentieth century, before the counter-culture movement of the 1960s, the use of drugs was restricted mainly to the lower working class (those with low-wage, marginal jobs) living in inner cities. In fact, popular ditties or jingles about slum-dwelling drug users were common enough in the 1930s and 1940s among the white middle class. Twelve-year-old school children, often unaware of its meaning, might chant a catchy tune like "Cocaine Joe and Morphine Sue were walking down the avenue, Honey, have a sniff, Honey have a sniff, Honey have a sniff on me." Popular swing or big band era singers would have tunes with lyrics like "I get no kick from cocaine . . ." ("But I get a kick out of you"). People in the 1950s and early 1960s were also mildly aware of drugs through stories of jazz band musicians succumbing to drugs—or, to the rise of the "beatnik" culture in which drugs (mainly marijuana and hallucinogens) played a part. Drugs were "handled" by "vice squads" in police departments or narcotics officers, but there was no "war" on drugs. Sentences were short. There was no need for a prison build-up.

The broad set of social movements of the 1960s—civil rights, consumer protection, student power, anti-war, environmental, women's

rights—included the smoking of marijuana for many movement people, along with vibrant musical innovation, as emblematic of a statement against conformity and movement membership (Trout, Tregea
& Simmons 1968). Drug use began spreading across the working class
and into what had emerged, due to economic growth in the 1950s and
1960s, as a "middle mass" or middle-class lifestyle. Major glossy magazines in the late 1960s reported 44 percent of people working in the
corporate advertising world smoked marijuana and did other drugs.
Feature stories on Hollywood actors getting busted for drugs became
common. Research showed by the early 1970s over 70 percent of high
school students had tried marijuana.

With time, cocaine, grown in South America's northern mountain
states, principally Columbia, became an imported drug of choice, edging out heroin from Asia's "Golden Triangle," and from opium poppies
grown in Afghanistan. As Colombian cocaine drug cartels grew in the
1970s and 1980s, and as powder cocaine use increased in Hollywood culture, middle-class white professionals began to use cocaine more. So, ever
more fields of coca were processed into cocaine. "Coke" imports into the
United States increased dramatically. Columbia drug cartels even owned
freighters and airplanes to deliver tons of cocaine into secret ports and
airfields in the United States.

With its pervasiveness and growing popularity, by the 1970s powder
cocaine, once confined to the inner cities, was now being used more
openly by the middle class at social events, in the office and factory, and
increasingly with teenagers buying from fellow students dealing in the
schoolyard, along with pot and LSD.

Those involved, and their parents and friends, concerned about bad
trips, drug reactions, mental health and career-threatening aspects of
what was illegal drug use, sought out private drug-treatment centers. For
those in student ghettos or poverty areas, without income or health insurance, neighborhood "drug-education centers" staffed with professional
and volunteer counselors became available, along with the low-income
out-patient clinics.

As drug use grew, drug suppliers knew that the unemployed in U.S.
cities would step forward as dealers. The volume of drugs into the inner cities fueled that location as the source for drug purchases. Cocaine,
"bud," hash, and other drugs were purchased by the working class and
middle class. Meanwhile the lower working class (or emerging "under-
class" of the jobless ghetto) was growing larger. There were now more
users in the city. The inner city drug market grew to meet the demand, as
did the number of young drug sellers.

Businesses—and the jobs they created—kept leaving for the suburbs,
with continued devastation of American inner cities. The word spread in

the inner cities streets of the profit to be made in drugs, stimulating many mid-teen school dropouts, who formerly quit school to look for legitimate jobs, to now be drawn into the economic crime—fast money—that street drug sales offered.

Drug sales became more professional and businesslike; indeed teenage youth came to consider drug selling a "business"—a good business, with high risk, but high rewards. Going to prison was part of "doing business."

Like any business with a steady market, if managed efficiently, one or more drug locations could prove to be a most profitable business. Such a business enabled the "owner" of that location (usually a street corner, or drug house) at the ripe age of nineteen or twenty to enjoy and use business "profits" any way he pleased—to help support parents or a child, or to buy new cars, clothes, attract women—in sum, to live an extravagant lifestyle. He could be a "player," with many women and financial security. He would have arrived, would now officially be "living life in the fast lane."

Sale and possession of street drugs *had* been illegal before 1986. The Marijuana Tax Act of 1937 criminalized pot. The Harrison Act of 1914 made heroin illegal, and the Opium Act of 1855 on the west coast first made opium illegal in California (Musto 1991). There were laws against cocaine. However, in the 1950s and 1960s, under the treatment ethic of "the rehabilitative ideal," drug sales and drug possession "crimes" were not politicized and the approach—short sentence with mandatory treatment—was not overly punitive. Few went to prison, and, if they did, the sentence for drug sales was generally two to five years, and people could leave prison earlier than their minimum with "good time." The incarceration rate stayed stable (around 100 per 100,000 population). People came and went from prisons without the prison system increasing in the number of prisons. There was no "war" on drugs, no "strategy of incarceration" to perform the convenient oppression of "handling" the troublesome inner city residents. The extreme joblessness of the "festering inner cities" had, in fact, not yet developed.

But, the United States has always had "swings in the pendulum" between tolerance and intolerance regarding "moral vices" such as alcohol and drugs (Musto 1991). For instance, the 1890s were awash with drugs and alcohol, but by 1920 the United States had Prohibition and a punitive "war on alcohol" era. Then drugs flowed again under a period of tolerance during the 1960s and early 1970s, only to run up again against a tide of intolerance driven by "tough-on-crime" politics in the 1980s and 1990s. Even with alternating eras of tolerance and intolerance over the decades, a rough stability in the rate of incarceration between 60 and 125 per 100,000 existed, up to 1984.

In the eighties, events were to change that stability. First, guns began flowing into the ghettos, especially into Detroit's inner city, which had formerly been without guns. The path to gang violence in Detroit resembled that of the gangster period of Prohibition in the 1920.

Initially, after Prohibition was declared, trafficking in illegal liquor was benign. But soon liquor sales became deadly as bands of armed gangsters competed for control of territories. So, in the same way, entrance of guns into the 1980s jobless ghetto quickly spelled competition and trouble in Detroit. There was an increase in the crime rate from 1986 to 1991. But it was not an increase in the *crime rate* that was scaring the U.S. public, so much as the alarming increase in the use of firearms in the city (Zimring & Hawkins 1997).

During the crack epidemic (1986–1993) homicides, particularly juvenile homicides, abruptly increased in Detroit's inner city as teenage drug sellers, youthfully headstrong and unschooled in guns, fought with youthful vigor and emotion to protect their particular piece of hard-won turf (Blumstein 2002). Sometimes these homicidal fights involved also the woman (or women) who went with the "player's" lucrative drug location.

News stories of the wave of homicides and arrests in Detroit created national attention and brought forth, in the summer of 1986, as we have highlighted, a moral panic (Chiricos 1995), in the form of the rushed passage of the federal Anti-Drug Abuse Act and its extraordinarily long mandatory drug sentences. This punitive response can be summarized as a fundamentally inappropriate response. Instead of focusing on the problems of the inner city—jobs, family support, housing, income, job skills and education—the United States began an incarceration binge.

Now, more than twenty years later, we *still* have the jobless ghettos (hyperghetto), but we also have this huge, world's largest, prison system (hyperincarceration). Are Tonry and Wacquant right? Did we need this convenient oppression of drug law prison growth as another in "a series of American cultural practices and legal institutions (operating) to maintain American patterns of racial dominance and hierarchy for (the last) two centuries . . ." (Tonry 2007:23).

DRUGS, GUNS AND THE INNER CITY—A "WAR" ON DRUGS

Many politicians seized on inner city drug crimes in the mid-1980s as a "wedge issue" to distinguish their political party from the "softer" (other) political party. The Republican Party was particularly good at this maneuver, but the Democrats found they needed to play catch up and be "tough on crime" too. Dismayed by urban violence, especially these drug-related killings in Detroit's ghetto, but also in other urban ghettos, and aware of the rise in drug use nationwide (by both whites and blacks), President Reagan seized the moment to announce, in 1986, a new "war" on drugs.

A new "federalization" of drug law, similar to the 1920s Prohibition Era, occurred (Heyman & Moore 1996). The new federal drug laws imposed stricter penalties and longer sentences for possession, use and sale of drugs. States followed with their own punitive, long-sentence penalties for "possession with intent to deliver," or "conspiracy with intent to deliver."

There followed immediate and frequent enforcement crackdowns. Daily police sweeps and arrests of inner city drug sellers occurred. At the same time, U.S. dollars for drug interdiction at borders, at sea, and in the air were dramatically increased, but with little effect. (Estimates are that drug border enforcement catches 2 to 3 percent of illegally imported drugs). President H.W. Bush, the first Bush President, however, was fond of advertising the "war on drugs," and was featured in late-1980s magazine "photo ops" at the steering wheel of "torpedo" speedboats meant for chasing drug smugglers off the coast of Florida and in the Gulf of Mexico.

With the prompt federal passage of the first Mandatory Minimum Drug Laws of 1986, in an atmosphere of moral panic (Chiricos 1995) many young drug sellers who had been living comfortably "on the fast track" on the streets of Detroit's ghetto abruptly found themselves detained on the streets, arrested, charged, convicted and sentenced, and condemned to prisons like Michigan Reformatory and Jackson Prison (see chapters 13–15) for harsh ten-to-twenty-year, and twenty-to-life mandatory drug sentences. As Schmalleger notes:

Mandatory sentencing is just what its name implies—a structured sentencing scheme which allows no leeway in the nature of the sentence required and under which clearly enumerated punishments are mandated for specific offenses or for habitual offenders convicted of a series of crimes. Mandatory sentencing, because it is truly *mandatory*, differs from presumptive sentencing . . . which allows at least a limited amount of judicial discretion within ranges established by published guidelines.

By passing mandatory sentencing laws, legislators convey the message that certain crimes are deemed especially grave and that people who commit them deserve, and may expect, harsh sanctions. These laws are sometimes passed in response to public outcries following heinous or well-publicized crimes. (Schmalleger 2001:374–75)

Did harsh mandatory drug laws really deter jobless youth in American inner cities from selling drugs? Schmalleger notes:

> An (evaluation of) New York's (1973) Rockefeller drug laws was unable to support claims for their efficacy as a deterrent to drug crime.
>
>   . . . Tonry found that . . . sentences become longer and more severe. Mandatory sentencing laws may also occasionally result in unduly harsh punishments for marginal offenders who nonetheless meet the minimum requirements for sentencing under such laws.
>
>   In an analysis of federal sentencing guidelines, other researchers found that blacks receive longer sentences than whites, not because of differential treatment by judges, but because they constitute the large majority of those convicted of trafficking in crack cocaine—a crime Congress has singled out for especially harsh mandatory penalties. (Schmalleger 2001:375–376; FAMM 2008)

Thus, the next fifteen years (1986–2001) would see the tremendous prison explosion of 1,000 new prisons known as The Incarceration Binge (Austin & Irwin 1997). Sentencing for drug crimes would get ever tougher and prisons nationwide would become ever fuller, reaching the capacity point, over and over again. Why did the people of the United States "let" a moral panic in 1986 over crack cocaine *lead* to such a twenty-year incarceration binge? Chiricos notes:

> Hysteria over violent crime is a classic example of "moral panic." This concept was developed by Cohen, who noted that at certain times a "condition, episode, person or group of persons emerges to become defined as a threat to societal values and interests" (Cohen 1972:9). He notes that typically the threat is presented in the media in a simplistic fashion; spokespersons such as editors, the clergy, and politicians man the moral barricades; and experts pronounce their diagnoses of the problem and present solutions. As the he emphasizes, the point of a moral panic is "not that there's nothing there," but that societal responses are fundamentally inappropriate. (Cohen 1972:204; Chiricos 1998:59)

So, the "war" on drugs with the police crackdowns and the long sentence mandatory minimums led to massive incarceration getting the now-reviled crack dealers off the streets and into prison. Then, another young inner city black youth would step forward to sell the drugs. But for every violence-prone, street-corner, gang-affiliated drug dealer there were many more "druggies" (white, black and brown) who bought the drugs and became addicted. These people often then, through drug abuse, started to do home invasions, petty larcenies (like shoplifting) or writing bad checks to support their expensive drug habit. These "persistent property offenders with a drug problem" go to prison and have become—in the "mixed bag" prison population that consists of several types of convicts—the largest single category of prisoner.

In 2007 the Michigan Department of Corrections (MDOC) admittance statistics report state prisoners charged with *drug-defined* crimes (possession, intent to deliver) entering the prisons are at an historical high of 21 percent in 2007, up from around 5 percent in 1980. While 43 percent of state prisoners admitted were "non-assaultive," 38 percent were "assaultive."

Some of those charged as "assaultive" are burglaries or home invasions which are often *drug-related property crimes.* "Home invasions" involve breaking and entering a home, while "burglaries" involve breaking and entering places that are not homes, such as warehouses or commercial buildings. The prison-admittance who are in the "assaultive" category can be broken down into a rough approximation of perhaps half who have violent tendencies (carry guns or engage in other opportunistic assaultive crime) and half who are non-violent (no guns or assaults, no other violence in their court records).

So, adding together drug-defined crime, the non-violent category of home invasion, burglary, and other non-assualtive convictions, a good estimate is that 50 percent *of those entering prison* are non-violent prisoners. That is, nationally, we have "one million non-violent prisoners" currently *entering* our prisons each year. The cost to Michigan taxpayers in 2008 is $32,000 per prisoner bedspace, per year. There is a tremendous cost in potentially misplaced priorities in state sentences when we incarcerate non-violent people for long sentence who we are *irritated at.* On the other hand, we want to reserve a prison bedspace for violent people we are *afraid of.*

So, in this regard, it is important to distinguish who *goes* to prison each year (prison admittance) and what types of people *are in* prison at any particular time (prison population).

Violent prisoners, as we've indicated, may represent only about one-half of all prison admittance. However, conviction for violent offenses typically involves longer sentences with fewer paroles at earliest release date. Convictions for many non-violent crimes (other than mandatory drug crime sentences) can be short sentences. We want to keep violent predators off our streets *during that period of their life* when they are violent. On the other hand, those with non-assaultive convictions are released more often at their earliest release date—they come and go from the prison. The exception, which we've been emphasizing, is the situation of overly long "war-on-drugs" sentences for drug-defined crime (e.g., the mandatory minimums and three strikes laws). So, those with a violent conviction in their record have longer sentences and are paroled less. Those with a violent conviction "pile up" in the prison and constitute roughly 75 percent of the *total prison population* at any given time.

So, yes, is can be said that our prisons are "full of violent predators." But only because many others come and go from the prison, leaving the more violent category of original offense, with very long sentences, to accumulate as a larger and larger part of the prison population. We need to distinguish between these three types of prisoner population: overly long non-violent drug-related sentences, other short non-violent sentences, and longer violent record sentences.

However, it's important to also note that not all "violent predators" are still violent predators after many years in prison. For instance, according to recidivism research, murderers are some of the *least* likely prisoner categories to reoffend when (or if) they are released. Many youth that, at seventeen, eighteen or nineteen got caught up in drug-related violence (turf war homicides and deadly assaults) and are serving very long sentences, mature-out in prison. They become non-violent people after staying so long in prison. After ten or twelve years they've wised up—but still have many years to go on a twenty-to-life, or parolable life, sentence.

Adding together the historical high of 21 percent drug-defined (MDOC 2007) and an additional estimate of 9 percent conviction for home invasion *where* the case file would show a non-assualtive individual with non-violent drug-related behavior, we have a reasonable estimate of a total of 30 percent of Michigan's state prisoners who come into Michigan's prison as non-violent offenders caught in the incarceration binge a as consequence of the "war on drugs." Why are we putting *these* people in prison, and for such long sentences? Blumstein notes:

> Unfortunately, our political system has learned an overly simplistic trick: it responds to such pressures (demand to do something about drug problem) by sternly demanding punishment. This approach has been found to be strikingly effective—not in solving the problem, but in alleviating the political pressure to "do something." . . .
> As a result, there has been a succession of punitive efforts to attack the drug trade. Many states have adopted mandatory-minimum sentences for drug dealing that are comparable to the sentences for homicide. The consequence of these efforts has been a dramatic growth in the number of arrests for drug offenses and the filling of prisons with drug offenders.
> . . . the growth from 1965 to 1992 in arrest rates for adults and juveniles for drug offenses, by race . . . (show) since the early 1970s, the rate for white adults has been fairly steady, rising slowly to about 500 per 100,000. On the other hand, the rate for nonwhites (primarily African-Americans) rose rapidly between 1980 to 1985, and then accelerated exponentially at an annual rate of about 15 to 20 percent per year until it reach a peak in 1989, and then continued at a high rate. (Blumstein 2002:466–67)

Writing in 1999, Marc Mauer notes that African Americans, who constitute 12 percent of the U.S. population, accounted for only 21 percent of the drug possession arrests nationally in 1980, and that, as the 1986 federal drug laws emerged, followed by state drug laws, the number of black drug arrests "rose to a high of 36 percent in 1992. . . . Importantly, for juveniles, this rate . . . climbed to 40 percent by 1991, before declining to 30 percent in 1995" (Mauer 1999:145).

Do African Americans use drugs a great deal more than whites? Mauer notes:

> Looking at the data for 1995, we find that while African Americans were slightly more likely to be monthly drug users than whites and Hispanics (7.9 percent vs. 6.0 percent and 5.1 percent respectively), the much greater number of whites in the overall population resulted in their constituting the vast majority of drug users. Thus, the SAMHSA (Substance Abuse and Mental Health Services Administration) data indicate that whites represented 77 percent of current drug users, with African Americans constituting 15 percent of users and Hispanics, 8 percent . . . it is difficult to imagine that African American drug use is of a magnitude that could explain blacks representing 15 percent of current drug users yet 33 percent of arrests for drug possession. (Mauer 1999:147)

Chiricos had identified the 1986 Anti-Drug Abuse mandatory minimum and massive prison build up as a fundamentally inappropriate response. He says:

> But instead of waging war on the inhuman conditions fostered by policies of disinvestment and de-skilling, that have hollowed our inner-city neighborhoods, we wage war on those individuals dehumanized by the lack of reasonable choices. Instead of waging war on unemployment, inadequate schools, and the loss of hope we wage war on individuals destroyed by those very conditions. Instead of waging war on the factors contributing to an increasingly isolated underclass—for whom life has less and less meaning—we wage war against individuals who seek meaning in drugs and violence.
>
> Instead of seeing the world as it is—one in which investment decisions by the owners of capital have caused the devastation of inner-city neighborhoods, communities, and families and the economic stagnation of almost all others—these moral panics force us to see as "in all ideology, men and their circumstances . . . upside-down as in a *camera obscura*" (Marx and Engels 1846/1970:47). The greatest victims of private and public policies that have literally determined that people will count less than profits are demonized by moral panics and herded behind ever-widening walls of exclusion.
>
> As noted above, the real danger of the recent moral panics is that they treat problems that have been *substantial* and *enduring* for several decades in many inner-city neighborhoods as if they are a *sudden* firestorm. An atmosphere of panic mobilizes demands for immediate repression and causes us to ignore the root problems of urban America, which have grown and festered for decades. The same media frenzy that raises *decisiveness* to the cardinal virtue

of public policy, lowers the chance that meaningful response to enduring problems will be undertaken. (Chiricos 1998:72–73)

WHAT EXPLAINS BINGE GROWTH?

The U.S. prison and jail system has "been on a binge," becoming the world's largest. Is this because the crime rate has been increasing? Hardly. While there was an increase in crime rates from 1986 to 1991, in fact, the U.S. crime rate has been falling since 1991 (Zimring 2007). Researchers note a steady decline of adult violence, particularly homicide and robbery. Blumstein notes:

> The decline in the 1990s is a . . . complicated story . . . the crime rate rise of late 1980s being caused almost entirely by offenders under age 25, whereas offending rates of older people displayed a steady decline. The sharpest decline in the 1990s has thus occurred among the young offenders. (Blumstein & Wallman 2000:4)

How are we to explain this massive 400-percent growth in the prison system (1986–2008) when the U.S. population in the same period grew only 25 percent from 240 million to 300 million? And even as there has been a decrease in crime, and even a decrease in violent crime? True, you cannot imprison so many without lowering crime. So, in this view, increasing incarceration lowers crime. However, the best research indicates that the incarceration binge lowered crime, at most, perhaps 20–25 percent in the 1990s. That leaves 75 to 80 percent of the fall in crime rate due to many other factors. Since the prison expansion did not occur in the context of an increase in crime, after 1991, why has there been such political support for a massive prison system after 1991?

We have explained that drugs were the primary reason for more arrests and convictions. It was the sharp punitive set of drug laws initiated by President Reagan and passed by Congress in the late summer of 1986 that launched the prison build-up (Figure 2.2).

Writing about his twenty-year prison college teaching experience, co-author Bill Tregea reflected:

> In 1986, I attended my first prison college graduation at Soledad Prison in California. Driving down from Berkeley for two years, I had taught business classes at the prison for Hartnell College. On the occasion of the graduation, about 150 prisoners and 50 teachers, administrators, and guests attended.
>
> In most college graduation ceremonies the discussion is about the bright prospects ahead, the promise of the future. (Tregea 2003:320)

But, while many prisoners were familiar with many drugs, these graduates of the Hartnell College Associates of Arts degree program at Soledad Correctional Facility who were also near their release date from the prison now faced a new crack drug epidemic that, at that time, was starting 200 miles south in Los Angeles. Simultaneously, politicians in Congress were calling for tough, new penalties. In describing the Hartnell graduation, Tregea continues:

> This prison college graduation was a ceremony of dark warning. The talk was about how the pull of the street, the lack of employment, inadequate transition services, combined with the virulent addiction potential of drugs and alcohol and money from the drug trade could spell disaster for many graduating prisoner-students. (Tregea 2003:320)

What were all the situational factors that could let this summer of 1986 drug scare, and the rush to pass the 1986 drug laws, escalate into a quadrupling of the U.S. prison system? There had been drug epidemics, drug scares and drug laws before—but we had never quadrupled our prison system before. What mainstream, "Big Politics," institutional "players" could facilitate such a growth of the criminal justice apparatus, (cops, courts, corrections), into a gargantuan organizational field (Stenson 1991; Scott 1992)? Why is crime—at certain times—so important to Americans? That is, what explains the *salience* of crime as peculiar to America, and how does that salience of crime underlie the tendency to use massive prison growth (Zimring 2007; 2006)?

It's true that between 1986 and 1991 the crime rate was increasing. This is an important point because the prison build-up movement could be seen as a design by a rational public to dampen down crime. And it is true that the growth of the prison system dampened down that late 1980s/early 1990s crime-rate growth by getting people off the streets and into prison. How much did incarceration of so many reduce crime? Establishing any "general formula" for how much effect increasing incarceration reduces the crime rate is probably inadvisable. Some researchers suggest that increasing incarceration rate between 1986 and 1991 decreased the crime rate by about 20 to 25 percent. Other estimates go as low as 13 percent and as high as 50 percent. In typical cost-effective analyses, the cost of financing the increase in incarceration is weighed against the cost of the crime deterred. John Irwin and James Austin note:

> Annual spending on corrections has risen from $9.1 billion to nearly $32 billion, far outstripping any other segment of the criminal justice system. . . .
> Significantly, the costs of crimes to victims is far below the costs of criminal justice. In 1992, the total costs of crimes to victims, as reported in the U.S.

Department of Justice's National Crime Victim Survey (NCVS), was $17.6 billion, or about $500 per crime; the majority of crimes had value losses below $100. These costs include economic losses from property theft or damage, cash losses, medical expenses, loss of pay caused by victimization, and other related costs.

. . . Given the enormous costs of aggressive imprisonment and it's doubtful effectiveness on crime, one must question the wisdom of our current sentencing policies. (Irwin & Austin 1997)

But it matters which decade you are talking about. The research is clear that *some* important reductions in crime occurred during the 1990s as the prison system grew (Conklin 2003:79–98). But, as we've entered the twenty-first century, a pair of the most careful policy researchers on the growth of "the prison state" have concluded, regarding the prison build-up, that "for many jurisdictions the point of accelerating declining marginal returns may have set in" (Useem & Piehl 2008:51–80).

The conclusion that all of our massive prison growth is "not paying off" anymore in terms of "cost-effectiveness" suggests that the problem of explaining the growth in the prison apparatus has become more than an academic exercise. People are really becoming concerned about overuse of confinement, especially governors and state legislatures. In order to fully address the *reasons* for the dynamics underlying the incarceration binge—which is that our premise *began* as a moral panic over a drug epidemic combined with a good dose of racism—and look at what explains the *continued* push for ever greater prison growth all through the latter 1990s and through the period of 2000–2008, we need to ask: why did we *let* drug laws and the prison build-up continue for fifteen years after the start of the decline in crime rates?

3

—w—

Prison Binge Growth Theory

The prisoner voices in the eighty essays in this book reveal their thinking and feeling as they enter the prison system. However, we need
to ask questions they, themselves, may not have asked: what "behind-
the-scenes" social dynamics are shaping this "experiential world" of the
expanding prison world? We suggested in chapter 2, "Premises of the
Incarceration Binge Culture," that the prison culture has changed over
the last twenty-five years to include the subcultural consequences of
overcrowding, double-bunking, more druggies, few correctional programming services, longer sentences, fewer paroles and more "revolving
door" offenders coming back into prison from mostly drug-related parole
violation—an in-prison "incarceration binge culture."

We reviewed the suggestion by Chiricos that a moral panic in the summer of 1986 over the crack epidemic led to the beginning of the prison
build-up movement. But why, over the previous twenty-five years—and
over the subsequent twenty-five years—did the society *ignore* the root
causes of persistent and enduring drug crime in the festering inner city?
Tonry suggests, following Loic Wacquant and Hofstader, that the U.S.
Republican party "southern strategy" used the simplistic trick of "getting
tough on crime" as a wedge issue to get votes; and, more deeply, that the
massive prison build up represented another "in the series of American
cultural practices and legal institutions (operating) to maintain American
patterns of racial dominance and hierarchy for (the last) two centuries
. . ." (Tonry 2007:23).

In this section we want to review several more basic theoretical orientations that can help explain the causes of prison build-up, in addition to

51

the drug laws and racism. These perspectives are offered as a tentative "binge growth theory."

BINGE GROWTH THEORY

Peter Kraska's 2004 reader *Theorizing Criminal Justice*, introduces eight theoretical orientations, each of which can be used as a *different* "theoretical lens," to answer the question: "What accounts for the growth of the criminal justice apparatus (cops, courts and corrections)?" These eight theoretical orientations are: (1) rational/legal, (2) systems view, (3) crime control vs. due process, (4) politics, (5) social constructionist stance, (6) growth complex, (7) oppression, and (8) late modernity. While the Kraska reader is meant to introduce criminal justice students to the issue of growth in the *entire* range of the "criminal justice apparatus," we want to focus on how his collection of perspectives can contribute to "binge growth theory."

We begin by integrating these eight theoretical orientations into three sets of interlocking explanations of prison growth. In summary, we argue that what may have started out as a rational public prison build-up movement responding to crime turned into a "binge growth" through the *orchestration* of continual massive prison growth over the last twenty years through these three sets of interacting social forces.

First, there has been a *rational and legal* response by an American public that, during the period in question (1986–2008), wanted to shift values from due process to a crime control model (Useem & Piehl 2008). This American public has been expressing both an increase in security consciousness (evident in all Western nations), and a peculiar salience of crime characteristic of America (Garland 2001/2004; Zimring 2007). While there was an increase in the crime rate from 1986 to 1991 that the original crack epidemic prison build-up movement tried to dampen down, there was also throughout the period of 1986–2008 a shift to crime control values, even after there was a decrease in the crime rate. At the same time there has been a simultaneous interest in community-level crime prevention. Americans may be beginning to connect with issues of community crime prevention (front end) and success in prisoner reentry (back end), but have not yet shown signs of analyzing the policies driving prison binge growth. *Wanting* a rational and legal response to crime that shifts values from due process to crime control is not the same as *getting* a rational and effective crime-control system. Overuse of confinement has begun to eat up state budget resources, at the same time that there are not enough resources for crime prevention. Would not a shift of some resources from the prison-build-up movement to an evidence-based crime-prevention movement be an alternative rational crime-control model?

Secondly, there is a history of *politics, media and fear* that combined with how the criminal justice network seeks coherence as a system acting to maintain its own interests as a growth complex. Similar to the rise of "tough on alcohol" during the campaign to build-up alcohol Prohibition, in the "politics, media and fear" view, what politician can oppose the "bandwagon" prison-build-up movement? Thus, an increasingly "bloated prison bureaucracy" is amplified by fear through a "governing-through-crime" political formula (Simon 2007) involving politicians as "tough." The media-driven drug scares and moral panics interact with the politicians' call to be "tough on crime." Thus, more laws increasing the sentence length occur, more prisoners stay longer in prison and the prisons grow. In this situation, the prison systems have "had the upper hand" in state budgets for decades. Will the American people "wise up" to this political quagmire, partly because they cannot afford it anymore, and support instead some sensible sentencing and parole policy? And, now that many effective evidence-based programs are known, why would they not wish a more rational shift of some resources to evidence-based crime prevention?

Thirdly, however, the *convenient oppression* that the growth of the U.S. criminal justice apparatus provides for "managing" the surplus labor in the jobless ghettos is a difficult reality to face up to. Yet, prison binge growth is coming up against the pragmatic concern of state budgets. The corrections budget has become the largest state general fund expense (CRC 2008; Council of State Governments 2008). Just as the federalization of drug laws that started the mass incarceration that spread to the states took a president to push the policy, so it will take a new focus from Washington to address the urban problems that have led to the existing incarceration strategy that is based upon "imprisoning communities." This is to ask: Can the American people and political leaders move away from hyperghettos "solved" by hyperincarceration and, instead, address the root causes of the festering inner cities? Can the taxpayers afford not to? To truly address crime we need to pay either way, and it's coming down to a choice: either through ever more prisons or through an increase in prevention. Is it time to face up to our "inconvenient oppression?"

Meanwhile, the emerging "prison state" happens separately from the person becoming a convict's own personal life experiences. Recent changes in U.S. institutions, as outlined by these three "binge growth theory" views, have helped "the prisoners' world" to grow "behind the prisoner-to-be's back," as they enter the experiential world of the largest prison system in the world.

A RATIONAL AMERICAN PUBLIC

Why would the American public want to build up the largest prison system in the world? One important understanding of why prisons have grown may be seen as a rational and legal response by an American public occurring in the late 1970s and 1980s: a shift in values from due process to a crime-control model. The American people, in other words, were *responding* to the Republican Party's "southern strategy." Also, *all* Western industrial nations have been expressing an increase in security consciousness even as there has been a decrease in the crime rate. From a "rational/legal" view prisons are *supposed* to grow because they have to, either as a natural reaction (increase in scale) related to an increase in crime and/or population growth, or as a result of an increase in *laws* requiring incarceration.

The American Revolution founded a constitutional democracy where a "rational" public could make laws debated-out in a legislature. During the Enlightenment period in Europe (1640–1830), also known as the "Age of Rationalism," the methods of science and critical thinking were expanded—confronting and largely replacing medieval tradition.

In the area of criminal justice the transformation away from medieval tradition started with Cesare Beccaria, who, in 1764, sought to sweep away the arbitrary judges and inconsistent laws of the feudal period and replace them with more rational laws created by a more rational process. Instead of the King declaring law, or law based only on tradition (common law), the laws would now also be made (with the subsequent help of the American Revolution of 1776 and the French Revolution of 1789) in the new democratic nation-state through legislatures.

In this view, people were seen as rational beings and would weigh the consequences of lawbreaking. Swift, certain justice, where the severity of the laws were proportional to the severity of the crime, was best—and punishment was to be "as analogous as possible to the nature of the crime." This rational approach could deter crime. Also, punishments that are more cruel and unusual than this can make men "grow hardened and insensible." Becarria (1764/2004) says,

> Crimes are more effectually prevented by the certainty than the severity of the punishment. . . . That a punishment may produce the effect required, it is sufficient that the evil it occasions should exceed the good expected from the crime, including in the calculation the certainty of the punishment, and the privation of the expected advantage. All severity beyond this is superfluous, and therefore tyrannical. (Beccaria 1764/2004, in Kraska 2004:26–27)

How, then, to explain the four-fold growth in the U.S. prison system from 1986 to 2008? From this *rational/legal* view, if the laws are rational and there has been a massive growth in prisons, it must be because there has been a massive increase in crime, due to either a population increase or a growth in criminal behavior, or both. However, the U.S. *crime rates have fallen* each year since 1991 and the U.S. population grew only 25 percent (not 400 percent). Another alternative is the massive growth in prisons could be because people wanted more laws.

Then, again, the view could be put forward that, after the initial prison build-up, the crime rates have fallen *due to* the use of incarceration during this period 1986–2006—an "incarceration effect." A lot of the bad guys are now in prison, reducing the crime rate. The best current research on this complicated question indicates that recent massive incarceration has reduced the crime rate by somewhere between 13 and 50 percent (Useem & Piehl 2008) or between 20 and 25 percent (Blumstein & Wallman 2000:6; Conklin 2003). There is room to argue that this "incarceration effect" is large enough to have some basis as rational policy.

So, because of *legal* changes in U.S. law starting with the federal law in 1986 and spreading to the states, street drugs (marijuana, powder cocaine and crack, heroin, meth, hallucinogens, club drugs) were now long-sentence major felonies and the United States would have to build more prisons and put more people in prison. And the prisons would stay full longer due to the "tough-on-crime" longer sentences brought about by mandatory minimums and "three strikes and you're out." And it is clear from the data in Figure 2.2 on the "Most serious offense of convicts admitted to state prisons (1980–1997), that *it is these drug laws that have been the main source of the expanding prison world.* We have made this point in chapters 1 and 2. Our need here is to reflect on the proposition that this is the result of a rational public. Is "binge growth theory" a rational process?

Consider Becarria (1764/2004) once more: Are these long sentences for drug dealing "in proportion to the evil they produce?" Is a "war-on-drugs" sentence for drug-defined law of twenty-to-life for carrying crack "with intent to deliver" a superfluous (unnecessarily severe) law? Is such a painfully long sentence for a seventeen-year-old, non violent, inner city first offender who got sucked into the street drug culture and was convicted of "conspiracy with intent to deliver" a severity tending to "harden" and "make men insensible?" Is the federalization of drug laws, and such long "war on drug" sentences at both the federal and state level "tyrannical?" These kinds of questions have not been frequently (or loudly) asked by the American public.

Yet, the "war on alcohol," during the Prohibition era, was resisted by a vast number of Americans who, through continuing their purchases of alcohol from bootleggers, supported the illegal alcohol trade. Today, in many U.S. urban communities drug use is common. And it has been growing in the U.S. suburban working class as well. Segments of the U.S.

people support, through continued street-drug purchases, the replace-ment drug dealer when the original drug dealer goes to prison. Beccaria was interested in rational law with proportional sentences that would *deter* crime. Yet, passing such harsh laws has not deterred drug crimes.

Becarria was concerned to overthrow the arbitrary and excessive pun-ishment of the medieval judges and prosecutors appointed by Kings. He sought a rational society of democratically made laws where "crimes are more effectually prevented by the certainty than the severity of punish-ment." Would Becarria be critical of the premises of the U.S. "incarcera-tion binge?"

Jeffrey Reiman reports in his book *The Rich Get Richer and the Poor Get Prison* (2004) that he asked his students to imagine

> that, instead of designing a correctional system to reduce and prevent crime, we had to design one that would maintain a stable and visible "class" of criminals. What would it look like? The response . . .
>
> *First.* It would be helpful to have laws on the books against drug use or prostitution or gambling—laws that prohibit acts that have no unwilling vic-tim. This would make many people "criminals" for what they regard as nor-mal behavior and would increase their need to engage in *secondary* crime (the drug addicts need to steal to pay for drugs, the prostitute's need for a pimp because police protection is unavailable, and so on). (Reiman 2004:2–3)

Is the time coming when the American people are past the *incarceration binge* culture? Could the American people push for and support a harm reduction and "health-and-wellness" approach to reducing street drugs? This would be a path similar to the U.S. history repealing Prohibition and adopting a wellness approach to alcohol—and in reducing tobacco use. The American people could then institute programs like the harm-reduc-tion approach in the Liverpool region of England—continued harassment of middle-level and large-scale drug traffickers, some decriminalization of certain drugs, combined with harm reduction for first and second of-fense, low level dealers and addicts (see chapter 1).

In fact, polls suggest that the public is of two minds—they want tough punishment but they also want their tax money to "do" something, to "fix" or reduce the drug abuse and addiction problem. A harm-reduc-tion approach would include education and treatment, and might result in a gradual cultural shift away from street drug use and abuse. A lot of money—tens of billions of dollars each year—could be shifted away from the punishment priority (prison system) to the rehabilitation priority through utilizing evidence-based crime-prevention programs.

The American people have been interested in effective community-based crime prevention for several years. David Farrington and his coau-thors, highly regarded researchers, have reviewed all the major empirical studies and come up with an important list of evidence-based programs of "what works in preventing crime." They have reviewed the research in the institutional areas of families, schools, communities, labor markets, places, police and courts and corrections. Some of the twenty-nine programs they have found empirical evidence for and that work to accomplish crime prevention include:

Families: Home visitation, parent education plus day care/preschool, school-based child training plus parent training, multisystemic therapy;

Schools: School and discipline management (crime, alcohol and other drugs, assaultive behavior); interventions to establish norms or expectations for behavior; mentoring, tutoring and work study;

Labor markets: Ex-offender job training for older males no longer under criminal justice supervision; intensive, residential training programs for at-risk youth (Job Corps);

Places: Nuisance abatement (crime, disorder, drug dealing); improved street lighting in open public places;

Police: Increased directed patrols in street-corner hot spots of crime; proactive arrests of serious repeat offenders; proactive drunk driving arrests; arrests of employed suspects for domestic assault; problem oriented policing;

Courts and corrections: Rehabilitation with particular characteristics (e.g. target specific problems of offenders, intensive treatment); prison-based therapeutic community treatment of drug-involved offenders; in-prison therapeutic communities with follow-up community treatment; cognitive behavioral therapy; moral reconation therapy and reasoning and rehabilitation; non-prison based sex offender treatment; vocational education for adult offenders and juvenile delinquents; multi-component correctional industry programs; community employment; and incapacitating offenders who continue to commit crimes at high rates (Farrington, et al. 2002/2006:408).

Many of these programs require money. One reason you may not have heard much about them (effective crime prevention), and you have heard a lot about the prison system (lock them up), is that a lot of media attention, political sound-bites and money have been spent on prisons and very little media attention, political sound bits or money have been spent on crime prevention. However, as services to children and families *before* offending, and as services to juveniles and adults *after* offending, these evidence-based programs can have a far greater impact on reducing the kind of crimes that lead toward prison (prevention effect) than building more prisons *if* state prison growth can be capped and state resources shifted to prevention (Irwin & Austin 1994:452; Petersilia 2003; Farrington et al. 2002/2006; Irwin 2006; Brown 2007). Once you see these options (prison and crime prevention) as *competing alternatives* for the use of state resources, it becomes possible to consider more seriously whether incarceration binge growth has been a case of policies of overuse of confinement (CAPPS 2008).

What causes drug use and drug-related offenses? There are often psychological and sociological reasons for heavy drinking and drugging that can be traced back to the family (child abuse and neglect) and the community (neighborhood poverty and gangs). Once you are addicted you've got a brain disease and so relapse is characteristic, making getting off drugs—and staying off—difficult. There is a need for access to drug-treatment therapy. And, of course, there is the drug economy that has entered the jobless ghetto. So we cannot solve the underlying problems of such communities and families without a massive shift of resources away from the overuse of confinement and into effective crime prevention and community development.

Could the American public shift from one rational paradigm (more laws, more prisons) to another rational paradigm (more family and community support and crime prevention)? This second rational paradigm would include a harm-reduction approach to drug problems, short "treatment-based sentencing," simultaneous early childhood development, parenting support, jobs, job skills and education and community development to address the "moral vice" problem of street drugs in the United States.

However, this is not what we've got in the United States. Instead, we have allowed the passage of harsh, punitive drug laws, and built up (overbuilt) our prisons. Would Becarria see the outcome of the quadrupling of our prisoners as a legal build-up, but not an overly rational result? What are the results? To repeat: Even in the context of a falling crime rate we have continued prison growth. Because so many prisoners are being incarcerated for drug laws, and because prisoners are staying in prison much longer because of the unprecedented severity of these drug laws, we have had to build a thousand new prisons. We also have had a "revolving door" of recidivism since the major reason for failure on parole, and return to prison, once released on parole has been "dirty urine," or testing positive for drug use—which, under the "war on drugs," is a violation of the terms of parole.

Becarria's voice (1764/2004) helped stimulate our founding fathers, through adoption of a constitutional system, to seek "a more perfect union." Has the shift in values to a "culture of control" and prison build-up movement over the last twenty-five years brought us a more perfect union?

Of course, regardless of whether the crime rate is increasing or decreasing, people can have *values* that are the foundation of how they respond to whatever level (and types) of crime there is. Herbert Packer, in his 1968 article "Two Models of the Criminal Justice Process," articulated two value clusters that characterize attitudes toward, and within, the American criminal justice system.

One value cluster is *crime control*. From this view the main value of the criminal justice apparatus is to repress or control crime. To do this, "efficiency" is necessary. The fact-finding administrative agency (police, Sheriff's departments FBI, other federal crime control investigating agencies) knows what it is doing, and should be trusted. The premise is that such criminal justice agencies gather facts and know who is guilty. There is a presumption of guilt.

The other value cluster is *due process*. From this view the main value of the American criminal justice process is its value on protecting the rights of the individual; ensuring their right to due process—such as evidentiary hearing, trial and appeal. To hold fast to this value, "obstacles" to the state's crime-control process are necessary: The state must "prove its case" in a series of required hearings with rules surrounding admissible evidence. The premise is that the state and criminal justice apparatus can make mistakes and should not be trusted. There is a value on the fate of the individual, and a distrust of state agencies, and a presumption of innocence.

Overall, writing in 1968, Packer believed that the American justice system is ambiguous on these values and at that time there existed a tension-filled "balance" between crime control and due process. Since Packer wrote, the American people have "leaned" markedly during the twenty-five-year societal incarceration binge culture (1984–2008) toward the value of "crime control." The growth of the prison system and its internal incarceration binge culture can, thus, be explained by a growth in the emphasis on the *value* of crime control and punitiveness.

Bert Useem and Ann Morrison Piehl, in their 2008 book *The Prison State*, argue that, to an extent, this growing emphasis on the value of crime control and the prison-build-up movement was not an outcome of irrational racism but a pragmatic and a rational social movement responding to the initial increase in crime rates during the period 1986 to 1991. However, they note certain limits to the "rational public" model:

> The prison buildup movement, we have argued, was a pragmatic effort to deal with an escalating crime rate rather than, as the critics claimed, an irrational expression of a disturbed population or an effort to achieve an otherwise extraneous political agenda. The critics include David Garland and Loic Wacquant, in a tradition that springs from the work of Michel Foucault. These attributions of irrationality, we found, do not fit the available facts. Yet, more generally, although social movements are pragmatic efforts to create new social forms, they are not deliberative bodies or research seminars.

They do not collect evidence on the structures that they are seeking to bring, or have brought, in being. Data analysis (with all its complications) is not part of their "repertoire" for contention. Social movements are rational, but they are not hyperrational. If successful in achieving their immediate goals, they may not know how, or even when, to stop. More prisons, even if effective up to a point, may have exceeded that point during the buildup, as well as damaged society in other ways. The prison buildup movement may have unknowingly gone too far. Although social movements are strong in their mechanisms of mobilization, they have weak brakes. (Useem & Piehl 2008:169)

There is also a third view set of social values, beyond the "just desserts" punishment crime-control model and the "right-based" type of justice rooted in the due process and evidentiary hearing aspects of the U.S. Bill of Rights. This third set of values view emphasizes "human needs" that transcend "crime control" and "due process." What does the community need? What does the victim need? What does the offender need? This can be more of a *harm-reduction model* and *restorative-justice approach* that de-emphasizes both crime-control "efficiency" and rights-based "due process" in favor of a community justice, victim-offender mediation and needs-based justice (Braithwaite 1989; Miller 1996; Clear & Cadora 2003; Sullivan & Tifft 2001, 2005).

After twenty-five years of "tough-on-crime" politics, is the United States ready to reassess its values, re-emphasizing human needs? Such a change in emphasis would require both a cultural and a political shift away from the incarceration binge culture in the United States.

Another aspect of a "rational American public" model would be the assumption that the American criminal justice organizations were, themselves, operating in a rational mode. Kraska (2004) outlines a theoretical orientation toward the criminal justice apparatus called the "systems view." Here, the criminal justice network of agencies acts similar to a biological system, or cybernetic system, where one action feeds into or is reciprocal and interdependent with another action. For instance, during the period 1965–1975 there *was* an increase in the crime rate, due mostly to the increase in the high-crime-rate age category of fifteen- to twenty-four-year-olds in the population—the cohort of the "baby boom" (Blumstein & Wallman 2000:4) (see Figure 6.2). As crime rates increased—due to the young, crime age baby boom—during that decade (1965–1974), interdependent actions between components in the "system" needed to occur. The police needed to make more arrests, the prosecutors had to prosecute more (or develop plea bargaining) and the courts had to be more active in hearing cases and sentencing to adjudicate (to probation or prison). Thus, there was a need for more adult probation officers, the state Department of Corrections (DOC) needed more prisons, and the DOC "Field Services" needed more parole officers.

Within the "systems" view the focus is not on the rationality of the laws or the rationality of the sentencing, but, instead, on the "rationality" of criminal justice agencies where rationality is defined as "efficiency" in the system. There is an emphasis on increasing the use of technology, and analyzing what really happens within and between criminal justice agencies as a network.

The systems view emerged first with the American Bar Foundation's mid-1950s set of "field reports" studying formal criminal justice agency activities. The existing view from the 1930s to the late 1950s was the "professional model," as exampled by earlier reforms in policing. This earlier professional model emphasized that more professional skills and demeanor by officers would solve most problems. A police agency needed professionally trained officers and good equipment. If there were problems, it was a problem of training—of becoming more "professional." However, the American Bar Foundation (ABF) studies placed a new interpretation on studies of how police agencies actually worked, emphasizing that "researchers should give more attention to 'the investigation of processes' (and) 'actual practices of arrest, search and seizure, handling persons in custody . . . and other such matters.'" Walker notes:

> These memos (from the ABF research directors) embodied elements of what would become the modern criminal justice paradigm: the problems of administration arising from the substantive criminal law; the pervasiveness of discretion; the extent to which illegal behavior (in police agencies) was not simply a matter of "bad people"; the fact that the various criminal justice agencies were interrelated in such a way that they constituted a criminal justice *system*. (Walker 1992/2004:54–55; Kraska 2004:54–55; emphasis added)

A certain problem arises, however, and that is that when working *within* the "system," and reforming its efficiency and professionalism, things appear to be occurring as a "closed system" (Scott 1992). However, the societal environment around criminal justice organizations was changing. As we've explained, during the 1950s suburbs were built away from the existing "main streets and city housing." This suburban development was based on federal housing mortgage programs, which stimulated suburban housing developments. Also, the federal highway system was building up by the late 1950s and early 1960s. As a consequence, malls developed at the edge of urban areas (in the new suburbs) to serve the new suburbanites—who often commuted back into the city to their jobs.

The downtown business and residential districts in the now "old" inner cities declined further. More factories and office complexes previously located in the city center began leaving the inner city and relocating in the edge cities, taking the jobs and tax base with them (Eitzen & Baca Zinn 2000: chap. 6; Garreau 1991). A pattern of "jobless ghettos" in major American cities developed as a result of the disinvestment, by the early 1960s. These developments resulted in economically devastated "inner cities" emerging in the United States (Darden, et al. 1987; Wacquant 2002; Wilson 1996).

Watts, such an inner city context in Los Angeles, had an "inner city riot" in 1965 and Detroit, also affected by this trend, had an "inner city riot" in 1967. Police were held in increasing disdain by inner city residents. As Louis Radelet and David Carter note in *Policing and the Community,*

> The riots and violent upheavals that occurred in various cities during the summer of 1967, and thereafter, marked a turning point in police-community relations programs. Suddenly, the nation was jolted into a realization of intense and profound divisions among its people, both racial and social. . . . There was widespread bewilderment (among police officers). Some simply withdrew from further efforts; many adopted a "get tough" philosophy. Another presidential commission, the National Advisory Commission Civil Disorders (popularly known as the Kerner Commission, after its chairman), proclaimed in its report that "our Nation is moving toward two societies, one black, one white—separate and unequal." As for police-community relations:
>
>> The police are not merely a "spark" factor. To some Negroes police have come to symbolize white power, white racism, and white repression. And the fact is that many police do reflect and express these white attitudes. The atmosphere of hostility and cynicism is reinforced by a widespread belief among Negroes in the existence of police brutality and in a "double standard" of justice and protection—one for Negroes and one for whites.
>
> . . . It is worth reflecting that a generation has passed since 1955. The police and civilian participants in the (community policing) institutes of the 1950s and even of the 1960s are today's "golden agers." The programmers have changed, as have the programs, but the apparent problems in the localities that are in the headlines as a result of flare-ups and tensions in police and community relations seem to be very similar to what they were in the publicized places of fifteen to twenty-five years ago. Racism, urban decay, rampant violent crime, citizen anxiety and fear, and the sharp increase in apparently permanent unemployment are all evidences of community deterioration. The link between these problems and police-community relations has long since been established and were clearly demonstrated in Los Angeles and other cities in 1992. (Radelet & Carter 1994:27–31)

The Democratic administration of Lyndon Johnson (1963–1968)—under pressure from the decade-old Civil Rights Movement—had just completed signing the historic 1964 Civil Rights Act to enfranchise African

Americans and make discrimination illegal. This was a political voting rights reform—African American and other "minorities" now had a voting rights law with teeth in it—but the *economic* problems of the inner cities described above (disinvestment, high unemployment, poverty, loss of a tax base for social services) was causing the inner cities to "fester," like a wound without healing treatment. The inner cities became "occupied" by white police departments protecting the nearby suburbs and enforcing order on an increasingly restive urban black and poor population.

Yet, this was a period in U.S. history when most people had been experiencing a tremendous economic boom for twenty years after the end of World War II (1945–1965). Journalists and politicians talked of "pockets of poverty." There were book exposés on the "remaining" poverty as "the other America." And there was a belief that all the American people could be brought along in the economic boom—that "all boats rise with a rising sea"—and that poverty in the United States could and should be eliminated.

President Johnson had, in fact, launched, in 1964, not a "war on crime" but a "war on poverty." He wanted to work toward reducing the national inequalities. He also appointed a Crime Commission, and the 1967 Kerner Violence Commission, in response to the urban conflagrations. America, in the 1960s, was looking at its social problems.

So, in this decade of self-examination-applying social science methods, the criminal justice network was forced to look at itself as an "open system" needing to respond to societal changes, such as the national crisis over urban policing, the Civil Rights Movement, Supreme Court rulings limiting police discretion, and rising crime rates. Walker notes:

> The principal findings that constituted the new (systems) paradigm included the following interrelated propositions: (1) the criminal process is extremely complex as a result of the nature of the substantial criminal law; (2) as a consequence, the police role is extremely complex; (3) the administration of justice is pervaded by discretion; (4) decision making is (or was at the time) unstructured by legal norms or formal controls; and (5) the various justice agencies make up a criminal justice "system" in which the actions of one agency affect and are affected by the other agencies. (in Kraska 2004:58)

Walker further notes that the ABF survey had an important effect on criminal justice education. Prior to the late 1960s there were no (or very few) "criminal justice" bachelor programs in the United States. However,

> Between the late 1960s and the early 1970s, criminal justice as a distinct field of study appeared. The number of college- and university-based academic programs increased enormously, and in many instances the term "crimi-

nal justice" replaced "law enforcement" or "police studies." The dominant model of criminal justice education became the "systems" approach, with emphasis on the *administration* of justice (as opposed to theoretical criminology), and with equal attention to the various components of police, courts, and corrections. This approach is reflected in the organization of the leading textbooks in the field today. (in Kraska 2004:62–63)

Notice how, as the American capitalist environment changed, bringing forth festering inner cities, the *focus* in criminal justice education turned toward problems of the *administration* of justice instead of efforts through applied criminology and social policy to *solve* the underlying urban problems. From the beginning, the emphasis of university criminal justice education programs, which were *born* out of the conflagration of the 1960s inner city violence, was a selfish "agency and system" orientation.

As mentioned, when working within the "system" (in police work, courts or corrections agencies) the system looks like a "closed system" within the linkage of cops-courts-corrections, or flow of suspects-defendants-convicts. Clearly, however, the criminal justice system is a more "open system" than "cops and robbers."

There have always been changing societal influences. Some of these influences included changes in politics, demography and economics: the laws the legislature makes, changes in the crime rate mainly due to demography (number of fifteen- to twenty-five-year-olds) and changes in structures of economic deprivational inequality—such as the emergence of inner cities and their continued festering. There are also changes in the culture: social movements, counter-cultures, trends in drug use and drug epidemics. All of these political, demographic, economic and sociocultural changes can be external factors in the environment for an "open system" of connected organizations such as the criminal justice network of agencies.

So then, what explains the growth of prisons from this "systems" view? It is still the *increase in crime rate*, or in *laws making drug-defined and drug-related behavior more of a crime.* In these circumstances the system must grow. More crime, and/or more laws, creates a "forced reaction" of prison growth. Also, note that the very academic discipline of criminal justice in colleges and universities grew out of a changing societal environment—the emergence of "festering" inner cities—that "required" a system view to examine the *efficiency* and changing administrative needs of the crime-control process within criminal justice agencies.

Could we have, instead, eliminated, or greatly reduced, the inner cities themselves as a "social problem?" This could have been accomplished through massive governmental economic development programs instead of what we did, in fact, get—a massive "more efficient" growth of the criminal justice administration and a quadrupling of the prison system (Wilson 1996). What were our values in all of this?

Just as our values shifted to crime control, and our criminal justice apparatus became more efficient, a parallel cultural and structural shift was occurring in our *type* of society, into what is now called "late modern." Late-modern society is theorized to be a more "risk-aversive" society, having a "safety-ethic" concern that is almost like a "fetish" for security.

In this "late-modernity" society view, time is compressed, life sped-up (Castells 1996; Harvey 2000). There is less room for error. Misfits are treated as person-categories (a risk) rather than humans that can respond to moral treatment (counseling therapy, education). The "problem communities" are shunted aside, instead of receiving large-scale crime-prevention programs. There is an "exclusionary society" resistant to reducing social class inequalities. There is a "culture of security consciousness" (Garland 2001), or "safety ethic" (Bauman 2000).

The criminal justice apparatus, and especially the penal system, is pushed to become more oriented toward "risk management" through (excessive) use of confinement. This management takes on a statistical form—actuarial techniques of counting what categories of people are more dangerous than others—and this approach *replaces* a former emphasis on individualized justice, treatment, access to programs, rehabilitation and restoration. There is a

quest to make human existence more predictable, safe, secure, and orderly. Late modern theorists note that this preoccupation with risk minimization has gone into overdrive in the last fifteen years. . . . (They) posit the ascendance of a powerful norm in late modern society—safety and security—that relegates other important norms, like individual liberty or tolerance of difference, to the back burner. (Kraska 2004:280–81)

Another trend contributing to "late modernity" is the rise of "neo-liberalism." This type of politics emphasizes an attack on state-centered governance "expounding the view that the interventionist welfare state has crippled economic dynamism by over-regulation"; an "assault on welfarism"; and the "advocacy of the free market as a model for most social order"; a cost-effective, results-based government; individual responsibility; and freedom of choice, especially emphasizing consumption (Kraska 2004:281–82).

Finally, in "late-modern, neo-liberal society" there is an acceptance of inequality and the trend is toward exclusion.

A society preoccupied with fear about danger and risk, and guided by free-market neo-liberal ideology, will by default define those members of society that pose a potential danger—and do not fit into the new economy—as the excluded "other."

. . . criminal justice behavior revolves around maintaining the barrier between the included and excluded . . . solutions such as mass incarceration or aggressive police patrol work targeted at inner-city hot-spots to confine danger and minimize risk. (Kraska 2004:284)

Presumably this "culture of security consciousness" is a rational evolution of the "quality revolution" in American lives regarding technology. Typewriters broke down and required regular cleaning; computers with chips made in "clean rooms" are a higher-quality device. So, even though the crime rate has been falling since 1991, our "safety ethic" has driven us—and our technological revolution may make us feel this is possible— toward a "zero-tolerance" security envelope around us.

While Useem and Piehl argue the prison-build-up movement was a pragmatic effort to deal with the escalating crime rate of 1986 to 1991, it is hard not to conclude—with a late modern fetish for safety and its tendency toward an exclusionary society—that there was an element of *fear* and racism cemented into the incarceration binge culture: "an irrational expression of a disturbed population" (Useem & Piehl 2008:169).

Politics, Media and Fear: The Binge Growth Complex

Pretty much all organizations want to get bigger: Executives and managers have more status the bigger the organizational budget and personnel roster, regular employees know their job will be more secure if the organization is growing larger, communities are happy to have permanent organizations. State prison systems, and their host towns, are not much different—opening up 1,000 new prisons between 1984 and 2001 created many new prison and community employment opportunities.

It is pretty clear to see that the criminal justice network seeks coherence as a system acting in its own interests—and as a growth complex. However, if you are going to have a growth complex, it helps to have normal organizational ambitions grow even more if the growth is amplified by fear. There is an aspect of the incarceration binge culture that is a "governing-through-crime" formula, with politicians being "tough on crime," the media driving drug scares and moral panics, and the criminal justice network itself in a mode of rapid organizational growth that is amplified by fear. Unlike decades before, when cops, court and corrections were a slow-moving, low-profile area of public bureaucracy, mere "street-level bureaucrats" (Lipsky 1980), in recent years politicians have learned to exploit complex crime problems in simplistic ways for political votes. This has had the consequence of politicians "fanning the embers of fear" in the public and then offering them "tough-on-crime" incarceration growth solutions.

In the "politics-causes-prison-growth" theoretical orientation the explanation of massive *growth* in the prison system is sought by looking at political orientations, ideology, legislators, policy making and its implementation and the role of media. The uses to which the criminal justice apparatus are put come largely from "the political climate" and power world, as discussed in chapter 1.

So, the 1950s and 1960s emphasis of short sentences, rehabilitation and drug treatment for drug addicts has, in the last two decades, become buried under a politicized drug war. Prisons and crime became highly politicized by the 1986 federalization of drug law (and earlier in the 1973 the New York state Rockefeller mandatory drug laws). This occurred under President Reagan, and politicians felt they could not afford to vote against this trend—just like, as we've mentioned, the politicians of the period between 1890–1920 felt they could not vote against "dry" proponents' legislation in the "war on alcohol." Criminal justice policy became a "wedge issue" or tool for politicians: "I am for getting those violent predators off our streets. And I am proposing a tougher law than my opponent, who is soft on crime" (Tonry 2001).

Seen in terms of political values, the United States underwent, from 1980 onward, a more "conservative" tilt emphasizing "right-wing values." Walter Miller, in 1973, noted the differences in political ideology of the "right" versus the "left."

> The *Right* constellation of values: There is excessive leniency toward lawbreakers, erosion of discipline and respect for constituted authority, excessive permissiveness; with assumptions that the individual is directly responsible, a need for a strong moral order, with a paramount importance of security.
>
> The *Left* constellation of issues include: We have a tendency toward overcriminalization (e.g. drug laws), too much labeling and stigmatization, overuse of confinement, discrimination; and assumptions that the primary sources of criminal behavior lie in conditions of the social order, that there is a need to alter the social conditions that breed crime, that the social and political order does not meet the fundamental needs of the majority of its citizens (health, education, jobs, environment); and that the criminal justice system is inequitable and unjust. (Miller 1973/2004, in Kraska 2004:113–14)

It is possible to argue that we need *both* of these sets of views. A thoughtful writer, such as Wright, asserts that it may be desirable to have "goal conflict" within the criminal justice system—that is, to have both "left" and "right" values at work (crime control and tough punishments but also due process and treatment and restoration) (Wright 1981/2004, in Kraska 2004:121–25).

On the other hand, this begs the question of which ideology, since 1980, has "won the day." Which way is the tilt? And, over the last nearly thirty years, it is clear that the more right-wing, conservative, punitive set of values has prevailed and that the criminal justice apparatus has needed to adjust to the political context or "swings in the pendulum"—building ever more prisons, with longer sentences due, primarily, to the punitive drug laws. In turn, the punitive drug laws were the outcome of a divisive political conflict that has involved the temptation to politicize crime. Writing in the early 1980s, Scheingold noted that crime was an issue that can provide "a simple and credible answer that the public is only too happy to embrace" (Scheingold 1982/2004, in Kraska 2004:126–27).

So, from the *politics* theoretical orientation, what explains the *growth* of the prison system? Is it increasing crime rates? No, the crime rates have declined steadily since 1991. Other external factors, the economy and demographics, have had ups and downs, but the prison system has continued to expand. This "politics" explanation of the expansion of the prison system is not a "forced reaction" to a larger population or increase in crime rate type of explanation, but rather an explanation emphasizing a political atmosphere of more crime-control values undergirding the creation of more crime *law*. The value cluster of "crime control" came to the fore with a more "right-wing" or conservative political *ideology shift*, and this explains the increased use of incarceration. And, this process of prison growth has *been caused, from the politics point of view, by politics itself*—and this includes the politics of self-serving aspects of news and entertainment media, politicians and the crime-control establishment.

What are we to conclude today, nearly thirty years later? Is crime control such a big issue these days? Are we tired of the "politics of tough?" Both state budget crisis and recent changes in the political climate and economy have polls showing that "education and health care were more important than crime." There is a "growing awareness among the general public that increases in corrections spending come at the cost of other governmental spending and services"(Vera Institute of Justice 2006).

In May of 2008 Michigan's Governor Granholm—in the context of a budget-strapped state—called for prison reform, including release of non-violent offenders (Granholm 2007). As of the Summer of 2008, the United States is moving into a recession. People are worried. They are worried about the cost of gas. They are worried about whether the United States can achieve energy independence. Many people are interested in promoting more sustainability and slowing global warming through alternative energy and lifestyle changes. Economic insecurity as firms downsize and outsource—and as the United States moves deeper into recession—seems a greater issue than crime rates. And, by the way, crime rates continue to fall (Zimring 2006).

Has the danger that some of our convicts sent to prison for non-violent drug crimes represent been exaggerated? Does our massive prison system—nearly twenty years after the last crime-rate rise (1986–1991)—seem to be somewhat an outcome of a fear-and-punishment response that does not solve underlying root problems? Is it time to recognize that our "prison state" is a fundamentally inappropriate response, and that now is the time to "put the brakes on?"

Kraska notes that a lot of criminal justice legislation and policy, media focus and public reactions are related to "moral panics," "drug scares" and other mythic and ritual-like social processes, rather than a rational "forced reaction" to a growth in the actual crime rate. The "crime problem," thus, is often not constructed on a basis of actual data—for instance an actual increase in crime—but in a *media-driven "story" that exaggerates* the situation into a "scare" or "panic." The public responds with moral concern, and the politicians dutifully step forward with simple, punitive legislation to take care of the problem.

In Michigan, in 2006, a prisoner mistakenly released on parole named Selepak killed some people. The media-driven moral panic pushed Governor Granholm to pull back from a planned release onto parole of thousands of non-violent prisoners. From the prisoners-awaiting-release point of view "One person spoiled it all for the rest of us." From the taxpayers' point of view, this "panic" postponement of prison release can be seen as unnecessary use of confinement. This overuse of confinement (at $32,000 a year per prisoner) cost the state hundreds of millions of dollars during a severe budget crisis—at a time when public school teachers, and other local and state services, were being cut back.

Marjorie S. Zatz, in her article "Chicano Youth Gangs and Crime: The Creation of a Moral Panic" (1987/2004) notes that in the late 1970s Phoenix newspapers, relying on information provided by the police, suddenly "depicted a serious flare-up of gang violence." Zatz, however, noted that "the interests of the police in acquiring federal funding for specialized (gang) functions" had a lot to do with the social imagery of Chicano gangs, as violent and . . . "different" (Kraska 2004:157).

However, "the problem" of gangs in Phoenix or gangs in any of the U.S. cities has been around for a long time, and, instead of a panic, a steady approach to solving the underlying sources of gangs and crime might seem sensible. Addressing areas of concentrated poverty and joblessness (such as the festering inner cities and some working class suburbs), drug addiction and the syndrome that includes family disintegration, child abuse and neglect, delinquency and alcohol abuse—as suggested in the harm-reduction model in chapter 1, and the list of evidence-based crime prevention programs in this chapter, for instance—might go further toward reducing gangs than a "moral panic."

Instead, however, the growth of use of incarceration is linked to a series of "moral panics" which are *socially constructed* and operate, at a mythic level, to generate *fear* and ritual pollution that must be cast out. Those engaged in the "big politics" of national issues and representing corporate and political power do not speak out against this fundamentally inappropriate response—they do not speak out for the use of resources to solve underlying causes (Reiman 2004). Instead, crime becomes a scapegoat for avoiding solving the underlying problems of our social order—solutions that would be inconvenient for the powerful.

This does not mean that we don't have a problem of crime, or that we don't need a criminal justice apparatus (Stenson 1991). However, the "moral panic" about inner city crack use, for instance, led to a "fundamentally inappropriate response"—too much emphasis on tougher laws and too little emphasis on reducing inner city poverty.

Victor E. Kappeler notes that: "Images of justice are not happenstance. While it is comforting to think of criminal justice as a fixed reality void of political and ideological influences, nothing could be further from the truth" (Kraska 2004:168).

Where do myths about criminal justice come from and how are they learned? Well, think about the fact that major media are *businesses* and have vested interests in the promotion of criminal justice myths that can create drama to keep us entertained. Kappeler (2004) notes:

> First, the public is fascinated by sensational crime. Crime has become a media product that sells perhaps better than any other media commodity. Attracting a larger audience translates into more advertising dollars.... Second, alternative explanations of criminal justice (than the myths) rarely resonate with the viewers.... Third, expression of views that contradict official government positions can lead to enhanced regulation of the industry and a loss of news sources. Media depictions of criminal justice are intertwined with government, money, and ideology. The media are therefore compelled to present a very simplistic, standardized view of justice that does not alienate those who either control or consume it. (in Kraska 2004:168–69)

Meanwhile, what had once been a few sleepy, rural and small-scale prison system facilities out of the limelight—a slow bureaucratic career organizational territory of guards, housing supervisors and wardens—has, since 1986, become not only a highly politicized and media-driven prison industry, but in some theorist's view, a type of "growth machine" expanding in its own interest.

It is possible to look at the *growth* of the massive U.S. prison system as partly an outcome of "bureaucracy building." From this view some aspects of prison growth are self-serving, creating jobs for correctional officers, those who supply prisons with goods and services and the construction industry that builds prisons. Also, with the advent of "privatization" of prisons this "growth-complex" view takes on a new alarm since, in the private prison, the profit motives may push to keep the number of prisons stable or growing (Mobley 2003; Perrone & Pratt 2006; Robbins 1997). Rural communities also may think they want the state to build more prisons in their area as a source of tax revenue and jobs (Beal 1998; Thomas 1994; Walsh 1994; Hernandez 1996).

Consider the California Correctional Peace Officers Association (CCPOA). This very large union has tens of thousands of both prison guards *and* parole officers in its ranks. There may be seen an *interest* on the part of parole officers to send parolees back to prison—thus continuing to grow the prison from both new-crime admittance and parole-violation admittance. This latent self-interest aspect has plenty of Californians worried that their tax dollars are unnecessarily tied-up in excessive confinement partly because of such "bloated-bureaucracy" interests of the CCPOA guards and parole officers (Petersilia 2003:240).

In this view, prisoners and parole violators become the "raw material" for an industry, or "prison-industrial complex." Because such a growth complex can become politically powerful, it can be perpetuated by policy favorable to it, such as legislative parole and sentencing laws. In California the CCPOA was the largest campaign contributor to two governors that ran for, and were elected to office in the late 1990s and early 2000s. The CCPOA is a powerful lobby interest group in California.

Kraska reminds us that the United States incarcerates five times more people per capita today than it did just thirty years ago. He notes:

> A number of scholars do not see this growth as merely a forced or rational reaction to a worsening crime problem (rational/legal and systems), or a pendulum swing toward retributive values (crime control/due process), or even the result of shifts in politics. Their position, while acknowledging a partial role for these forces in the initial stages of development, stresses that today's criminal justice apparatus constitutes a *growth complex*, an entity that has taken on a life and logic of its own for its own sake. (Kraska 2004: 178–79)

Shelden and Brown ask "Why has a 'crime control industry' emerged at this point in American history?" They answer, such a growth complex reflects the workings of capitalism: "That is to say, it is driven by a need to make a profit anywhere possible and the need to control an inevitable and growing 'surplus population'" (Kraska 2004:198). Is it possible in our "the-rich-get-richer" society where "the poor get prison," that there is some *convenience* for the powerful not to fix the inner cities, reduce poverty, increase jobs and generally support programs to reduce the syndrome of family disintegration, child abuse and neglect, delinquency and alcohol abuse, that are the roots of crime?

Convenient Oppression: Binge Growth and High Impact Communities

The convenient oppression existing in the growth of the U.S. criminal justice apparatus is this: hyperincarceration provides a way for "managing" the surplus labor in the jobless ghettos through an incarceration strategy. This "symbiotic relationships" between certain impoverished inner city neighborhoods and the state prison system can result in a strategy of "imprisoning communities" (Clear 2007).

Certainly over the last few decades inequality has increased in the United States. We've developed festering inner cities, towns devastated by plant closings, lowering of manufacturing wages and benefits, a growth in low-wage service jobs and temporary and part-time jobs, cut-backs in the social welfare safety net, lack of health care for many—even poverty in the suburbs. Now, in the Summer of 2008, the United States is moving deeper into recession. Some look to the crises and contradictions of political economy—surplus population, class oppression (lowering wages, reducing security, breaking unions, increasing profits), inventing scapegoats—and see a nation in need of progressive values and social movements.

Conservative Americans with "right-wing" values typically do not focus on the reality of inner cities, plant shutdowns, low wages, economic insecurity, but see, instead, a prosperous America led by "freedom-to-choose" free-market business values. However, economic insecurity conditions "marginalize" people, requiring them to live in low-rent districts. With less power, under these conditions of inequality, people have less "enfranchisement" or status in the society.

Kraska notes that the criminal justice system can be seen as a means to oppress those who are marginalized in U.S. society. The criminal justice system is riddled with class inequalities and racial disparity. By focusing on lower-working-class crime, the "under" class, the criminal justice system diverts attention from the rich and powerful, the "over" class. As we noted in chapter 1, the definition of what is crime—and how to reduce crime—is driven by those in the "power world," those with economic, cultural and political power.

People in American inner cities have little or no political power. Michael Tonry (1995) writes that the "abandoned" American inner cities that have festered since the 1950s (e.g., 1965 Watts Riot, 1967 Detroit Riot, 1992 South Central Los Angeles Riot) have continued to exist *because* of a type of neglect he calls "malign." In fact, in addition to "neglect," the black and Latino inner cities have withered under a "war" on crime and drugs that has ruined lives and weakened the high impact community. Tonry states:

> It was foreseeable that wars on crime and drugs would worsen racial dispari-
> ties in jails, courts, and prisons. Any experienced police officer, for example,
> would have known that the War on Drugs' emphasis on arrests of low-level
> drug dealers would have little lasting effect on the drug trade but would
> result in many more arrests of young males from deteriorated inner-city
> neighborhoods. And that is what happened. (Tonry 1995:v)

No war against crime will ever be won. Crime rates are the product of demography (number of fifteen- to twenty-five-year-old males in the population) and such underlying criminogenic social and economic factors as: lack of adequate child development, lack of home ownership, unemployment or underemployment, poor education, alcohol and other drug abuse, weak parenting network, family stress, hopelessness, anger and rage among youth, dysfunctional families and peer influences (gangs). Recall that 80 percent of state prisoners have a history of child abuse and neglect, have not finished high school, and have few job skills. Yet both Reagan and Bush I administrations slashed the federal safety-net funding for education, housing and social programs for the cities. "Presidents Reagan and Bush *promoted a strategy of federal disinvestment in the inner cities,* (accelerating their deterioration) and diminished the scope and quality of urban public services. The Reagan and Bush administrations thereby increased criminogenic pressures in the cities" (Tonry 1995:40; emphasis added).

At a time when drug use in small university cities was mildly tolerated, and drug treatment still remained the mainstream solution in suburban communities, the 1970s saw big-city policy over "drug crime" enter the "big-politics" realm, politicizing drug crimes with stiff mandatory penalties, as exampled by the state of New York and the 1973 Rockefeller Laws. With the 1986 drug laws the tactical policy program chosen was the arrest, prosecution and lengthy incarceration of street-level dealers who were disproportionately black and Hispanic. "What was clear both then and now is that a program built around education, drug abuse treatment, and social problems designed to address the structural social and economic conditions that lead to crime and drug abuse would have much less destructive impact on disadvantaged young blacks" (Tonry 1995:123).

However, how do we explain, in fact, what happened? Why was street-level enforcement and prison binge growth the chosen tactic? Tonry argues that the choice of arrest and lengthy incarceration of street-level dealers was a *political* decision that had "foreseeable disparate (racial) impacts," and that the disadvantaged black Americans were *used* "as a means to the achievement of politicians electoral ends" (Tonry 1995:123).

Tonry wrote these words about cynical politics in the early 1990s. At that time the incarceration binge had reached 1.3 million prisoners in U.S. prisons and jails. As we write, fourteen years later, the U.S. incarceration rate has continued to soar to rate close to 600 per 100,000 and with an increase in the number of those incarcerated in prisons and jails to 2.2 million in 2006. Prison populations are now 48 percent African American. Christian Parenti (1999/2004) writes:

> To reiterate how this buildup occurred, recall that politicians in the age of re-structuring (lowering wages, reducing security, breaking unions, increasing profits) face a populace racked by economic and social anxiety. The political classes must speak to and harness this anxiety, but they cannot blame the U.S. class structure. So they invent scapegoats: the Black/Latino criminal, the immigrant, the welfare cheat, crackheads, superpredators, and so on. These political myths are deployed, first and foremost, to win elections. But the eventual *policy byproducts* of this racialized anti-crime discourse are laws like three strikes and mandatory minimums. Most important, of course, are the drug laws. Drug offenders constituted more than a third (36 percent) of the increase in state prison populations between 1985 and 1994; in the federal system drug offenders make up more than two-thirds (71 percent) of the prison population. (Parenti 1999, in Kraska 2004:272)

Todd Clear, former president of the American Society of Criminology, has studied the impact of high levels of incarceration in the disadvantaged neighborhoods of America's largest cities where as many as 20 percent of adult men are locked up on any given day, and almost every family has a father, son, brother or uncle who has been behind bars. His 2007 book, *Imprisoning Communities: How Mass Incarceration Makes Disadvantaged Neighborhoods Worse*, makes several points:

> The extraordinary growth in the U.S. prison system, sustained for over 30 years, has had, at best, a small impact on crime.
> The growth in imprisonment has been concentrated among poor, minority males who live in impoverished neighborhoods.
> Concentrated incarceration in those impoverished communities has broken families, weakened the social-control capacity of parents, eroded economic strength, soured attitudes toward society, and distorted politics; even, after reaching a certain level, it has increased rather than decreased crime.
> Any attempt to overcome the problems of crime will have to encompass a combination of sentencing reforms and philosophical realignment. (Clear 2007:5–6)

Clear, in emphasizing the need to really address community well-being in the inner cities, argues we need to "reconceptualize the correctional project":

In the end, we cannot reform sentencing procedures without reconceptualizing the correctional project itself. It goes without saying that the narrow range of concepts about corrections that we hold currently cannot help. Phrases such as "getting smarter rather than tougher," "providing more programs," and "investing in reentry" are not bad ideas, they are just irrelevant to the problem of mass incarceration of people from poor communities. To deal with that problem, we will have to make community well-being a central objective of our penal system. We will have to embrace an idea of community justice. (Clear 2007:13)

Times change, and with them their demands. As many state budgets have been in crisis since 2003 (and particularly in Michigan) there has developed a tightening noose around state prison systems pressuring them not to expand (Jacobson 2005). Some legislators are looking at clearer parole guidelines to help increase the percent released after their first parole date (CAPPS 2008). Reentry initiatives are trying to slow down the recidivism rate (MPRI 2008; CEA 2005).

There have been some changes in thinking about the "imprisonment binge" now that many states have gone into budget crises. Certain states have repealed mandatory minimums, or scaled back the length of some sentences (Michigan 2002, New York 2005), and a handful of states have begun to emphasize a sentence to mandatory treatment instead of prison for drug cases (Arizona 1996, California 2000). Drug courts to accomplish oversight of this approach have increased. Michigan's Governor Jennifer Granholm had plans in the Spring of 2007 to release 2,500 to 5,000 prisoners, out of the state's 52,000 prisoner population (plans that got delayed due to the Selepak murders). The plans are to release those who are already past their parole date, or older and infirm prisoners.

But the "tough-on-crime" rhetoric, so characteristic of the last thirty years (1980–2008), *continues* among state and federal legislators. Are we on the cusp of social change toward community well-being, or are we at an impasse where, because we are unable to solve root-cause problems, we will remain locked into the perpetual incarceration machine (Richards & Jones 1996)?

Rise of Convict Criminology

Many people who are convicts change and mature. While this varies by state, once released, between 30 to 70 percent of those leaving prison do not recidivate (return to prison). (Michigan's recidivism rate is close to 32 percent while California's recidivism rate is close to 70 percent.)

Out of the ashes of the "war on crime" and "war on drugs" some handful of ex-cons have been "making good" in the academic field after getting some prison college, being released, and going on to graduate education.

Dr. John Irwin, professor emeritus at San Francisco State University, author of several books long used in criminal justice classes, is himself an ex-felon. He tells the story of growing up in his younger days in the late 1950s that, among some in his neighborhood, it seemed cool to be a safecracker. Irwin decided to be a safecracker. Then, he reports, "They made it harder to crack a safe." He moved on to robbery—a big mistake—and he went to prison for five years. He was, of course, labeled a criminal.

But convict John Irwin got the opportunity to take some college courses while in prison. He began to affiliate himself as a student. Upon his transition after release from the prison in the early 1960s, and with this new "student" identity, Irwin went on to complete a Ph.D. at the University of California–Berkeley, publishing his doctoral dissertation, *The Felon*, in 1970. John Irwin subsequently became a professor at San Francisco State University.

Over the years between 1972 to 1995, about 10 percent of prison convicts in the United States had access to prison college through the Pell grant programs. Then Congress ended prisoner eligibility for Pell grants in 1994 and the prison college programs ended.

However, a small number of ex-felons who had been imprisoned mainly for drug or drug-related crimes, and who had taken some prison college while it was available, hit the academic trail upon release to continue their higher education. In 1996, Chuck Terry, one of the academic ex-cons, finishing his Ph.D. at the University of California–Riverside, organized (with help from Joan Petersilia) the beginnings of a movement that would subsequently develop as "convict criminology." This network of ex-con academics, leaving prison and entering the nation's universities and colleges, have gone on to have an influence on academic criminology. Several ex-con academics now mentor new "convict criminologists" coming up through graduate education.

The ex-con criminologists made it out of street-drug culture and crime to education, jobs and health. They often have a critique of the U.S. incarceration binge. Several dozen of these ex-con academics now teach at various colleges and universities in the United States and write books and papers analyzing the prison system from prisoner and ex-con perspectives. Insights from these ex-felon professors are included in this book. As Ross and Richards say in their "Introduction" to *Convict Criminology*:

> The outlines of the new school of convict criminology's mission and purpose emerged as writers shared the experiences they have had with prison and academia. This represents an effort to revitalize the criminological literature with research validated by personal experience. Together, these

academic authors critique existing theory and present new research from a convict or insider perspective. In short, they "tell it like it is." In doing so, they hope to convey the message that "its' about time" (Austin and Irwin 2001)—time served, time lost and time that taught us the lessons we share. (Ross & Richards 2003:9)

Hopefully readers of this collection of eighty prisoner portraits will find that these prisoner-voice essays "tell it like it is."

Conclusion

So, we see that social knowledge about the criminal justice apparatus is perspectival knowledge. How do you know what you know about crime and punishment? We are like "fish swimming in the stream"—we don't "see" the water until we are taken out of it—for instance, by considering different points of view. In chapters 1 through 3 we see that there are several historical contexts, cultural and political insights and theoretical lenses we can use to explain the extraordinary quadrupling of "the prisoners' world" population and binge growth of the U.S. prison system.

Who are these "person categories" in our "late-modern" society? The rest of this book presents many prisoner voices on "the prisoners' world." We start the next section with prisoner voices on their life before prison—their home and their pathways to prison.

POSTSCRIPT

The prisoners' world since 1986 has been an experience of the incarceration binge culture—overcrowding, long sentences, more flops, more druggies, more revolving door re-offenders. And this "binge culture," beginning to build up around 1986, has already been a long "historical period." The binge growth world of prison experience has been not only part of prisoner experience but also a part of the American peoples' experience for the last twenty-five years as they have seen the power world shift from the "rehabilitative ideal" toward zero tolerance of street drugs, heard the politician say "we must get those violent predators off our streets" and participated in the pragmatic prison-build-up movement that was also characterized by a retributive and vengeful "lock-them-up-and-throw-away-the-key" mood. But, as state budgets require examination of corrections as the largest component of the budget—sparking a new pragmatic concern to "put the brakes on" the prison-build-up movement—and as a sense of justice returns, will the binge growth culture end?

II

—ɯ—

LIFE BEFORE PRISON

W ho are the prisoners caught in the incarceration binge? Recall that 50 percent of prisoners entering prison are non-assaultive. Politicians, during the binge growth historical era, themselves fearful of losing an election, and thus helping to drive fear in the public with their "I'm-tough-on-crime" rhetoric, would not talk much of prisoners' homes and families.

In life before prison he—the prisoner—was "free." Once incarcerated in the prison world he sees his *self* and self-reflection increasingly from within the prison context. But prisoners want to hold on to a rapidly diminishing memory of a "self" that was familiar before prison.

The prison world is a big, impersonal bureaucratic system. Michigan's forty-two prisons as of 2008 hold 52,000 people. Each of the forty-two prisons (approximately 1,500 population each) is like a small city and prisoners are often shifted around from prison to prison, reinforcing the prison system bureaucratic world as the world in which his life is lived. Yet, each man that enters abruptly left, and often remains emotionally attached to and self-identified in and by, the outside world. A world in which he is not a number, a cellmate, a defined "deviant"—but rather a world in which he is a son, husband, father or boyfriend, long forgotten friend, neighbor or homie. In sum, each prisoner on the outside world had a home, a family and a life of growing up. It is important to return to our prisoners' roots, and to see his pathways to prison.

Eighty percent of prisoners have a family history of child abuse and neglect. Typically messed up by his family (Newbold 2003), the person raised this way, in turn, messes over other people in a way, or to an extent, that others—or the police enforcing laws—draw lines. Frustrated, irritated or angry with him—and sometimes afraid of him—there are charges, prosecution and conviction. He (or she), now a convict, enters prison. Ninety-five percent of prisoners are male. Along the way there were tipping points that turned him to crime. His life before prison—a blend of free will and determinism—was partly *determined* for him (parents, upbringing, festering inner city neighborhood) and partly was a matter of his *poor choices* (issues of developing responsibility, maturity and self-leadership).

4

—ᴍ—

Families and Home

INTRODUCTION

In contrast to the publicly held stereotype of all criminals as violent "animals," recall that according to the Michigan Department of Corrections (MDOC) 38 percent of those *entering* prison are non-assaultive, and another 21 percent are drug-defined or drug-related convictions. In prison for long periods, many mature, even those with assaultive convictions, and pose little risk later in their life. The risk posed by many prisoners is overdrawn by politicians and the media (CAPPS 2008).

From our experience as prison teachers we've found that many prisoners—at least in the prison setting—tend to be submissive. Many are deeply repentant, almost to a fault, and are lacking in self-esteem. Some feel guilt for what they have done to their families.

How do most prisoners feel about their families? Depending on the growing-up process each experienced, feelings may range from respect and near-adoration ("I'm sorry I let my family down") to disrespect and absolute hatred ("I feel my family is the cause of my being here in prison").

Such feelings by the prisoner may differ between parents. Most usual may be a response like: "I hated my father who beat us and finally deserted us. While I loved my mother who loved us and tried hard as a single mother to raise us right." On the other hand, less often one may hear "My dad was great and always there for us while my mother drank, took drugs, and didn't care about us." As mentioned, data show that over 80 percent of Michigan prisoners have had a history of child abuse and neglect.

Family feelings may differ between races. African American prisoner/ students, we found, may usually look first to their mothers as the strength, inspiration and guidance for their lives. Rarely do they mention fathers because in ghetto families fathers or dominant males had left their family—due to unemployment, street culture involvement and going to prison—and were unable to carry financial responsibility, or were long gone from the household.

White students mention mothers less, with fathers being much more visible, usually as a role model and the teacher of male virtues such as responsibility, courage and so on, with the father instructing the son in "male" activities like sports and hunting.

Grandmothers are especially revered by black men and women because so many children in inner cities were raised by their grandmothers. For many reasons the mother cannot adequately care for her child. She may work full-time, sometimes at two jobs. She may be young and inexperienced, essentially still a child herself (note two students mention 15-year-old mothers). She may be a single mother with all the burdens listed (young, must work). Or, the mother has left home, perhaps abandoning her child(ren) because she is an alcoholic or drug addict. In juvenile court the probate judge may search those attending for a grandmother to take responsibility for the child(ren). Foster homes are scarce. So, for all these reasons and more, the grandmother is left to raise her grandchild.

As prison college teachers we started out nearly every teaching day sitting for half-an-hour or more in the prison lobby. We were always instructed to arrive a half-hour before class due to uncertainty in getting through the gates "at the last minute." Sitting in prison lobbies over twenty years we have spent time—many hours—observing visitors. We've also passed by the visiting room on each walk into the inside-prison classroom building. Then, again, in our college classes "on the *inside*," we noticed how many (if any) prison college students got a "call out" for a visit. We have observed that the longer a man is in prison, the fewer visitors he has, and the more those tend to be family. Observing any prison visiting room will verify this. The current lady friend, workmate or homie has long since ceased to come. However, his mother or grandmother continues to drive the many miles to the prison or take the prison visitor bus or a cab every month to visit her child or grandchild in prison.

FATHERS

Prisioner Essay #1

My Dad

Me and my dad went up north to Rose City to some land that my brother-in-law owns and my dad let me use his very first rifle. It was a 30.06 and boy, did it have some kick.

Well, the first day out hunting my first time my dad had me sit in the blind with him and told me where to watch. And we just sat there waiting for deer to come by, talking about things we never before had the chance to talk about. Like my girlfriend, and was I ever going to introduce her to him, and I told him that I thought that he didn't care about my social life and he told me that there are a lot of things that he would like to know about but I never gave him the chance to ask.

Well, sitting there that afternoon talking to my father about the past eight years of my life we missed our chance at two bucks—a younger and an older—who just walked right on by, like a father and son passing another father and son.

Well, that time that I spent with my father up north deer hunting meant more to me than anything that I could have ever done with my friends that week. My dad got to shoot an eight-point buck and I got a doe that week and when we got home he taught me how to cut up the deer and how good it is to eat.

Well, it just so happens that was my dad's last year hunting because he died the following year. But that time with him will always be the most memorable time in my life and I just wish that I would've had more time with him sooner.

—⚘—

Prisoner Essay #2

A Good Mother and Father—But I Chose the Streets

My family is loving and caring; it is now ten of us including me; I have four brothers, three sisters, a mother, and a father.

I was raised the second child born with my mother, father, and two brothers. Me and my brothers are very close. We all look after each other the way full-blooded brothers are supposed to, and we would never let anything happen to either one of us. We helped each other with whatever the need be, would never tell on each other or get anyone of us in trouble. If one gets in trouble all of us would go down for it or none of us would.

We have never been separated. Throughout our childhood, we always got what we wanted and what we needed—our parents had good jobs. My mom worked for General Motors and my dad drove a cement truck. We lived in a good neighborhood all of my childhood years. We stayed in a good school district and went to good schools until I was about ten. That's when my mom sold her seniority at GM. And she and my dad were going through their tribulations at the same time. They used to argue and fight until they got separated. My dad moved out and me and my two brothers stayed with our mom until we got older and started selling drugs and making unproductive decisions and mom couldn't control us.

So we moved to Tennessee with our dad and he was doing good but we were still out of control. He tried to reshape our perceptions but he couldn't because we choose the streets over everything. So we left Tennessee to go back to the neighborhood and we did everything we wanted to because we really didn't have guidance then.

But one thing had changed when we came back to our mom and it was a baby sister and my mom was really struggling. Because she had to quit her job because she was pregnant and couldn't work, that really made me and my two brothers sell drugs.

And once my sister got a little older my mom started back working so she didn't have to struggle anymore. She was a hardworking self-independent woman that was responsible enough to accept her responsibilities. As a mother she did her best to raise her children, and loved and cared for the young men that she raised to be healthy and strong.

While my dad met a young woman about five years ago, had a son by her and moved to the old neighborhood I grew up in, nevertheless he helped my mother, brothers and sister because he is a kind-hearted, loving father who is man enough to accept his responsibilities as a man and father.

Even though me and my brothers are grown and in prison he still does his deeds as a father while he also has two baby daughters and two young sons out there to take care of; he still supports us financially and mentally. That's a good father and mother, they both sacrificed for their children and they both care and love us.

SINGLE MOM

The number of black prisoners raised by single mothers is extraordinarily high. Often, there are two and even more children in the one-parent family.

Obviously, the job and responsibilities of this single woman are difficult, to say the least. Not only must she fill the traditional time-consuming mother role of housekeeping, nurturing and childcare but she must also play the father role as provider, judge and disciplinarian.

Many women are simply not up to this Herculean task and the family becomes dysfunctional (see below).

A few are up to it and do an exceptional job. Usually despite a life of poverty, the children she raises go on to become well-educated and productive citizens.

Too often, though, the sons of single mothers simply go on to prison, sometimes arriving angry and rebellious. As is often the case when this happens, however, with time and maturation—or as the prison system calls it, "aging out"—these prisoners have time to reflect on their lives and especially on parental influence.

Prisoner Essay #3

My Mother

In my family there are four of us. My mother: myself, and my two younger brothers.

My mother tried her best to raise her three boys as a tight-knitted family. Other than her husband who was killed by the police when I was about two-and-a-half years old, I've never known her to have a steady man around. It's always just been her and her boys.

My mother has always been very religious, she used to have us in church two to three times a week, involved in all types of programs, and constantly kept a strong hold on our activities. She also could sing and play the piano real well. I'd have to say she was on professional status, but she just never pursued a career in singing. She only played and sung in church and she always had us there with her.

She tried teaching us to sing and play instruments, but that didn't work. I, being the oldest, ended up playing the drums, and eventually went on to DJ a little, but I also ended up in prison, so that's as far as I got musically. My brother "D" who's under me, ended up going crazy. As far as I know, he don't really do anything. Except take medication.

Before I went to prison at fifteen years of age, he was thirteen years old and he was a normal thirteen-year-old. Once I left, he started selling drugs for one of my cousins and ended up getting gaged up. He never been the same since. In many ways I blame myself, because had I been a real big brother, things would be different with him.

—ɯ—

GRANDMOTHERS

Prisoner Essay #4

Tribute to a Lady

She is a pillar of strength, the epitome of a saint. Who could possibly be compared to a grandmother?

Grandmothers have more knowledge, understanding and experience than a dozen different scholars all rolled into one. My grandmother in particular is a perfect role model.

Since I can remember, my grandma has been there, to support me through the good times and the bad. I remember my first motorcycle ride and, believe it or not, it was my grandma who gave it to me. It was on her 125 Yamaha Enduro. I sat astride the navy blue gas tank, holding on to the cross bar, as we cruised around the city. It was an exhilarating experience that I will always remember. However this is just one of the many, many wonderful memories I cherish of my grandma.

She has taught me many things about life that have shaped the way I conduct myself in public and in private. For instance, how to speak to my elders. Look them in the eye and speak clearly, this way they are aware that I am speaking truthfully and not trying to get one over on them.

I remember once how this all came about; I had been out playing in the yard when Grandma called me in for dinner. "Go wash your hands for supper" she said. "Alright" I replied. Being seven years old you really can't comprehend what grown-ups fascination with washing your hands before you eat is, so I went into the bathroom and ran water over them and came back out. "Did you use soap?" "Uhm yeah?" I replied hesitantly. "Anthony!?" she replied in that grandmotherly tone of are you fibbing? "What!?" I said exasperatingly. Finally I gave up the ruse and asked her how she could tell that I hadn't used soap. That's when she gave me the advice on how to look a person in the eye and to speak clearly.

She's taught me many things including how to be a gentleman by always being polite, courteous, and helpful whenever possible. Always be respectful by addressing people by ma'am and sir. All of these pieces of advice are just a few of the characteristics that my grandma has instilled in me and that make my grandma the strong-willed, saint-like person she is today.

My grandma has angelic-white hair, deep-set brown eyes, naturally rosy cheeks, and an infectious smile, which adds to my perception of her as a saint and also contributes to her lovability.

Born in the 1920s, she has seen and been through more than I can imagine. My grandpa and her struggled through some hard times, including a depression, World War II and Vietnam to raise six children. My grandpa went off to the war while my grandma awaited his return from war. She worked in a department store while he was away. Later after the war she became a full-time housewife and mother to six children, which had to be one of the hardest jobs in the world. Just when things started to get better another war broke up and now she had to wait and worry as two of her boys went off to defend our country in Vietnam. Both of them returned home safe and maybe not too sound.

Shortly after the return of her sons, I came to be. There wasn't too much I could say or do to get one across or over my grandma that she hasn't seen or heard in the past.

She has lost her husband and youngest son within a five year period. And has a grandchild in prison, yet she still keeps our family together. She has faith. She is my faith.

Even though age is catching up with her, in my eyes she will be ageless. I believe she is the perfect example of a humanitarian. Her beliefs and values have become my own.

I haven't exactly been the most gracious grandchild, I have tried to become a better person. Like my "Grams" always tells me, "You can accomplish anything you set your mind to do!"

Everything this lady has told and taught me has kept my head above the cesspool I have been floating around in, for the past ten years.

For her and myself, I will continue to be the person I am, a tribute to her wisdom and experience. I will be forever grateful and in awe of her, and try to better myself in every way, every day.

—ɯ—

DYSFUNCTIONAL FAMILY

Introduction

The statistics on prisoners from a dysfunctional family approaches that of prisoners from one-parent households. The frequency of prisoners from broken homes is high and the person reared in such a family is generally affected for life.

What constitutes dysfunctionality? Any definition may encompass a near-endless array of permutations and combinations. The situation may be one in which both parents, either married or not, have a substance-abuse problem—addiction to alcohol or drugs—and may abuse the child mentally, verbally, physically or sexually. They may have poor parenting skills. They may neglect the child, or denigrate or ignore the child. They may indulge in deviant, inappropriate or criminal behavior in front of the child, and so forth.

The situation may be one in which one or the other parent has deserted the home and family while the remaining parent may exhibit such behaviors. And so it goes, endlessly.

Whatever the particular situation and results, one prisoner can usually recognize the overall memories, effects and syndrome of growing up in such a family in himself, and in other prisoners.

Prisoner Essay #5

"What Family?"

My home describes drugs, sex and violence, which were very normal because I saw it every day of my life. There were no free meals, fancy clothes, or love. Up until I sold dope I never had a bit of hope. I learned hard work from my grandfather who worked hard for his money, and I kept with this until now I'm in prison. I still believe in working hard for money. But drugs seem to be my job of choice from the early age of twelve. My mother bought us clothes so when I learned I could buy my own shit by selling drugs it was all she wrote. My home describes neglect, abuse, substance abuse and mental abuse and so forth. Home, what home? Never had one!

—⟋⟍—

Prisoner Essay #6

A Dysfunctional Family

This is the story of my family. It's definitely not your average American family. That is, unless your family is really messed up.

I guess the first place to start with is my mother. She herself didn't have a very good mother. And unfortunately for me, it ran in the blood. Considering how she was raised I think she did a decent job.

After her, I believe we should example my father. My biological father that is. I have only even seen him twice ever. The first time he was in a wheelchair on an oxygen tank, and he called my mom a bitch. The next time I saw him was at his funeral. Which is the only time and place I really ever saw my brothers or half brothers. But I know they turned out good. I think they all went to college.

But the man who raised me and kept me out of prison, almost out least anyway, was my stepfather. He was a really good person and the best influence I had in my life. He even went to college. He'd dead now though. My mom went to jail for smuggling marijuana into Carson City Correctional Facility and got busted. After that I guess he couldn't take it any-more. He was found with a bullet in his head and a pistol in his hand.

After I get out of prison (God willing) I am going to take his name—or at least his last name. You see, my biological father has other boys to make his name live on. But my stepfather unfortunately doesn't. So I am going to try to make his name live on as long as the good Lord will allow.

Then there's my grandmother. She just recently became a ward of the state. You could tell she wasn't a really good mom. Once when I was a little kid five or six years old, out of the blue she says, "when you are six-teen you can quit school." She gave birth to four girls and one boy. None of which went to college. She even did time in prison too.

Speaking of her kids, I guess they are next. I already mentioned how many kids she had. Two of her daughters are dead. One died in a car wreck. Another died in a fire with her four-year-old baby girl. My mom's only living sister I think is dying. I think its AIDS. Her son, my uncle, is an alcoholic. Or at least he used to be. I guess I lost pretty much what was left of my family when I got arrested.

I know they are not much but they are my family. I guess I turned out good considering the people who think they raised me. But after coming to prison I am a better man. I don't steal, I don't rob, rape, kill anyone. I am a lot better now. I understand that laws are put in place to keep people safe and have a chance to enjoy life. Not just to keep me from having fun. So I guess it really did work out for the best.

—⁂—

A NORMAL FAMILY

The opposite of a dysfunctional family is the "normal" kind of family most of us were raised in. With all its clashes of personality, habits, disci-pline, feuds, bad mistakes—even traumas—you name it, in the long run, the family pretty well sticks together and nurtured each other.

The essay that follows, "Twenty Years—And Still My Family" is the description of the family of a lucky prisoner that has not only stuck to-gether but still considers him a valuable member—even after his twenty years in prison.

Prisoner Essay #7

Twenty Years—And Still My Family

I don't really know what to say about my family except for they're my family.

They still consider me a part of the household even after the twenty years I've been in prison.

I talk to them on the phone often. Every blue moon one of my brothers might come visit, but only with my mother. Even at thirty-four and thirty-two my mother still takes care of them. Hell, she still takes care of me.

She usually comes to visit alone regularly. She is the only who writes, my two brothers don't write well. But they're all still there and down for me. It kind of bothers me sometimes because of the expectations that they have of me.

In many ways my family has made it clear to me that no matter what happens, no matter where I am, I am still a major part of the family. And, that when I come home, I have to put the family back on track, which makes me have to be concerned, think, and care for four people instead of just one. Being away so long makes that kind of hard to do, especially coming from a confined environment.

I guess another way to look at it is like saying each player has a role, but the team can't produce as efficiently or effectively with one member missing. So, either you have to replace that team member, or wait until that team member can return to, or begin to do, his role again in order to make that team a complete and effective unit.

Even though the team still plays, they won't be capable of playing up to the level they would if all of the members did their role. My family is like that united that, to them, there is no one else that can fill that role or position. So even though they're still playing the game (living) as best as they can, they're still waiting on their other member which is (me), to re-join the team or family so we can get back to the level, or a higher level than we were at before I left.

When I was younger, before I came to prison, and a little bit after, I never looked at family in this manner. I guess I just thought about myself. Now that I can see things a bit better, I can appreciate a family, which directly affects my behavior and actions, because I'm not thinking just for self, but for family as well, which is a unit of people.

—〜〜—

HOME

Introduction

What are prisoners' homes like? Well, there are many types of homes described by prisoners—prison is a mixed bag. Since 48 percent of people in prison are African Americans and most are from "imprisoned communities" (Clear 2007), the housing is characteristic of poverty areas. In terms of what goes on in the house, as we have seen, there is generally some dysfunction in the family. Most prisoners, however, enjoyed their home growing up or as an adult. At least their home seems better to them now as they look back from a prison cell. Note the emphasis in some essays of how the prisoner wants to state the level of luxury he was able to sustain. This is characteristic of many prisoners the coauthors met in prison college classes who wanted to show (or show off) that *they too could afford all this stuff*. This could be interpreted as a somewhat defensive attitude characteristic of some who may have come from disadvantaged neighborhood that is near nicer suburbs—a social-psychological outlook of "relative deprivation." A strong sense of relative deprivation is a contributing factor in developing criminality.

PRISONER ESSAYS: BY JACKSON PRISONERS

Prisoner Essay #8

My Home is My Palace

My home is my palace. A step above the ghetto norm. A place of rest and relaxing. It's made of bricks and has four bedrooms with ceiling fans in them plus the basement. It also has a beautiful view from the front porch with a couple of bushes lining the front walkway. Inside it's huge with oak railing leading upstairs as soon as you walk in. The kitchen is undergoing remodeling, while the living room is painted sky blue with a chimney for cozy winter nights.

The things that I've furnished the house with are essentials to every home but maybe a little more ritzy than others. I have a leather couch jet-black that seats four and faces the windows. I have a Zenith Movie Screen that sits near the stairwell and the side windows, which are small but illuminated and accent the living room. I also have borders running around the ceiling to bring a touch of glamour to the scenery. The carpet is thick and also sky blue with trinkets of white speckles all through it. It may not be a million-dollar home but it's something I can call my own. Along with the feeling of self.

—w—

In the next essay, "Home—Almost Paid For," we find a black prisoner and family living in a home even more luxurious than that just described. Is this for real? Did drug money pay for this? Or is it an "estate of mind."

Prisoner Essay #9

Home—Almost Paid For

My home is this wonderful place about 5,000 square feet of loveliness. A large in-ground pool, three-car garage, privacy fence around the entire place, five-bedroom three-and-a-half bath. Three fire places, large study, large dinning room and a view of the lake from every room facing the back, a dockage to the lake. Plasma TV throughout the home, great landscaping to complete this beautiful estate of mine. What a wonderful home.

—∿—

A real-life young, white skateboarding "druggie" from Southern California describes his "squat."

Prisoner Essay #10

A Squat in Santa Monica

Sometimes I think about places I've been, but none compare to home. Not the home where my mother lives, but the old, rundown squat in Santa Monica, California.

When I first saw this abandoned house, it looked like it was ready to become a parking lot. Although the blue paint is chipping off the lapboard siding, the house is structurally sound. The windows may be covered with plywood and the front porch is caved in, but that didn't matter, as long as the floors, roof, and stairs were in decent shape.

This house was built around the turn of the century, so the lumber was very good. Besides, wood doesn't rot as quickly in Southern California as it does in Michigan.

The only entrance into this abandoned boarded-up house is through the rear basement window. As you crawl through on your stomach, feet first, you kinda sense what it means to squat a rundown house.

Because of the boarded windows, it is dark inside so you need a flashlight or a Bic Lighter. It's always good to have light, you never know— since the bathrooms don't work in this house—what you may step on. Warning: Squatting is Hazardous.

Anyway, once inside the basement, with the light on, you must turn left to go up the stairs to the first level of the house. This is the worst level because of all the junk on the floor. Not to mention Jester—someone I once knew—got killed in the front room on the first floor.

When going to the flight of steps that leads to our room, you had to pass the room Jester was killed in. This is bad because of all the memories of Jester that would come up just then.

Turning to the right you begin once more up the next flight of stairs. This is your last chance to turn around and go out, once you're in the room, you're in till morning. Too much traffic in and out of a squat is bad; it draws too much attention from the police.

Now that you're on the second floor of the house, you march directly to the back. To the left is where you find my door, right next to the rest room. A very bad place, however it's good for that morning run to the toilet in spite of all of the bowel that necessarily winds up on the floor.

This is home. "Squatters" rights.

—∞—

Prisoner Essay #11

The Country is Really Cool—Sort Of

Before I start describing my home, let me begin by telling you I live in the country.

Among the trees, by the side of a paved road lies a redbrick house. Along the front is a flower box and a set of wrought-iron patio furniture. My home has a chimney on one side next to the driveway.

There are trees around that keep the house shaded in the summer. There is also a downside to all the trees—raking up the leaves in the fall.

Trees have other uses besides shade. They are great for tire-swings and tree-forts.

Tree-forts are cool because they are above the ground, where pesky moms and dads do not like to intrude.

My tree house and tire swing are behind my house, located in the country. By the way, have you ever been to the country?

Well if you haven't, don't be so quick to judge, because there are a lot of things to do around your house, in spite of being bored most of the time. Beneath the canopy of leaves—in your tree house—and between the tree trunks there are a lot of things to look for such as birds and animals.

—∞—

PRISONERS ESSAYS: BY GUS HARRISON PRISONERS

In the essay, "Finally out of the Projects," a black, thirty-five-year-old prisoner remembers moving out of the projects. The second essay,

"Dancing for Joy on Our Summer Porch," reveals that, while they shared the house with memphites (insects), they loved their home.

Prisoner Essay #12

Finally out of the Projects

I remember moving from the Human Gardens to a home on the West side of Detroit back in 1976. The home was very different from the projects and it was very nice. At that time I was about seven years old. There was myself, two brothers (younger) and my mother. The house was at that time very middle class and the neighborhood was white. The basement was cool, because it had a bar in it and lots of room to play in. As I got a little older, I would use the basement as my all-purpose room. DJ-ing, dancing, working out, etc.

My two brothers and I slept upstairs on the second level. We only had two levels and a basement; on the first level was the kitchen, dining room, Den, my mother's bedroom, a living room, and a closed-in back porch.

We also had a nice backyard with an apple tree and a pear tree.

Prisoner Essay #13

Dancing for Joy on Our Summer Porch

We moved to Gable Street. It was a nice house considering we had just moved from the pole-town Hamtramck district. Our house had a nice wide porch, which we found ourselves dancing for joy on every hot Summer evening. Our house was white trimmed in black, two rooms, one bathroom and a redecorated attic with carpet from the attic down to the living room. A lot of Memphites were born in this house; especially the basement, but for the most part it was our house.

5

—⁓—

Pathways to Prison

INTRODUCTION

Prison has many categories of prisoners, and there are many pathways to prison. However, over our twenty-five years as prison teachers we have found, and the prison essays in chapter 5, "Pathways to Prison," reveal, that somewhere in middle school or high school, learning about street drugs relates strongly to winding up in prison.

Now we have presented in chapters 1 through 3 certain issues. For instance, there have been, for a long time, laws against street drugs. The Marijuana Tax Act of 1937, the Harrison Narcotics Act of 1914 outlawed heroin and long-standing laws against cocaine—there has been legislation outlawing meth (speed), PCP and most hallucinogens—all laws passed in the 1950s, 1960s and 1970s—made street drugs *illegal*. Therefore, when our convict essay says, about pathways to prison, "I started to get into drugs," we know—since the predominant societal approach to street drugs has been making laws and law enforcement (rather than, say, the harm-reduction and restorative-justice approach)—that they may well be on their way to prison.

However, these essays are not about the 1950s, 1960s or 1970s—they are about the period between 1981–2008, and especially from the 1986 crack epidemic onward—where there emerged not just a continuation of the existing laws, (with short sentences and a treatment approach), as we've explained, but a "war" on drugs—the incarceration binge. Now there were long sentences. Also the "bad neighborhoods" that were always there "on the other side of the tracks" before the 1960s became, since the mid-1960s, *jobless* ghettos. The reciprocal effect of "white flight" and capital flight, and unemployment, crime and drugs increased the deterioration of these inner city neighborhoods. The drug economy, by the late 1970s and early 1980s, now dominated "what was going on in the streets." So, "getting into drugs" as a pathway to prison now included more possession, more dealing, more gangs and more drug-turf violence. Schools deteriorated and the dropout rate began to exceed 50 percent.

Teens and earlier are a time for learning about sex, alcohol and other drugs and crime. Peers are the usual conduit. Kids may challenge each other with dares. Recent research indicates that teens in general have not developed fully their cognitive ability to distinguish high risk from less risky situations. But juvenile delinquents on a "pathway to prison" engage in many more risky behaviors than other youth their age. Many chilling examples of dares are recalled in prison college classrooms by prisoners, including: (1) crawling with others through a mile-long drain tunnel shore to shore from Detroit to Windsor, Ontario, under the Detroit River; (2) swimming alone across a busy waterway loaded with container ship traffic somewhere in the state of Washington; (3) rolling under the wheels of a moving freight train in Detroit and emerging unscathed on the other side.

We all know that anybody, anywhere in the class structure, can get involved with drugs. But systematic sociological research suggests certain social contexts hold more "risk factors for drug use." These include: "Social norms favorable to drug use, availability of drugs, extreme economic deprivations, neighborhood disorganization, parent and family drug use, positive family attitudes toward drug use, poor/inconsistent family management practices, family conflict and disruption, association with drug-using peers, low commitment to school, alienation, early onset of drug use" among other risk factors (Abadinsky 2008:185). This list pretty well describes the inner city neighborhood, family, peer and drug economy *social context* that many prisoners are exposed to as they grow up. Under these circumstances the dare of learning drugs becomes more frequent than in other social settings. And with the harsh sentences after 1986, the dare of getting into drugs had more consequences.

In the prisoner essays that follow, in addition to childhood dares and risky behavior, certain distinct pathways to prison related to drugs present themselves.

LEARNING DRUGS

Prisoner Essay #14

A Drop-Out at Seventeen, I Started Going Straight Downhill

From kindergarten to the third grade I did pretty good. I never had a lot of trouble out of other children because I was liked by all. When I moved to a new neighborhood that's when my skills were tested.

I ran into a new style of children. They were more materialistic and a lot more spoiled than my last friends.

So to keep up with this new breed of friends I felt like I had to start dressing and acting like them to fit in. So I did and it worked a little bit until it was time for middle school to start.

When I started middle school it really was a change for me. I had been used to going to school with only black children, now I was going to a school where it was 50 percent blacks and 50 percent whites. Now I had to adjust to this new situation.

The peer pressure here was 100 percent more than in my new neighborhood. Now I found myself having to make another big change. This consisted of my getting smarter in this new school because everybody was very smart. Then I had to get me some "top-of-the-line" clothes to stay in style.

I now ran into a very big problem with my mother. She wouldn't buy me the "top-of-the-line" clothes that everyone else wore until I made better grades. Now I had to get these clothes with or without my mother's help.

Now I'm looking for ways to get money. So I pick up some guys in my neighborhood that always seem to have these brand new outfits all the time to hang out with, and this was the start of me getting in some big trouble. By the time I was fourteen, I had been in and out of inner city police precincts for stealing cars more than five times. To me I was starting to make my mark in this new neighborhood.

Now came the age when I went to high school. These were the best years of my life. I met my first real girlfriend in high school and I was introduced to a new kind of hustle. It was selling dope, and the money was very good.

Now I had the best-looking girl and making some nice money, but I wasn't going to classes and that was bringing me down. I also got my girl pregnant at the age of fourteen and now I was going to be a father.

After my girl had her/our baby I found that this was the biggest obstacle in my life. I found myself wanting to be a gangsta and a father, so I made it work for me (the gangsta and father thing). This was a big problem for my mother, because she wanted the best for me and my daughter.

I had dropped out of school and moved away from home by the age of seventeen because there was too much controversy at my mother's house.

From the age of seventeen to twenty-one, I started going straight downhill at a rapid pace. I found myself doing drugs that I had once said "never, not me, not in a 1,000 years." So I never recovered and caught a case that landed me in jail till this very day. The end.

—〰—

Prisoner Essay #15

The Same Old—Skip School, Drinking, Smoke Pot

I'm seventeen now and in prison, but the story starts when the teenage years are about to get underway. As they do, I began to fall farther and farther down the wrong path. The skipping school comes back and the drinking starts to take its course. Along with the drinking and skipping school comes the pot. The three together are not a good combination.

Well, first things first. I'm starting junior high now. For the seventh and half the eighth, everything goes well. I still attend school every day, do all the work, and get pretty good grades. Then it all starts to fall apart.

About halfway through the eighth grade year I start skipping school and shortly after I start drinking and smoking pot. Again, it's me, Chris and David that start skipping school. At first we'd just skip school, go to David's house and play video games or just hang out.

David's older brother, Jon, would be there and most of the time he would be drinking. Seeing this a lot we got interested in trying it. . . . The first two or three times weren't all that fun. By the sixth- or seventh-grade drinking experiments, though, we were hooked. The school skipping was now up to about once a week.

Well now the ninth grade is getting started. During the summer we drank almost every night. When school started none of us felt like going. So we basically didn't. We only went maybe two or three times a week and that was a good week when we made it three days.

Again, about this time, David's brother, Jon, started selling pot. Naturally we got interested in trying this, so we did. Chris was never one to use pot, but me and Dave loved it. We would be high all the time. Almost every waking hour we were high or trying to get high.

We were the same in tenth grade. Skipping a lot of school, drinking and smoking pot. Little did I know that I'd be in prison before the tenth grade year was up.

One day me, Steve, Dave and Chris were skipping school at Dave's house as usual, but something happened this day that changed all our lives forever.

That takes the story to about where I am today. Now, only seventeen years old and in prison (MR). Hopefully I won't do all the time I got. Hopefully I'll get back on appeals. But for now I just got to sit in prison and wait.

—⚬—

Prisoner Essay #16

Selling Drugs for $800 a Day to Help Single Mom

I'm a twenty-six-year-old man who's serving a sentence of two years for a gun in possession during a felony and four to ten years for assault-with-the intent to do great bodily harm less than murder. In which I have approximately one year served.

I'm here because I was lost. I didn't know where I was headed. I knew what I should've been doing but didn't know how to go about getting the ball rolling.

It all started back in high school (ninth grade). My mother had just stopped smoking crack and my father was still in his addiction. He began when I was at the age of five and mother began when I was at the age of eleven. My mother was a single parent on welfare who could barely afford to feed myself and my two younger brothers. So I started selling drugs. Every person that was already in the game took an instant liking to me. They said that I had potential to be great in this game. I started off getting "fronted" sacks, but that didn't last long. I realized how much money could be made by entrepreneurship. So I can talk someone into teaching me how to "whip" (cook cocaine to crack). I established a "front" in front of a gas station by the bus stop. I started to make $800 per day. That was excellent for a fourteen-year-old man. I put a "man of the house" in the house at fourteen.

My mother saw the path I was beginning or had begun to take and tried to stop me. She stressed school and how it was pay off in the long run. Hell, I figured I would be a millionaire at this rate by the time it would be time for me to graduate. I was very intelligent. I received a full four-year paid scholarship to Eastern Michigan University at thirteen years old. It was called a Wade McCree scholarship. Myself and about twenty other students in the city received one. All I had to do was graduate from any high school with a 2.0 grade point average or better.

But, I couldn't go to school in rags. I cared too much about what people thought about me. So by the time I did wake up and see school was the way, I was already seventeen and I wasn't about to be sitting in a class with sophomores. My pride wouldn't let me.

So with my drinking, smoking weed, buying clothes, tricking with women and helping moms out, my $800 a day became about $100 per day. That don't include the bonding my supposed to be friends out of jail and paying for numerous abortions.

—⚓—

Prisoner Essay #17

Party til You Puke—Crack in Detroit

Here I sit in prison doing time for a crime against society, my crime second degree home invasion, the sentence ten months to fifteen years; am now doing a twenty-four-month flop.

I was heavy on drugs (crack cocaine) and my so-called friends were people just like myself, working people, but none-the-less drug addicts and alcoholics, thieves and liars.

Criminal activities was what we all did to survive on the streets of Detroit, and also to support our habits.

My circumstances at the time was that I have five children who don't have anything to do with me, family that don't care, and a "forget you" attitude, I'm looking out for more me.

These were my circumstances and attitude before and during my latest arrest which sent me to prison where I now sit doing time. In middle school it was pretty much the same: sex, drugs, and rock-n-roll—you know party till you puke. In high school, now that's funny, I never made it past the first two weeks in high school before getting kicked out, then sent to a reform school for teenagers.

Now here I sit in prison doing time for crime. In my preteen age I was subjected to crime and drugs as far back as I can remember, at least going on thirty years back.

—⚓—

Prisoner Essay #18

Growing up with Physical Abuse

I am serving parolable life in prison for second degree murder. This stems from the beating death of a person over drug money owed to the victim. I have served fifteen years on this sentence,

I came from a lower-middle-class family whose parents were classified as hard workers. We had a small farm and they also held jobs at factories to help supplement their income. There were nine of us in the family, seven of us being children. As children we were introduced to hard work at an early age. We worked in fields harvesting fruits of every kind. The work was hard and the days long. I ran a tray line around 5:00 am and then did chores, mostly carrying water and grain to the animals. In order to watch any T.V. we had to churn butter or crack open walnuts. I believe my mother enjoyed this harder-than-necessary way of living.

My mother remarried when I was five or six. My father had died when I was three. This stepfather was only interested in work and money. He had no time for us. It wasn't long after when our new home was finished being built. It was only a mile away so there were no changes in schools or neighbors. Things did change at that point in our lives within the family.

My mother became increasingly unhappy. She would come home from work and do nothing but yell and hit us. This eventually turned into regular beatings. My sister had so many bruises on her once that the school called home. I received the blame for it. The rest of us would be relieved when one of us was being beaten because it usually meant that no one else would get it that night. Once in a while our family would get together for group beatings.

My mother's control of me was complete. I did nothing she didn't direct me to do. As I entered junior high school I wanted to be more involved with friends and sports. That would never be. I was expected to attend school and I didn't dare fail a grade for fear of the worst. During this time I often spent much time confined to my room "cell" wishing my mother was dead.

At age fourteen, I was introduced to marijuana. I smoked it when I could get it. I was smoking cigarettes at this time also. My parents neither smoked, drank or did drugs. I moved up to amphetamines (speed) and also selling it. At age sixteen I was turned in by my mother for possessing five-and-a-half pounds of marijuana. I chose treatment over jail. I hated my mother for this and when I returned to the yelling and beatings I returned to the drug-abuse, doing up to four-and-a-half hits of acid at a time.

My grades in school were C's, D's, and F's by now. I had no interest in anything but getting high. When I was broke and couldn't buy drugs I sniffed record cleaner. I was beaten one night for several hours because my math teacher informed my mother that I was failing.

I in turn took my anger out on animals. I tortured cats at first. I eventually built a satanic altar and sacrificed small animals. I then moved up to shooting a friend, hanging a cousin, and sniping joggers. None of these resulted in death or convictions.

I was breaking and entering buildings, and stealing money from my parents whenever possible. I worked in a factory and never seen a red cent plus my parents were keeping my social security check all those years.

Soon I discovered my stepfather's checkbook and felt justified writing several people's checks in his name. His friend held me while he (stepfather) called the authorities. I broke free and hid in the swamp. Even though I was surrounded I escaped by slipping through a drainage tunnel.

I lived in the woods for a month or so until I caught on fire one rainy cold night. I decided to go into town in search of food and company. During this time I reflected on how bad life was. I wanted to join the Navy and fly F-14 Tomcats but my Navy testing would only allow me to be a mechanic. That would have been better than this. I thought about suicide but I had no weapons. I then decided to climb a tree and jump out of the top of it. Halfway up I slipped and fell into a thorn-apple tree. That ended my attempt at suicide.

An aunt finally found me and told me to call home. I did so and was offered a place up north if I would get off drugs and go back to school. It was November, I was cold and hungry and didn't turn it down. A couple of my sisters joined us. A month later I found some marijuana while hunting. This was sprayed by the DNR but I smoked it anyway.

The weather was bad. Lots of snow that winter. My sister went off the road near the house and a neighbor went to assist her even though he was drunk. He sexually harassed her which led me to pay him a visit the next day. I found him in the garage. I told him why I was there and he apologized, offering me some marijuana. I began to pay him regular visits. Eventually I bought marijuana from him as well. I owed him and ended up doing odd jobs for him which included stealing fire wood. I soon moved up to transporting pounds of marijuana from Traverse City to his home.

As time went by I couldn't pay my debt and soon was giving him only what I could. My friend (and codefendant) decided to run away so I picked him up and hid him out in my place. We all used drugs together.

One night the drug dealer (victim) supposedly slapped around my friend (co-defendant) demanding the money we owed. Upon my return from town we discussed our options and decided to rob and kill the dealer. We beat and stabbed him to death, taking what we could of his money, pot and stuff and headed south. We were arrested two days later near Fennville, Michigan.

In the county jail I received my GED and started a course from MSU in ecology. Upon my incarceration in the MDOC I took some (prison college) business courses. Every waking moment I am thinking about freedom and what it is going to take to gain my liberty.

I was introduced to horticulture while at M.C.F. and gained many certificates. I was able to become lead landscaper and then lead greenhouse worker. Horticulture will be my ticket to success if I am ever released.

June 30, 2001, I was stabbed to death in prison. A guard was instrumental in bringing me back to life. I received open-heart surgery at Hackely hospital in Muskegon. I experienced some strange things during this time. After my operation I was placed in the hole or administration segregation for manufacturing a weapon. This offered me time to reflect upon my life and experiences.

I was transferred from the hole to Adrian to this prison (Gus Harrison), as mixed up as ever. I finally landed a job in this prison's greenhouse.

I somehow draw up the needed motivation everyday to try to better myself. I have over a dozen horticulture books that I study almost daily, hoping to have a reason to better myself. I've taken conflict resolution workshops and several drug therapy classes. I have grown to believe that if positive change is to take place it has to come from within. I do not want to die achieving nothing in this life. So, I strive to learn more and to better myself as much as possible.

If positive thoughts and actions can redeem a felon then I wish to apply for it. I've given up the pursuit of the petty prison life for a real life with meaning and purpose. Forgiveness would be nice too.

—〽—

ENCOUNTERING—AND DROPPING OUT OF HIGH SCHOOL

Introduction

The United States prison and jail population is composed of one of the nation's largest pools of uneducated men and women. As we've mentioned, almost 80 percent of today's prisoners entering Michigan prisons have no high school diploma and few job skills (MDOC 1996). Most states are the same, with more than three-fourths of prisoners nationwide being high school dropouts. (Federal prisoners have completed high school before incarceration more often.) Both authors, in their twenty-five years as prison college teachers and post-GED workshop facilitators, found this statistic regarding the low educational attainment of state prisoners to be true—and troubling.

Who are these high school dropouts? Recent research indicates that about 30 percent of high school students nationwide drop out. For inner city high school students the dropout rate is over 50 percent. Many Michigan state prisoners come from the states' inner city neighborhoods—economically deprived metropolitan neighborhoods in Detroit, Flint, Muskegon and Benton Harbor.

What is there about these inner city prison college students we have taught over the years that relates to the special characteristics of our 2.2 million incarcerated men and women? One of the short answers is that they were high school dropouts.

Teaching on the main campuses of regional community colleges the authors find 100 percent of typical classroom students have graduated from high school. In our prison college classes, however, only one or two students out of twenty-five possessed a high school diploma *before* coming to prison. Of these, perhaps only one had gone on to college, and then for only a term or two. Often no students at all in class had graduated from high school.

The Michigan Department of Corrections reports that most prisoners have entered prison at an eighth-grade reading level, or less (DeRose 2006). Many have needed Adult Basic Education (ABE) in prison. The prisoners in our prison college classes (1981–2000) had all completed the GED in prison and then gone on to enroll in prison college.

Many state prisons now require that prisoners begin working toward completing the GED in prison. There are GED prep classes, taught by civil service prison GED teachers. In Michigan, since 1998, prisoners must be working on the GED in prison as a condition of release on parole. When there were prison college programs in U.S. prisons, teachers in the prison college were hired and paid by the particular colleges which were running the prison college program as an adjunct campus to their own main campus. The money to run prison college from 1972 to 1994 came through federal Pell grant money, since, until 1994, prisoners qualified for Pell grants as low-income students.

Each of the essays on high school that follow was written by high school dropouts who eventually landed in prison and completed their GED in prison in order to subsequently enroll in prison college. They recollect their feelings when in high school.

After reading their comments, it will become obvious that when in high school (on the outside) these prisoners were not scholars, nor did they wish to be. Studying and school were not their thing. In their opinion, this was only for college-bound nerds, and at this point in their mid- and late teens, college was not in their plans.

Indeed, usually no one in their families had ever gone to college and it was not expected that they would go either. The young people wanted simply to be done with school, to quit boring classes. Often their parents had not disciplined them to the persistence required for academic success. Or they didn't listen. Many were drawn into street life, drug dealing, drug culture and criminality, and were "living off crime" (Tunnel 2000; Wright & Decker 1994; Tregea & Larmour 2005b). It was only after being in prison, and often spending time being in the alternative community of the school building prison activities (Newman 1993), rather than spending time in the yard—and reflecting on their past lives—that each came to the conclusion that studying and school now seemed a path out of the prison world (Tregea 1998; Duguid & Pawson 1998; CEA 2005; Tregea & Larmour 2005c). The experience of prison college often changed their self concept (Wenda 1997; Duguid 1992; Duguid, Hawley and Knights 1998; Tregea 2003).

PRISONER ESSAYS

Prisoner Essay #19

Not Cool to Study, But Don't Drop Out

In high school in the 1980s in Saginaw, Michigan, I hung around with a crowd that looked down on people who did well in class. It was not cool to spend time studying, or do good on tests and exams. My crowd was into things like skipping class, smoking, drinking and doing the popular street drugs. I guess I belonged to a crowd that would be considered by most to be trouble makers. On the other hand it was not cool to completely fail at school or drop out all together. We looked down on flunkies or dropouts—they were seen as not cool or complete bums.

—⟋⟍—

Prisoner Essay #20

Homework? Nah—We Did Drinking and Partying

During my high school years, homework was more likely to be done by the female student than the male. There were males on the sports teams who may have studied some, or were required to maintain a grade to play team sports.

A few males who studied perhaps as hard as some females were known as our bookworms.

The friends and school chums I remember did little homework, we spent more time drinking and partying.

The females seemed to prefer the more rowdy type of student. If you were "cool" and could dance, getting a date would not be one of your problems.

—⚹—

Prisoner Essay #21

The Status of those who Studied in High School

High school was a brutal time for most of the people I knew. We were the kids that didn't study and only showed up to class every so often. Those kids that did apply themselves in high school were considered preps or nerds. To me, the preps were sort of snobby because they kind of understood things about life that I didn't and usually peered down on me and my pre-drop-out friends. The preps were cool back then, but they secretly did the same things I did. The only difference was that I skipped school to smoke pot and drink and they saved those activities til after class when their homework was done.

The nerds were something different. The nerds were loners and no one really knew where they lived or their names unless they incidentally sat in the next seat over in class. Commonly, those were the kids that always had some pothead peeping over their shoulders during a test.

—⚹—

The following essays were written in 2005 by prisoner/students at Gus Harrison facility, Adrian, Michigan. Regardless of a wide time gap existing between the first set of essays written in the 1980s and 1990s and the second set in 2005, we note that the results regarding encounters with high school for both sets of prisoners are similar.

Prisoner Essay #22

I Got Heavy into the Drug Culture—My Coach Had to Sit down with Me

I've always been the cool one. Ever since I was an early teenager, even before I had gone to high school, I had lived in different states, ran-away, had my first felony and been with enough women that I knew that high school was only for three things, sports, girls and more girls.

At the end of the eighth grade I went to high school orientation. My high school wrestling coach said that he would introduce me to the rest of the team. I had been wrestling for almost seven years at the time and was slated to go very far in my high school career. If all went well, I'd be a Michigan State University freshmen in less than four years and at university-level wrestling, and everyone, including myself, couldn't wait. Mason high school is a great school, great teachers, staff and sports staff.

My mother and stepfather spoiled me, though, when they learned that I had made varsity wrestling while still in my freshman year. I had a car, and all of the right friends, not a jock. You couldn't really classify me into a certain group. But if you knew me, there were a couple things that always followed, trouble and more trouble.

I had a new group of friends my second year in high school. The bad-asses, the fighters, guys and girls that liked to party and just have fun. My friends knew my background, that I used to live in Lansing and still had friends who were heavy into the drug culture. I was really the only guy that could get drugs at the time and I began to sell drugs and use them on a more regular basis. The drugs took time away from my ability to wrestle. My coach heard rumors going around school and he had to sit down with me. He told me all my hard work would be down the drain unless I took a different path. I refused to listen.

—◊—

Prisoner Essay #23

The Streets Taught Me to Make Fast Money by Any Means

I went to Inkster High School. At first my encounter with high school wasn't so bad. I started out doing good, I went to school everyday, in my ninth grade year getting good grades and I passed all of my classes.

But as soon as I went to the tenth I was a little distracted by the peer pressure, which led me to making unproductive decisions. I was a popular individual in my city and school so I had a lot of students in my school that looked up to me and thought I was cool because I sold drugs and smoked weed. I had my own nice car and a whore, name-brand clothes and shoes and a lot more of the nice things the average teen doesn't have a lot of at the age of fifteen.

I was a bad influence on the peers who I affiliated with, because I used to get the girls to skip school and ride around the neighborhood with me, and smoke weed all day while I sold drugs. And I used to always try to have sex with all the popular girls in school because I was what is known as a Boss—always on top and in control—and I knew they would do whatever I asked because they looked up to me all through my high school years. When I was in the eleventh grade I used to make the girls do my homework for me so I knew I was passing. And at the same time while in school I sold weed everyday in the back hall because I was molded by the streets to make fast money by any means.

But I can remember at the end of my eleventh grade year when my high school days were almost at the end. I was making $560 dollars every two days from selling weed to the students at school. The money was good until the students were getting caught smoking in the bathroom and they finally got somebody to tell on me.

So one morning I came to school, and as soon as I came to my locker, I was rushed by the police and school security. They took me into the bathroom and searched me and they found four bags of weed, which was fifty six grams, two ounces. I was arrested. I was charged with possession with intent to distribute. I bonded out of jail and was expelled from the Inkster school district and I never went back to high school. But I finally got a GED in prison.

—⚞—

Prisoner Essay #24

Expelled from School, Now Highest Prison GED Score

I had a bad habit of getting into trouble. I got expelled from the seventh and eighth grades. I liked school and was very sad about being expelled. School was a hangout to me. I did not care about grades, because I didn't get good ones.

My home life was good earlier, but later it seemed as if I didn't care anymore. It was like I could get away with anything.

When I was fifteen I got arrested for the current charge I'm doing time for now. I came to M.R. (Michigan Reformatory) when I was sixteen. I had an attitude about this, so I was very violent and troublemaking then. I think I did this to cover up my real feelings of being scared.

I finally ended up in another maximum-security prison when I was nineteen for a couple of years. I just got back to M.R. in February (1994) of this year.

I only finished the eighth grade in school. After studying with a prison GED teacher, about two years ago I took my GED exam. I'm proud to say that there has been only one other person who got as high a score as I did in all of GED history here at M.R. and he tied it.

—⚞—

Prisoner Essay #25

My School Years? It's Like My Education Has Just Gotten Started

My education was limited. I went through all the grade schools and middle schools but my high school years were very short. I only went for one year then quit school. I started working and getting high all the time. I didn't complete my education until I was sent to prison. That's were I got my GED and then went on to career and technical education class here in prison and got a certificate of completion in custodial maintenance technology. So I didn't get to enjoy all the high school experiences the way most people get to. It's like my education has just now gotten started because now I want to learn everything I can so I can show my kids how important it is to get your education, so you can do whatever you set your mind to and accomplish everything your heart desires. I want to be living proof of that for them. That's why my education has just got started.

—w—

AUTHOR'S REPORT #1

"Leaving Home—and Going Straight Downhill"

After high school, the urge to leave home commonly rises in many young people. Some want to drop out of school before graduation and get a place of their own.

Many reasons are given for wanting to strike out from the family. The young adult may want more adventure than the hometown offers. They may want to work and make money. They may want to go off to college. They may want to marry and start a family. They may want to escape domineering, abusive or "smothering" parents. Some parents "throw in the towel" on their child at fifteen and say "You're on your own." Or, a single parent many simple lose control over their child(ren). Many prisoners admit they wanted to leave home and parental control in order to pursue a carefree life of drinking and drugging.

Coauthor Marjorie Larmour taught prison college English classes in which she utilized Gail Sheehey's award-winning book, *Passages* (1976). This book examines stages of life the average person passes through. In her chapter "Pulling up Roots," Sheehey describes breaking away, leaving home—this late teenage stage most people go through. Instructor Larmour had her prison college class students in the 1980s and 1990s do a critique of Gail Sheehey's 1976 *Passages*.

Several African American prisoner/students wrote that the black American experience is different than Sheehey's archetype of teenage anxiousness for a "road to autonomy." Some African American prisoner/students asserted that Sheehey's "Predictable Cries of Adulthood" is not applicable to the working-class poor. One black student wrote: "a major stumbling block that bars an expeditious, chronological, and successful transition (for) working poor individuals is their 'weak' financial infrastructure. They lack a solid economic base, which first must be formed before their focus of obtaining autonomy can become a goal that isn't unrealistic or premature."

This student notes that, while the working-poor parents endure continual stress and anxiety, and have trouble establishing a secure financial base for their children:

> In the long run they (the working poor parents' children) will become stronger psychologically—or be consumed with worry. If the former prevails, determination will build until they become content under all circumstances. If the latter becomes their state, more often than not, they will seek outlets to escape the reality of their status quo. Usually, and in most cases, many seek refuge in mind-altering vices—drugs.

The writer notes that many working people, and especially the working poor, "moonlight," or work second and third part-time jobs. In contrast, teens with parents who have good-paying jobs feel, themselves, financially secure and have more of a sense of independence which "gives the teen time to refresh their spirit and enjoy other things in life: vacations, education, entrepreneurships, and participation in important social events."

But, beyond the class analysis comparing the financial stability of well-to-do and the grinding stress for working poor, this African American prisoner/student notes that it used to be common for blacks to "never leave home."

> In black families, contrary to Ms. Sheehey's descriptive experience of "pulling up roots," it was not unusual up until the late 1960s, to find up to four generations (of African Americans) living in the same home, even fearful to venture anywhere in the country without being in the company of family members or friends and acquaintances.

Social class differences, racial or ethnic differences, and historical race discrimination were factors highlighted by African American prisoners as examples of why—and whether—young people "pull up roots." A white prisoner/student notes that age differences matter—the fourteen-year-old may want to leave home, but the eighteen-year-olds may want to stay.

> Today, children have become more dependent on the comforts and security of home. Unlike the early 1970s when Sheehey was writing, today parents are not in the home as much. In my case, being from a single-parent household, mom was gone most of the time. She had to work two jobs to take care of me and my two siblings. With this being the case, we were home by ourselves most of the time. With all that freedom at home, why leave?

One prisoner noted that kids will stay until they are basically forced to leave, and some choose a community college in the area so they can still live at home. He puts it this way:

I think that the kids today may want to leave before the age of fourteen, not eighteen. Around fourteen they begin to feel like they can take on the world, and that they're too old for their parents' advice. I had the same type of attitude at that age. By the age of sixteen, though, they begin to grow out of this stage, and reality starts to settle in.

To add confirmation to this view, this typical prisoner/student noted that his mother had to face this issue of early teen rebellion with his younger brother: "When he was fourteen, he was relentless, and constantly defying her. He's sixteen now, and sees much of the errors he was making. Now he has moved on to the stage where he actually fears the prospect of leaving."

However, many of the prisoner/students in Larmour's English II classes thought that Gail Sheehey's "Pulling up Roots" chapter actually "hit the nail on the head" in describing the outlook of the typical eighteen-year-old accurately. In Sheehey's overview, she had noted college, military service and short-term travels were all customary transitions toward independence—a "first round trip between family and a base of one's own." These types of options allow a teen to become self-led and independent and explore the world, giving a young person a chance to become self-sufficient.

A prisoner/student notes that parents are always saying to teens: "You think you know best, but you don't."

I believe teenagers pull away from their parents at this age because parents start pushing them to go into the direction the parents want them to go instead of helping their teenagers to go into the direction the teen feels is more suitable for themselves. So what happens? Teenagers are drawn to fads that are mysterious and inaccessible to the parents. She states: "For allies to replace our parents, we turn to our contemporaries."

He concludes that the late teens may seek help from another, other than parents, by getting married and, in this way, "he or she often wins his or her chance to become self sufficient." However, as several prisoner/student essays in the next sections—"Party Life" and "Drug Selling: Life on the Streets"—reveal, sometimes turning to teenage contemporaries does not lead to the kind of self-sufficiency that is sustainable.

While the first two prisoner/students analyzed class, race/ethnicity and age circumstances in leaving home, and two commentators thought Sheehey was "right on the money," the next prisoner/student analyzes a generational difference, arguing that the "kids of the seventies are not your kids of the nineties."

I give credit to Sheehey for being right on track according to her time. Born in 1937, and spending her teenage years in the 1950's, her opinions reflected these years. Life was a whole lot different then. A typical family consisted of dad as breadwinner and head of household, while mom worked at home taking care of cooking, cleaning, and laundry duties. Kids were expected to go to school and do well. The economy was good and the family structure was solid. I'm sure the kids of the 50's had the natural desire to leave and explore the world, but there was not an urgency to do so. In 1976, when Sheehey wrote this passage, she lacked the ability or insight to perceive the change that was about to happen in the future family structure.

If we were to summarize this prisoner/student's late 1990s views, they indicate several social changes since Sheehey's 1976 book, *Passages,* such as:

- Many of today's youth are not granted the type of economic or family security offered by the parents of previous years
- Today, family values are at an all-time low
- Divorce rates are at an all-time high and teenagers are having babies at younger ages
- Kids having less supervision
- Ineffective parenting
- A lower self-worth
- Unlike the 1950s, today's parents are often forced to work two jobs to adequately support the household
- Parents too exhausted and busy to participate in the extracurricular lives of children
- Kids are left to deal with many minor day-to-day dilemmas on their own, forcing them to concentrate on worldly issues rather than school and enjoying their youth
- Because of typical family moves after divorce, kids are often stripped of the friends and neighborhoods familiar to them and placed in an unfamiliar situation
- Left with the feeling of abandonment and home life insecurities, they turn to the streets—peers, gangs, teen girlfriend/boyfriend—in search of role models and secure friendships

This prisoner/student noted that Sheehey had an exceptional ability to understand the conflicts associated with life in the 1970s, "Unfortunately, in the 1990s, reasons for leaving home are much more complex—family values and family structure have changed."

In these several perceptive English class student views, prisoner/students in their twenties and thirties gave background factors (class, race/ethnicity, early versus late teen and generational explanations) affecting the leaving-home decision. An older prisoner, in his fifties, however, reflects on how the American dream can morph, and someone who made it successfully into their late twenties can drift into poor choices, crime and pathways to prison.

Prisoner Essay #26

The American Dream Morphs into the "Nearing Thirty" Set of Bad Choices

As children, whether or not we're consciously aware of it, we set goals for ourselves, dreams and aspirations begin to manifest themselves in our minds. We have a vague idea of what we would like our station in this world to be, by the time we reach the age of sixteen.

By the time we become young adults—between the ages of seventeen and twenty-one—the "seeds" that we have sown concerning our future, begin to grow and take shape. Things that seemed unattainable or intangible are within our grasp; the education, careers, and family we used to dream about as adolescents, become a reality that we can "see" in the immediate future and we begin to strive for it.

For instance, the person who spent countless hours fantasizing about life on a college campus, pursuing a chosen vocation, graduating, acquiring a profession in the field of our choice, getting married, buying a home and raising children or any of the above realizes: "There is only one course of action at this particular time in my life." And at that point an individual takes the necessary steps. No one interferes with whatever it is he or she so desires. This "course of action" comes in different forms, embracing responsibility, and being diligent and tenacious in pursuit of one's goals.

Those characteristics are often misinterpreted as selfishness, and in all actuality it is, but being thought of as such is a small price to pay for what we want in life.

More often than not, however, once we obtain that which we desire—nearing the age of thirty—we fall into a monotonous routine that we begin to resent. And suddenly we find ourselves seeking something new and different—perhaps something illegal, or a type of criminality—to add excitement to our lives. For some, this is when the "American Dream" becomes a nightmare. The sense of responsibility, sanctity of the marriage and duty to loved ones are set aside for whatever illusions you've conjured for yourself—be it drugs, thrills, danger, excitement. In the end—everyone loses.

The biggest losers are the innocent; children of broken marriages, and the offended mate. All because what we want is hardly ever enough.

—ɷ—

LIFE IN THE DRUG CULTURE BEFORE CATCHING A "CASE"

Somewhere between high school graduation or dropping out of high school and the present, our prisoner got into trouble ("caught a case"), was arrested, charged, convicted with a felony and landed in prison. The average sentence served in Michigan prisons is seven years—but an "average" figure clouds over two distinct modes of people being admitted to prison as new or return prisoners: a large violent or assaultive offender mode, and a even larger non-violent or non-assaultive offender mode.

The case "caught on the street" for our prison college men writing essays for this book may have been one of a dozen or more of the assaultive crimes, such as: homicide (often street gang retaliation shootings), attempted homicide, aggravated assault ("with intent to do great bodily harm"), assault and battery, serious domestic violence, rape ("criminal sexual conduct"), child sexual abuse, some cases of home invasion or burglary where there is assault or a weapons charge, robbery, car-jacking, arson and some of the drug-related crimes involving drug trafficking that also involve assault, guns or other violence.

As prison college teachers we are supposed to be non-judgmental. Educational culture does not judge on the past but on the present and the future: what you know, what you can learn, how well you do on the test. The word "education" is based on a logic of eduction—drawing out the potential of someone, forward looking. However, prisoner students would sometimes want to talk to us at the class break in the halls about their past, about "their case." After learning a lot of the "cases," in order to stay neutral and non-judgmental in our teaching, we learned to say: "Spare me the details."

While these assaultive convictions—people "we are afraid of"—represents less than half of the *prison admittance,* (38 percent in Michigan), since prisoners with assaultive convictions are *sentenced* to longer prison terms and *paroled less often,* the percent of prisoners *inside* prisons that have assaultive convictions is very large, perhaps 75 percent, since these offenders accumulate in prison. Up to three-quarters of the composition of state prison population at any point in time, thus, were originally convicted for a violent offense.

We've made the point before, but it is worth repeating: there is a certain exaggeration in saying "prison is full of violent offenders." That is because, as MDOC professional staff and risk-assessment researchers themselves know, many prisoners with long sentences become more mature over the years, while "aging out" in prison, and represent a low risk later in their life.

Prison admittance for non-assaultive convictions is more than half of the prison *admissions* and includes people we are "irritated at." These are the convictions for such behavior as: larceny theft (shoplifting), bad checks (uttering and publishing), some of the home invasions (burglary) where there is no gun or assaultive record, and some of the drug-defined crimes (felony drug possession, possession with intent to deliver), driving under the influence (DUI), negligent homicide or reckless endangerment (e.g., car crash due to negligence), statutory rape and minor felonies (some of the less violent assaults, fleeing and eluding), and so forth.

A lot of the non-violent prisoner behaviors were drug-related. Most of the home invasions, shoplifting (larceny) and bad checks and illegal use of credit cards (uttering and publishing), for instance, are committed by persistent property offenders with a drug addiction problem. This category represents about 25 percent of the prison population. First time, non-assaultive offenders generally stay in prison two to four years, much longer if it is their second or third felony.

Prison college students' lives before prison involved drugs—either using drugs or selling drugs, or both. Take pot. A lot of people have had a little bit of experience with marijuana. Some get caught. Many federal or state sentences for "possession" of small amounts of marijuana will result in short jail sentences, probation, some community service, a fine perhaps.

However, our prisoner/students tended to have a *lot* of drug experience. Possessing large amounts of marijuana when arrested might indicate, to a prosecutor, "possession with intent to deliver." Possibly this might be plea-bargained down to simple possession, if there are no priors—and result in a year or less in jail. Very large amounts of marijuana will usually result in a sentence of "possession with intent to deliver" where plea bargaining is not possible because now the offender must receive a mandatory sentence from the "mandatory minimums" legislative sentencing guidelines, which might result in up to five years first offense at the federal level and two to five at the state level for first offense, the sentences often served consecutively at both state and federal prisons.

For other drugs, like cocaine or heroin, first offense for possession of small amounts may be jail or may be shorter prison terms. But for amounts over fifty grams of either of these two drugs, first offenses can range from three to twelve years at the state level; and the sentence goes up under sentencing guidelines for larger amounts, and/or more prior convictions. For any schedule I or schedule II controlled sentence, having *prior convictions* can result in much longer sentences. A second offense in a federal case can lead to a sentence length of ten to twenty years.

Before 2002, Michigan had a set of mandatory minimums in the state's 1998 sentencing guideline laws that could result in "twenty-to-life" sentences for possession of 650 grams or more of crack cocaine! In December of 2002, after pressure on the Michigan legislature from Families Against Mandatory Minimums (FAMM 2008), state Representative McConico helped pass state legislation that rolled back such long sentences in certain drug cases. Still, many states have long sentences, especially for third-offense drug convictions. Many "three-strikes" state laws mandate a *life sentence* (without parole) for a third felony conviction—in some states only if the third felony is a violent offense, but in other states simply *any* third felony will mean a life sentence.

The two types of drug offenses—felony possession and felony drug trafficking—would in many cases be incurred by two different categories of people. Middle-class, working-class, and lower-working-class whites from suburbia and rural areas may often be primarily drug users (although some may have sold drugs, grown pot, or manufactured methamphetamine). On the other hand, poorer lower-working-class, "under"-class, or inner city African Americans may more often be primarily drug sellers (although often using marijuana and sometimes getting messed up with hard drugs and becoming unable to be good drug-selling businessmen/gangsters).

DRUG USE AT "STEVE'S PLACE"—OR "LIFE AS A PARTY"

White drug users, especially many school dropouts already heavy into the drug culture while still enrolled in high school, primarily looked on possessing a "stash" and *continual* drug use as a way to maintain their drug-culture lifestyles—a continual upbeat of staying high (with marijuana, hallucinogens), or alternative meth or cocaine (stimulants) with heroin and alcohol (depressants). They are "polydrug" users and often can have mental health problems as well, sometimes before such drug use, but most certainly, for many, *after* such polydrug use. This is a *different* pattern than occasional use of alcohol, marijuana and/or club drugs that some "jock, prep or nerd" regular ("non-criminal") youth may have. But there can be a "slippery slope" of falling into addiction for anyone using many of these drugs.

However, those into the continual use of drugs were already known as the school "druggies," "potheads" or crack addicts, and gave this as the reason they dropped out of school and moved away from parental control—that is, so they could pursue a free lifestyle that involved permanent partying, drinking and drugging and "having fun." As one prisoner says: "You want what you want when you want it." This concept is known as "life as a party." There are both psychological (child abuse and neglect, oppositional-defiant personality disorder, etc.) and sociological (immature adolescent culture, peer influence, gang) explanations for these continual "party" behavior patterns.

Using their own house (when parents were not home), an apartment, room or a trailer in a mobile home park as their party site, they strived to maintain a constant supply of street drugs and alcohol. Of course, enough cash was needed to buy fresh supplies. While many drug addicts do work jobs, at least part-time, still, working legitimately in order to get cash—and having to get to work everyday on time—can become incompatible with a drug-culture "party" lifestyle. Work may be unstable or not pay enough for the drug lifestyle, an expensive lifestyle that tends—to sustain the social status of the person leading the "party" mode—to push the participant leader to buy, use and share "only the best" (best food, best restaurants, best drugs, best alcohol and so forth).

The drug-culture lifestyle can be sustained, at least for a while, with the help of other "druggie" friends. These buddies, who hang together, may be ready to participate in illegal activities (home invasion, shoplifting, bad checks)—and other property crimes of opportunity (where stolen goods can be sold or fenced)—in order to keep the party going. They can be quick to suggest new ways and fresh targets that they have "cased out" for finding items to sell for cash (fencing, selling to acquaintances) that, under "desperation," they can turn to in order to keep the party going. As Wright and Decker note, three-quarters of the subjects of their study of burglary (home invasion) in St. Louis

> said they used the money for various forms of (for want of a better term) high-living. Most commonly, this involved the use of illicit drugs . . . For many of these respondents, the decision to break into a dwelling often arose as a result of a heavy session of drug use. The objective was to get the money to keep the party going . . .
>
> Lemert (1953:304) has labeled situations like these "dialectical, self-enclosed systems of behavior" in that they have an internal logic or "false structure" which calls for more of the same. Once locked into such events, he asserts, participants experience considerable pressure to continue . . . Implicit in this explanation is an image of actors who become involved in offending without significant calculation.
>
> Their offending is not the result of a thoughtful, carefully reasoned process. Instead, it emerges as part of the natural flow of events. In other words, it is not so much that these actors consciously choose to commit crimes as that they elect to get involved in situations that drive them toward lawbreaking. (Wright & Decker 1994:38–40)

DRUG SELLING AS LUCRATIVE JOB—LIFE ON THE STREETS

The African American prisoner, on the other hand, if we trace his life back before prison, is generally poor, from the inner city, and often from a single parent home, is more apt to sell drugs themselves *on the street* for cash, the more sales and the more cash the better. The money goes sometime to support a single parent, or if the seller is a father himself at a young age (which is common) to support his girlfriend (his "lady") and child. If he is still in school, he may sell drugs on the school ground to other students.

On the inner city street corners, gangs may fight for drug-selling turf, often using guns. Thus there is violence tied to efforts to control territory in this type of drug market. The drug seller looks on his drug selling as a "job" every bit as much as the legitimate job of the "square john," a job he learns "on the job" from his peers in the gang on the street corner. Indeed, often it is almost a "family trade," taught him by relatives (older brothers, cousins, uncles, mother, father), and he becomes a second-generation drug dealer.

Blacks will have the front porch to "keep the good times rolling" at their houses or nearby street-corner venues. This part of "street-culture" life as a party is more tied up with display of the results of successful drug sales: "only the best" cars, jewelry, women, restaurants—an ability to gamble with real money—and some recreational drugs. But then it's back to work, selling drugs.

Both white drug user and black drug seller drop out of school in order to pursue their drug activities—the drug-culture lifestyle or the drug-selling lifestyle. However, while the black seller speaks openly of leaving school to join the "street culture" or "corner society," devoting his time to hanging with other peer drug-sellers at locations while conducting "business" with his "crew," the white user rarely mentions "the street" or "street culture." A "party" for whites into the drug culture is held and continued behind closed doors with the aim of maintaining the ambience of an exciting life experience among friends constantly punctuated with alcohol and other drug-induced continual highs, and is rarely held on a street corner or front porch.

Also, and a significant difference, while the precise goal of the white "party" drug user is to keep using ever more drugs, to consume ever more alcohol—the other, the drug seller, rarely even uses hard drugs. In fact, other than "bud" (marijuana), he disdains their use. "After all," said one young drug seller, arrested and imprisoned in Michigan Reformatory, showing his business sense, "how can you do business if you a crack-head!"

Prisoner Essay #27

My Thoughts on "Life as a Party"

My thoughts on "life as a party" is pretty simple. I am doing this time now for exactly what you were describing. My case is second-degree home invasion and it was done for the sole purpose of buying drugs to show myself worthy to be with the "in crowd" so to speak.

My life-as-a-party lifestyle was for excitement, social status among other addicts and also so I could keep money always in my pocket, it was for the women too.

Sometimes I needed that extra courage in order to do certain illegal activities and drugs or alcohol was a courage booster; then usually after the crime occurred it was more drugs and alcohol to celebrate the victory or defeat. You can say they both go hand in hand—where there's crimes there usually are drugs not too far away.

Crime will always be a part of drugs and vice versa. Most people, as I did, need an extra boost of courage to commit crime. As for many felons drugs and alcohol had some factor in the crime itself.

Prisoner Essay #28

"Life as a Party" Has a True-to-Life Ring for Most Prisoners

To me "life as a party" has a true-to-life effect on most inmates I've met in the prison system. I personally lived an irresponsible lifestyle from about age thirteen, when I first started using marijuana and other drugs. The most important thing for me day to day was to have fun! As a kid that was fairly easy because Mom and Dad kept food on the table, and provided me a warm place to sleep.

But after growing older, living on my own and being forced to be responsible, "life as a party" became much harder, since I never paid attention in school to counselors or teachers when being told to plan for my future or being told anything really.

Just 'cause I was grown up in years—didn't mean I was grown up emotionally. I still wanted only to get high, laugh a lot and be popular.

I couldn't do that and take care of my basic needs on the low-skilled type of jobs I'd gotten. So I personally chose to steal, hustle and sell drugs to keep up that lifestyle. I'm not sure about anyone else, but I could never "grow up emotionally" while I lived that way. Until my forced sobriety, in prison, I never wanted to change.

Prisoner Essay #29

Living on a Street Corner

Living on a street corner, or living "out there" in a life of crime, you can live making money and save it whether it be by crime or legitimate. The money you make can go to the act of helping or destroying yourself. A person on the street expects to get something better than what he already has, whether it be selling drugs or stealing. The whole point is to make your situation better than what it currently is, which is basically you want what you want when you want it.

Now using drugs and alcohol does have an effect on you whatever you do in your life. However, if you are a street person you will most likely do something that will result in you being imprisoned for a period of time. No matter how severe your crime may be, if drugs and alcohol play a role you will still be held accountable, mostly to blame.

A lot of times people get arrested for crimes and may have smoked a little weed, but does this mean that drugs made him or her commit a crime?

—⁂—

Prisoner Essay #30

Street Culture is a Way of Life

Street culture cannot be described. It is a way of life. No sane person with common sense wants to live in poverty, living day for day in a dog-eat-dog world. A society that breeds on each other, where ones turn to drugs as a way of escape from the ugly reality of his or her bad choice, a choice one made early in life, and with no supervision to correct one's mistakes. Only in time the supervision comes—when ones come into contact with the justice department. Then, those who party, gambling with their freedom, those who think that way soon come to learn the true reality about life, after or during twenty-five to fifty, somewhere in that time being it going to sink in on them, that being "with it" is better than sitting in a 6 × 9 cell wondering if they are going to make parole.

—⁂—

Prisoner Essay #31

It Couldn't Be Much of a Life

I don't really know much about the drug culture and life as a party. I've only used little or no drugs in my life. But from what I've seen on T.V. it couldn't be much of a life.

—⁂—

Prisoner Essay #32

The Life I Chose was Forced on Me

I can't relate to the topic because the life I *chose* was *forced* on me. Can you understand that? Try to come up with a theory or hypothesis for that. The people who were interviewed for this topic must have come from stable families with both parents and may have had some financial stability. The people interviewed were probably European (white). They are the people who get out and commit these crimes because they think that those acts are cool. Or they're being rebellious against their parents. Then you all interview them and think that they speak for everyone. Well, screw that theory. You have people who had to rob, steal or sell drugs because that was the only way of life they knew, the only way they knew the man of color to get ahead. So we did what we knew how, to get ahead, until we *learned something different*. This is what was taught to us by our fathers and uncles. The only men in our lives were drug dealers and addicts. So don't let a study of morons influence your decision on crime by men of color as something we do or have done because we wanted party. *It's offensive.*

—∿∿—

Prisoner Essay #33

The Criminal, in His Mind, Has a Job

He was broke and wanted to "get money" by any means necessary. "Life-as-a-party" philosophy could be described as impulsive and irresponsible. I don't think the criminal doing the crime would consider it as "life-as-a-party." "A lifestyle of crime" is quick and easy to the criminal compared to working a "legitimate" job or going to school, earning a degree, and preparing for a "better life." I'm not condoning or siding with the criminal but I find it difficult to say or agree with the "life-as-a-party" concept. The criminal in his mind has a job—selling drugs, robbing—and the money he earns from his "job" he will, like another human being, buy the best he can with his "paycheck." What the criminal does not understand is he is "setting" himself up for having to feed his impulsiveness by having to deal drugs and sell more and more

—∿∿—

Prisoner Essay #34

Most Motivated by Economic Factors

I think most felons are motivated by economic factors more than a party lifestyle, at least from a black perspective, which is the only one I can speak from.

—∿∿—

Prisoner Essay #35

The Reality that this Lifestyle is about Nothing Comes into View

People in lower-class society want to be praised, socially accepted and liked by the majority of the townsfolk. By their feeling this "need" they will not go about it in the positive ways, i.e., job, volunteer, college. Because that is considered the "square" approach to life's goodness and riches, so it seems that they appeal to more people by selling drugs, robbing, breaking and entering and then "sharing the spoils." This approach gets them the "pat on the back," sex relationships and so forth that otherwise they wouldn't of had. The drawback from this, in my point of view, is that, when caught and sent to prison, the reality that this person and lifestyle is about nothing comes into a clear view and I think this destroys the person's value of self worth and esteem drastically. And with prison not being the place for constructive reform, the person turns to religion, gets a GED, learns a few quotes from the Bible and mimics some person he values in order to say, "I've changed." In reality this false sense of change often leads to more criminal behavior.

—⚮—

Prisoner Essay #36

They Use the Streets as an Opportunity

Growing up on the streets to me isn't a party, it is a way of life and survival for that person on that corner every day and night, trying to make a living. He or she sees it as a full-time job until they're able to achieve what they're seeking out of it. We have to understand that a lot of people are growing up in poverty with no help from their parents. So they use the streets as an opportunity where they can get on their feet and come off the corner. The things they do aren't by choice, it's by force to their plights.

—⚮—

Prisoner Essay #37

No Party until a Person Makes Enough to be on Top

There is no party in the drug life, from what I've seen or how the movies tell it, until a person makes enough money to be on top. Then is perhaps when he starts partying because he's the boss and he's making $20,000 a day in drug sales. But, how many people make that? I don't know of anyone. The people I do know is just using drug money to pay their rent. Or car note. Or sell drugs because they can't pull in enough money from their job to support their children and life. Some people sell drugs to support their habits. If they are supporting their habit, then how much money are they really making? Any time a lot of people get together it can be viewed as a party. Shoot, a rave with a lot of young people be a "party" and at twenty dollars a pop, the drugs or dope man will find them. I've never done drugs so, I can't relate. As you can see, this is a narrow topic. I tried to answer the question to the best of my ability.

—⟋⟍—

Prison administration often tries to suppress gang behavior in prison. Marie Griffin, writing a reaction essay to a lead article on "Gangs, Guns, and Drugs: Recidivism Among Serious Young Offenders," in *Criminology & Public Policy*, May 2007, writes:

> In the face of marginalization, multiple failures, and few conventional paths toward success, gang identity offers status, companionship, and social capital inside and outside prison walls. According to Fleisher and Decker (2001b:69), "gang identity is a proxy for a person's social history, for better or worse." Whether on the street or inside prison, oppressive measures to incapacitate and suppress gang behavior, when not used in concert with meaningful social interventions, underestimate the importance of gang identity and may well act as an additional structural pressure facilitating the growth of prison gangs. (Griffin 2007:228)

Prisoner Essay #38

Life on the Corner: Living-out the Self-Image of Gangster

Life on the corner can be to some the greatest of adrenaline rush, the excitement of living-out the self-images from your values of what a gangster or drug dealer is. Often, one cannot differentiate between the two, one being what's real or what's not. This internal vision of self manifests itself in weakened resistance to anything street. So, alcohol and drugs become your way of life to socialize and have fun because if you're not drinking and doing drugs you're not cool.

POSTSCRIPT

Prison is a mixed bag—many different family backgrounds, many pathways to prison. However, drugs loom large. Leaving home, getting involved with drugs and "going straight downhill" appears as a common experience for many who wind up in prison. Experiences of leaving home and teenage life are particularly full of trouble for those who fall into living life in the drug culture. The longer they stay in drug sales—or the deeper they sink into "life as a party"—the more likely they are to "catch a case." Drug selling as economic crime may mean "life as a party" to some, with the drug sales as a way to support the street-corner culture lifestyle. For others, the argument is made that the economic conditions of the inner city—high unemployment, poverty—*force* inner city youth into the drug selling lifestyle: it's what going on in the streets and they are almost compelled to become involved. Finally, however, for either path, as the convict enters and "wakes up" in prison and sees his life wasting away, the "reality that this lifestyle is about nothing comes into view."

III

—ഝ—

ENTERING THE
PRISONERS' WORLD

INTRODUCTION

In describing typical prisoners' families and homes we found many types of families and homes. However, we found that the pathways to prison all seemed to center on "dropping out of high school, hanging out with a rougher crowd, learning drugs, and going straight downhill." However, the path is not inevitable. A strong policy commitment to evidence-based crime prevention can really work for early and middle childhood (Farrington et al. 2002/2006), especially if joined by a "reconceptualization of the correctional project" toward community justice (Clear 2007). In chapter 1 we assessed how, for first- and second-offense adult drug offenders, a firm focus on harm-reduction approach could replace the failed "war on drugs," which accounts for up to 30 percent of state prison admittance, and over 40 percent of federal prison admittance. And we've made the point that the underlying problems of the inner city need to be solved.

As prison teachers we spent the fourteen years from 1983 to 1997 working at the Michigan Reformatory (MR) where we saw the seventeen- to twenty-five-year-olds enter the "adult system," often with prior experience in the "juvenile justice system." We saw our classroom ages, and ethnic composition, get younger and get blacker. The racial disparity in prisoner composition was caused by the adoption in 1986 onward of law enforcement of the new, long-sentence drug laws using an enforcement approach focusing on retail drug trafficking: picking up young, urban, black street drug dealers—a law-enforcement approach bound to result in a disparate impact on African American youth (Tonry 1995, 2007).

125

While most of these seventeen- to twenty-five-year-olds needed to be off the street, their *sentences* were definitely too long, some twenty to life (for drug dealing only, no violence). So, as prison teachers, we saw the racism implicit in not enhancing economic opportunities in the inner city neighborhoods, but, instead, sending them to prison. But, also—because of the very long sentences—we saw the *same* prisoners ten, fifteen, twenty years later over in Jackson or at one of the other of the eleven Michigan prisons we taught in.

The prison world that these young, right-off-the-streets prisoners entered was, since 1986, greatly expanded, into an "incarceration binge culture." The prisoners were becoming different: overcrowded (now with double bunking), more black prisoners, more drug-related sentences, longer sentences, more parole denials and more ex-convicts reentering into the mix from failure on parole. Entering this new "managing-the-dangerous-classes" penal system now meant fewer prison programs, less focus on cultivating individual responsibility, the elimination of good time and no more early release to correctional center halfway houses. The legislature needed to be "tough on crime." In 1992 Governor Engler changed the parole board, now there would be a governor-appointed parole board replacing the previous civil service parole board. Now there were no effective parole guidelines: no amount of prison accomplishment made much of a difference. Prisoners were often denied parole. This new "incarceration binge culture" inside the prison awaited the "war-on-drugs" prisoner.

Chapter 6 describes the details of "Getting into 'The System'": awaiting sentencing in jail, the trip to the prison in a Sheriff's van to the prison system's Reception and Guidance Center for the thirty- to ninety-day orientation, how prisoner classification works and prisoner essays on coming to prison and going through orientation. The situation of scarce bedspace as the U.S. prison system quadruples is presented by coauthor Marjorie Larmour as she describes the problems of handling so many prisoners for correctional facility administrative staff officers.

Chapter 7 introduces the reader to how prisoners experience their first time in a prison cell. The descriptions are graphic. The first set of cell descriptions span the period from 1981 to 1986 when an adult prisoner at Jackson, the "Big House" prison, would climb four stories to a single bunk cell. The second set of prison cell stories are set in the period of the late 1980s through the 1990s and up to 2008. Now prisoners are describing the two-man cell and noting aspects of the overcrowded prisons, such as getting along with their "bunkie." Some stories tell of personal transformation during the long hours, long days and long years in that cell.

Chapter 8 describes the "Daily Work Routines" of typical prisoners. Recall that Gresham Sykes had noted in 1958 that life in prison during time spend outside the cell is made up of a set of interactions that build up a "society" integral to the prison. For Sykes, "the prisoners' world" emerges as a subculture through *interaction* at: mess hall, chores, exercise, work, recreation, school and religious activities" (Sykes 1958:5). Prisons rely on prisoner labor, such as laundry for 1,500 people, shoveling snow from the walks, janitorial cleaning and "custodial maintenance" and emptying trash cans. These routine duties bring prisoners in contact each day with others in the prison through a daily "detail" (or prisoners' day assignment sheet). During the period 1972–1995 when prisoners were eligible for Pell grants and 770 prison college programs were up and running, a prisoner could have a daily "education detail"—an assignment to study hard and go to classes. Several of the prisoners whose writing appears in this book were full-time prison college students during the period (1981–2000) when Michigan prisons had prison college classes available. (A court-ordered prison college program existed in two Michigan prisons, from 1995 to 2000, after the end of the Pell-grant supported programs.)

Correctional officers (guards) and other correctional professionals work the three daily eight-hour shifts. Prisoners must present their "detail" (days approved activity slip) to the guard posted at the gates leading from housing unit to each activity area: work, school, medical, visit, etc. This presents a situation wherein prisoners meet and interact briefly with guards and officers all throughout the day. This creates another realm of "the prisoners' world": how the day's experience of interacting with correctional officers and program professionals went. "Bunkies" might talk of "how was your day at work" much as a couple at home—but every day at prison usually holds more uncertainty about "how things went with the guards" than a household conversation about "how things went with the boss."

Entering the prison world includes entering a situation of daily uncertainty that, for some, disciplines them to become inner focused: control your temper, and do your time.

6

—⟋ɯ⟍—

Getting into "The System"

INTRODUCTION

When the "pathways to prison" lead to prison, what are the steps along the way? Typical steps for those who eventually enter prison include: moving from the juvenile justice system involving contact with the police to the local juvenile court; an adjudication which may indicate juvenile probation; failure on juvenile probation resulting in commitment to juvenile detention. If detention does not deter, the youth may experience several such detentions and then be sent to a yearlong juvenile residential treatment. Further failure to change behavior may subsequently involve further adult crimes (at age seventeen or older) resulting in contact with the adult justice system. Now becoming involved (again) with police contact (arrest), adult court (conviction), adult probation, prison, reentry and parole or release. The following short stories reveal young adults' first experience with juvenile detention, jail and prison.

Prisoner Essay #39

Juvenile to Adult Court

It was June 1985 and I had just gotten a call from a friend. We had Honda Elite motor scooters and my friend says, "Hey, I'm on my way over." Five minutes later the doorbell rings. Without thinking I rush to the door, open it and there are four detectives. They grab me, handcuff me, and I'm escorted to the back of the car where I sit between two of the biggest humans I've ever sat next to.

I'm driven to the juvenile detention center. The door buzzes and I'm escorted to a holding area. Shortly thereafter it's clothes off, shower, and I'm given oversized pants, shoes, underwear and shirt. The intake officer says you're going to 5N.

We take an elevator up to the fifth floor and I enter the dorm-type setting but it's shaped like the letter A. I am paralyzed with fear. The guard yells "Take it down" and that became the new phrase that let you know its time to lock in.

—*m*—

Prisoner Essay #40

Fear in Super-Slow Motion

It was late in the month of July 1999 that I found myself sitting in a standard-size classroom being orientated to the life of prison. My first reaction to this new way of living was of shock, fear and not knowing what to expect. However, as I sat in that classroom with other inmates, I realized that I was not the only person there afraid of the unknown. I must admit that there were a few guys in that room who knew more than enough about prison life than I wanted to know.

The topics that day ranged from diseases and protection from catching them, to how to live without ending up in trouble. Rules of the prison were also discussed in depth. This sense of fear continued in super-slow motion. I do not know if this fear of what will lay ahead of me was due in part to the wild stories that I was hearing. How easy it could be to contract something from another person from something as simple as smoking his cigarette. To this day I still remember just about all that had happened, shock embedded the memory in my head.

—*m*—

A typical "flow chart" of the steps of "getting into the system" common to many people's experience who've been prisoners is presented in Figure 6.1. Difficulties after release, such as parole violation or being arrested for a new crime, result in return to prison (recidivism).

PRISONS ARE A "MIXED BAG": WHO GOES?

Some children grow up in circumstances and engage in choices that put the youth at risk for juvenile-status offenses and youth crime. They become adjudicated through the Family Court (Probate) as a delinquent.

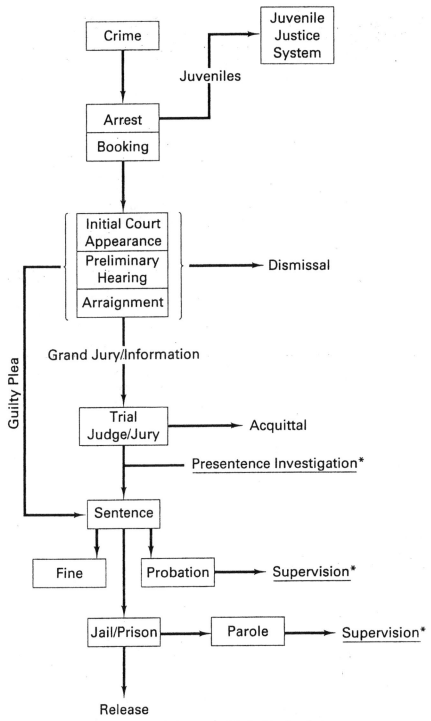

Figure 6.1. Probation and Parole in a State Criminal Justice System

As Figure 6.2 shows, "crime is a young persons' game." Most criminal offending occurs between the ages of fifteen to twenty-four years old (Blumstein & Cohen 1987). Often the under-seventeen-year-old "persistent offenders" will then enter their adult years with a series of young adult prior criminal convictions, leading to their "getting into the system" (Moffit 1997). Youth may do home invasions and shoplifting and sell drugs, frequently to support a "party life" and a drug addiction. Other youth may have a sense of hopelessness, anger and rage, acting out with violence and assaults (Green 1993). Still others are drawn into the gangs and drug trafficking (Griffin 2007; Spergel 1995). Some youth, especially young African Americans, accumulate several minor "priors" in their court records because they're "on the streets" and the police, on "search-and-destroy" missions to dampen down youth crime in that neighbor-

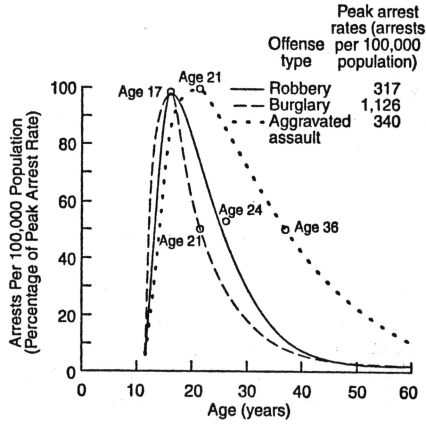

Figure 6.2.   U.S. Age-Specific Arrest Rates (Arrests Per 100,000 Population of Each Age for 1983). ("Characterizing Criminal Careers," *Science*, Blumstein, 1987)

hood area, "write them up" frequently (Miller 1996). Community crime-prevention efforts can build social supports for such youth (Berger 1985; Rosenbaum, et al. 1998), and many youth are resilient (Higgins 1994), responding to mentoring. For others these efforts fail.

Frustrated parents may seek help through the justice system or with parenting skills (Patterson & Forgatch 1987). Police and school officials may guide a youth to teen court instead of into the formal juvenile probation system. But, when these efforts at diversion or probation fail, a series of stints in juvenile detention may follow and, for some, longer-term residential treatment.

As the youth ages and problematic behavior continues past the age of seventeen in most states or as sentencing-as-an-adult requires, he or she may find themselves facing a prosecutor and judge, and being sent off to an adult community corrections, probation, jail or prison sentence.

As one prisoner in a later prisoner essay in this chapter emphasizes, in the Reception and Guidance Center for classifying entering prisoners there are "all types of convicted felons. Murderers, druggies, burglars, drunk drivers, assault and battery, child molesters—you name it, they had it."

Some people may go to prison for situational deviance in their adult years where the circumstances have little to do with upbringing or neighborhood of their youth. There are adult prisoners who are mentally ill. There are drunk drivers that harm people. There are sex offenders. There are some drug-related convictions where the prisoner disagrees with the law.

As mentioned in chapter 3, "Binge Growth Theory," the American people are of two minds, supporting "tough" punishment but also interested in making people rehabilitate themselves. Many people feel that we ought to put "people who frighten us" in jail or prison—but handle "people who only irritate us" through some kind of community corrections (probation, day reporting, jail work release, electronic tethering). But crime policy has become very politicized with legislatures deliberating on sentencing grids, and judges required to sentence "within the grid."

While prison is a mixed bag, as we have emphasized, the largest mode is persistent property offenders with a drug problem. And, if they have prior offenses, they often fall into a longer sentencing "grid." Even so, as discussed in chapter 2, the crime rate has been going down since 1991. Again, to repeat: our prisons grow ever larger not because of national population growth or an increase in crime rate, but because of drug laws, longer sentencing, fewer paroles and lack of adequate prison programming for successful reentry—and because the United States has, among industrialized nations, more inequality, more festering inner cities, more poverty, gun violence and stress on families than does Europe, Australia or Japan.

PAROLE FAILURE: "GETTING BACK INTO THE SYSTEM"

Young men, property offenders and individuals with extensive criminal histories are most likely to recidivate; and failure to pass a drug test while on parole has been one of the single most common reasons for return to prison. Because the largest source of prison admittance is failure on parole, "Failure to consider the needs of offenders returning to the community may undermine the ultimate effectiveness of deterrence and incapacitation-based justice policy" (Huebner, Varano, & Bynum 2007:189).

The United States has a high average recidivism (return to prison) rate compared to other Western European industrial nations. However, U.S. recidivism rates vary by state. California has a very high recidivism rate, over 70 percent. Even so, many prisoners, up to two-thirds in some states, get out and are "making good." Michigan's recidivism rate is around 32 percent. What accounts for success on parole or reentry?

The fact that many prisoners *mature* in prison is an important insight provided by both MDOC statistics and academic research. The fact is that the *older* prisoners become the less likely they are to return to crime after release. Again, as Figure 6.2 shows, "crime is a young person's game." Some older prisoners need help immediately after release and get structured supervision and support through parole agents and prisoner reentry programs. However, many of the ex-offenders, once released, will do well enough on their own, if just left alone. Wardens themselves often talk of their role in keeping people in prison as one of "burning some years off of them." The politics of "tough-on-crime" rhetoric, such as "keep those violent predators off our streets," loses sight of the fact that many convicts "age-out" and represent a low risk of re-offending in their later years.

Yet, "getting back into the system" through parole violation is a major source of prison admittance. Most criminality after release is not violent offenses but, rather, the recidivist is often a late-twenties, early-thirties, persistent property offender (home invasions or burglary, larceny) with a drug problem (drug use, drug selling) who fails a drug screen (parole violation).

To reduce the obstacles to reentry and improve success on parole and after release, new efforts, such as the Michigan Prisoner Reentry Initiative (MPRI) pilot projects, with a pilot budget of $13 million from 2005–2007 and a fully-funded, but modest, regular budget as of mid-2008 of $34 million per year, establishes a community coordinator in each county with state money working with a local county steering committee that lines up the resources prisoners need for reentry.

In the Michigan MPRI, prisoners are transferred to prisons close to the community in which they will reenter. The Steering Committee analyzes and prepares reentry services, and then a volunteer Transition Team enters the prisons doing "in-reach" to work with reentering prisoners, connecting them up with housing, job, drug treatment, clothing, job training and education, and so forth. The goal: to reduce recidivism by maybe 5 to 10 percent, (e.g., reduce Michigan's recidivism rate from 32 percent to 27 percent). Each person not going back to prison saves $32,000 a year.

As important as better programs for reentry are, success on parole would benefit even more from shorter sentences and a presumption of parole at earliest release date so as to not lose family and community ties (Austin & Irwin 2001; CAPPS 2008). Also, there are just a few urban neighborhoods that most prisoners come from. Shorter sentences and more success in parole can reduce the devastation to such "high-impact" communities that "churn" people going to prison, coming out, and going back to prison (Clear 2007; Lynch & Sabol 2001), but there must be a shift to "reconceptualize the corrections project" to make these high impact communities better, and more just, places to live and work (Clear 2007).

Crime prevention is always short on resources. As reentry programs cut recidivism, it would be possible to *shift* some of the saved resources (from the need for fewer prison bedspaces) into these enhanced prison reentry programs (back-end) and other evidence-based crime prevention programs in the community (front-end) listed in chapter 3. However, in states like Michigan, when there are severe budget problems, so far nearly all the money that is beginning to be saved by the beginning of better success on parole goes back into the state's general fund for other priorities, such as state-supported higher education. Crime prevention remains starved for resources. Meanwhile, new prisoners keep going off to prison for new crimes.

GOING OFF TO PRISON

Going off to prison is not the instantaneous transaction many newly sentenced prisoners might imagine. Waiting apprehensively in the local county jail, they may picture "Like, one day you're still comfortable at home, next day you're spending hard time in a cell somewhere."

No. It's a slow, troublesome, two-step process.

First, you go from that local jail to something called a Reception and Guidance Center (RGC). It's located fairly close nearby to the prison, usually as a separate unit attached to a regional state prison. There you sit in a temporary cell for weeks or months before finally "going off to prison."

Why sit and wait? Well, let's put it this way. You may already know all about prison, and anywhere from 30 to 70 percent of the people heading there usually do. But prison officials, who are now responsible for your incarceration, don't really know much about you. In Michigan, if a youth is handled "formally" in the juvenile system, their records may be public until they are thirty-four. But, juveniles who are handled informally through the juvenile justice system (e.g., teen court) can have their records expunged.

How can the MDOC assure public safety? They are taking charge of you, yet they may not know a thing about you. At the same time, hopefully, they may need to facilitate a better person getting out. As mentioned, it costs a lot for the state of Michigan to "house" an average prisoner—and average of $32,000 to be exact.

Prison administrators are responsible for the care and custody of inmates. In short, they have to learn all about this somewhat valuable "commodity" they are entrusted with (care and custody), especially what level of security threat you pose to others when inside the prison. That's what RGC (Reception and Guidance Center) used to be all about, as you will learn from the prisoner essays in this chapter.

So that's what the prisoner is about to get as his introduction to prison— a thorough screening. This screening, testing, assessment decides, among other important things, just where—at what security level—to place this still unknown person; and what his or her potential for programming should be for eventual release.

Starting in 2003, however, Michigan's Governor Jennifer Granholm, the state legislature and the Michigan Department of Corrections Director, Pat Caruso (MDOC), committed to launch the Michigan Prisoner Reentry Initiative (MPRI). Now prisoners entering Reception and Guidance Center (RGC) go through *additional* interviews and tests establishing what education and behavior programming they need to be working on while *in prison* to be ready for release and improve success on reentry (Petersilia 2003; National Institute of Justice 2001; MPRI 2008).

The average stay in prison for Michigan's 52,000 prisoners is seven years. Of course, that means some stay much longer and many stay from two to four years. Eleven thousand are released on parole each year. Therefore, it's important to get going on how to be "making good" on the outside after release while you are still in prison—that is what the premise of the new MPRI is all about.

RECEPTION GUIDANCE CENTERS (RGC) AND ORIENTATION

Introduction

The subject of prison orientation may be discussed from two viewpoints—the prison administration view and the prisoner view. The prison administration view is to screen, classify and disperse an incoming group of prisoners as fast as possible, and make room for the next incoming groups. The prisoner's often opposite view is that this little-understood, ultra-slow, apparent arbitrary, lengthy "temporary" incarceration by prison officials which stretches into boring weeks—without access to much yard or work details—is simply the prisoner's first introduction into the "hurry up and wait" tempo of prison life.

ORIENTATION AS A PRISON ADMINISTRATION FIRST STEP

A. Assigning Inmates to Prison

Prison classification is a method of assessing inmate risks that balance security requirements with program needs. In the following discussion, we will follow the North Carolina Department of Corrections description of this process, which is similar in each state.

Newly admitted inmates are transported from county jails to one of several prison receiving centers in their own state. For example, in 2007 there were eleven receiving centers in North Carolina. The number of reception and guidance centers varies by state.

At the Reception and Guidance Center the risk assessment process begins. Prison classification specialists develop an individual profile of each inmate that includes the "Presentence Investigation Report" from a probation officer that was first submitted to the sentencing judge (offender's crime, social background, education, job skills and work history), medical and mental health screening and criminal record, including prior prison sentences. Based on this information, the offender is assigned to the most appropriate custody classification and prison. (In Michigan, as of 2008, under the new MPRI regime, this is called the "Compass" assessment).

From this initial classification, inmate behavior and continuing risk assessments by prison staff will determine the inmate's progression through the various custody levels to minimum custody and eventual release. Prison managers classify inmates for possible work assignments and lay out reentry planning around rehabilitative self-improvement programs that will be required (assaultive offender programming, substance abuse treatment, mental health assessment, English as Second Language, Adult Basic Education, GED completion).

As prisoners serve their sentences, those who comply with prison rules, do assigned work and participate in corrective programs may progress toward minimum custody, often as they near their Earliest Release Date (ERD). Prisoners who violate prison rules are punished and may be classified for a more restrictive custody classification and be transferred to a more secure prison. Inmates are then required to demonstrate responsible and improved behavior over time to progress from this status back to less restrictive custody classifications and prisons.

Thus, the incoming prisoner who is now locked down in his temporary cell for perhaps weeks, is undergoing a screening testing procedure. When finished, this lengthy process will turn him from a newly sentenced "civilian" nonentity into a distinctly classified, photographed, fingerprinted, numbered and ID-member of the prison bureaucracy. He is now ready to be accorded a security status, assigned to a facility appropriate to that status (minimum, medium, maximum security), and soon to be shipped out to a permanent cell in what is likely to be an overcrowded facility.

Prisoner Custody Levels

While states differ in their terminology, prisoners may be classified and assigned to the following general custodial levels: maximum (level 5), close (level 4), medium (level 3), minimum I (level 2), minimum II (level 1), and minimum III (trusty). The classification levels are in descending order of perceived safety risks to prison guards, staff and other inmates presented by the prisoner. There is also a category called "protective housing unit" (PHU) or "administrative segregation" (AD SEG) for special-case prisoners. There is also a category called "super-max" with twenty-three-hour lockdown and individual cells and small individual exercise pens. In super-max prisoners have no circulation among the "general population" (other levels), which means no release to general "yard."

Within this mix of custodial assignments, inmates also may be subject to various control statuses. The control statuses include maximum, intensive, safekeeper, disciplinary, administrative and protective. Michigan has no death penalty but other states do. In such states there is another custody assignment—death row (such as at California's San Quentin Prison).

An unruly prisoner may be placed in disciplinary and/or administrative custody or segregation for a period of time for protection of other inmates and staff. Other prisoners such as overly immature, fragile or homosexual may be placed in protective custody for their own safety. Each custody level is usually housed in a separate cell block or building.

Prison Security Levels

Prisons themselves may be classified and designated by security level, or there may be two or more units with different security levels within a single prison facility.

Maximum-security units are utilized to confine the most dangerous inmates who are a severe threat to public safety, correctional staff and other inmates. Inmates confined in a maximum security unit typically are in their cell twenty-three hours a day. During the other hour they may be allowed to shower and exercise in the cellblock or in a "private" exterior, single-person exercise cage. All inmate movement is strictly controlled with the use of physical restraints and correctional officer escort.

Close-security prisons or units are typically comprised of single cells and divided into cellblocks, which may be in one building or multiple buildings. Cell doors generally are remotely controlled from a secure control station. Each cell is equipped with its own combination plumbing fixture, which includes a sink and toilet. The perimeter barrier is designed with a double fence with armed watch towers or armed roving patrols. Inmate movement is restricted and supervised by correctional staff. Inmates are allowed out of their cells to work, attend education or corrective programs in the facility. Some of the essays in this book came from prisoner students in Jackson Prison's "level 5" central complex.

Medium-security prisons (level 3 in Michigan) usually have double fence perimeter with armed watchtowers or armed roving patrols. There is less supervision and control over the internal movement of inmates than in a close-security prison. Most inmate work and self-improvement programs are within the prison.

Minimum-security prisons (level 2 and 1 in Michigan) are often comprised of nonsecure dormitories, which are routinely patrolled by correctional officers. It may have its own group toilet and shower area adjacent to sleeping quarters that contain double bunks and lockers. The prison generally has a single perimeter fence that is inspected on a regular basis, but has no armed watch towers or roving patrol. There is less supervision and control over inmates in the dormitories and less supervision of inmate movement within the prison than at a medium facility. Inmates assigned to minimum-security prisons generally pose the least risk to guards, staff or other prisoners, and the least risk of escape.

Minimum custody inmates at minimum-security prisons sometimes participate in community-based work or events. For instance, prison softball teams may play a local city or college team on the prison field, or minimum-security prisoners can work on road improvement with Department of Transportation employee supervisors, or on other community work projects.

B. Why Classification is Needed

Classification is a key process in solving many of the problems of jails and prisons. Various primary and subsidiary roles are performed by control classification systems in jails and prisons.

Tim Brennan (1998) discusses reasons for these classifications in his "The Roles of Institutional Classification," a listing and brief, partial discussion of which is presented below.

Inmate, Staff and Public Safety

Failure to separate predators from victims is likely to result in victimization and an unsafe, anxiety-provoking environment (p. 169).

Classification for Rehabilitation and Reintegration

Correct classification aims to protect the prisoner's rights to avoid deterioration of social skills, to have access to rehabilitation programs, and to be placed in the least restrictive environment (p. 169).

Provision of Appropriate Service

Classification is a basic mechanism for identifying the various vocational, educational, physical and mental health needs of inmates (p. 170).

Efficiency and Rationality in Resource Utilization

Valid classification becomes even more crucially important when there are severe resource shortages (when there is a need to) make the most advantageous use of physical, financial and human resources (p. 171).

Management Planning

Enormous financial savings result (from objective classification systems) because planners (in the absence of such classification systems might have) overestimated the need for expensive maximum-security cells and underestimated the need for minimum-security space.

Social Control and Discipline

Classification is strongly linked to the control and management of inmates' behavior since it governs access to rewards and may circumscribe privileges. For example, misbehavior is often "punished" by reclassifying the person to a less privileged level, while good behavior is rewarded by reclassification into custody levels having greater privileges (p. 172).

You may have heard of the old saying that to control behavior you can use "the carrot or the stick." Remunerative controls—the reward or "carrot" of being allowed to move down the ladder to a minimum-security facility with more yard and other activities can be a good source of social control and reduce the risk of prison riots (Reisig 1998).

C. An Ex-felon Professor Writes: Entering Prison and Orientation

In a refreshing book *Behind Bars: Surviving Prison* (2002) authors, Jeffrey Ian Ross and Stephen K. Richards cover all aspects of prison life. They write, "everyone goes through the same routine upon arrival in prison. . . ."

Receiving and Departure

Upon arrival at the prison, you and your fellow fish, as new prisoners are called, are marched inside and go through R-and-D (not research and development, but Receiving and Departure), where you will be strip-searched, deloused, and issued a uniform. Then you are placed in a holding cell, called a "bullpen" or a "fish tank," reserved for new prisoners. . . .

Once dressed out, you'll be fingerprinted, have your mugshot taken, and ordered to undress for a strip search. . . .

Orientation and Fish Tier

In some joints, there may be a rudimentary orientation program, where you, one of the new fish, are issued an inmate rule book and allowed to ask questions. These sessions are essentially dog and pony shows; most new inmates learn the rules and procedures from other convicts (Ross & Richards 2002:65–67).

As a new prisoner, you are technically unclassified, have not yet received a work assignment, and are not allowed phone or commissary privileges. You are typically locked down twenty-four hours a day on the fish tier. . . .

You'll be introduced to your new cellmates, who will probably begin sizing you up, trying to figure out whether you are friend or foe. After surviving your first terrifying twenty-four hours at the institution, you will gradually meet a cast of characters that includes fellow convicts, correctional officers and administrators—citizens of a new world which operates by a different set of rules (Ross & Richards 2002: 67–68).

FEDERAL PRISON ORIENTATION

A "Federal Prison Orientation" list, below, that outlines contents of a counseling package offered to new federal inmates and their families is similar to a packet provided incoming prisoners at all state Reception Centers.

FEDERAL PRISON ORIENTATION

It's important that prisoners and their families understand what to expect as a person enters the prison system. This counseling package offers familiarization with the following:

—Overview and history of the Federal Bureau of Prisons (BOP)
—Administrative structure of BOP
—Designation of institution's Security Level in which client will be placed (complete analysis of placement determination)
—Intake screening and orientation
—Temporary work assignment
—Classification meeting (what to expect and how to prepare)
—Importance of assigned Case Manager
—Disciplinary policy
—Program reviews
—Performance pay
—Furloughs and escorted trips
—Telephone privileges
—Visiting policies
—Education opportunities
—Recreation
—Transfers
—Drug Program (one year off sentence)
—Intensive Confinement Center/Boot Camp six months off sentence)
—Personal property
—Correspondence
—Incoming publications
—Religious programs
—Inmate accountability (counts)
—Record office
—Good time reductions
—Psychology Department

www.prisonconsultant.com/fpo (updated 15 January 2004)

D. Prisoner View on Entering Prison and Orientation

In our first story, "A Place Like No Other," an average young African American from Detroit's inner city, who has not traveled outside the city, or his immediate "hood," takes the two-hour trip to Jackson Prison, perhaps his first real journey outside the city limits. He enters a cavernous five-story cell block, one of the eleven such "Big House" towering blocks that still existed at the historic old "Jackson" walled prison in the 1990s.

He enters a bedlam of eternal noise—up to 900 prisoners in one five-story block with cells around the walls and a central "arena"—officers' orders, clanking cell doors, prisoner catcalls between cells. A generally petrified entering prisoner faces a spectacle—open shower at one end of the ground floor, along with milling prisoners at ground-floor tables in the middle of the "arena" with echoing cat calls and taunts. Long rows of cells stretching five stories high with narrow flights of metal stairs attached against the wall at one end, with just a simple rail winding up, separating the climber from the open pit, far below.

As coauthor Bill Tregea recounts:

> In the Spring of 1981, I began teaching at Jackson Prison. On my first day, I met Paul Wreford, the director of the prison college, in the main lobby. . . . Then, I walked through the high-security gates for the first time, wondering if I would ever get out; loosing my sense of freedom, and thinking of all the awful things I had ever done, as the metal grilles closed behind me . . . I entered the prison with trepidation. After my second week of teaching literature, the guys in class told me, "This place is going to blow." The next week Jackson Prison rioted, classes were canceled, and the spring semester was never completed. (Tregea 2003:313)

Jackson Prison in the 1980s was a dangerous place, crowded, with a loosely monitored mass of 600 to 900 prisoners in each of twelve large "Big House" blocks. There were two guards on a shift. It is no wonder that young prisoners entering Jackson Prison's RGC for the first time became open-mouthed and terrified when they looked at the cell conditions. Jackson prison was, in fact, so bad and dangerous during the 1980s that, after the riot in 1981, a federal district judge took oversight of the prison and required the state to rebuild the entire 7,000-person prison into sets of smaller "unit-management" areas of 250 men, with better supervision, at a cost to the state, over a fifteen-year construction period, of $116 million.

PRISONER ESSAYS

Prisoner Essay #41

A Place Like No Other . . . this Place

(Riding out from county jail to Jackson Prison, SPSM—RGC)

A place like no other. This place, like no other place you could imagine. I was brought here by the county officers from Oakland County. One morning after I was in custody for three of four days, this county officer came by my little housing room at the jail at four in the morning. He told me to get up, you are riding out this morning. So I jumped up out of bed put on my clothes, packed up the few little belongings that I had inherited in my brief stay. My hair comb, paper, pencils, and envelopes.

When I was completed with packing up my things I was escorted down to a bullpen. I had some thoughts in my mind—this must be how animals feel. Being herded around from cage to pen, or vice-versa. I was waiting in this bullpen for three or four hours until an officer said it was chow time. There was standing room only. Another thought rushed into my head. Now I know what sardines feel liked being packed in a can. For chow these trustee's passed a plastic tray through a hole in the door.

One prisoner at a time squeezed over and through another until he was in place to get his morning chow. After I saw this stuff on this plastic tray, I didn't recognize any of it except the carton of milk. My brain was really working.

I was thinking to myself that my dog at home eats better than this. Well I am happy to say that I didn't eat very much of it and I'm still alive. When we were through with this stuff on the tray we were instructed to pass the trays back under the bars into the hallway.

Fifteen minutes later my name was called to come out of this big cage. I squeezed through the other men, to the hallway where the officer pointed me to a line of guys with waist chains and handcuffs.

It's time for a ride not knowing where I will end up. We rode for a while till I fell asleep. I took a little nap. I woke up after a time, not knowing where we were, so I started looking for familiar sights and signs.

I didn't know any of the sights we were passing until we went by a sign reading Jackson.

The van that we were in pulled up in front of this big fenced-in area. We were ready to pass the guarded gates. We entered and pulled up in front of this door. All the guys in the van were unloaded one by one and lined up like ducks in line. When all of us were emptied from the van we proceeded into the building. We were stripped down, washed, inspected, and had to dress in blues. We sat at a desk for a while and these people would ask some questions and so on. Now it's time for us to move to where we will be staying. About five guys and I were escorted into this big building. (A cavernous, five-story "Big House" cell block.) I thought man, is this place big. Every man in Michigan must be in here.

—⚹—

Some prisoners, both new incoming "fish" and long time veterans, upon entering (or reentering) prison resolve to go straight.

One of our incoming prisoner/students wrote:

Lying around in my cell with my thoughts, it got me to thinking things over and why my life had been. When I realized that this could be the start of changing myself and what I could do to change me, I felt an inner peace I have never felt before.

What a significant point in my life. A few years before I came to the realization that out of every bad situation good can come out of it if you look for the good instead of dwelling on the bad. Now all I had to do is start the good process from this bad situation. What good could I do? Make myself into a positive person instead of living the negative type of life I had led.

Besides fear of the unknown, usually unexpressed, many new prisoners come to the prison world loaded with bravado. Often, however, the bravado is short-lived.

Prisoner Essay #42

My First Taste of Prison

(Riding out from Kalamazoo County Jail to Reception Center at Riverside Correctional Facility, Ionia, MI)

I remember the day I got my first taste of prison.

Thinking back to the time when I was transferred from Kalamazoo County Jail to RGC in Ionia. It was about 7:30 in the morning and you could tell that the sap hadn't showered through the clouds. I was walking to the car thinking to myself that one day I would write about how the ground was moist from the mist of rain and the reflection of the car's window was like a mirrored reflection of me and the trees behind me.

The car ride was quiet except for when the officers were asking me how I planned to do my time. My first instinct was to snap back at them "I don't plan for shit like this." But instead I said "I haven't given much thought to it." The officers could tell by the tone in my voice that I really wasn't in the mood for talking. I pretty much thought how this would be the last time I see a Wendy's for a while.

When we arrived at RGC the officers said for me to take care of myself. Then they walked me through the prison doors.

Once inside, an officer barked at me "strip naked." I hesitated long enough for the officer to notice that I just wasn't going to jump at everything that he said. When this officer said for me to strip again, he added, "you can do it the easy way or the hard way." I did it the easy way. All I thought to myself, "you can do it the easy way, or the hard way," I was referring it to the way I was going to do my time.

To this day I don't mind doing time the easy way.

—⟋⟍⟍—

Prisoner Essay #43

RGC (Jackson Prison Regional Guidance Center)

I was sentenced on June 14, 1993, in Midland County District Court, Midland, Michigan. The very next day, I was sent to the Regional Guidance Center, known as RGC, located in Jackson, Michigan. Jackson Prison is the biggest walled prison in the United States. The RGC facility is known as quarantine and brings in all new and old returning convicted felons coming into prison for screening, in order to place each in the correct facility.

I remember being scared and afraid. What had I gotten myself into? I asked myself while I was standing in a ten-by-ten steel cage with other convicted felons entering prison. One at a time, the Sarge would yell to get in a single file. We all got into a file, one at a time.

We could not take any possessions with us, except religious materials and a couple of pictures. Each one of us was stripped down to our underwear.

One officer said, "Spread 'em" "What do you mean?" I asked. He said "Grab a hold of your cheeks and spread 'em." I decided I wouldn't want that job—to look at somebody's butt all day. Then a shower about thirty seconds. Then we were issued prison blues, a bed roll, sheets, socks, underwear, a coat and shoes. We put the clothes on and all got our picture taken and a number that will be with us the rest of our life. One officer said, "All you got is just a house number. We don't want to hear your bull."

RGC held all types of convicted felons. Murderers, druggies, burglars, drunk drivers, assault and battery, child molesters, you name it they had it. This housing unit is called "Eleven Block." We went through all the routines coming into quarantine. They treated us like animals.

One officer said, "Follow me," and we went up a couple flights of stairs. We met another officer who said "One at a time, I will call your name and number." The officer called me and gave me a lock number for cell three gallery four.

"Continue down the two flights of stairs and to your right," the officer said. So I and a couple of other new inmates went down the stairs to an opening.

"Wow" I said. I was surprised by what I seen—rows and rows of cells. We were standing at the entrance of Seven Block. I looked to the right, then I looked straight up. There was four tiers with at least fifty cells on each tier. I looked to my left, it was the same—cell after cell.

Right ahead of me was the base floor, with fifty tables with four seats at each table. At the far end there was a flight of stairs going up to the fourth tier.

I walked beyond the tables toward the far end and up the stairs to the fourth floor (tier). While on the way up the stairs, I could hear the inmates who were locked up saying, "Hey fish, your number is still wet," "Hey white boy." I just paid no attention.

I walked down the gallery toward the third cell, other inmates in cells asked me, "Do you have a cigarette?" They call them "squares." "Do you have any stamps and envelopes?"

The gallery was about fifty feet high from the base floor and I grabbed the steel guard rail. Then I finished walking down the gallery to number three.

My cell was six by nine, an electronic steel door with bars, at the far end with steel bars on both sides. There were solid cement walls, a steel bed and a concrete mattress, a sink and a toilet, a locker that looked like the one in high school, a regular chair and a shelf-type desk. I made my bed, got comfortable, and fell asleep for a couple of hours.

I was awakened by a clanking sound and looked down the hall. An officer with a steel bar in his right hand was checking the steel bars on each of the windows and back of each cell.

I asked my neighbor what the schedule was around here. How long do you have to be in quarantine before being transferred? First, he said, you will be having a psychological test, a complete physical, eyes, ears, blood test, and dental. Once you are all checked out, they will classify you for what level you are going to be transferred to.

What is the schedule around here? Like showers, meals and phone? He said he would let me know when. It was about five o'clock in the evening and I was going to ask him about showers, phone and meals when an officer came up on our gallery and flipped a switch and the electronic doors were unlocked. We all got out of our cells and rushed down the gallery and down the stairs across the base floor toward the front of the tables. We all stood in line waiting for a tray with food on it and a drink. Each of us were singly put into a seat at a table

I noticed that everybody was eating fast. So I started easting fast too. It probably only took two minutes to eat what should have taken at least fifteen minutes. We each took care of our trays.

Back up the stairs and up to the fourth gallery; back down again. When do we get freedom? I hated being locked up.

There wasn't much to do that night. All I did was sleep. The next morning I woke up about 5:30, hearing a racket. Looking down on the base, I saw they were getting ready for us to have breakfast.

An officer came up to our gallery and flipped a switch to open our doors and down the gallery, down the stairs, across the base floor toward a line of inmates, waiting to be served a tray, we went, then to an assigned seat at a table. Again you had to eat within two minutes. Take care of your tray and back up the stairs to the fourth gallery to be locked down till lunch.

In the mean time your bed had to be made before 7 a.m. You also had to be dressed in the full prison clothes they issued you.

Lunch time was 11:30. Again, an officer came and pulled a switch to open the doors and we went back down the gallery and down the stairs, across the base floor, to a line of inmates waiting for trays with their lunch, assigned to a seat. Again only two minutes to eat. We took care of our trays, back up the stairs, down the gallery to our own cells, locked down again.

At one o'clock, an officer came by and said ready to go outside, he unlocked the doors, down the gallery we went, down the stairs to the base floor and out a door. Sunlight at last.

I ran to a line of inmates who were waiting for the use of a phone. An officer was taking ID's so nobody would cut in line. Once on a phone you only had ten minutes. If you didn't use the phone there was a little track you could walk on or the basketball court that only blacks used. I hardly ever seen a white person playing basketball.

We only had one hour for yard, only on the weekdays. No weekends, rarely, unless holidays. Back inside, up the stairs, down the gallery to our cells, locked down again, only for one hour or less.

Time for showers. We all were dressed in our underwear. The officer would come and open our doors just on the fourth gallery. But each gallery would take their turn.

Down to the showers we went. The water was scalding hot. You couldn't even stand under the water for more than a minute, it was that hot. Back to our cells, locked down until supper, we had showers once or twice a week. We got issued clothes once a week. We were locked down at least twenty-three hours a day.

Once you were classified for the level of incarceration facility you are going to, you are transferred to another facility in a week. I couldn't wait to get out of RGC. I hated quarantine.

—⚏—

The prisoner essays above were written by Michigan prisoner/students in the prison college program at Jackson Prison before those programs ended. The following short essays were written by Gus Harrison prisoner/students in post-GED reentry workshop classes from 2003 to 2005.

Prisoner Essay #44

Prison Orientation Means "Self Orientation"

Prison orientation was more like an out-of-body experience to me. I remember leaving the courtroom and yelling to my mother and girlfriend that I will be home in "six months." But that's not how things worked out.

My first orientation was looking up at the gun towers and barbed-wire fences and saying to myself, "I'm finally here." Like I knew it would happen one day and as soon as my shocked feet touched the concrete, it was like I saw myself here before. It was strange, because I was not nervous. It was like I knew what to expect. "At least," I thought, "My orientation was far more than a learning experience. It was a self evaluation, a change to really find out who I was and what could and could not break me (mentally as well as physically)."

I quickly found myself adapting—I couldn't understand how or why—but, like I said before, it was like I had been here before. As I moved to different institutions and came across different personalities attitudes and backgrounds, I understood the way I adapted. The way I did it was because a lot of the people around me were from the same place I came from or had similar backgrounds: family, culture or upbringing. And I adapted because I understood them. So that's why I say my first prison orientation was learning self.

—⁂—

Prisoner Essay #45

Prison Orientation: A Wake Up Call

At orientation they tell you all the rules and about how many prisoners had HIV. It made me wonder what was going on in prison. They tell you who runs the prison, where things are at, like the school, chow hall, law library and the housing units. Then they tell you what the prison offers to help you with rehabilitation, which nowadays is very little. To me orientation into prison was a wake-up call that let me know I have to change my way of life or spend it in prison going through orientations at other prisons.

—⁂—

Prisoner Essay #46

Vacation

When I first arrived to prison, I was transferred to the Riverside Correctional Facility for orientation. I was a very young guy of seventeen and the majority of prisoners there were my age. I am a quiet person, and so I kept to myself and silent. After three to six months, finally I settled at the Michigan Reformatory (MR) and felt that I could do anything I wanted because at MR there were many friends from my neighborhood, and plenty of drugs flowing throughout the facility. Therefore, I felt, thought and acted like I was still on vacation.

Prior to being in prison, I had received a Mechanic Trainee Certificate, and had $1,000 worth of tools and a toolbox. But all I could get was a job in Detroit as just a gas attendant. However, in prison I completed all my reception and guidance requirements (RGC) and soon transferred to the MDOC Special Training Opportunity Program (STOP) in Lansing, where I received my Mechanic License. Then I worked at National Machine Repair where I became a certified Millwright.

—⁓—

Prisoner Essay #47

Learn How to Do Time

One thing I learned during my prisoner orientation was how to do time. They taught us what to learn to do time, such as, making the very most of our time.

Another thing I learned were the basic dangers of everyday prison life. For example, the dangers of getting HIV or hepatitis viruses from sexual intercourse and by tattooing and sharing needles.

And last but not least, they told us the basic things to do to get out and never come back. For instance, avoid tickets, fulfill requirements. They also told us that there were things we could do to greatly improve our chances of parole, like the extra school and trade classes offered.

These are the most basic elements that I believed they tried to teach us: to do time, the dangers of prison and getting out and staying out.

—⁓—

Prisoner Essay #48

You Know without a Doubt Who You Really Are

When first entering the prison, the emotional feelings were of fear and excitement—fear because of the unknown, and excitement of the new, this kind of knowing and acceptance of "now I know I'm here," and it hits you, the reality of the situation.

Whatever you thought you "knew," you suddenly realize that you had no idea. From the guards talking down to you to your having "no fear" mentality. This is real life on the inside, and you must be, in your own mind at least, ready. If you're not, you might lose it—your mind, that is. The shock of the first night hearing grown men cry, knowing this is your home for the next nine years. And you know without a doubt, who you really are.

Prisoners Essay #49

My First Time: That's When the Jail Learning Began

My first orientation was some twenty-two years ago. I was eighteen years old. And I was coming from Detroit House of Corrections (DHOC) after being sentenced to five to twenty years for armed robbery and two years for the gun. I arrived at Riverside Correction about January of 1985. It was like being at some kind of youth camp. There were about 200 to 300 young boys between the age of seventeen to twenty-five. And most of us were locked up for armed robbery or drugs.

> *Day One* at Riverside was nothing but being in a room all day only coming out for lunch and dinner. So, I just sat back and listened to the other guys talk shit. I did a lot of push-ups and sit-ups all day.
> *Day Two* was the day when all clothing and health items were issued out to us. We were told the "do's and don'ts" of the place: like no smoking in your room, no two in a room, no fighting.
> *Day Three* was all medical-type issues. And it also was the first day that we were allowed to use the phone.
> *Day Four* was the first day we were sent to the yard and were allowed to be together with each other. You had East Side Detroiter, West Sider, YBI, BK Pony Boys, Projects Boy. All kind of guys. And that when the jail house learning began. . . .

Being around such a diverse group of people taught me all kinds of new things. Some good and some bad. Like: how to deal and how to sell drugs in an organized fashion. How to put a hit down on a person with a jailhouse knife. Also, how to make a bitch, knock a woman, and squeeze a lamb. What was most interesting to me was the different style and hustle and outlook on life from guys from G.R., Flint, Pontiac, Benton Harbor, Saginaw, Detroit—East and West. Some were drug dealers, some were into robbery, some were B & E artists, some were booster, check writer, bank robber and etc. I learned many things.

One thing that caught my eye was the value of tobacco—how a person could lose their life over cigarettes or a fag. Yes, another man would be ready to kill because you look at his boy, sissy or whatever you may call "it." But I must say that in the end, it came down to respect of yourself and others. That what could keep you breathing long enough to see another day or year. . . .

Prisoner Essay #50

Institutionalization

The ride always went from giddy to nervousness, but after being there more than once it was more like going home than experiencing a new phenomena.

Going through the old bubble, the first two times there was a color TV with a so-called AIDS video. It showed a group of addicts stealing to support their drug habit, and the shooting up. I remember that video showed over and over again while I sat in the waiting room to be dressed out in prison blues. It was torture to sit and watch people get high over and over again.

Another thing I remember about the first two times is that we came from a county that delivered us last, so we had to wait for the other counties that came first to go through. This was a hardship in that we weren't fed until we were dressed-out. So we always missed lunch.

You ask what is the big deal about eating. When your life is restrained down to the basics—breathing, eating, shitting, showering—when you lose one of these simple pleasures, it hurts. And, knowing that the people who now control you don't care how much it hurts makes it that much more painful to bear.

My third time through the bubble, instead of dressing you out, they gave me a jumpsuit to wear. Until I could go to the quartermaster. That I could live with. It was having to walk around in the Michigan March weather that froze my balls to see the psychiatric nurse. She wanted to know why I was shivering. Another example of institutional neglect.

The fourth time I went through the passage to prison we pulled up to a fence and pillbox that looked like "Checkpoint Charlie" of the old East Berlin photos. We were marched into a brand new concrete structure that reminded me of book in the county jail. A room for each purpose. One for filling out your health questionnaire. Are you suicidal? What is your waist size? Do you have any assets we can seize? Finally a picture and talk to a nurse inside before you went to quartermaster in your overalls.

Why so functional? Because instead of thirty or forty prisoners a week, it was now forty to fifty each day of each week. We had now become parts of the Department of Corrections factory.

SCARCE BEDSPACE

Introduction

A major problem in today's swollen and overcrowded prisons and jails is where to find a bed for each prisoner. Of the 6.5 million American people being supervised in the U.S. criminal justice system (probation, prison, parole), as we've noted over 2.2 million people are incarcerated in U.S. prisons and jails. Of this, in 2006, there were 1.5 million prisoners in federal and state prisons, and 700,000 in local jails. A major problem in our prisons and jails is locating and allocating scarce bed space (beds in cells).

Twenty years ago, before the national incarceration rate went up from 150 per 100,000 to nearly 600 per 100,000, and for a century before that—as incarceration rates stayed right around 100 per 100,000—prisons would periodically get overcrowded and typically more prisoners would be released into parole (Abadinsky 2006). But, with the exception of the Prohibition Era's "war on alcohol," where new, "Big House" prisons were built, most of the cycling involved in overcrowding leading to release on parole as a safety valve did *not* involve a massive prison build-up. Releasing people acted as a "safety valve." There was no need to build new prisons.

But now, in the twenty-year "war on drugs," we have created many more prisoners with longer sentences and fewer paroles, with many states eliminating "good time," and adding "three strikes laws," and eliminating halfway houses through "truth-in-sentencing laws." These *policies,* (and not an increase in crime), have caused a build-up of longer-term prisoners and a perpetual prison bedspace crisis. And this is a bedspace crisis that persists even after the building of 1,000 new prisons nationwide since 1986.

So how is the bedspace problem handled? As described, next to some prisons in each state will be regional reception and guidance centers, or RGC. Here, incoming prisoners are screened, classified and dispersed to other permanent facilities in the state.

The problem is twofold. One, to locate bedspace in the prisons where prisoners *exiting* RGC will be headed. This, however, is not the highest, immediate, concern. The first and immediate problem is to locate bedspace for prisoners *coming in* to this small, already overcrowded RGC (where they are already double-bunking), resulting in a constant search for housing to handle the steady flow of incoming prisoners (often backed up into local county jails). Since prisoners will stay at the RGC for several weeks before they move out, finding bedspace in RGC can be a real problem.

The coauthors took a tour, as guests of the warden at San Quentin Prison, of the Reception and Guidance process at this California prison.

We visited a room within one of the prison blocks in the RGC unit devoted to this single foremost mission—to find bedspace for income prisoners already en route to the RGC. Here, two busy overworked people, a Special Officer and his prisoner-clerk helper, are daily working to solve this urgent problem in their particular RGC.

In viewing this "microcosm" of a problem, we can visualize the larger problem of "allocating bedspace" in thousands of facilities nationwide, even as the number of prisoners annually increases. Where to house every prisoner?

Locating Bedspace

As soon as his security level is established through a series of tests and evaluations, the prisoner will be assigned a cell in an appropriate facility (max, medium, minimum).

Many aspects need to be considered. For instance, a sentence may have mandated a certain program be pursued or treatment be taken during incarceration. These programs include drug abuse treatment (AA, NA) and residential substance abuse treatment facility placement (RSAT facility), assaultive-offender program (AOP), mental health, basic education (adult literacy, ABE, ESL), high school equivalency degree program (GED) and so forth. Some of these program may be required as a condition of parole. However, these programs may be available in some prisons but not in others. So, prisoner placement in facilities matters very much to prisoners and their families, especially near the end of their sentence if they have not yet gotten access to programs required for parole (CAPPS 2008). Additionally, prisoners are screened in their health status and given information workshops on HIV/AIDS (see page at end of this section).

All of the "get tough" measures we've described *lengthened the prisoner time spent in prison* and resulted in a drastic slowing down of the normal freeing up of bedspaces. States have had to add a second, and even a third reception and guidance center to their prison admittance system. Such a new regional RGC facility was opened recently (1996) as a part of San Quentin Prison (SQ) in California in order to receive and process the growing prisoner load for just the northern part of California.

San Quentin: An Example of Allocating Scarce Beds in RGC

For prisoners departing from San Quentin's RGC for a permanent cell in any of Northern California's overcrowded prison facilities, the search for bedspace in these other prisons around the state is hard enough.

But the bedspace search actually is a full-time task for two people to just find a vacant temporary bed at the Reception Center inside the walls at San Quentin itself.

The authors know. They were able to watch the hectic process in 2000, at the height of the imprisonment boom. Like many other prisons, the San Quentin Prison was forced to go to double-bunking for regular prisoners (two prisoners to a cell). At the same time, the prison staff also had to find available vacant temporary cells for prisoners entering RGC's Orientation program.

Recidivism rates in California have been exceedingly high, from 60 to 80 percent, so, many prisoners rotated through the system in a "revolving door" effect, resulting in constant using up of valuable bed space. With California's "three strikes" law in effect, and drug testing for parolees strictly enforced on the outside, prison staff are doubly worried about bedspace and recidivists. (Not to mention the concerns of already two-time prisoner loser recidivists themselves who worry about getting another "third-strike" felony—even a non-violent felony—and a life sentence).

In 1990, before the full effect of the imprisonment boom, the authors had visited San Quentin. In 2000, the two authors made a second visit to San Quentin Prison, California's venerable oldest prison, located on San Francisco Bay.

The RGC is an area of the prison not usually visited by public tour groups. Here was the special cell-assignment operations room where bedspace within the prison was being assigned. San Quentin had long been a multi-level prison that included the state's Death Row block. By 2000, in order to accommodate a ballooning state prison population, a portion of the prison had been converted into a reception center.

Incoming prisoners would spend up to a month at SQ (San Quentin) RGC orientation and then the newly classified would be sent to a permanent cell in an appropriate prison in Northern California.

As we entered the small room at the end of Block Two, accompanied by a California Department of Corrections Assistant Deputy Warden, we observed how stressful it was just finding bedspace at San Quentin's RGC. (Excerpt written by Marjorie Larmour, from Larmour & Tregea, *The Imprisonment Binge: Or The Great American Drug Bust*, 2002:268–73).

AUTHOR'S REPORT #2

Bedspace Tour: Allocating Scarce Beds in RGC at San Quentin

"You want to see how we handle the scarce allocation of cell space for just the Reception Center?" he asked, swinging suddenly around to us.

"Sure," I said

"Well, I'll show you room 2A first, then."

"Lead on," I said. I thought, no official tour here, with jokes and all. This man is putting first things first, and it's clear that a flood of prisoners is his first and daily worry.

We followed him across the square toward a row of blocks.

"When the press comes through, mainly on some execution stuff," he continued, "I show them room 2A. It's hard to get folks' attention how bad off our prisons are these days."

His voice was matter of fact as he turned from the square to enter the first block, a square old structure with large "A" imprinted on the side.

Once inside, I was struck with a muted wall of noise, which resounded in the echoing chamber, not something I remember hearing on my last visit ten years earlier in 1990 (Larmour & Tregea 2002).

Where was it coming from? To my left the two long rows of cells extended five stories high the length of the block along one of its sides, just as they had in my previous visit. But now each contained two men. Double-bunking was in force. The newly different "wall of noise" now made sense.

Frowning toward Bergman, I spoke louder. "Double bunking sure makes a difference in the noise level."

"Yes," he smiled. "It got much worse. It was even worse than this, but an inmate won a court case. Now men can have radios only with earphones."

The cell assignment room marked 2A was the first as you entered the cell block, a small eight-by-ten cubicle. Quietly we approached and were able to stand in the open doorway silent and observing before the room's two occupants, absorbed by the cell-tracking task at hand, noticed us.

The small staff workroom, I could see right away, was actually just another cell, the last in line and nearest the door. It had apparently hastily been cleaned out to make an ersatz office.

What I saw stunned me. Headlines about prison overcrowding I'd read over the last fifteen years of the "war on drugs" abruptly boiled down to two men and a pegboard in a tiny cluttered room located at the end of an ancient cellblock.

Occupying much of one wall, which was painted off-white like the rest of the cell block, was a huge wall chart, perhaps five tall by seven feet wide, depicting individual cells—rows and rows of cells—and on hooks attached to each cell symbol dangled labels or tags with names of the cells' occupants. There were perhaps three or four hundred hooks on the chart.

The officer's job, helped by a prisoner/clerk who manned a desk and phone in the far corner of the impossibly crowded room was, in effect, to change a nametag, which represented bed occupancy, as the clerk handed him a new tag. In short, to keep prison occupancy up to date. It boiled down to when one man was paroled or sent to another facility, another promptly took his place, you might say, before the sheets had even cooled.

A prisoner clerk had the official task to take calls that came in constantly to his desk from somewhere giving a name, hand a slip with the name together with some hurriedly scribbled detailed information on a crumpled list to the officer standing beside the chart some four feet away, and wait while the officer searched out and located the name on one of the myriad pegs.

The crumpled list, I could not help but notice, even from my observer's position, and from stray bits of overheard clipped exchanges between the two during the process, contained an incredible amount of discernible information about each man—his name, AKA, prisoner ID number, social security number, date of birth, race, dates of previous incarceration if applicable, any tickets, parole date, and other comments. All of it was crunched like a human DNA genome string into code so that it occupied only a single line after the prisoner's name.

The amazing performance continued, each incoming name needing to be speedily searched out, changed and checked off with utmost accuracy. What was disturbing was the realization that something like this was happening all down the line. After San Quentin RGC, in the facility where the newly classified inmate was to be sent, a similar search for bedspace would be underway. Or, once at the other prison facility, if he were transferred, the same search would occur for bedspace for him. Wherever the man was sent, another search began.

We two prison instructors had entered, been introduced, and remained watching, fascinated, the two of us crowding into a corner, trying to keep out of the way of the fast-paced action in this cramped room.

Soon the officer at the pegboard—Officer McNeil, it developed—began throwing comments to us over his shoulder.

"That's G. R. Martinez coming back," he announced, as he took one label down and hung up a tag scrawled Martinez, G. R., the clerk meanwhile searching and checking off from the list.

"You have to understand," officer McNeil was saying to us, "Recidivism is very high. Most of these guys, over half, will come back. Maybe real soon."

"How high is the recidivism rate?" I asked.

"Official figures put it at about 60 percent but"—he frowned—"I don't know, I might peg it closer to 80 percent."

"Eighty percent!' I whooped.

"Unofficial like I said," he added quickly.

"Wow," I thought. "Sixty percent is bad enough. Michigan's rate is 30 to 60, depending on how you measure it—meaning for every two prisoners paroled, one and more come back. But 80 percent!"

More names were handed to him. "Transfer guys," he muttered and scratched his head. "Gotta' figure where to put them."

Even while figuring, he glanced at the next incoming name. "Yep, there's Sanborn back again. He was in here last year. I know 'em all. They send 'em to us."

One label tag came down and Sanborn, E. L., went up. He continued searching for spaces for "the two transfer guys." Then, turning to us, Officer McNeil sighed. "It's truly a revolving door. Nothing here makes them change. They don't learn a new skill for instance. A trade to get a job. Don't get a degree in something."

I know," I was quick to agree.

It was the same old story as in Michigan, I reflected sadly. The same in every state prison system. Few job skills learned. All the 770 college programs offered in state prisons had closed down after the 1994 punitive ending of Pell grant eligibility for prisoners.

Once more at the board, the officer shrugged again. "We're bustin' at the seams. But nobody out there cares these days."

"Yes," I said quietly.

How right he is, I thought, equally depressed. As we left the small room, the officer and his clerk returned once again to their seemingly endless job.

PEER-LED HEALTH ORIENTATION
CLASS FOR INCOMING INMATES

Part of what faces incoming prisoners are health risks. What follows is an excerpt from a "Collaborative Program in Prison HIV Prevention for Incoming and Current Inmates" at San Quentin State Prison.

Program Description

A peer-facilitated intervention for incoming inmates reaches approximately 12,000 new inmates per year. As new inmates arrive at the Reception Center of the prison, small groups are escorted to the health orientation classroom for the educational intervention. This class was instituted when inmate focus groups stressed the need for HIV prevention education at prison entry. The warden mandated the program in 1991 for all new inmates and a classroom is provided for the program.

The purpose of the program is to increase awareness of risk factors among new inmates, personalize risk, increase risk perception and reduce the risk of HIV, STDs, hepatitis and tuberculosis in prison and after release.

Inmate Peer Health Educators deliver the educational presentation, document the attendance and maintain the classroom and materials. A bilingual/bicultural Spanish-speaking inmate peer educator is available to meet with monolingual Spanish speakers. This program was formally evaluated and peer educators were found to be as effective as a professional HIV educator. We also found that inmates preferred peer educators (Grinstead, Faigeles, and Zack 1997).

Health Orientation Class Outline:

1. Introduction and peer educators' personal stories about the impact of HIV
2. Modes of transmission: the four body fluids, sexual transmission, transmission by needle sharing
3. Review safer sex and injecting practices
4. The role of alcohol and drugs in HIV transmission and prevention
5. Testing for HIV in prison and in the community
6. Other health concerns: STDs, hepatitis, tuberculosis

Immediately following the Health Orientation class, all participants are offered voluntary HIV testing. Approximately 50 percent of class participants voluntarily sign up for HIV and hepatitis testing.

http://www.caps.ucsf.edu/projects/maporient.html

7

—ɯᴜ—

Cells

AUTHOR'S REPORT #3

"The Big House: Cell Life at Jackson Prison"

Coauthor Bill Tregea started his prison teaching in 1981, working in Jackson Prison's maximum security "central complex" (Level IV and V) with the Jackson Community College prison program. To get to his prison college class each day he walked through two gates ("the bubble"), then through a rotunda ("control"), then a long hall and then another sets of gates into central complex yard. He then continued walking, alone, through the central complex yard, a grassy area. The central complex yard, surrounded by high walls and massive five-story cell-block buildings (housing unit), was usually empty. A few birds and a cat could usually be seen. But the worrisome spot was the accumulation of high-security-risk prisoners waiting in front of the "school gate." Piling up and milling around in the yard driveway by this school gate, the prisoners were on their own turf. Once inside the school building and in the school halls, school offices or classrooms, the prisoners were on "our turf"—that is, the teachers, librarian, writing center director, counselor, prisoner clerks and administrator's turf. I was always a bit wary waiting for the guard to process us all through the gate: the small crowd of twenty or thirty prisoners and a few teachers funneled past the guard at this bottleneck, showing our "pass" or our "ID," one-by-one. I tried to calmly wear a mask of cool indifference.

Another "tight spot" it seemed to me in my first weeks was, after being processed through the one-at-a-time school gate, we all went up the flight of stairs together—teachers jammed in with the prisoners. After a few weeks, however, I felt we "were all in it together." After a few years, I had forgotten these earlier small fears—they had become buried in semester-after-semester "walk-in, walk-out" daily prison teacher routine—a purposeful, dull routine characteristic of prison life. Imagine needing the patience to "stand in line" on some daily basis for several years and you've got an approximation of prison life. Still, it was just thirty feet from the very "bottleneck" that a woman correctional officer was killed by a prisoner in a corner of the auditorium—the only Jackson prison guard killed in the twenty years I taught there. I reflected: there were *two* murders in my neighborhood during this same twenty-year period. In some ways, at least as a teacher, I was safer "inside" than in my own neighborhood.

What must this prison life be like for actual prisoners? While I calmly parked my car in the lot, walked in on my own, showed my prison staff ID to get through the "bubble" (first set of gates), and had small worries waiting around a crowd of prisoners at the school gate, one Jackson prisoner student describes his arrival like this:

> I saw a long building that looked like Dracula's castle with bars on all the windows. The guards, hanging onto the gate separating the bus cockpit and passenger area, yelled:
> "Alright you dirty swines, time to move out!"
> One of the guards picked up a twelve-gauge shotgun, and quickly pulled the pump to load a shell. The other guard placed the barrel of a chrome-plated pistol in his lap. Surrounding the bus was a regiment of armed guards in riot gear.

After describing big, burly guards escorting the prisoners off the bus, and in describing the final steps toward his cell, he commented:

> I walked down a long, narrow walkway to a cell with a small opening that I could hardly fit through. This was going to be like living in a bathroom. The bed was where the bathtub would be, and the bed was bolted to the floor. The bed was placed inches from the toilet. Who would believe that some people actually enjoy living in a bathroom?

In 1994 coauthor Bill Tregea had the opportunity to teach a "Crime and Deviance" class in Hillsdale College's Sociology department and arranged to take a half-dozen (mostly college age women) in a tour of Nine Block at Jackson Prison. This was the old "Big House" type of cell block. Mostly these nine-block prisoners were "trustees" and would be out within a year. They took classes at Jackson's "South" complex Levin School building, where Tregea had been teaching for twelve years.

As our Hillsdale College student tour entered the cavernous "Big House" block set-up, with central first floor and then four floors of cell tiers rising up on both the south and north walls, it was like entering a cave. The walk up the precarious stairs all the way up to the fourth tier—and then the walk along that narrow fourth-tier walkway—was unforgettably terrifying for both students and teacher. One prisoner/student in a prison college English class described these old Big House cell tiers this way:

> "Up the stairs to your right, fourth gallery, cell sixty-four," the guard stated, after I had shown him my ID card and informed the officer that I had just arrived from another prison
>
> I apprehensively approached the flight of stairs, and began to climb them like you would a giant ride at an amusement park. The only difference was the ride wasn't amusing.
>
> Once I reached fourth gallery, which was the highest floor in the prison, I had to walk about half a block down a narrow catwalk to get to my cell.
>
> The only thing between me and plunging fifty feet to my death was a four-foot guard rail.

As might be expected, traits and characteristics of a man or woman remain the same whether that person is in prison or not. If a person is neat, he will remain so. If untidy, he will always be. If cynical, cheerful and so forth, he will remain the same.

In the comments from Marjorie Larmour's prison English class, as the men described their cell, their personality traits and characteristics are clear, and their need to adjust to life in a cell. Upon entering his cell, "a damp, gloomy pit," the transfer prisoner who was escorted to nine-block, fourth gallery, cell sixty-four, was shocked by the unkempt-ness, stating: "It looked as though it was alive with filth." He describes how he talked the guard into showing him where some cleaning supplies were located so he could clean his cell, then:

> As I reached the top floor with a mop in one hand and a bucket in the other, I was terrified by the oncoming traffic, on the narrow catwalk, yet the other "drivers" passed me like Germans pass Americans on Germany's Autobahn.
>
> Clinging toward the cell-side of the catwalk—and not wanting to look down four stories to the open floor below—I waited for everyone to pass by me before traveling any further.

He finally reached his cell and began to transform "the gross slimy hell hole" into what he hoped would be a "clean, hygienic place to lay my head." He reflects:

> My days in the gloomy pit have turned into weeks and weeks to months and months to years. There's not a night that I don't wish that I was at home. I remember my mom telling me as I was growing up: "You never miss your water, until your well runs dry."

Can there be privacy in prison? Many prisoners try to respect each other's privacy, but it's hard to come by. One prisoner/student put it this way:

> In spite of the size of the unit, I can find my comfort in being by myself. On some occasions, I can use my memories, along with my vivid imagination to have my love with me. Against all odds, I try to seek joy in a bad situation. Before too long, however, someone will always interrupt me from my moments of happiness. Behind the bars of a cell there is little privacy and very little joy.

How would you describe the actual living areas of the old Big House blocks and the still-used, tall, many-floor "tiers of cells" housing unit set up? In each block there are about 350 cells stacked 5 high. Each cage is open on both ends so, as one prisoner notes: "it has the effect of a zoo on the mind." Another prisoner student writes: "Every time someone uses the bathroom you get the effect that this person is in your room. The smell is all in your cage." What do people in prison think about? This varies, but one prisoner commented:

> It's a hurting feeling to know there's no love in this place. It all makes you very hateful toward others and that's not good at all and the people that run places like this know the effect of this place on you. It plays games with your mind and then it's a trap—yes, it's a trap. They tell you when you leave—those that get to leave—that once you go, you'll be back.

The sample comments above from prisoner/students about their cell life are from the 1980s, before double-bunking. Then came the 1986 federal "war-on-drugs" laws, and the long mandatory minimum sentences spread out to, and were adopted by, all the states. The result: the rapid building of 1,000 new state prisons. And still, the increasingly overcrowded prisons had to move from the single-bunk arrangement to double-bunking the cells.

PRISONER ESSAYS BY GUS HARRISON PRISONERS

Coauthor Bill Tregea, after the end of prison college in Michigan in May of 2000, began teaching volunteer classes at the local prison near his employment at Adrian College, Adrian, Michigan, about forty minutes south of Ann Arbor. During the period 2001–2008 he asked his prisoner/ students to describe their cells and their cell experience.

Prisoner Essay #51

Cells across America

My first cell was in Green County Jail in Xena, Ohio. Just that morning I had been working as a lab technician at the donor center inside the hospital complex on Wright Patterson Air Force Base.

I was the sergeant in charge of the donor floor when four men in blue suits accosted me on the donor floor with a secret grand jury indictment. I was arrested for aggravated trafficking in LSD. I was led away in handcuffs in front of my coworkers through the medical center full of military personnel and their families, and subsequently deposited in the Green County Jail.

I was twenty-one and had never had any dealings with the criminal justice system. After having my rights read to me and deciding not to make any statements, they put me in a small room of cement with a hole in the center of the floor. There were no lights and nothing to sit on but the cold concrete floor.

After being locked-up most of the day incommunicado, the door was flung open, and I was given my bond paperwork. Because this was my first case ever, and being in the military, I was given a personal bond.

The last cell I'm currently incarcerated in is a two-man cell here at Adrian Regional Facility (ARF, or Gus Harrison Prison). It is larger than any other two-man cell I have been confined in, in Michigan. It is a cell in a Regional Institution that was built in the late 1980s by the last Democratic governor before Engler, but they ran out of money before it could be opened. Of course, John (Engler) wrangled federal monies so he could open those regional prisons. These were the last prisons built in Michigan, but you can be sure if more money could be found to open more of them, they would have been built.

The worst cell I was ever housed in was at Macomb County Jail. It was April 2002 and there was a warrant out for me for violation of probation. While I was on the run, I was also in a methadone clinic. Someone who owed me money gave me some Xanax in lieu of the monies they owed me. I took the Xanax and promptly went into a blackout.

Later on that night, over twelve hours later, I was accosted by the Mount Clemens police. After they tried to interview me, and I was still too high to give any kind of intelligible answers, I was put into the back seat. Knowing I still had more Xanax on me, I took the rest of the pills to avoid another felony charge.

Many hours later I stumbled into Macomb County Jail with no knowledge of what had transpired after I swallowed the pills.

I was told that I had OD'd (overdosed) and that I was taken to the nearest hospital to have my stomach pumped. Luckily, I didn't have to remember any of it. But I was put into a "Bam Bam Suit." That is a quilt overcoat that hooks together over your shoulders with Velcro straps. Also, I was given a quilt blanket about four feet in length.

They deposited me in what is called a "high-observation cell." It is a cell with a cement block on the floor with a sticky plastic mattress to lie on. Also, the cell door is completely see-through so the officers can look into the cell 24/7. Your most private acts, like trying to take a shit, are on view for a cop all day, every day.

When chow comes it is served in a Styrofoam container that smells like the food with the worst smell. If you have smelled broccoli, then imagine everything in the tray smells and tastes like broccoli. Also, because you're the last served, everything is at room temperature; cold or all the same low temperature. And the final indignity is there is nothing to eat with. No plastic spoon, fork or knife. You have to tear the corner of the Styrofoam tray to dig out the congealed mess.

The only way I could get released from this torture cell was to plead my case with the head psychiatrist on why I tried to kill myself. After many tries and pleading, she finally decided that I wasn't a harm to myself anymore. I was released from my "high-observation" cell to be placed in a communal cell that at least had a shower. After eleven days of smelling my own ass, I could at least wash off the charcoal that was still plastered on my face and ass from when they pumped my stomach.

My favorite cell was in quarantine at three-block in Jackson Regional Guidance Center (RGC). It was a one-man cell. I had been in a one-man cell at the old seven-block when quarantine was there, but in seven-block, when you went to take a shit, you had to face the inmate across from you. In three-block, however, there were ice machines, in the unit. There was power in the cells, so that when I had bought my TV, I could watch whatever I wanted, read whatever I wanted, shit whenever I wanted, and be completely at ease when the cell door was closed. What you lose most in prison, besides your freedom, is your right to privacy.

There have been many more cells in my past. From county jails, to prisons in three different states: I just wanted to give you a taste of the cells I have lived in.

Prisoner Essay #52

My Escape: Demolition of My Cell

A lot of guys think of their cell as temporary. I don't. I know I'm not going to be in a cell forever, but it is where I live right now. I try to keep it as clean as possible. Every one of my meager belongings has a specific place where it is kept. I hang pictures from home on the walls. I try to make it as comfortable as possible.

I don't just consider it as a residence that I inhabit and decorate, but also as a dwelling that I built. Every crime I committed and bad decision I made is a brick in my cell. If I would've changed my life a long time ago, the walls would be short and I could very easily have jumped over them. As the years passed by, the bricks stacked up higher and higher. Even as I got deeper and deeper in the consequences of my actions, it's still possible that I could've managed to climb out.

The crimes I was sentenced to prison on were the bricks I used to build the roof. Now, here I am, but I'm planning to escape.

I don't have to worry about the fences with the razor wire or the officers guarding the gate. I'm not even concerned with the locks on the door. It's the bricks of my cell that I'm focused on. The determination I have to change is the sledgehammer I use to demolish my prison.

It's more difficult to tear these bricks down than it was to build them up. But, the task is not impossible. Every time I clean my cell, I'm chipping away at the mortar. When I look at pictures I've hung, the walls are crumbling behind them. When I make my surroundings more comfortable, I'm really just preparing to leave. And when my cell is torn all the way down to bare earth, and the soil is exposed, a new seed can be planted.

Prisoner Essay #53

Building up Hate, or Becoming a Man

No one could imagine the things that were going through my mind sitting in a county cell awaiting and knowing that you are about to go to a place you only heard about or saw on television. Sitting in a cell by yourself, listening as those who had already been to prison recite their war stories about what goes on behind the walls in Jackson Prison. I was so scared the following day when the deputy called my name, because I knew then that my life was about to change in every way and what made matters worse for me mentally was knowing that there was nothing I could do to change my fate, unless I took my own life.

After being cuffed, shackled, then placed on the bus, I was seated in the far back with two other guys who had been to prison several times between the both of them, and I guess the fear showed on my face, despite how hard I was trying to look calm. They kept saying amongst themselves that young guys get raped and killed in Jackson—they knew I was listening, so they just kept on talking. It took only a couple of hours for us to make it to Jackson, and when we pulled in, to me, the place looked like an old high school surrounded by gates and Constantine razor wire, but when we were escorted inside I saw clearly that it wasn't a school, it was the devil's play room.

I went through things in the first five minutes that were, to me, the most degrading, humiliating and dehumanizing things a man could go through, although the two I came in with went through the process of stripping, showering in front of other men, then bending over and spreading their behinds open, as if it were a normal thing in everyday life.

After that we were given our state-issue clothing which consisted of three pairs of state blues, nine underwear, three t-shirts, eight socks and two sets of long-john thermals. The guards took each of us to the cell that we would occupy for the next 90 to 180 days. Walking down the rows of cells stacked up in four galleries was to me sort of an initiation because every cell you walked by, men were screaming at me, telling me they would kill me, rape me, hell, everything you can imagine, they were yelling.

When we got to the fourth gallery, the officer yelled, "Break cell twenty-nine." The cell door came open and the CO (correctional officer) pushed me inside, my eyes were closed and didn't open until the cage door slammed shut. I sat down on the steel bunk, with a one-inch-thick pad that was to sleep on, and put my head in my hands and cried, realizing that this was how I was going to spend the next seventeen years of my life.

I spent the next ninety days building up as much hate as I possibly could because I knew hate would carry me further than love ever could. I came to this realization because everyone who had ever told me they loved me, loved me enough to leave me in my darkest hour. I knew there would be no one who would visit, no one I could call, and no one to write to. Hell had come to earth and this was my life.

After 180 days in "Reception and Guidance" they broke my cell door and told me to pack up my things—that I was being sent to a new world. I packed up everything quickly and stepped outside the cell. Once again, my eyes were closed, and only opened when the cage slammed shut. It was then that all my faith in God, hope, love, dreams and people went away, as if they never existed in my heart. I was headed to a place that I was either going to learn to become a man, being only twenty years of age, or become the monster the jury depicted me to be.

—❦—

The following are earlier thoughts on cells in 2004 and 2005 from prisoners in Bill Tregea's post-GED 2003–2005 reentry workshops at Gus Harrison prison. These essays were after the "war on drugs" had resulted in double-bunking.

Prisoner Essay #54

I Start My Day by Looking at My Family

This is what the word cell means to me: Taken from my home, and my family, locked in a six-by-ten slab of concrete no bigger than a walk-in closet. This is where my life has taken me.

To keep my mind occupied, this is what I have done to my cell. I have a bulletin board for all my pictures to hang. I have two sons I keep close to me by having their photo hung there. Everyday I wake up I always stop to look at them, that's how I start my day. I have other pictures of my family that are very close to me that are also hanging on my bulletin board. My bulletin board is very important to me because that's where all my loved ones hang.

My cell is very small. I also have a bunkie, so there are two people in this small place. There are two desks against the wall about two feet from my bed, most of the things go in my desk cause I have no where else to put them.

I sleep on a bunk bed, I have the bottom bunk so I don't need a chair to stand on to get up in my bed. The top bunk is pretty high it has no steps and if you're short you might have a hard time getting up there, I know I do. My bed is very hard, it's made out of steel with a thin green mat they call a mattress. The bed is against the wall in front of the door so anyone who walks by can look in and watch you sleep.

My toilet is also in my cell, it's made up of stainless steel with a sink on the top. If you gotta use the bathroom and your bunkies in the room, than you gotta hang up a sheet for a little privacy.

Across the room are two lockers, one for me and one for my bunkie. The lockers are very small, but I guess that's cause there isn't enough room. However there's enough room for my personal clothes for my visits.

Well, inside this cell is some place I really don't want to be, but this is what the word cell means to me.

—ﾟ—

Prisoner Essay #55

Share and Share Alike

Anyway, what keeps me at peace is prayer and having a virtuous woman. I try to stay out of the cell most of the time, especially whenever my bunkie must use the toilet and/or his showertime and afterwards. I try to let my bunkie at least watch a program on my TV every so often. I found out a long time ago about how he handles the clean up duties, so I requested to do all of the cleaning up by myself.

—⚉—

Prisoner Essay #56

My House: Office, TV, Kitchen, Stinger—and Open the Window
When Using the Bathroom

My home away from home: the multi-purpose prison cell. It is an ingeniously designed room with a hundred different uses. Probably the only
place where you might find so many uses for such a single small space.

My prison cell, A.K.A. my house. Whether I like it or not this is the
place where I spend most of my time, and sleep. Where, when I get tired
around 8:00 p.m., I rest for the night. A place where my anger boils at
times and I toss and turn, unable to get to sleep. Or where I doze off just
to kill a little of the time.

The office, where my desk is securely attached to both my floor and my
wall, is the place where I choose to do most, if not all, of my typing and
writing. Also, this is an excellent workshop area to run my business of
making greeting cards to sell or to send back home to my mother. It is also
the only place for me to keep my television and the rest of my appliances.
Or the shelves that I may put to use by making my very own, little, private library. I tend to watch a whole lot of television in my house (as we
like to call it!). It's what I am afraid to admit I do with the majority of my
invaluable time.They say if you can't stand the heat, then stay out of the
kitchen. And so try to get out of the kitchen I must. For the seldom occurring very few meals I try to prepare in the amazing new kitchen that was
transformed almost magically into my very own and very small kitchen.
To be honest, it will not make anyone jealous or envious. Yet whether I
am just trying to fix myself a snack or am making what may seem like a
complicated meal, it will definitely get the job done. However one may
choose to break the rules that seem to be enscribed in stone for some of
these officers as are the ten commandments to the many Christians and
Jews—to make what is called a "stinger" from an extension cord. With
this contraband item one can heat water to cook soups, macaroni and
cheese or, even for many, coffee. Beware if you decide to use one of these.
After all they are contraband.

You can really get stuffed eating so much food all of the time in here.
And sometimes we need to find a place to put it. This is the part the bathroom is used for. Basically the bathroom consists of a toilet with a built-in
sink. And then a mirror that you can shave with. That is, of course, if one
can look at himself in the mirror. But with all of us being prisoners we
can't all keep our heads high with pride. Also there are a few things you
need to do when you use the bathroom in prison. The first thing is to open

the window if it's not too cold out. Then you put up a sheet and if you're lucky enough to have incense you need to burn one. Once all of those are complete, you can start using the bathroom. Just flush it quickly after you feel something drop. In prison we call it a writsy flush. Now that is all about the bathroom of an actual prison cell.

When things start to get boring, as they generally tend to do, you can turn your multi-purpose room into a den or game room. You might be very surprised by the sheer number of card games there are. Even solitaire has over a hundred different versions and types of games to play. Plus there is always chess. And one good thing about chess is that it exercises the mind. Many people don't know that the mind, just like the body, needs to be exercised to be kept in top shape.

Once it starts to become too cold to be outside, a cell can become a very cozy place in which to hold off the long winter. Be it the sun and clouds, or the moon and stars, it seems to become a big window. And if you look close you may be able to see through the screens and bars, over the fence razor-wire, out to freedom—out above the horizon.

However, the single and most important place my cell somehow magically transforms into is a house of God, a church of Christ. It is in this room that I say my prayers to my God the Lord. The same God that King David and Solomon prayed to. In my own little private church is where I sing and rejoice because I am happy. It's also the cruel place where I cry out in distress because I feel in my heart as if I can take no more.

Only in prison you find ingeniously designed cells. With many more uses than in some people's entire household. This is my house. Where I live, in my cell.

—❧—

Prisoner Essay #57

A Place of Loneliness, A Place of Waiting, A Place of Change

My cell feels like the loneliest place on earth. When I'm in it I'm thinking about my family and friends.

When you're sitting in a prison cell it's as if everyone has forgotten you were ever alive. You sit there hoping for a letter but they come far and few, so you start thinking that no one cares, but you still don't give up because you know there is more to life than this.

A cell can also be the place that takes you away from everything you have to deal with day to day—so a cell can be what you make of it, not what it makes of you—but everybody that's in a cell has their own way of looking at it.

I decided to make my cell a place for bettering myself by writing letters and studying the Bible and learning from my mistakes, so I can leave this cell behind for the things that are yet to come.

So no matter what your cell may be to you, a place of loneliness, a place of waiting, or a place of change, you'll always have the hope of leaving that cell behind you and moving on with life, but don't ever forget about that little cell because it will be right there waiting for someone to fill it whether it be you or someone like you. But that little cell will still be the same.

—ɯ—

Prisoner Essay #58

A Quiet Drama, Building and Building—Trapped Inside

When I enter the cell I am plagued by the reality of the living hell. The gut-wrenching pain haunts me endlessly! It's much like a quiet drama that keeps building and building without end. The cell reminds me I'm trapped inside a world where the fibers of dread, contempt, lost hope, despair, love and rage come and go. When the door opens from the cell and it's time for the yard, I realize the yard is yet another cell to remind me of this living hell.

—ɯ—

Prisoner Essay #59

A Life Not Yet Completed

You see it everyday, like a giant aqua-green cave. The door to my cell, this color is ugly, looking at it makes it worse, walking through it, with its small slit for a window, more like a mocking Cyclops eyes from some medieval or Greek myth. My so-called name tag adorns the bottom of the window, to remind the guards who I am. I wonder if they could forget. Would they? This monster of a door is controlled by the guards, they open it with a clang and buzzing of electric motors. Open now to expose the inside. At least the inside isn't aqua green.

You walk through. My room is kept up at least. If my mother taught me one thing, it is to have to be clean and neat. Even here. For having a toilet one foot from your bed, it smells good in here. I have contraband incense and I don't care if I get caught. If I don't, then the arid musk of the toilet who lives so close to me, well, let's just say he is a grumpy one. He is a stainless steel sculpture, sticking out of the wall like a decoration gone bad. To flush him invokes a kind of noise that can only be compared to what survivors of hurricanes must hear when the wind rips through their house, it can and will wake those who are even the most devout of sleepers, but it must be done.

Tidy is the word that comes to mind. Having two males live in the size of a small bathroom, there isn't much room for the flop of your shoes-off-at-the-door mentality that you had while staying at mom's house.

I have my family pictures tacked up, so I have my daily motivation knowing why I don't do something stupid. My cellmate doesn't have one picture up, he says it reminds him too much of things that hurt. I understand him. It hurts me also to look at my son everyday and know I'm not there, but then again my pain is motivation. So they still hang there, captured memories of a life not yet completed.

8

—ɷ—

Daily Work Routine

INTRODUCTION

The daily routine for prisoners at prison facilities all across the United States—whether they are federal or state prisons—remains remarkably the same. Prisoners rise at about the same time (early), spend similar structured and closely monitored days, especially weekdays, and retire (lights out) early.

Workdays are usually divided into structured units—work (morning and afternoon), chow (three times a day), yard time (recreation) during early morning and evening hours after dinner, free or leisure time after dinner for a couple of hours spent in TV or lounge room until lockdown in cell. Finally, reading, studying or radio or TV until lights out.

Rules and methods are essentially the same in each prison. These include rules about work details, count, pay, punishments (lockdown in cell, or worse, "the hole"), call-outs, passes, tickets, phone lines and visits.

Security levels may differ in regard to privileges granted—more or less of yard time, free time or access to certain work details.

One account of a workday at one prison facility could be replicated almost hour by hour by a similar account at any other prison across the nation.

This chapter begins with such an account, a description of a workday at the Federal Prison at Fort Dix.

Perhaps what is unique about this description is not the workday—it mirrors others—but the fact that the describing was done by a prisoner now serving time in Fort Dix Prison himself. Michael Santos, the writer, has already served several years of a long-term sentence, and still has a few more years to go. This description and other writings by Santos on prison life appear periodically on the internet (and his new book *Inside* appeared in the late summer of 2007).

A. DESCRIPTION OF THE WORKDAY:
THE FEDERAL PRISON AT FORT DIX

Guest Essay #1

From: Michael Santos (on web), at: www.michaelsantos.net

> . . . prisoners are waiting at the door of each building prior to the morning's announcement. As soon as they're able, five- to six-hundred prisoners are moving on the compound;
>
> Between 6:00 a.m. and 7:30 a.m., the prison is pretty much opened to the inmate population . . . the prisoners may walk around the compound or meet in some of the common areas that are open.
>
> Several prisoners exercise early in the morning. A few prisoners begin their days running around the track, many more walk and quite a few will train with weights.

Workcall

> The complexity of the prison changes at 7:30 a.m. each weekday . . . to one that is controlled much more tightly.
>
> The workday for most inmates begins at 7:30 a.m. . . . . Several hundred prisoners work in UNICOR, the large prison factory with operations in most every federal prison. Here at Fort Dix, UNICOR operates a computer repair factory, a factory that refurbishes toner cartridges, a factory that manufactures mailbags. . . .
>
> Besides the factory, prisoners may be assigned to Central Maintenance Services (CMS), where they are responsible for performing electrical, plumbing and construction services. . . . They may be assigned to food services, where they will prepare and serve the food or clean. . . . Prisoners may work for landscaping, education, health services or they may be assigned as clerks or orderlies who perform janitorial services.
>
> A prisoner needs the small amount of money he earns ($25 a month) to purchase not only "luxury" items, like food and athletic clothing. But he also is required to purchase his own cosmetics, aspirins, stamps, telephone credits, and other items necessary to live in prison. Strict rules prohibit prisoners from "conducting a business" or "providing

anything of value to another inmate," but many prisoners . . . disregard these rules and perform services for other prisoners, like ironing or cleaning rooms. . . .

Programs

. . . several programs begin after 7:30 a.m. Classes . . . to earn their high school equivalency certificates; some courses . . . from a local community college; arts and crafts programs . . . offered by other prisoners; psychology counseling services begin at this time, also.

Call-out Sheet

. . . the prisoners must formally enroll (for programs). . . . The prisoners will be placed on a call-out sheet, which enables them to leave their housing unit or job detail to access the program.

Pass System

If a prisoner wants to leave the housing unit after 8:00 a.m., but is not on the call-out sheet and not scheduled to be working at that time, he must request a pass from the unit officer. The pass authorizes the prisoner to walk around the Fort Dix compound, to participate in education or recreation activities, or to sit at one of the tables outside (in the yard). If a prisoner moves to one of these areas without a pass, he may receive a disciplinary infraction for being "out of bounds."

B. A PRISONER VIEW ON WORKDAY AT JACKSON PRISON

During the era (1972–1995) when Pell grants were available to state prisoners, an inmate who had completed the GED could get a "workday" assignment that involved going to vocational trade school during the day and prison college at night and on weekends.

Prisoner Essay #60

Daily Life in Prison—One Day

As I awake, I feel the presence of other people around me. I realize where I am. I close my eyes and pray for it to only be dream, but know it's real. I'm in prison!

I start my day out by getting up at 5:30 a.m. to clean up by washing my face and brushing my teeth. As I walk down the long housing-unit hallway, I see others doing the same.

I enter the bathroom and see others standing over little sinks, staring into mirrors that are scratched and distorted. The floor is usually wet by this time, glistening with water.

I finish up and return to my bed, which is just big enough for one person. I sit on my bed and look around, my eyes are finally coming to rest on my desk. I see my cigarettes and coffee cup sitting within easy reach right beside my TV. I get my coffee cup and walk down the long hallway to where the hot water is waiting. I return and make my first cup for the day and smoke my first cig.[1] The day has begun.

Next comes breakfast. They call over the P.A. and tell us its time to eat. As I approach the set of double doors I already know what's on the other side of them—a long walk to the chow hall. I walk out the door and the fresh air hits me in the face. I walk down the sidewalk until I pass the gun-tower and come to a road that takes me past the school, church, quartermasters and finally I am at another set of doors that takes me into the chow hall.

As I go through the doors I always notice a foul smell, which is usually coming from our food. The chow hall is a big room with lots of tables for us to sit at after we have been served. There is a dividing rail to make up two separate feeding lines off to the right of the room (I go through this three times a day).

I return to my housing unit until they take a body count. At 8:00 a.m. count is clear for us to go on the yard if we don't have a work assignment.

The yard is on the other side of the camp. There is a softball field with a walking track around it, and a weight pit for us to work out in. Off to the side is a store, horseshoe pits, tennis, handball and basketball courts, phones, picnic tables and bleachers for us to sit on. Yard lasts until 10:45 a.m. at which time we return to our units for count.

After lunch, I go to school down at the auto shop where I am studying to be an auto-mechanic.

The auto shop is a big building on the outside, but as you step through the door it becomes real small, due to the fact that there are five cars, one tractor, and a van inside it, not counting all the tools and car parts. The first thing you notice is the strong smell of gas and oil as you enter the building. There is a tool room where we get the tools of the trade, and right beside the tool room is the classroom where you can look up info in the books that are on desks and chairs if you want to do some studying.

After auto shop I then return to my housing unit to pick up my book for college and return to the classroom for college and return to the chow-hall for dinner. They clear count at 4:45 p.m. and I am off to school for the final time of the day.

As I approach the small one-story building, I wonder, what is in store for me today inside the little school.

I enter the school to walk down a hallway with classrooms on both sides of the hall until I come to my final destination (a prison college English Class).

As I enter the room the first thing I see is the smiling, cheerful face of my teacher standing beside her desk greeting her students as they enter, that is if she isn't too busy helping a student out already. You would notice all the desks facing the front of the room where the teacher desk sits. There are three rows of lights on the ceiling, and a bookcase on the far side wall, cabinets on the near side of the room and carpet on the floor. Behind the teacher's desk is a blackboard so she may write down some learning tips. As the end of class nears, I know that I will soon be back at my desk doing the college homework that she gives us for the day.

Now class is over and I head back to the unit and my confined area called home. We have a recreation room ("rec room"), where we have a pool table, weight machine, TV and card tables for us to pass the time. If a person like me, who is enrolled in prison college, can ever find time away from his college homework, which usually takes until about 10:00 p.m., by then I just want to lay back on my little bed and watch some TV or read a good book until I fall off to sleep, because I know that I have to wake up and do the same thing all over again.

What I am trying to say is that one day is just like the next and one day just leads into the next with very little difference between the two.

There have been no workday details that involved attending and studying for prison college classes since prison college was eliminated, so when these prisoner students in the 2005 Fall volunteer post-GED workshop at Gus Harrison Prison (Adrian, MI) wrote short essays on their "Daily Routine" they do not talk of prison college.

Prisoner Essay #61

I'm the Night Shift Laundry Man

My day starts late, sometimes after 2:00 pm. When yard is called, I have about two hours to sit outside or to use the phone, I always look forward to calling my two sons and their mom, sometimes the conversation with their mom doesn't end as peaceful as I would like it to. I have a problem with saying the wrong things.

After we lock down for the night I start work at 10:30 p.m. I'm the laundry man, I do laundry for most of the prisoners in my unit. The job is very dirty with a smell that no one would like. After hanging all the clean laundry bags on the inmate doors I head in for bed at about 4:00 a.m.

—⚒—

Prisoner Essay #62

Brown Snowman

Late in the midnight hour it began to snow, as if thick cotton balls were being dumped out of a sack from the sky. I think: "I hope it all melts before the night is over." Watching it snow for a couple hours I fell asleep. I was in my comfort zone when, suddenly, my cell door "broke" with a clank and I was awakened by a loud voice saying all yard crew workers "suit up" for snow duty. I sat in my bed and looked out my window, noticing that the snow was all over the place like spilled flour over a black kitchen table. I hurried and put all of my gear on, starting with the longest and state blues, and then with the full-length brown body suit for winter outdoor work that I called the guerilla suit. I hated doing this, only because of the hours, and this particular day I was awakened at 3:30 a.m. My job is shoveling snow.

—⚒—

Prisoner Essay #63

I Do My Job

To start my day off at 0245 is not the way I would choose, but there is a job to be done and it is my responsibility to do it.

I am a laundry man—six bags into the washer, hot for whites, cold for colors. Then there are the complaints—my favorite part of the day—because it means that someone is just as angry as I am. The biggest complaint is my clothes ain't dry. But it's a part of the job. Everyday is almost the same. There are, however, those days when someone's laundry is lost, and it is an all-out investigation as to where the laundry might be . . . another six bags into the washer, another six bags in the dryer, another six bags returned to their owners, and another two complaints. But, at the end of the day, everyone is happy because their clean laundry is there to put on after a shower. And not one thank you. This is my daily routine.

—⁓—

Prisoner Essay #64

Work Keeps Me Motivated

I became certified in custodial maintenance and blood-borne pathogens in 1992. Since then, no one will pay me for the professional job that I perform. For example: I clean doorknobs, windows, sweep, mop, wax and clean floors. Whenever I work, it's not that I'm trying to take over someone else's job, but I just do the best job possible as if any residents or thing belongs to me. And this is one of the things I've learned since being incarcerated and I prefer to do: that is work!!! Also, work keeps me motivated. It doesn't matter if you do your job or not because I will help you if you like me to.

P.S. (water fountains, showers, etc.)

—⁓—

Prisoner Essay #65

Trash Man and Prisoner's Rep

Around 4 a.m. hygiene time I just roll out of bed—a half-hour to yard. I rush to get ready and get to the weight pit for two hours—then back in to shower, sleep, lunch time and time for work. I empty all the trash cans in the housing unit, wash off the sinks, clean the shower and mop the floor work. I'm done until 9:30 p.m., then I do the same. In between this time I advocate prisoners' issues as I am the elected non-white black representative. I am given a list of issues that I must sort through as I am the mediator for prisoners to guards, all the way up to the Warden. I answer as many of the questions I can from personal knowledge, and discard some matters, and list valid problems for the other representatives to review as a whole. And then we select the ten most important issues to submit as our agendas. I also sit as the non-whites inmates benefit fund member, me and another prisoner. We are in charge of all the prisoner-benefit funds that are generated from commissary sales, photos, pop can returns and so forth. We have to make sure funds are distributed properly.

NOTE

1. Smoking was later banned inside housing units in Michigan prisons.

9

—⚒—

Correctional Officers

INTRODUCTION

To understand the prisoner response to correctional officers it is necessary to look at the role of correctional officers (CO's) from two perspectives—that of the Department of Corrections (DOC) and that of the prisoner.

The primary mission of any DOC is "care and custody," to keep prisoners safe and absolutely secure while completing their sentence. The correctional officer trainee is usually required to spend time at the DOC Academy learning how-to-do-it training—techniques of cuffing, handling prisoners, pistol practice, riot control, officer ranks and duties, some legal training and supervision techniques. A few community college courses are sometimes required, such as client relations, prisoner psychology, criminology, prisoner legal rights and sociology. Correctional officers are taught to attend to the prisoner primarily with methods of control.

For the prisoner the personal relationship between prisoner and CO is uppermost. While the prisoner's personal safety, sometimes even his life, may depend on the CO's subduing another enraged, unruly prisoner, yet apart from technical control skills, the CO "should have compassion." The prisoner wants to be seen, and treated as a fellow human being—with understanding, a certain empathy, dignity and respect—one who has made a mistake, true, but still the same fellow human as the correctional officer.

During the period in which the prisoner essays for this book were written (1981–2005) the prisoner population was always increasing and pressure to bring in more correctional officers was constant. In order to meet the DOC's recruitment needs, qualifications were lowered. The Michigan community college requirements were, for instance, reduced from five courses completed before hire, to two courses completed within eighteen months after hire.

Recruiting descriptions, of course, always accentuate the career's positive points (good pay, fringe benefits, many openings, job security), avoiding the negative (often overwhelming boredom, uninteresting, and conforming). It helps to have served in the U.S. armed forces to be hired. Because prison guards are part of state civil service, some people enter correctional officer work looking to transfer out, after a few years as a guard, to other state employment. Others leave corrections and go to the local police or sheriff's departments or private security work. A commonly held view by the public is of one prisoner accountable to a single "guard," a sturdy figure seated somewhere just outside the prisoner's cell, complete with a ring of jingling cell keys on his belt.

To the contrary, over a single day, a prisoner may be in contact with—that is, be monitored by, show ID to, verify pass—with several CO's, perhaps ten or more. So the day is structured by correctional-officer contacts. A common view of prisoners reflecting on CO's is a wish that, before beginning their DOC position, the officer-too-be could spend observational time in prison "walking in the prisoner's shoes" to gain increased understanding.

CORRECTIONAL OFFICER JOB DESCRIPTION

A description by a woman correctional officer from the website www. au-badge.com follows.

> I have worked for the Tennessee Department of Correction since 2000. As a Correctional Officer, my duties involved direct inmate supervision. In the housing unit (or "guild" as they are called at my facility) I was assigned to on any particular day, it was my responsibility to insure that the inmates were fed, and made it to all appointments or scheduled activities. It was also my duty to perform routine random cell searches for contraband, and to correct (or prevent, if possible) any violation of state or institutional policy through the use of observation, verbal warning, work sanction, written disciplinary report, or in some instances, physical force.
>
> As a Correctional Corporal (my rank since 2001), I became an entry-level supervisor. My primary duties were supervising Correctional Officers and supervising/controlling the movement of inmates outside their Guilds. I made sure that all COs knew that they could call on me or any supervisor for assistance if needed, and I offered one-on-one counseling and guidance when I observed an obvious need. I also performed interim and annual job

PART A CORRECTIONS PRISON PERSPECTIVE: INFORMATION AND RECRUITMENT MATERIAL

Image and Recruitment

- Exam #4012: Entry-Level Security (Corrections Officer and Forensic Security Aide)
- Exam #4081: Corrections Supervisors (State Employees only—Assistant Resident Unit Supervisor, Corrections Security Inspector, Corrections Shift Supervisor and Resident Unit Manager)
- Exam #4091: Corrections Resident Services (State Employees only—Corrections Resident Representative, Corrections Security Representative, Corrections Transportation Officer and Special Alternative Incarceration Officer)
- Exam #9031: Supervisors (Office Supervisor, Departmental Supervisor, Physical Plant Supervisor, Electrician Supervisor, Janitor Supervisor and more supervisory jobs)

For these jobs, the Department of Civil Service administers an exam, and maintains an applicant pool that state agencies utilize when they have vacancies.

For the remaining classifications, a vacancy-driven process is in place. Applicants must apply for each vacancy they are interested in applying for.

Employment Restrictions

An applicant who has been convicted of a felony cannot be hired, in accordance with Public Act 140 of 1996. In addition, no applicant can be hired who has pending felony or misdemeanor charges (includes deferred sentences), or who has a controlled substance violation in any jurisdiction, including military controlled-substance-related discharges. In addition, an applicant who has been convicted of any misdemeanor shall not be eligible for employment until one year after satisfactorily completing any sentence imposed, including probation. Also, an applicant who has been convicted of domestic violence cannot be hired into any position which requires the possession or use of weapons or ammunition. Any new applicant hired into a position by the Department of Corrections must successfully pass a drug screen.

For more information regarding employment with the Michigan Department of Corrections, please contact:

Michigan Department of Corrections Recruitment Section
(517) 334-6775
(Requirements for Employment in Michigan at: www.michigan.gov)

The Michigan Department of Corrections is an equal employment opportunity employer.

performance evaluations on the COs assigned to me. Otherwise, I stayed out of the way so the COs could do their jobs.

From a February 15, 2005 story, "Lock Up A Corrections Career," in *Decision Times*, journalist Jessica Lawson describes how "Good-paying jobs in jails, prisons often go first to former military." She writes:

LOCK UP A CORRECTIONS CAREER

Jessica Lawson

A military background—with its discipline, structure and regulation—fits neatly with the work environment found in jails and prisons, said Florence Schrauben, recruitment manager for the Michigan Department of Corrections.

"We're a paramilitary environment," she said. "Those who have been in the military understand that."

To that end, Schrauben said the department often goes to job fairs throughout Michigan that are sponsored by veterans groups.

Corrections-officer salaries vary widely, depending on whether the facility is privately run or is operated by government on a county, state or federal level.

A study by the U.S. Department of Labor's Bureau of Labor Statistics put the average annual earnings for corrections personnel in 2002 at $32,670, with the middle 50 percent of this work force segment earning between $25,950 and $42,620. The lowest 10 percent earned less than $22,010, while the highest 10 percent made more than $52,370 a year.

Pay aside, ex-military people interested in careers in corrections should consider other benefits. Many corrections officers also get health coverage, vacation and sick leave, uniforms and, depending on whether their facility is government-run or private, pensions and 401(k) retirement savings plans.

"Corrections facilities are small cities," Sondervan said. And, as with actual cities, there are many jobs to be had within their walls, from social workers, teachers and health care to maintenance, warehouse and food service. . . . Most positions in corrections are those perhaps most commonly associated with the field: corrections officers—the people with uniforms, guns and clubs who provide security and keep prisoners in line.

Michigan applicants need only have a high school diploma to be hired, but within 18 months on the job, they must have completed fifteen college semester credits in a human-services-related field such as criminal justice, psychology or corrections. . . the Michigan corrections department promotes from within, so advancement is likelier for those who pursue advanced education beyond the required fifteen credits.

Education aside, there are other ways to make a good impression on those who have the ability to promote you. Some suggestions:

- Seek out a variety of jobs within your facility, or rotate/transfer to other facilities.
- Become multi-talented. Learn a variety of different sub-skills.

- Seek out opportunities to go to ACA conferences, Sondervan said, and take advantage of the opportunities for training that are offered in your county or state.
- Ask your warden to be a mentor or to appoint you a mentor.

"If you do those kinds of things, the promotions will take care of themselves," says Bill Sondervan, director of professional development for the American Correctional Association.

[From: www.armytimes.com/story.php?f=1-292313-599975.php]

TYPICAL PRISONER EXPERIENCES AND VIEWS

A Typical Prisoner's Daily Contact with CO's

Let's walk through a particular day with one prisoner. We'll call him Joe. What correctional officers (CO's) does he meet during this single long workday?

After having his cell door electronically unlocked about 5:30 a.m. (CO in Control Center), Joe walks downstairs to take a shower (monitored by shower CO), dresses, walked downstairs to door of cell block where he shows prison ID to officer (block CO), walks on path to chow hall (passing yard CO), takes tray, food, sits at a table somewhere (two or more chow CO's). From chow, Joe heads down another path to the auto-mechanics class, showing his prison ID and detail for the class at the door (vocational training CO).

Class over, he retraces his steps—to chow for lunch and back to his cell for a count (same COs as morning, still on same shift).

After yard time for an hour after lunch (showing pass to unit CO at door, then yard CO monitoring yard), Joe returns to study in cell until chow time. Now he sees the same correctional officer duty stations, but there is another shift (3–11 shift) on duty, and so these are different officers. Then, after chow, back to cellblock for books, (show ID and detail), then to evening college class. Again, showing ID and detail at door of school building, (school officer CO). Class over, Joe retraces his steps, returning to cell for count, stopping to show his ID to the second shift officers. He may want to use the phone (phone CO) or buy something at the prison store (store CO). Finally, lights out and door locks (unit control room CO).

So, in the course of a workday, then, the average prisoner makes official contact with correctional officers at least ten times—often the same officer when coming and going, sometimes with different officers on different shifts. The important thing to realize is that the balance of power in all cases is weighted toward the officer. The correctional officer can reprimand, or punish by issuing a ticket. There are published rules and, in exceptional cases, a prisoner grievance against the officer may be feasible.

But other than the rare instance, the prisoner is essentially powerless. The prisoner is so vulnerable to the correctional officer he must accept the reprimand or ticket without comment.

Thus, the onus of self-control falls almost entirely on the prisoner. For instance, if a correctional officer "gets up on the wrong side of the bed," or if things go wrong in the officer's homelife, the CO may easily be inclined to take his anger or frustration out on the prisoner. And this does happen, as noted by prisoners in their essays.

Of course, correctional officers are trained "not to take any guff" from prisoners. On the other hand, as the prisoner in Essay #66 (below) says:

> They come in (the officers) with a mindset that it's us against them. Or, every convict is trying to con them. Or, they're convicts, they are the bottom of the barrel—why should I treat them with dignity or respect? They are scum. They've got or deserve everything that comes to them.

On the other hand, if the prisoner is inclined to become irritable and lose his temper, he may, and usually does, end up with a ticket and punishment time "in the hole." With contact with so many correctional officers each day, over many months and years, it is hard to *not* get a "ticket" during a stay in prison!

Actual Prisoner Opinions of CO's

Coauthor Bill Tregea taught "Advanced Skills Training and Reentry" classes at Michigan's Gus Harrison Prison in Adrian, Michigan. These reentry workshops, taught from 2003 to 2005, were for level-two prisoners, some of whom would be returning to the community within a year. In addition to providing information to the prisoners about their eligibility for Pell grants, once released, details about community college programs and discussing reentry issues with them, he asked them to write a short essay on "What They Would Say to Correctional Officers."

PRISONER ESSAYS

Prisoner Essay #66

Where Would You Be If People Didn't Give You a Second Chance?

I really don't see how a change in treatment of prisoners will be made by staff unless they actually have done some time, which probably isn't likely, because in order to obtain such a job, you would probably have to have a clean record. Or another aspect of understanding is to have had or have a loved one incarcerated.

But they come in (the officers) with a mindset that it's "us against them." Or every convict is trying to con them. Or they're convicts, they are the bottom of the barrel. Or, "Why should I treat them with dignity or respect? They are scum. They've got or deserve everything that comes to them."

The bottom line is, people have to have compassion for other people. They (the officers) have to understand that all people make mistakes. The majority of the prisoners I've come in contact with are remorseful and truly sorry about the crimes they've committed. So they deserve another chance. What would you do or where would you be if people didn't give *you* a second chance?

The officers also have to have good people skills. They should be made to develop them before graduating. I've noticed that their mentality is one way. Their way. There is no form of compromising among inmates and officers. And understanding is the best thing in the world.

—⁓—

Prisoner Essay #67

Potential Guards Should Understand Prison before They Take the Job

I am a father of five children—three girls, two boys—single, never been married, and I am serving "ten months to two years" and "ten months to fifteen years" concurrently here.

But as for a criminal justice student, I am not sure if they'd be able to relate to those of us in prison for the fact that, unless they are placed in these situations, so to speak, watching films and reading textbooks are okay for knowledge—but real-life experience is totally different than school books. Although this book our essays are going into (*The Prisoners' World*) may be helpful in the sense of getting an idea of what real life in the prison system is, the fact is that prison is *hard*.

As I have said, "textbooks are okay," so are films. But, to get the real picture, you'll have to spend time in a prison, more than a usual one-time prison tour. I believe that correctional duty training should consist of at least one tour of different level prisons from camps to level-six facilities every two to three months for at least one year to get the real feel for what goes on inside Michigan's prisons. If you do this, you'll probably be surprised at how many students may have a change of heart on their choice of career.

Back in the past you'll probably remember that high schools had career day and some students went to work with their parents to see if they might be interested in that occupation or that field of expertise. So, this is what they should do with the correctional duty student. Theory is good but hands-on experience is best.

—∭—

PROFESSIONAL TREATMENT AND CORRECTIONS

We have described the prison correctional officers: "people with uniforms, guns and clubs who provide security and keep prisoners in line." There are other state Department of Corrections employment roles in the "small cities" that are corrections facilities, including social workers, teachers, health care professionals, maintenance, warehouse and food service.

In particular, criminal justice students should know about several of the more professional treatment and corrections roles that are available either through promotion or through academic credentials. For instance, all the prisoners who have written essays in this book were facilitated in getting out of their housing unit and over to the school building for their "education detail" through the work of the prison's "Special Activities Director." The role is frequently carried out by a person with a bachelor's degree in criminal justice. This is the person who negotiates with the prison administrative staff to arrange for classes taught by prisoners teaching other prisoners, and approves volunteers coming into the prison and offering special classes or workshops. This role may help coordinate other special activities such as sports, weight lifting contests and hobby crafts. During the prison college years (1972–1995) the Special Activities Director helped facilitate the in-prison college program.

The career step for a regular correctional officer's next move up is to become an "Assistant Resident Unit Supervisor" (ARUS). Typically, this promotional step requires completion of the bachelor's degree. After being a Assistant Resident Unit Supervisor, the next step is to become a "Resident Unit Manager" (RUM). Moving further up the administrative ladder, there are typically two or three "Assistant Deputy Wardens" (ADW) supervising functional areas of the prison; and an "Inspector," who works with the Warden to oversee all operations. Finally, there is the Warden, who supervises the entire prison operation and maintains liaison with the community and the headquarters of the state Department of Corrections in the capitol city.

There are other professional roles. There are usually one or more "Correctional Counselors." This role may require that one be working toward completion of the bachelor's degree. The Correctional Counselor does not, however, do much "professional counseling" or therapy but, rather, operates as a communications functionary, receiving communications from prisoners and *processing* their requests and needs through the prison bureaucracy.

Truly professional treatment (therapy) and correctional counseling involves the availability of a psychologist—someone who has received a Masters in Counseling degree or a social worker with the Masters in Social Work (MSW) degree. Not every prison has such professional counseling personnel on staff.

Some prisons will be chosen to house more of the older (aging) prisoners and will have a medical wing with a doctor and nurses. All prisons have a chaplain on site, and the services of a legal aid lawyer (who typically visits several prisons during the week).

Michigan has, as of the Summer of 2008, just created its first (and only) Residential Substance Abuse Treatment (RSAT) facility. At that facility there will be professional substance abuse counseling (with therapists who have Masters degrees) running therapeutic communities. Some of the prisoners from around the state's forty-two prisons who have drug addiction problems will be transferred to this single, special facility. Considering that 80 percent of state prisoners have a substance abuse problem and that substance abuse relapse (dirty urine) is the number-one reason for failure on parole, it is unfortunate that there is only one facility for 1,500 out of the 52,000 state prisoners in Michigan.

We have made clear that while 50 percent of prisoners who enter state prison are non-violent, up to 75 percent of prisoners in prison at any one point in time are assaultive and have some conviction for a violent offense in their "jacket" (prison file record). Part of the job of a state prison system is to assign prisoners to mandatory treatment. One such mandatory treatment program is "Assaultive Offender Program" (AOP). And, there are a handful of other such mandatory programs, such as "Sex Offender Therapy," "Anger Management," "Domestic Assault Treatment," and some volunteer-run programs such as "Parenting Skills," "Marriages that Work" and "Picking Better Partners." Typically these programs are contracted out to professional therapists and counselors who run the programs. Prisoners become anxious about the level of professional treatment staffing and availability of these mandatory programs, since the prisoner is often required to have taken the AOP, for instance, (and other mandatory programs) as a condition of being granted parole, but the programs may not be offered in the prison he is currently at. The Michigan MDOC has, as of 2006, begun shifting prisoners who need such therapy to the prisons where the therapy is available.

POSTSCRIPT

A new prisoner has intense fear of the unknown. The new and the old prisoners alike are processed through the steps entering prison—quarantine, classification, assignment. The youthful offender might "act up," the older repeat offender knows the ropes. Once released, being on parole is sometimes known as "the speed trap." Most repeat offenders during the period 1981–2008 return to prison because of failure on parole.

Starting in 2005, the MDOC has tried to operationalize the MPRI approach, starting prisoners right out in Reception and Guidance with a prisoner plan for success after release that follows the prisoner through his (or her) time in prison, but this change is still just getting going as of 2008. This would be a change. During the incarceration binge historical period, as prisoners did their time toward release, it was hard to get needed correctional programs, adequate vocational training, and—once there was the elimination of correctional halfway houses—little support on parole. The sometimes-bitter essays by prisoners about "hating quarantine" may be replaced with appreciation for a prison plan for success, if the Michigan and national prisoner reentry initiatives work out as planned.

Still, even as Michigan plans, through the Michigan Prisoner Reentry Initiative (MPRI), for more success in reentry total (MPRI 2008), state prison population remains at 52,000 in 2008 and its budget and prisoner numbers are expected to grow (CRC 2008). Closing two prisons recently has only meant other Michigan prisons have become more crowded as prisoners were transferred in. Prisoners sitting in cells who have a drug problem may now, as of the Summer of 2008, be transferred to a new, entire prison facility devoted to therapeutic community drug treatment at the Cooper Street Residential Substance Abuse Treatment (RSAT) facility. Yet, 80 percent of the 52,000 Michigan prisoners have substance abuse problems and Cooper Street facility is the only RSAT facility (serving approximately 1,500) out of forty-two prisons.

Nearly 80 percent of Michigan prisoners enter prison with no job skills (some of them say they "have never had a job" and have been selling drugs or "living off crime" since dropping out of high school) (MDOC 1996; Tunnel 2000). The daily work routine provides little more than entry-level job skill training, at best. There are thirteen prison vocational programs, yet only 25 percent of the 11,000 prisoners leaving Michigan prisons each year have received any vocational training.

Correctional officers, according to prisoners, should understand the prison and the prisoner, yet under pressure to add new guards to its already large staff, the expanding Michigan prison system has *reduced* the community college requirements for new officers.

There are sincere efforts from Michigan's current governor, Jennifer Granholm, and Director of Corrections, Pat Caruso, and her Field Operations and Research Director, Dennis Schrantz, to apply evidence-based practices that work to prison reentry. The MDOC, as of the summer of 2008, is going through a lot of organizational culture change. A lot is now riding on the Michigan Prisoner Reentry Initiative to improve success in reentry, reduce recidivism and save money. Entering "the prisoners' world" introduces new prisoners to a new incarceration world. The orientation, cells, daily work routine and daily interaction with correctional officers creates an "inward" and increasingly preoccupying "prison world"—an experiential world to which the prisoner becomes accustomed. The prison self can become immersed in this world and lose contact with "the real world."

IV

—ꟷ—

PORTRAITS OF
THE PRISON SELF

INTRODUCTION

We've presented descriptions and prisoner essays on entering the prisoners' world: the ride from jail, orientation, staff problems finding bedspace, prisoner's view of their cells, daily work routine and interactions with prison correctional officers. After he has a cell assignment and work detail, and knows how to attend required correctional programming, and has the routines of chow, yard, recreation and housing unit life down—the prisoner begins to "do time."

Once duly incarcerated, and thus "settled into" the prisoners' world, the prisoner increasingly adopts the "ways of the prison" and sees his *self* and self-reflection from within the prison context. Of course, prisoners are kept busy in prison, and thus their prison workday routines, prison programs and prison free time encapsulate their identity within "prison life."

Prison free time and classes they may take, however, can create small "alternative worlds" on inside-prison culture. When prison college was available (1972–1995) prisoners had the "alternative community" of the prison college classrooms, complete with teachers to talk with, a college office with a college clerk to hang out with for a moment, a computer lab, a prison college library, a writing lab—but that all disappeared in 1995.

Chapter 10 describes other ways prisoners spend their free time. Some prisoners write poetry and a few write stories, often attempting to create prison literature about, and from, a prisoner perspective. As the "ways of the prison" sink into the prisoners' outlook, religion can take hold. There is prison religion—from the Native American sweat lodges to the African American Baptist (gospel singing) meetings, to earnest prison black Muslim conversions. Some attention is paid to personal growth—the "self work" necessary to improve or alter self-concept. Some do cell cooking.

There becomes "each other" as a prison way of relationship and subculture. Guys' "buddy up," women create "families." We've mentioned the problem for offenders with long sentences, but who will get out in a few years, sustaining an effort, in their self-concept, as a "going to go straight self" while meeting and interacting with others in the yard—where the "yard is the street." So, "getting into the mix" in the yard can lead to "trouble," since there are more "weird people" in the yard (Owen 1998:83). The prison yard social pull and tug between personalities, gangs and social statuses tends to reinforce criminality. Once inside, away from the yard, some engage in homosexual life within prison.

Chapter 11 "The Homosexual Prisoner" describes consensual male and female homosexuality, as well as the more troubling reality of violent homosexuality and sexual victimization. Coauthor Larmour describes teaching prison college classes in "Block Five" (an Ad Seg Unit) at Jackson Prison with a class full of "couples."

Then there is also other prison deviance, such as drugs and contraband as types of activity around which there may be some excitement and an identity as a "player" within the joint. Chapter 12, "Drugs and Contraband," describes the issue of what is contraband in prison.

Thus, the prison self deepens into an almost comfortable and familiar "prisonization"—a total immersion in prison culture that loses contact with the "real world." When, finally, for most (95 percent of prisoners return to society), the prisoner get near his release time (called "getting short"), he becomes anxious since he is now going to reenter "the real world." The time spent becoming comfortable and familiar with the prison life now makes it very hard to "make it" in the now unfamiliar mainstream culture on the outside. A lot of time has been lost and a lot of change has happened in the meanwhile on the outside.

10

—m—

Prisoner Free Time

INTRODUCTION

Despite a myth of the lonely prisoner staring at the wall for empty years, as we've described in chapter 7, "Daily Work Routine," prisoners actually have little free time except on weekends.

PRISONERS ARE KEPT BUSY

Everyone is usually required to be out of their cells for most of the day. Prisoners must be signed at each "detail," or activity, for certain hours each day. Correctional officers (CO's) have daily schedules for each prisoner, and prisoners move around to each "detail" over the day. If a prisoner is needed for a prisoner visit, phone call, or to report to an Assistant Deputy Warden's office, or whatever, officers can tell exactly where that prisoner should be at that particular time of the day, and can call him on the CO's walkie-talkie or over the loudspeaker. It is only at super-max prisons with twenty-three hours lockdown that prisoners stare at the wall for empty years.

A prisoner is usually required to either work—at a prison factory, prison laundry, truck repair shop, boiler plant, kitchen, building maintenance, custodial, painting, electrical and so forth—or attend school and a prison program—or both. Prison programs the prisoner may be required to attend can include: Adult Basic Education (ABE), high school general equivalency preparation classes (GED), English as a Second Language

(ESL), Assaultive Offender Program (AOP), Substance Abuse Treatment possibly at a special prison facility often called a "residential substance abuse treatment facility" (RSAT), Alcoholics Anonymous (AA), or Narcotics Anonymous (NA).

Then there are activities that prisoners might want to sign up for by choice, like post-GED workshops, prisoner-taught classes, parenting skills, marriage class, church activities, weightlifting or hobby-craft. Vocational education or skill training may be available. In nearly all states there is currently only a very small budget for the federal Youth Offender Program (YOP) where those twenty-five and under can take a few college class credits. From 1972 to 1995, however, there were prison college Associate of Arts degree classes to complete. Some of these essays were written in prison college classes during that period. Since 1995 the state-funded prison college option has been available in a few states (Ohio, Indiana), and only at a very few prisons in each state, if at all. (In California the only prison college is the Patten University volunteers who run a program at San Quentin prison). As of 2007 Michigan had a federal budget for less than 200 prisoners in the YOP program—out of a prisoner population of 52,000. In Michigan there are severe "politicized" restrictions on any "state appropriations" being spent on prison college (Michigan STEPP 2008).

Other prison programs might include "Reentry" or "Success-on-Parole" workshops for those soon-to-be-released. Beyond these prison-required and prisoner free-time choices, a prisoner may find other ways to get away from the cell. He may have a pass: a pass to go on a visit, a pass to go to the hospital, a pass to spend time in the prison library (usually a very popular place) or a pass to take part in a prison activity like working on the Prison Newsletter, or be part of the very occasional prison sports team to meet with a college from the outside, or a once-a-year weightlifting contest.

Beds must be made and cells neat and shipshape for inspection before leaving in the morning or whenever for any activity. Not being at said scheduled place, arriving late or leaving early, are grounds for being ticketed as "out of place."

Recreation time in the yard—or "yard time"—is scheduled and limited (one to two hours a day). There are only a few minutes during the week to shop for sundries at the minimally stocked prison store (where your few cents an hour at work details can be spent). Usually the limited time in the yard is also the only time that telephone calls may be made. During "yard" prisoners line up at the outside pay telephone booths to make "collect" calls home, for no more than ten minutes each. At certain times of the day a "call" will come over the loudspeaker for "med-line" (pill dispensing). At that time prisoners on medicines go to the Medical Dispensary.

Such regularly scheduled times—yard, store, med-line—are usually announced by loudspeaker heard throughout the prison in the prison blocks, offices, classrooms, at yard and along pathways. Frequent notices are given, such as "attention: yard is now officially open" or "yard is now closed" or "store is open" or "prisoners report back to their cells for afternoon count," or "Prisoner Max Johnson has a visit," or "attention: med-line," and so on.

PRISONERS DO HAVE SOME FREE TIME

So, as we've described, prison life is a pretty busy time. What, then, does the prisoner do with his leftover free time? When a top football or basketball game is on Saturday or Sunday afternoon TV, all TVs in cells and lounges are on! Such broadcast sports is one of the major forms of camaraderie for prisoners, who also follow sports by reading the library newspapers and on TVs and radios in their cells.

As a matter of fact, betting on football and basketball games are probably the "number one" recreational activity in most prisons.

During yard time there is always a softball game in the dirt diamond playing-field. Usually the field is surrounded by a cinder track where walking occurs. At the edge of the yard prisoners will be busy weightlifting and there is a basketball court where shooting baskets is being diligently pursued with perspiration flowing freely. But—only for the hour of yard.

In quiet areas throughout the yard, during this break time, other prisoners are seated at permanent tables talking with friends or yard acquaintances, playing cards, checkers or chess with others, playing guitars and singing, or sitting alone and reading, writing letters or just getting some sun. Of course, in winter, yard is cold and fewer people gather there, preferring to hang out in the block where there is TV or ping-pong.

Indoors, in a small but popular prison library, prisoners read the donated magazines, newspapers and books, which may be checked out. Some may work on legal briefs in the law library. A law library is required in every prison to pursue the right of appeal.

There may be hobby workshops such as woodcarving, jewelry making or leatherwork. Prisoner-made products can be sold to relatives and visitors in a craft store usually located in the prison lobby.

In fact, any skill that can be turned into a small moneymaking project to supplement a prisoner's less-than-meager income is always sought.

Prisoners with minimum paralegal skill or with college credits as a paralegal hire themselves out—or contribute "pro bono" as "jailhouse lawyers"—to work with prisoners on preparing legal briefs to try to get an appeal hearing. Occasionally one of these briefs might be pretty good, and their case will make it into appeals court.

Prisoners with electric know-how fix appliances, lamps, radios and television sets. Sometimes there are prisoner-taught classes in the school building on electricity, math, Spanish or how to make a business plan.

Some inmates help other inmates to learn to draw, paint, do acrylic or to indulge in any kind of hobby.

Prisoners translate informational material, read letters or write letters for other prisoners

Inmates crochet woolen caps, bed socks, scarfs and sweaters for themselves and, usually, by request, for others.

Prisoners sew and repair items of clothing by hand, patch jeans, darn socks, mend tears. Many buy sewing machines and (depending on the rules of the prison) make "custom" shirts and special items for other prisoners on order. "Designer" dresses made to order for prison "drag queens" are especially popular and bring raves from other gays or homosexuals when shown off on prison paths or paraded in the yard.

As prison college teachers, we have at times assigned prisoners to write a journal. Occasionally, also, a prisoner will show us a poem or a story they have written. We have some prisoners who have written about their identity, about their personal transformation, and about cooking up food in their cell. These stories follow.

AUTHOR'S REPORT #4

The Prisoner Student: Participation in an Alternative Community

From 1972 to 1994 prisoners were eligible for Pell grants and, fueled by this federal money, 770 prison college programs were up and running in the United States. But, in 1994 the U.S. Congress ended Pell grant eligibility for prisoners. Nearly all of the primarily community college Michigan prison college programs ended. However, in Michigan a court order kept two prison college programs going until May of 2000.

Over a twenty-five-year period of prison college and volunteer class teaching, starting in 1981, both coauthors have seen the nation's massive prison system quadruple. We've explained that the main cause of this unprecedented growth has been the still-mandatory sentence "war-on-drugs" laws and an incarceration rather than a harm-reduction strategy.

Alternative Community

As teachers, our experience of this war-on-drugs prison buildup was an *in-the-classroom experience.* It is important for the reader to understand that, for prisoners, the school buildings that, during the day had GED classes, had, during the period 1981–2000, prison college classes going in the afternoon, evening and weekends that were prison college program classes. The prisoners themselves had an opportunity for an *in-the-prison college program experience*—college classrooms, college halls, college computer labs and college support offices were a "zone" that became an "alternative community" for these prisoner students over these three decades of the prison college era. So, during the 1972 to 2000 period, in Michigan, in addition to experiences in Reception and Guidance, cells, daily work routines, yard, chow and interactions with correctional officers at break from the unit for yard, chow, med-lines or work details, some roughly 10 percent of state prisoners were enrolled in post-secondary correctional programs in the "school building" of their prison.

These prison college programs had their own "space" or place in the prison; a set of rooms set aside for the prison college program which became, as mentioned, an *alternative community* for the prisoners: a place to hang out and a place to do college work where, for a few hours a day, perhaps two or three times a week, they could "try on" different roles, become "normal" in the role of student and begin affiliating themselves as a student. Alternative community provides a space for personal transformation: teachers don't judge, but ask "what do you know?" and "how will you do on the exam?"

Since May of 2000 there have been no accredited prison college programs in Michigan. However, volunteer classes can also offer, on a more modest scale, a sense of "alternative community" inside the classroom in the prison. When leading a volunteer class the instructor creates a personal space during a two-hour session—a space for growth: to educe, to bring out potential. Education is forward-looking, open—and thus an alternative community of personal transformation.

In this author's report we present several settings of personal expression and growth: English II prison college class assignments, such as journal writing and poetry, Mexican-American and Native American prisoner/ students in a college class expressing their culture (and the international drug trade culture) and stories of personal transformation brought back from the cell to a volunteer class and shared with others in a social science and personal writing group.

Prisoners' Journals

Most prisoners say prison is a place they want to forget, not remember. Not many journals or diaries are kept. Where you might find a journal, however, is at a desk in a cell occupied by a student enrolled in prison college who is taking an English course.

An assignment to keep a daily journal is frequently used by English teachers everywhere. As they usually explain to their students, journal entries should include not just the routine happenings of the day as recorded in a diary. They should also articulate the writer's deeper thoughts and philosophies about life, as well as creative ideas, descriptions, cogent paragraphs and so forth that might be used in a future essay or story.

The journal's practical purpose, of course, is to give students practice in writing and encourage a previously untapped, unused or unrecognized flow of creative ideas. It also provides students the opportunity to reflect on their lives and goals. Coauthor Larmour regularly taught an English II class where one assignment was to keep a daily journal.

One prisoner/student exposes us to some sensitive and beautifully reflective writing by a man long used to such lonely exercises. He is a prisoner serving a life sentence. Like other lifers who are now considered nonviolent, not a threat to other prisoners or staff by the MDOC, he is allowed to take prison programs, and so is enrolled in a prison college class.

He was caught up in the inner city's crack cocaine epidemic. Due to the addictiveness and sudden violent unfamiliar emotions crack cocaine unleashes in a frequent user, he committed a murder he cannot even remember. As police will testify, such an event in crack addicts is not uncommon. He was given a life sentence.

One can only marvel at how this lifer has maintained a level head after all the years of the pain of addiction, prison, regret and remorse. Here are two excerpts:

A late 1990s fall day:

> I think that for people in prison one of the heaviest forms of suffering we experience is loneliness. You can see it in the way we cling to anyone who offers a little caring and concern. When people come in from the free world to conduct Bible classes, to give musical shows, or any number of things, we flock to them like parched men to water. And those of us who have family or friends outside are constantly trying to wrap them up with strings. We lasso them with guilt and all kinds of emotional obligations to try to keep them near. We seek, in any loving, caring being, salvation from our own sense of emptiness. We are driven by a belief that if only we find someone who'll accept us, forgive us and love us, everything will be alright.

Even though in prison for a life sentence, this writer makes one observation that is shared by some—that if they had not been caught and convicted, they would be dead.

> Time is the invisible enemy of incarceration. Time is slip-siding away like tiny grains of sand falling freely through an hourglass. That's how I see my

life passing before me. An indifferent, cruel, aging time that I can't have back. To live in the moment is all I can do. To live one day at a time brings true meaning to being incarcerated. Although, being locked up can be a strange blessing, had I not been thrown off the merry-go-round of life, I might be dead. For a lot of us, prison was a savior from death. Incarceration is an opportunity to reflect, make better choices and find a new direction at the crossroads. It's a time to empty out the attic of old habits, thoughts and fears. It's a time to fill the empty space with rewards—exciting thoughts, hopes and dreams.

Still, for this prisoner and many others, the memory of crack is strong, even ten years into a long sentence. Our journalist writes: "I was so infatuated with you (crack) that I put you before my mother, my brother, my friends and most of all, before myself."

—◊◊◊—

MEXICAN-AMERICAN PRISONERS

While Latinos number 3.5 percent of the total population, 4.7 percent of them are incarcerated (U.S. Census 2000). Mexican-Americans are a large ethnic group in U.S. prisons and jails, especially in California, Texas and the American Southwest.

Those in prison represent a mixed bag. Some Mexican-Americans are peaceful and nonviolent. They may display a true reflection of their own south-of-the-border culture—gentleness personified, placid, soft spoken, caring for others, such as children and the elderly. Extremely religious, they are faithful churchgoers and observant of religious holidays.

Other Mexican prisoners fall at the opposite extreme—super tough and violent—exemplifying the worst and most dangerous of American barrio street culture. Former gang members, they often end up in super-max prisons where they run prison gangs and are feared even by super cautious guards. Often in and out of prison, they are long familiar with guns, knives and homemade "shivs." In short, approach at your own risk.

Jorges was one of the prison college clerks in a minimum-security prison in Jackson State Prison. He was a prime example of a gentle Mexican-American. Everyone knew Jorges, the office clerk, and could expect a cheerful wave if he happened to look up from his computer through the big glass window and spotted them in the hallway.

Small, slim and dark, he was a breath of fresh air in a life of constant prison monotony that could get anyone down if they let it. But the prisoners knew that Jorges wouldn't let it. He could always think of ways to bring cheer where there was none. For instance, he always brought cheer and celebration to every holiday, no matter how obscure, and expected his fellow prisoners to do likewise, even if most were not sure what day it was they were celebrating.

All the prisoners counted on Jorges to cheer them up when they had a spell of the pervasive "prison blues," which everyone had every so often.

So it came as a sad surprise when one day the usually cheerful, bubbling Jorges appeared, glum and long-faced, to circulate a poem he had written describing how depressed he felt. As he explained, he himself had the "prison blues." Four of the concluding lines of the blues prose poem are below—Jorges is a "wretched leaf," blown like a leaf in the wind off course, but, finally working his way out of the blues, he has come to the ground:

> Oh mister wind, I feel your push, but for some reason I do not move. Oh mister air, I feel your touch. I feel you vibrate all inside of me. What is going on? What could this mean?
>
> Oh mister light, can you explain? Why can't I breathe? Why do I feel life? Come forth and shine on me so I can see.
>
> Oh blessed life. Look at what I've become! No more a leaf nor a seed, but a sprout of a tree!
>
> Oh blessed life I will ever hold. No more will I drift to the unknown. I have a direction! I know where I lay! No more will I be the same old wretched leaf!

—⚋⚋—

Coauthor Marjorie Larmour notes that an English writing class taught in prison can turn up unknown quantities in every other seat. She reflects on her class.

Take that gentle-talking black guy in row three. Despite his gentle speech and harmless looking ways, his past is violent. He is a two-time rapist.

That handsome white guy in the first row, smartest one in class, ready to explain the macroeconomics problem on the board, or argue politics with the teacher? Again, his past betrays him. He is a four-time recidivist pedophile. Can't stay away from children or prison.

What about those three guys who like to sit together, who laugh and kid each other constantly? Are they quite as cheerful and benign as they seem? Don't know. They're each in for murder and serving life sentences. Each killed his wife. All of them are smart, work in the college library and are classed as non-violent, meaning they wouldn't hurt a fly. Now.

On the other hand, the swarthy looking guy seated in the second row, a criminal killer type if I ever saw one, has no prior criminal record at all.

He's in for only one year for the mildest of drug crimes, and writes the loveliest poetry in class.

The student sitting next to him, the one with ugly razor scars on his cheeks, and gums where his front teeth should be, is also a first-time offender. He supports two small children at home and is saving to somehow pay for a dental job in preparation for a job interview when he is paroled next year. So go figure.

Take the thirty-five-year-old Mexican-American prisoner/student sitting quietly, reflectively, in the back row, the one with the typical dark hair, dark eyes, dark complexion and small dark moustache of a Mexican.

He writes knowledgeably and well about smuggling drugs into the United States from Mexico. It's obvious he's been there and done that. Plus he also writes excellent stories about his past, about growing up in Texas near the Mexican border, graphic descriptions of exploring beautiful old Mexican churches when a boy, about summers spent as a teenager on his grandfather's sprawling ranchero in Mexico, with thrilling accounts of wild boar hunts on horseback with bow and arrow.

Then comes the "iffy" part—there are "recollections" of his grandfather issuing orders from his seat in the huge mahogany "don's" chair as he rules over his (apparent) drug trafficking Mexican mob or "family." Loyalty to the death to the "family" is demanded and, like the actual Italian Mafia, orders are disobeyed only with the most dire, cruel and predictable consequences. It is a fate well known to all Mafia "family" members.

Eventually, as we discover from our Mexican student/author, members of the Mexican mob plot against and kill the ruling grandfather, leaving the grandson to exact revenge for the killing in true Mafia style, and how he, the grandson, is now the young killer seeking revenge. An excerpt:

After two years of investigation, I finally found somebody to turn on two of my Godfather's associates. I knew his associates wouldn't pull the trigger themselves, but they would give the order. The two gunmen were from out of town, but I knew where to find them.

I took the two associates to a "secluded" area outside of Tampico. I tied them to a tree and gut shot them both. I wanted them to suffer, to let them know that I kept my word. As I walked away from the tree I heard them yelling at me, "The others will come for you. Saul can't protect you now!" I knew someday they would come for me.

(Later) the gunmen met similar fates. . . .

. . . I walked out the basement door and made my way down the alley. I stopped behind the Chevy Blazer. The Associates never changed the style of vehicle they drove. And they always traveled together. I knew someday they would come get me. I was waiting.

"Open the door and tell that man to come here," I said.

The Associate in the drivers' seat replied, "Please don't shoot."

"Call him over here now. Sixteen hollow points go a long way," I said sticking the gun in his ear.

The driver honked the horn and flashed the lights. The man by the door ran back to the Blazer. As he leaned into the open window I pointed the gun at him and told him to get in the front. I knew someday they would come get me, I was waiting.

I directed the driver to an old abandoned warehouse about thirty miles out of town.

—∿∿—

NATIVE AMERICAN PRISONERS

Many prisoners have probably the next-to-lowest self-esteem in the world.

Their entire self-identity and worth is reduced to a number, a several year sentence and a cell. As citizens, they have no vote and are termed "animals" by the outside world. When released from prison, many of them broke and jobless, they are not permitted to take certain jobs and have little to look forward to except more discrimination as ex-felons.

But when it comes to racial discrimination, the Native American, both in and out of prison, must certainly be low man on the totem pole.

In Michigan, for instance, only 0.6 percent of the state population is Native Americans, yet Native Americans are 1.4 percent of those incarcerated in prisons or jails. This contrasts with an under-representation of whites with 80 percent of the population being white but only 44.6 percent in prisons or jails.

Outside of prison some of the Native Americans who live in high-unemployment reservations live on food stamps, bolstered too often by alcohol. For some it's a ramshackle home on a rundown reservation in the middle of nowhere; and, he is labeled a drunken Indian when he goes into town. Young people from the reservation seeking an advanced education are sometimes snubbed in colleges. For many, dreams of a career or decent life "in the mainstream" are forgotten as they drift back to the warmth and security of the reservation.

And there is a "nugget of truth" in the stereotype of the drunken, brawling Indian who lands in prison, charged with assault in alcohol- or drug-related crimes.

In prison, the Native American is discriminated against. Other prisoners may come from parts of the country where Indians are looked down upon and they bring their long standing prejudice and labeling to prison with them.

The red man feels different and isolated behind bars in the white man's facility and sticks to his own people, ways and customs.

Like in all states, the Michigan Department of Corrections is required by law to allow all religions to conduct weekly services and prayer meetings for prisoners. Native American prisoners conduct a weekly meeting in each facility where they chant, conduct the age-old ceremonies, and repeat the well-known prayers.

The sweat lodge, where Indian men, stripped naked, enter to pray over steaming kettles of water, is a most important part of every Indian village and life. The dome-shaped lodge is constructed of logs and branches, with a fire pit and kettles in the center and door of wood or animal hides to enter. Before ceremonies, water is brought to steaming.

After long demands by Indian prisoners, state Departments of Corrections began allowing their Indian prisoners to construct sweat lodges on certain of its prison properties and hold weekly ritual ceremonies there. No one—prison staff or other prisoner—must be allowed to observe the secret proceedings, however.

Such a sweat lodge, constructed by Indian prisoners at Jackson State Prison, is tucked in the farthest wooded corner of the prison land inside the perimeter fence, the sweat lodge is virtually invisible and, as prison staff and the coauthor will confirm, no one is allowed near.

Personal names are all important to the Native American since one's name encapsulates virtually the whole history of one's heritage. In a sense then, almost like a self-fulfilling prophecy, the name that is given the child serves to almost anticipate the person's future.

This is why, most importantly, the Indian prisoner or student prisoner insists on the Department of Corrections and the schoolteacher getting his name right.

The following brief excerpt written by a Native American prison college student whose MDOC last name was "Bigmeat," describes the real origin of the name in his tribe, how it became misinterpreted as a name, and the importance of handing names down in Indian culture, generation to generation.

The clan name is a part of each Indian nation. It identifies each clan and their role in the making of this way we came by this place.

Together with your own name given to you by your family, it is told to you by your family during your early years and while growing up so that if ever asked "who are you and where are you from" you can tell them in great detail and watch them be amazed at your knowledge of self.

The Cherokee people, a farming people, have different clans.

My family were cattle herders and had a great many head of cattle. One of my ancestors, "Ka loun a hes ki," had large numbers of cattle. All of these animals were not his sole possession but rather a steady supply of meat and milk for the entire tribe.

In the late 1800s, settlers and people of the Christian faith came to the land and introduced the Bible to many of the "savages." It was unheard of for a man of Christian faith not to have a Christian first and last name.

Through English translation the man known as La-loun-a hes ki, meaning "Big Herd," now had the last name, Big Meat. As most of his people were taking to the Christians to get their names, "Ka lou a hes ki" refused to acknowledge this name given to him.

PRISONER POETRY

> If I had the wings of an angel
> Over these prison walls I would fly.
> I'd fly to the arms of my darling
> And there I'd be willing to die.

This mournful prisoner ballad is about as old as walled prisons themselves. And its theme—loneliness, isolation, dejection of the forgotten prisoner—is still with us in the never-ending poetry being turned out by prisoners in today's modern prisons.

Poetry is big in prisons. Fully three columns of any weekly prisoner newspaper may be devoted to poems sent in by prisoners. Some prisoners will read every word avidly, and send responses to be published in the following week's poetry columns. Prison poets will argue and discuss content and poetry technique. Religious poetry can spark heated debate that approaches the violent.

Nationally, several prisons have prisoner newsletters, and there are journals with prisoner writing, both of which often include some poetry in their pages. [Unfortunately, the Michigan Department of Corrections (MDOC) eliminated prison newsletters a few years ago].

However, while poetry is big, prose and storytelling is virtually an unknown art in informal prisoner writings. "Nothing happens around here," they say. "What would I write about?"

Poetry is not taught in prison classes. But in the mind and memory of the prisoner, the imagination goes on—unstructured. Prisoners turn to such unstructured poetry by and for themselves, for their lady friends, and for other prisoners to read. Here is one prisoner student poem:

Prisoner Essay #68

I Study Them from Afar

Once again I am awakened to hopes and dreams
A long time has passed since I have had them.
These are my aspirations, my golden path.

But the question is: Can I follow the path? Or will I be detoured as I am now?
Stuck behind iron bars and steel fences,
This place of shadows and fears, with faces with no identity and noises with no
  shapes.
I hate this place, yet I admire it also
The sadness and sorrow, the hidden pain and tears
One can learn so much from just watching these men
The things they feel are expressed in plain view to all who can see them
And I can see them
I see the beauty of rage and anger, the true vulgarity of hate and resentment
These things help me to grow, as if I were feeding off them.
So I study them from afar, keeping myself safe from my own wretched emotions.

PERSONAL TRANSFORMATION

In the Spring of 2009, coauthor Bill Tregea offered an eight-week "Social Science and Personal Writing" class, an equivalent of a one-credit college class. His students read chapters from an introductory social science book and wrote essays. Instructor Tregea found this Saturday afternoon volunteer class group of twelve prisoner students to be very thoughtful—they had formed as a "self-help" group using the class as a time and place to build up a group discussion, a discussion of personal transformation different than the usual "yard" talk (of how to do crimes better next time). Instead of a dysfunctional stability of honing past practice in criminality, this group was determined to turn the opportunity to be in an "alternative community" offered up by coauthor Tregea's volunteer class into a "counter-narrative" to the yard talk. Here are a few of their insights.

PRISONER ESSAYS BY GUS HARRISON PRISONERS

Prisoner Essay #69

Some from Bad to Good, Some from Good to Bad

For the past fifteen and a half years I've been an inmate in the Michigan Department of Corrections. I've been asked to write truthfully what I have observed, and believe.

Even though we are prisoners, and have long been afraid to face the truth in our own lives, some of us have found the truth by faith through the work of the Holy Spirit. A prisoner held within the boundaries of three fences with razor wire lives in isolation from true friends. There are no true friends among the inmates because they seldom learn to really trust one another. The prison personnel working for the State seldom show any personal interest in the inmate. To them it is merely a job and they tolerate us because we are here. The attitude of everyone is an attitude of mistrust. There is unwillingness on the part of most to really learn what is in an inmate's mind, to try and discover what he truly wants in life, and to help him find a sure and positive answer for the days and years ahead.

Some prison officers come to work just to make life harder for the inmates. They will yell at an inmate, make sarcastic remarks, and treat them as a real lowlife. According to the officer, it's always the inmate's fault. They fail to realize that a lot of inmates are old enough to be their dad, and treating anybody like they do, whether in prison or out, is wrong.

It reminds me of a story of a dog that ran free until it was caught and put in a cage. At this time the owner fed the dog every day, and slowly cut the dog's food in half. Then he began hitting the dog with a stick every other day. Then every day, he would hit the dog. Finally, the dog, after weeks of being hit, bit the man.

It's the same way with a man. You can take away his freedom, you can take away part of his food, as long as he still has friends and family. Now the State is trying to take that away. They tell you who you can and can't call on the phone. They tell you who can and can't visit you. What's next? Are they going to start with who you can and can't write? They don't want you to have any outside contact with people. They say you can have your own clothes, then they are taking them away. They say you can have hobby craft, but you can't order enough to make projects. If you are at one correctional facility they will ride you to another one for no reason other than taking you away from your family. Some inmates will get to five or six different facilities or more in a year, costing the taxpayers millions of dollars a year. Once again, this reminds me of the dog in the cage.

To know that the State believes they can set a man free under such conditions and start on a new road to life is one of the most unrealistic things I have ever seen. My heart reaches out to these men in here. However, many of them have such distorted thoughts toward life, they seem impossible to reach, and yet I know all things are possible. Let me say it again, that I am seeing it work here in prison through the lives of transformed men. Some from bad to good, some from good to bad. This restoration and conforming to a manner of living is far greater than being converted. With this uppermost in our minds, what's next?

We have a complete change of attitude toward the desires of other people, with a willingness and the ability to live as a free man with others. For some reason, the State does not want to restore and prepare men and women who are in prison to live in the free world. For some the understanding of the State's promise is being shaken. What is wrong?

It is quite simple. *We* need to think carefully about future plans because *the State* will do nothing but keep you down. Everywhere you see the State at work, in prisons, asylums, mental hospitals and county jails—it's all the same: lock them up and throw away the key.

I know life on earth is filled with many temptations and many tempting things appear to be good. Then, when it is too late, we find we have gone in the wrong direction. We wonder how we became involved. How could we have done such a thing, when we were trying so hard to determine good from evil.

On the way to health care one morning, as I passed through the door, the officer said "Good Morning." And he used my name. Suddenly, I realized that I had seen this man dozens of times, yet had never noticed him as a person. He knew my name, but I didn't have the vaguest idea of his. I glanced at the name tag on his uniform. "Good Morning Mr. ____," I responded, and tried to think of something else to say to let him know that I was interested in him as a person.

I've had two heart attacks, both in 1996. At that time an officer came to my rescue and saved my life. I'm now at a different facility, even so, there is an officer that asks me daily how I am feeling. Some officers seem to have concern for inmates no matter who they are. Officers should be screened and trained a lot more than what they are. Some officers shouldn't even be working around people, let along working in a prison. A prison should be built for older inmates who cause no trouble. The prison would be cleaner and quieter, and the State would need less security.

They need to take the guns out of young guys' hands and put a diploma in their hands. They need to take the bitterness out of their minds and put a trade there. Give them the help they need so they can become a productive person in society; however, the State doesn't care about inmates. If God can forgive the sinner, then the State should be able to give a man or woman another chance in society.

Prisoner Essay #70

"Prison's Moral Lesson: Become Apathetic"

In my particular writing, the moral is one which is very unique. The pain, the anxiety, the reality is enough to stop the heart. What you will hear will be my interpretation of my accounts of entering prison.

First, on the streets, I was dumb, addicted to dope, so I committed some crimes for which I saw no repercussions. I never, in a million years, would believe I would end up here. I heard of prison, but never *knew* about prison. If you were to have asked whether I would end up in prison, I would have laughed. Then I got arrested. . . .

Then and only then did I realize that I messed up. The phrase "hitting rock bottom" came into play. Just the realization of it made my heart stop. At this point the worst part was to tell my mom what had happened. Then, the prison stories from the county jail . . .

Then the stories of prison from the ex-prisoners were scary at best. The rapes, the stabbings and the "prison sex." This made my time in the county jail become very nervous and uneasy. The fear became so intense, I could barely sleep at night. I couldn't stomach the thought of *me* going to prison. Then came the point where I was to get transferred to "the joint."

This point was tremendously terrifying to me. The skyscraping fences with miles of razor wire. Then the shackled walk through the fenced-in hallway. My stomach drops, my legs give out, I begin to perspire.

Then the intake, the most degrading point of my life. The orientation consists of how to not get HIV/AIDS. Not quite adequate enough for what is to come. The next part was the initiation of what we were about to embark.

As I approached my cell (five stories up), reality struck me like a baseball bat. The cell is fifty years old and small, very small. The only thing you have is yourself. It gives you time to ponder on what is to come next. Then we enter the congregation of all the inmates together.

The life inside differs from the life outside. The inmates become apathetic, showing no emotion. They become cold. Because in here, sympathetic people become preyed upon.

The basis of the experience is a never-ending one. In this situation, your mental comes into play. Your overall awareness of people's *true* colors shines like a light. Everyone in here eats the same food, wears the same clothes, and does the same routines. This allows people to just be them. My emotions are so dulled, when I get out I will be permanently scarred.

It is a place where nobody cares about you, not even the CO's. This place is very petty. This is a place where people get killed for fifty cents.

The moral of my essay is that the way to adapt is to trust no one, and show no emotion.

Prisoner Essay #71

"Outgrow the System?"

I'll never forget the pain and hurt I saw on my family's faces the day the judge sentenced me to fifteen years in a prison cell. As I was being taken out of the courtroom, I glanced over my shoulder and saw the tears running down my kids' faces. It killed me. I lost my heart that day in March of 1998. It's been a nightmare to close my eyes, and dream about promises I couldn't keep. I've been forced to live in a world all of its own. It's been a long, cold-blooded journey that'll never really end until I die.

I live in an eight-by-ten cement cell, there's nowhere to run, nowhere to hide. Survival in here is based on the strength of your heart, and mind. It's a man-made hell: the everyday deaths, rapes, fights and chaos become a part of life.

While locked in this cell, I've sorted out the real from the false: my feelings, my thoughts and actions that consistently resulted in pain, in shame and in isolation. I've come to realize the only way to beat the system is to outgrow it.

We've got to keep in mind that being ex-felons our criminal history is in a database waiting to jump out and bite us in the ass. Then we'll be right back in a cell like a caged dog.

For you that's never been to prison, you'll never know what freedom means—until you've been where I've been and seen what I've seen.

—〰—

PERSONAL GROWTH AND SELF-CONCEPT

In a Summer 2005 seven-week "Going Home" workshop, given at the Gus Harrison correctional facility by coauthor Bill Tregea, prisoner/students discussed the importance of "self-narratives." They read chapter 5, "Making Good: The Rhetoric of Redemption," from the book, *Making Good: How Ex-Convicts Reform and Rebuild Their Life*, by Shadd Maruna (2001).

The prisoners were asked: "What is there about the psychology of human beings that makes personal growth possible?" Below are short comment-essays by prisoners who had briefly reflected on such additional questions as: "Can I change myself?" "Where did I go wrong?" and, "Can I start 'Going Right'?"

Prisoner Essay #72

Human Psychology

A person's background has a lot to do with how a person develops, also it can determine how your life will turn out. However, a good background doesn't mean you'll be successful, it has a lot to do with how much you have learned as an individual. Your life is your own, you have the power to become what you believe you can be.

Everyone makes mistakes, but those who learn from their mistakes are the ones most likely to be successful or show growth by action.

You can be subjected to the wrong lifestyle, people or community. This will place you in a situation to choose your road where some make it, but a lot don't. This is why the statistics of failure are so high.

—⁂—

Prisoner Essay #73

Personal Growth

Psychology is the mind-set of the human being. When the individual starts to know his/her way of thinking and starts to change it for the better, that's when growth starts to form. There are two kinds of knowledge: knowledge of the light (good) and knowledge of the darkness (evil).

"Knowledge of the light" is the knowledge of doing what is right and good for oneself and humanity. "Knowledge of the darkness" is the knowledge of doing evil and wrong for one's self-gain.

When someone has been doing wrong for so long they become master of the darkness and the gain is so rewarding until they get caught; that's when they start to realize themselves for what they are worth and what they have to offer to others.

That's when knowledge of the light comes into play, when you start to realize that you want to do something good, then you start changing the way you think. The more you educate yourself, the more you change for the better.

—⁂—

Prisoner Essay #74

What Makes Personal Growth Possible?

We humans have the ability to "reason" and to "dream." This allows us to see alternatives to our current situations. I think all people want to "do" the right things but don't always know how. Interaction, and life experiences, can allow any and all people to learn. But as humans we also have "desires." If a person "desires" growth and change he can learn from those experiences and interactions.

I am currently in a controlled setting and my activities are monitored and controlled, but my thought processes are still my own. I have been able to learn, and find alternative actions from reading, talking with friends, family and classes like this. In the knowledge of my different actions I am also able to change the way I feel about myself and my future. I am also in "control" of my own dreams and fantasies. No matter what actions are taken from me as a human my thoughts are still my own.

—⚏—

PRISONER CELL COOKING

As almost anyone familiar with prisons or prisoners soon discovers, dislike of prison food is practically unanimous throughout the prison system. Indeed, prison riots have been sparked simply to protest against the chow.

Prison dinner hour comes uniformly early—in most prisons, generally around 5 p.m. One result of this serving hour is that prisoners are able to attend classes, group meetings and ministerial outreach services in the evenings.

One reason for cooking in your cell is the almost universal hatred of the food served at "chow" hall. Prisoners say when they can afford to do it they would simply prefer to skip dinner entirely and cook up something on their own in their cells from items bought at the prison store. Another reason, as prisoners will point out, given the early hour of dinner, without a bedtime snack, it's a long twelve-hour stint between dinner and 5 a.m. breakfast.

Other reasons: Dislike of some menu items, religious sanctions, health diets, a cold or temporary illness.

Whatever the reason, cell cooking is common. Recipes are exchanged and "old faithful" recipes handed down one inmate generation to the next. Coauthor Marjorie Larmour reports on her first thoughts on prison chow—an attempt to be constructive—during her first year of prison teaching.

AUTHOR'S REPORT #5

"A Proposal for Skilled Prisoner Cooks"

Glancing over the weekly menus posted on prison hallway walls and reading off the delicious sounding fare—round steak, baked potato, steak, stuffed pepper, baked beans, homemade pies, ice cream—I thought that I might willingly exchange my hastily wrapped peanut butter sandwich for a free seat at a prisoner table.

I could see prison trucks (after they had gone through the "sally port") delivering fresh meat and green vegetables daily to the kitchen back door. With all this fresh food coming in, obviously, because prisoners complained so much about poor food, something was going horribly wrong in the preparation between truck of meat, cereal and produce and chow table. And the raw foodstuff was not low quality. A look the annual state prison budget for prison food shows more spent per prisoner for food than was spent per-capita for food for dormitory students at Michigan State University (MSU).

And, I reflected, MSU happened to boast a world-renowned School Hotel and Restaurant Management (Institutional Services) that drew chefs from famous restaurants all over the world to recruit their cooking graduates!

I queried the students: "Who prepares the prison food?"

A shrug. "Who knows? They're all prison guys at the bottom of the DOC's prisoner job placement list. The no-brain types who can't get on the waiting list for the factory or paint crew or better-paying jobs. They get kitchen or server or chow hall cleanup. Nobody wants the lousy job."

His neighbor chimed in. "Oh, and level 4 guys in maximum security. They get a lot of KP. Officers assign it so they can keep an eye on them."

"Great!" I thought. Expensive ingredients prepared and served by scruffy bums who never read a cookbook. A sure recipe for turning out garbage.

At this point, early in my prison teacher career, I even went to the time and trouble of drafting a proposal to the prison authorities about how a fine prison college opportunity for a program in food preparation presented itself here.

My plan: In cooperation with Michigan State University, graduate students from the university's Department of Institutional Services would teach prisoners courses in Culinary Arts for credit and the chow hall would be the laboratory. A triple bonus: The university would get a culinary arts internship site, the prison could create skilled cooks who should be able to get good jobs and not return to prison, and the prisoners, for the same budget, could get better fare. Also, the state budget for Corrections would cut costs of wasted food. No more prison food riots.

So, what happens to the great ideas like this in a prison bureaucracy guided by a politically cautious governor and legislature? This story about my "skilled prison cooks" proposal became a self-deprecating joke for my prison teacher colleagues, a joke about how naive and hopeful we can be when first starting out teaching in prison, before we learn about the purposeful design of dullness that is prison.

So—how hungry are you? Try this recipe for "The Cook Up."

PRISONER ESSAYS

Prisoner Essay #75

The Cook Up

I will be explaining how to make a penitentiary cook up. Since we are limited in prison to only a few food items that we can buy at the prison store there have been very imaginative ways to create a meal. I will be explaining the basic cook up.

First of all, the equipment you will be needing is three 40-ounce bowls and a big fork or spoon and a knife.

The ingredients are as following: two Manchon Instant Lunch California Vegetables (package) soups, one Ramen (packaged) noodle soup—beef or chicken—whichever you prefer. One Sandler's Beef summer sausage or two beef deli sticks (obtainable from the prison Commissary for a cost). Any meat substitute can be used. If you are a vegetarian then just subtract the meat. It will taste just as good. Also needed are Cactus Annie's refried beans or chili mix. I prefer the chili mix myself. Also you need Cactus Annie's jalapeno cheese squares, some honey and, finally, a bag of nacho chips.

The first thing you do is crush up the Ramen noodles and vegetable soups. Put them into a bowl of boiling hot water and let them set for about ten minutes.

While you are waiting for the noodles and soup to simmer you can be cutting up your meat into small bite size pieces. Then place that into a bowl as well.

Take your honey and drip it into the meat while stirring it. Do this until you feel almost all of the meat has honey on it.

Now you are ready for the final step in preparing the meat. Place the bowl into the microwave (available in the housing unit prisoner TV lounge) and cook the honey-marinated meat for about one minute depending on the meat. For summer sausage or beef sticks heat for forty-five seconds.

In the third bowl you place the Cactus Annie's chili mix or refried beans. Add half-an-ounce of water and heat in the microwave for six minutes. Sometimes that's not sufficient. You can tell by biting into one of the beans. If it isn't soft, then heat it up for an additional two minutes. If needed repeat the process.

By this time, the noodles should be done. If they are soft then they are done. Drain all the water out of them and add the flavoring packet that comes with the Ramen Noodles. Stir until all the noodles turn from white to brown or yellow, depending on the flavor.

Now add the meat and stir well. Be sure that the meat is spread out evenly. You don't want to eat half of the meal without biting into a piece of meat.

The chili mix or refried beans should be added to the noodles and meat now. Make sure to stir well again. If needed, pour all the ingredients from one bowl into the other bowl. That way you'll be sure to get everything on the bottom.

The meal is practically finished. Two more things should be done at this point. Take the microwaveable cheese and heat it for approximately forty-five seconds. Once it is hot and melted, add it to the rest of the meal and stir well. Again, if you need to, pour it all into another bowl.

Finally, crush the nacho chips into small pieces—the whole bag. Add this to the cook up and stir well. This ingredient is added last so it won't get soggy. It's best if eaten right away and crunchy.

Dig in and enjoy. You have just made a meal penitentiary style, called a cook up.

11

—ᨊᨙᨑ—

The Homosexual Prisoner

Standing at six-foot-five, weighing in around two-sixty, and going "straight ahead" at his teaching of economics, psychology and management like an on-time train, coauthor Bill Tregea was often known over his twenty years of teaching prison college by his prisoner/students as a man who is "all business." Yet Bill Tregea reports "I was approached once after a class by a winsome and earnest male prisoner. He said: 'You'd be good.' I knew what he meant. I just smiled, and changed the subject."

Instructor Tregea could smile and chuckle about this encounter as he left the prison and the last lobby gate clanged shut behind him. But the experience of prison homosexuality is much more complicated for prisoners themselves.

CONSENSUAL HOMOSEXUALITY

Since the gay and lesbian liberation movement of the 1970s there has developed greater tolerance and acceptance of homosexuality in U.S. society. This shift has also entered the prison world. Robert Johnson (1987/1996) reports research estimates that about 10 percent of prisoners are "actively engaged in sex." He notes:

> Homosexual outlets . . . are more readily available, partly because prisoners can move about fairly freely in today's prisons and because the stigma associated with such conduct has been sharply reduced in society and in the prison. Thus a contemporary prisoner at Lompoc, a federal prison, told one researcher that "most dudes with homosexuals are married" (to them) (Fliesher,

219

1989:162). Such marriages may involve formal ceremonies of sorts; when sep-
aration or divorce occurs, personal crises may ensue (Fliesher, 1989:163) . . .
there isn't any . . . concerted effort to curb the sexual appetites of the estimated
10 percent of his fellow inmates who were "actively engaged in sex" during the period of Fleisher's study (1989:157). Still, for most prisoners today,
homosexual outlets are unavailable, and others who seek such relationships
may be unable to secure satisfying homosexual arrangements. Furloughs and
conjugal visits must be earned; not all prisoners are eligible, and those who
are must often wait years for the privilege. (Johnson 1987/1996:84)

The issues of voluntary or consensual homosexual relationships in
prison are complex. It is not a "voluntary" or real-world environment and
free choice is constrained by envy, disdain, power tensions and identity
issues in the prison environment around sexuality. Pollock observes:

Most prisoners, male or female, whose pre-prison sexual orientation is toward the same sex may not openly advertise that fact in prison or may not
involve themselves at all in prison sexuality. In fact, they may look with
some disdain upon the sexual activities of "jail-house turnouts." Other relationships are not advertised as romantic relationships and are camouflaged
as friendships or hidden from view to avoid the attention and envy of others.
(Pollock 1997:241)

Of course, being in prison means being without an association with
women (other than guards). The pains of heterosexual frustration can
"call into doubt the male identity of the lonely convict." Johnson notes:

Two salient problems emerge. One is pressure toward homosexual satisfaction of one's sexual needs, which provoke anxiety in many prisoners. The
other is the tendency for male personality traits such as toughness to become
exaggerated in the absence of the moderating effect of women. . . . (Johnson
1987/1996:82)

On the other hand, John Irwin notes:

Most prisoners . . . are . . . made anxious by prison homosexual patterns,
not so much because they feel "pressure toward homosexual satisfaction
of one's sexual needs," but because they are regularly . . . disturbed by the
complex and unique prison homosexuals—the punks and queens. Many
heterosexually oriented prisoners, . . . who have grown up in prisons (such
as state-raised prisoners) or have spent many years in prison, engage in sex
with other prisoners. (Irwin 2005:158–59)

Irwin is suggesting that as time in prison wears down the originally
heterosexually oriented prisoners slowly, year by year, first a mild "act"
and then a few years later a more advanced "act" occurs, and gradually
such prison homosexuality becomes permissible. Irwin emphasizes:

most male prisoners do not engage in homosexual behavior, but they are nervous about it. Always present are prison sexual predators in search of new victims they can seduce or rape.

. . . alert on the issue of homosexuality . . . there is constant tension.

Because of the prison-induced distortions—exaggerated "machismo," homophobia, and distorted sexual preferences—released prisoners have special problems adapting to outside social arrangements and relating to conventional members of the opposite sex. (Irwin 2005:159–60)

Coauthor Tregea works with a long-time local director of parole in Lenawee County, Michigan, on parole success issues. This long-time parole agent notes that in his view: "These guys coming out of prison need mentoring work on how to get along with women." A local judge in the same southeast Michigan community emphasizes that his "Picking Better Marriage Partners" workshop for prisoners at Jackson Prison is a very popular course. These local Michigan insights confirm what John Irwin indicates as a "special problem" for male prisoners reentering society in "adapting to outside social arrangements and relating to conventional members of the opposite sex" (Irwin 2005:160).

Lifer Victor Hassine feels that while the majority of prisoners do not engage in homosexual behavior, prison administrations appear, to the prisoners, to actually favor homosexuals.

Consider this: only homosexual prisoners can enjoy sex in prison (other than masturbation). Among the prison population this creates for heterosexual prisoners a perception, argues Hassine, that the prison administration "has lost its ability to be fair." In trying to explain why prison administration appears to prisoners to be an administration favoring homosexuality, Hassine notes: "As long as the heterosexual prison population is forced to endure administratively sanctioned homosexuality while being denied their own conjugal rights, tensions between homosexual and heterosexual inmates will continue to mount" (Hassine 1996:112).

Coauthor Tregea notes he once looked out of the classroom building window while teaching a class to see a fight in the yard between two men. His prisoner/students knew what was going on and explained the fight was precisely caused by tensions between heterosexual and homosexual men.

Pollock reports that later research, in the 1990s, indicates that in contemporary prisons, male prison homosexuality "may not be as violent or coercive as earlier described." Regarding male prison sex roles, she notes there is a difference between punks and queens:

Queens—those who openly adopt a feminine manner and dress (as a woman) in a prison for men—are very much in demand. If they have the protection of a stronger inmate, they may operate in a semi-autonomous manner and pick and choose partners at will, for monetary or other reasons. In many respects,

queens may be more comparable to butch roles in women's prisons, while
there is no true comparison to the role of punks or boys. (Pollock 1997:241)

This book's coauthors, Tregea and Larmour, have taught prison college
classes since 1981, mostly in general population "school" buildings. Some
of our classes, however, were occasionally in protective housing units
(PHU) designed to keep certain prisoners out of the general population,
such as young men, avowed but weak homosexuals, and troublemaking
queens. Teaching a class of a dozen or more homosexuals in PHU makes
the situation obvious. Even in the many regular general population classrooms we have, as prison college teachers, encountered open "couples"—
and queens—in several classes over the years. But in describing his early
years of prison college teaching Tregea reports:

> In 1983, at Riverside (Michigan), a weathered brick prison built in the 1930s,
> two women prisoners appeared in my Business and Management class. Their
> long hair, lipstick, eye makeup, dresses, and movements attracted me. Still
> a novice prison teacher, I wondered which wing the women lived in. After
> two weeks the other guys in class finally laughed at me and said, "You were
> really taken in by those two!" Who, of course, were men. (Tregea 2003:317)

PRISON WOMEN'S HOMOSEXUALITY

Prison scholars have long noted that women prisoners tend to form pseu-
dofamilies. Thus, Cole and Clear note women prisoners have "families"

> in which they adopt various roles—father, mother, daughter, sister—and
> interact as a unit, rather than identifying with the larger prisoner subcul-
> ture. Esther Heffernan views these "play" families as a "direct, conscious
> substitution for the family relationships broken by imprisonment, or . . . the
> development of roles that perhaps were not fulfilled in the actual home en-
> vironment." (Cole & Clear 2000:278)

These prison women families serve an economic function, too, sharing
resources and helping to socialize and provide clear roles, while in prison.
Some research suggests that prison lesbians had longer sentences, were
arrested younger, were more likely to have been previously confined,
and have served more time (than heterosexual women) (Cole & Clear
2000:279). As Clear and Cole conclude,

> Giallombardo suggests that in most respects the prison subcultures of men
> and women are similar, with one major exception: The informal social
> structure of the female prison helps inmates "resist the destructive effects
> of imprisonment by creating a substitute universe—a world in which the

inmates may preserve an identity that is relevant to life outside the prison." The female inmates are somewhat collectivist, with warmth and mutual aid extended to family and kinship members; male prisoners adapt by self-sufficiency, a convict code, and solidarity with other inmates. (Cole & Clear 2000:279)

Both Tregea and Larmour, having taught in women's prison, can attest to this collectivist atmosphere among the women prisoners. The warmth and aid among women prisoners is extended in a pronounced way to their families, to parents that visit, and especially to prisoners' children who visited often at the women's prison where we taught (Scott facility, Plymouth, Michigan) and who enjoy special playground areas provided by the DOC.

The women, so many of whom enter prison with the lowest of self esteem, go out of their way to notice and applaud each other's efforts toward even the smallest of achievements—stopping smoking, losing weight, receiving a certificate in some prison program, getting good grades in a GED or prison college class, writing poetry that appeared in the prison newsletter.

As in male prisons, female couples "pair off" and remain loyal to each other as "husband" (butch) and wife. At least one pair, sometimes two pair, would appear in our prison college class, sitting together and whispering, exactly as gay couples in a male prison.

The violence associated with homosexuality as seen in a man's prison seems to occur less in the women's prison setting.

VIOLENT PRISON HOMOSEXUALITY

The prison populations have increased fourfold since 1981 resulting in overcrowding (see chapter 6). This is due, of course, to the rapid expansion of the prison system since the 1986 drug laws and underlying racism involved in an incarceration solution for the festering inner cities (see chapters 1 and 2). We have witnessed this incarceration binge in Michigan as dozens of prisons were built and double-bunking became prevalent during our twenty years of prison college teaching (1981–2000). Overcrowding has increased homosexual activity in prison. In his description of living in prison, "lifer" Victor Hassine notes that when two strangers are randomly assigned to a small cell, one man may be an aggressive homosexual.

Rather than an expression of love, or caring, or even passion, a type of prison rape may occur that is not reported.

Most victims of rape in prison do not report it because of the consequences. They worry not only about reprisals but also about exposing their humiliation to other inmates. If a victim reports the incident, he will be locked in the Hole indefinitely for his own protection and pressured to testify against the rapist. This means paperwork in his files, possibly even a published court decision graphically detailing his ordeal. The preferred option is to grin and bear it rather than have one's reputation dragged through the mud. (Hassine 1996:112)

The first American women's movement, in the late 1890s, pushed to establish a juvenile justice system separate from the adult system to treat adjudicated youth. Children and youth were increasingly seen as having developmental rights. Decades later, when the devastation of the U.S. inner cities began in the early 1960s and subsequent expansion of the inner city underground drug economy occurred in the 1970s and 1980s, sparked by the crack epidemic, which led to tougher street life and more violence among youth under seventeen years old, younger male youth were drawn into street-corner drug sales and gangs. Then came the rush to punish, with the mandatory minimum drug laws in 1986. The U.S. view of youth—in the inner city at least—then changed from "child developmental rights" to controlling "thugs."

As a result of the then-new "war on drugs" (1986 to present), the punitive "tough on crime" political atmosphere meant politicians pressured prosecutors and judges to "try more youth as an adult" and "waive them to adult court," resulting in more teens going to adult prison. In Michigan that meant young, under-seventeen males, going to high-security Boys Maxi School at Milan, and to various "boot camps." Those seventeen or over went to Michigan Reformatory, a maximum-security prison for those aged seventeen to twenty-five. In some states prisoners seventeen and older go directly into the general population of prisoners in prisons with much older adults. In all such facilities, there are older men and younger late-teens mixing together, from all sorts of neighborhoods, family backgrounds and sexual orientations. One consequence? More homosexual, identity-related, prison suicides.

SUICIDE BY YOUNG HOMOSEXUALS

The evidence indicates that homosexually oriented men account for more than half of the more serious suicide attempts by male youth in North America (Bagley & Tremblay 1997).

Even though the gay movement of the 1970s was underway in places like San Francisco, old beliefs about homosexuality still went unchanged in much of the nation.

Homosexuality, little understood, was considered to be unnatural and immoral.

Psychiatrists, before the gay and lesbian movement, had recommended ideas such as that homosexuals were sick, morally vacant, predatory and in need of help.

Adult males engaging in same-sex sexual activities of any kind were "criminals" and laws since the 1800s in Canada, England and Britain in the United States, made sure that all homosexual acts were criminalized.

All boys were being taught that the rejected and often-abused, easily identifiable "sissy" in early childhood would, by adolescence, be transformed into the "fag."

Youth Sexual Victimization Cycle in Prison

Suicide by young male homosexuals in prison may occur due to these youth suffering not only an exaggerated amount of "normal" verbal abuse but also an intensified and dangerous level of physical aggression by tough, physically strong predatory males.

It must be remembered that contemporary attitudes about homosexuality existing outside the prison world are not complicated by the tensions of prison life, as we explained earlier.

In the conditions of currently overcrowded prisons many teenage prisoners (seventeen- , eighteen- , nineteen-year-olds) may be pressured into homosexual relationships. Slightly built young men entering prison are sexually approached. Some are raped. There can also be gang rapes. As a consequence of this threat, some of these teenagers enter into a homosexual relationship with an individual tormentor as a way to protect against gang rape.

> If teenagers are anything, they are resilient. When a young felon gets raped and victimized, he overcomes the trauma by incorporating his violation into part of his lifestyle. If you can't beat 'em, they reason, join 'em. So these young victims tend to go out and find victims of their own in order to regain some of the respect they feel they have lost. This practice creates a cycle of victimization of and by youth, thereby proliferating the practice of violent homosexuality. (Hassine 1996:115)

PRISON CONDITIONS RELATED TO HOMOSEXUALITY

Double-celling in overcrowding prisons contributes to both violent and consensual homosexuality and makes it difficult to control violent homosexuality. There may also be understaffing, which results in less supervision. In an overcrowded and understaffed situation, prison guards may appreciate TVs—and homosexuality—in cells, to keep prisoners busy. As

Hassine notes: "two lovers in a cell with a TV will find very little reason to leave their cell," and this makes less work for guards (Hassine 1996:115). Hassine notes, however:

> Most guards tacitly approve the practice of homosexuality. . . . This policy has often backfired, however, since one of the most common causes of violence in prisons are inmate love triangles and lovers' quarrels, which can lead to murder, maiming, savage beatings, and revenge by the willful infection of AIDS.
>
> Homosexuality in overcrowded prisons may solve some short-term problems, but it lays the groundwork for long-term consequences. Encouraging involuntary homosexuality on a large segment of the prison population ultimately leads to (1) more violence between inmates, (2) the proliferation of diseases, (3) the spread of sexual dysfunction, and (4) more hatred for the system which promotes this practice. (Hassine 1996:115)

We can safely reduce overcrowding not by building still more prisons but by rethinking our drug laws, moving to a harm-reduction model, releasing more prisoners that are past their parole date and reducing sentence lengths so people are not prisoners for so long (Austin & Irwin 1997/2001; CAPPS 2008). And we can reduce the dysfunctional tension of prison homosexuality through enhancing continued contact with heterosexual family and marriages, even giving furloughs for both heterosexual marriages and homosexual civil unions on the outside. Reducing overcrowding and moving toward a prison policy that fosters conjugal visitation, as is done in Germany and some other European prisons, would be good reforms for America.

Meanwhile, in part to protect the homosexual prisoner, especially the excessively young and/or fragile prisoner, all prisons maintain a separate and segregated unit called Protective Housing Unit (PHU).

Coauthor Marjorie Larmour describes a semester teaching in the Protective Housing Unit (Ad Seg) at the old Jackson Prison, Central Complex.

AUTHOR'S REPORT #6

"Five Block"

It was with a bit of trepidation that I walked from the college office to begin teaching a class within the somewhat mysterious "Block Five," a specially assigned block, its former teachers usually acknowledged their alumni status with either a shudder or a smile and wink. Block Five was the Protective Housing Unit for the homosexual, the young or frail, prisoners who have committed homicide or drug-smuggling in prison, and occasional "notorious" or politicized criminals.

After climbing the stairs this first day of class, and being let in to the empty classroom by the guard, I waited for students to arrive. Twenty-four students—a big class—had signed up according to my roster. Hm, I mused, hope I could control the class.

Still I waited. And waited. Finally, I approached the guard, enquiring: where were the students?

He laughed outright. "Don't worry. You'll know when they arrive. They should be along any minute."

I returned to the window with its quiet scene overlooking an almost-empty central yard just visible over the wall.

Block Five prisoners attended classes by leaving a gated door from their block that led into the central rotunda of the main prison office building at the old Jackson prison. This central rotunda was just inside the main gate—the "bubble," or initial set of two gates—where inspecting guards and metal detector and an adjacent, thick glass-walled "control room" were located. It is through this "bubble" that all prison staff, other employees, volunteers and visitors must enter and depart. Once past "the bubble" you entered the rotunda which, at the old Jackson prison, was a beautiful ornate circular room with marble floors, across which the students must walk before mounting the equally ornate curving staircase to the second floor.

Five minutes later I heard a far off rumbling coming from the direction of the stairs. And the scraping of many feet. Something was moving en-masse over the marble floor of the rotunda below.

The rumbling grew louder and closer—with, now, the loud clumping of feet—many, many feet. Then something seemed to be rushing pell mell up the stairs.

In a near panic I turned from the window.

The sound of voices rose above the din. Many voices. Many loud, very energetic voices, the kind I recognized could only be made by pent-up vocal cords. It could only be the sound of young men who had been cooped up in six-foot-by-eight-foot cells for too long.

The door burst open and there they were. Twenty-four of them, at least twenty-three. Scrambling for seats, with three or four couples pushing to assure side-by-side seats for themselves. Chairs scraped. Books banged on tables. All the while the talking continued.

A prisoner/student at the end of the closest table to the desk turned to me. "You're our new teacher. You'll have to excuse us—all the racket. They keep us locked down for so long every day, we're kinda noisy when we get out."

"Yeh," echoed his neighbor, "maybe an hour yard time, then it's back in the cell."

"Yeh," spoke up another neighbor. "Really protective custody. We might as well be in the hole."

So, the class soon got underway, with books out, and work being done, more or less in a quiet, somewhat organized fashion. Being done, that is, by most of the class. Despite my urging to "get with it," one or two of the homosexual couples remained in their own world apart, whispering and giggling together like ten-year-old girls and paying just about as much attention.

But regardless, the class progressed, with roll completed and only one student missing. I was about to mark down absent for this student (two absents a term and the student is dropped), when the classroom door was gently pushed aside and "she/he/it" arrived.

To say that the arrival was made with bells and whistles is an understatement. I glanced toward the door and my jaw promptly dropped. The students looked at me and promptly began to hide snickers.

"It" undulated over to the window where I stood. Watching the grand entrance and stage walk, one almost expected an opening drum roll and loud refrain of "Hey, Big Spender" from Neil Simon's play *Sweet Charity*.

Flickering long mascara eyelashes lazily somewhat in my direction, she breathed, "I'm here," and wafted a perfume much like Chanel Number Five my way.

"Well, so you most certainly are," I thought, almost disbelieving my eyes.

Before me, indeed, stood a real drag queen, as professional looking as one ready to go onstage at the best gay bar or nightclub along San Francisco's Barbary Coast. This "gal" was ready to play Las Vegas—to a round of applause, I might add

I too felt applause was in order. But I instead turned sternly to the students who, at my obvious confusion, were close to exploding with mirth.

"Continue reading until the end of the chapter," came the command. "While I enroll Miss—Mr.—the new student."

Amazed as she stood there extending an enrollment card, I took it all in. The coiffeured black wig, dangling earrings, roughed cheeks, grey eye liner, pencilled eyebrows, and lipstick meticulously applied so as to bring out the luster of her white teeth as she smiled at me and gave a little wave. (Now I understood why the guards at the main gate often retained my cosmetics as contraband.)

"Hope I'm not too late," she half-murmured.

"For what?" I almost asked. Then recovered. "Well, yes, we have started, but that's all right. Let me just get your name and number now and we can get you a book and class material at the break."

"Whee" I thought, "that perfume is almost overpowering" But soon, chatting casually together, I found something else strangely overpowering—that was the continuing thought that I was talking to another woman. The feeling became stronger and stronger. Her soft gentle way of speaking, lilting laugh, engaging smile, a small rolling way of walking, a practiced mode of conversation, a relaxed way of sitting—it was all down to perfection. And I was starting to go right along.

As a matter of fact, when she, woman-like, complimented my outfit in the same way Corporal Klinger (from the TV series *MASH*), connoisseur of women's clothes, would have done, it brought a tiny glow of appreciation.

Once more, I had to reflect just where I was and again look down at the name I'd just entered on the roster sheet—Henry Appleton. Prisoner I.D. 182175.

"Have a seat anywhere," I said to Henry. "I can get a book and handout material for you at the break."

I watched fascinated as she undulated across the room to the far table. A dozen pair of eyes, I noted, also followed the journey.

How does she move in that tight skirt, I wondered? It was a purple fitted gown with mid-calf hem adorned at the neck with a string of pearls. Below the hem one could see black net hose covering a pair of very shapely legs. Her black high-heeled pumps went tippity tap on the old wooden floor.

Slipping gracefully into an empty seat, she had smiled over at a very young looking guy with fresh crew cut and open book. "Mind if I share?" she breathed. ""Uh—no—course not," he stammered, turning beet red.

Settling in, she crossed her legs—revealing black net hose up to and beyond the knee. Again, a dozen pair of eyes followed every movement.

"Well class," I said sternly, "let's pick up the reading on page sixty," and ten pair of eyes snapped back to the books.

At the break I walked over to "Henry's" vacant place and left a book and handouts that had been distributed to the others earlier.

But after the break, Mr. Appleton had not returned, nor did he show up later.

"I guess our new student is dropping already," I commented to the friendly student up front.

"Not to worry," he answered. "He does that all the time. Comes at the beginning of a class, then that's it."

"Oh well, I'll give him one more class, before dropping him," I said. He replied, "I wouldn't hold my breath."

His neighbor smiled wickedly. "No, I think Elaine just likes to advertise a little at the beginning of the term."

"Elaine?" I asked. "I thought the student's name was Henry."

Again a smile. "It is. He wants to be called Elaine but the DOC won't do it on the official forms."

"Hm," I commented.

The college semester in Five Block went just fine and I almost grew to welcome the clatter of the arriving students. We never did see Elaine again.

12

—ɯ—

Drugs and
Contraband in Prison

INTRODUCTION

D rugs and alcohol have always been available in prison. However, as the inner cities festered and the street drug sales economy grew, more drug-oriented gang members, drug-traffickers and many more drug addicts entered prison. After the 1986 "war on drugs," federal and state punitive sentencing mushroomed. The illegal drug market inside the prison changed. Powerful drug-dealing prison gangs and staff corruption emerged:

> One impact of drug use (in prison) is an increase in violent assaults . . . drug deals that do not work out may result in assaults; (and) incentives increase for "rip offs," robberies, or thefts of drug caches. . . . Drugs have increased the power of those who market them, and marketing is controlled to a large extent by gangs . . . or by organized crime figures. . . . Once an officer has succumbed to the temptation to bring in drugs, his authority is basically destroyed, and inmates who threaten exposure can control him.
>
> (Yet) drug use may be so pervasive in prison that officers overlook the smoking of marijuana or the drinking of prison "hootch." (Pollock 1997:249)

Ex-con academic Stephen Richards, convicted in 1982 of conspiracy to distribute marijuana, (who's appeal case to the Supreme Court failed), wound up serving eleven years of correctional custody in nine prisons. He writes:

> many of the older (1980s) federal prisons were plagued by rampant staff corruption and theft. . . .

Every joint I was in was flooded with drugs and alcohol. It was common to see convicts smoking pot, snorting cocaine, shooting heroin, or drinking either homemade or commercial liquor. . . .

At (Federal Correctional Institution) FCI Talladega low-flying planes did air drops at night. Every morning prisoners would check the "yard" looking for rubber balls or waterproof packages filled with dope. A less high-tech approach, used at many prisons, was to simply throw or use slingshots to deliver tennis balls with drugs inside over the wall or fence. (Richards 2003:146)

In Michigan, recently, a similar approach to getting drugs into prison has been used, apparently successfully. This was revealed in the context of a state budget crunch. Funds for the guards' union had been cut back leading to a letter of protest from the union. The letter cited many prisoner violations the guards were unable to prevent or stop due to staff cutbacks. One such violation was the finding of drug packets which had been thrown over the wall.

These stories about air-drops and sling-shot tennis balls and drug packets thrown over the wall seem dramatic. However, most illegal drugs enter the prison carried by guards or visitors. For instance, guards are rarely, if ever, strip-searched or "body cavity" searched. Many dozens of correctional officers flow through the set of entry gates each day, for each of three shifts, without significant search. The lure of extra money can appeal to guards—and some prisoners have access to money on the outside to pay these guards to be corrupt. Likewise, dozens of visitors come each week that are rarely if ever strip-searched. While they are watched closely in the visitor room, there is seldom more than one or two guards overlooking the visitor room and contraband can be passed to prisoners, who may not always be strip-searched after each visit.

Periodically there is the need for state departments of corrections to "clamp down" on correctional staff, to reduce drug smuggling, and to restrict those who may visit prisoners. The Chair of the Michigan Senate Judiciary Committee commented during a 1998 hearing seeking to expand drug treatment in prison that "It is impossible to keep all drugs coming across the U.S. border and it is equally impossible to keep all drugs from coming into our state prisons."

John Irwin served five years at Soledad (1952–1957) before getting his Ph.D. at UC–Berkeley. He has long been a model of the "prisoner voice" as a criminologist of prisons and prison conditions.

Irwin reports that at the Solano State Prison he studied (level II and level III, pop. 6,000) about 20 percent of the prisoner population are *Paisas* or Mexican nationals. They come from, and are oriented to, Mexico, and some have been involved in drug trafficking. These *Paisas* still have connections with drug dealers after they go to prison, and they smuggle and deal drugs (Irwin 2005:98). Such prisoners attempt to get drugs smuggled into the prison hidden in mailed packages or carried in by officers (Irwin 2005:104).

Of course, the overwhelming majority of visitors, volunteers and staff would have nothing to do with smuggling drugs. Both authors of this book have walked in and out of a dozen prisons hundreds of times over twenty-five years of prison teaching—never been strip-searched—and, along with nearly all staff and visitors, wouldn't touch drug smuggling into a prison "with a ten foot pole." Yet, it happens. Irwin notes:

> The prison administration vigilantly attempts to prevent drug smuggling. . . . Some prisoners who have a strong urge to use drugs, time on their hands, and a willingness to take risks, constantly invent new methods to obtain drugs.
>
> (Most) often, though, they make cash transactions through outsiders, who purchase drugs directly, pay smugglers, or deposit money in the prisoners' prison accounts. (Irwin 2005:104)

Irwin reports that money and hypodermic needles are sometimes hidden in the rectum as "keister stashes." Another problem of drug use in prison is that the prison underground economy cannot keep a constant supply available, so supply is irregular. There are added health risks like HIV and hepatitis C infection from sharing needles.

While it sounds dramatic to say that prisoners use drugs—and in the "Big House" atmosphere of the 1970s and 1980s this was more prevalent—it's not *that* prevalent today. Irwin, who did a recent (2005) study of contemporary state prisons, emphasizes:

> most prisoners, even many who were regular drug users on the outside, avoid drugs on the inside.
>
> In a federally funded study of drug use in several California prisons, urine analysis of randomly selected prisoners was conducted at three level III prisons, and only 3 percent of those sampled tested positive for drugs. (Irwin 2005:104–5)

Also, being caught in prison drug smuggling can land a prisoner in the dreaded SHU unit (Segregated Housing Unit) where prisoners have little face-to-face contact with other prisoners, do not work in prison industries, and typically leave cells only for brief showers and ninety minutes of daily exercise (often in small private walled or fenced yards). Irwin writes:

> many of the persons in SHU are there because they have been inaccurately identified as trouble makers . . . suspected but not guilty of having

committed serious crimes in prison, such as homicide or drug smuggling. Once these bystanders have acquired a "jacket" or label as a gang member or a dangerous prisoner, they are closely watched, even harassed, and accumulate many disciplinary actions. They often end up in SHU. (Irwin 2005:135)

CONTRABAND IN PRISON

There has always been trading of illegal items in prisons. Pollock argues this is:

an integral part of the (prison) male subculture (although not as prevalent in prisons for women). The value of reciprocity—a sharing of resources—is emphasized to some degree (Strange and McCrory 1974). But more often "conniving"—"getting over" on someone by taking advantage of them—is accepted and respected (Hayner and Ash 1939). The prison's illicit trade system has been described as a coping mechanism that achieves two purposes: First, it is a means of obtaining contraband items that make prison life easier; second, it is a vehicle that provides excitement and risk to an otherwise dull existence. (Hayner and Ash 1989; Pollock 1997:236)

Contraband is any item that is possessed in violation of prison rules. Pollock notes: "Contraband obviously includes drugs or weapons, but it also can be money, cigarettes, or even some types of clothing" (Pollock 1997:236).

Pollock describes the "power-holders" in the prison setting are often linked to key roles in the underground economy.

Selke (1993) provides a more recent account of the power-holders in the inmate economy, including the drug dealers, the kitchen staff (who can steal food), the hospital orderlies (who steal medicine or can cut through red tape to get a prisoner to the doctor faster), the barber (who has access to weapons), and the administrative clerk (who has access to records). (Pollock 1997, 237)

In the "Big House" prison "blocks" of 600 to 900 prisoners, having contraband was easier. The current smaller "unit management" pod of 250 prisoners make it harder to deal in contraband, but it still exists. As Bernard and McCleary note:

The underground economy . . . is a complex adaptive system. . . . When shortages appear in the official economy, the underground economy steps up production to fill the void. It assures inmates an uninterrupted supply of necessary goods and services, though at a cost. Although all inmates benefit from this underground economy to some extent, benefits are not distributed equally.

The underground economy also creates expectations among its component members, forming the basis of an underground society—a "Kingdom of Inmates." (in Hassine 1996:35)

THE NEVER-ENDING FLOW OF CONTRABAND

The attempt to stem the flow of illegal items (contraband) is never-ending. To illustrate, a story in the July 6, 2005 edition of the *Baltimore Sun*, with headline "Contraband Floods Maryland Prisons," begins:

> A black market bazaar of heroin, marijuana, pornographic videos, tobacco, cell phones and top-shelf liquor is routinely being smuggled past security checkpoints and into Maryland's troubled prison, an investigation by *The Sun* has found.

The newspaper had reviewed hundreds of pages of contraband reports filed by the state's nine largest prisons for a ten-month period ending April 30, 2005. *The Baltimore Sun* found:

> Heroin and other illegal drugs are making it into almost all of the state's prisons, occasionally in large quantities. For example, at one prison alone . . . of 121 cell phones recorded on contraband reports for the nine prisons examined, 92 were found in one prison. The phones present a security problem because they allow inmates to arrange drug deals or to continue to direct outside criminal enterprises while serving time.

TEACHERS AND CONTRABAND

At required orientation meetings before each term, Department of Corrections officers would brief prison college teachers on the prison rules and realities, including regarding bringing contraband into the prison, often unknowingly.

For example, many articles the teachers considered harmless were disallowed as contraband—such as money, maps, newspapers, food, drink, cosmetics, or medications. If such items were brought through, they were confiscated by the inspecting officer at the gate. However, the teachers could then pick up such confiscated items on the way out of the prison. The preferred routine was for teachers to leave all these items in a locker in the lobby. We were also warned to keep our cars locked and windows rolled up.

We were warned never to reveal to prisoners our home address or phone number. "Remember, prisoners get out," they'd say. Or they know people on the outside that might make an unwanted contact with you.

Importantly, they warned, don't succumb to requests by prisoner students to bring items inside the prison for them—innocent-appearing things to us, like books, newspapers, magazines, writing paper, pens. Or to make phone calls on their behalf.

Again, as an officer would explain, acquiescence on the teacher's part to any of these requests might be the beginning of a blackmail attempt in which the inmate would then go on to suggest the teacher bring in contraband like drugs or money.

Inmates are adept at exploiting any opening to obtain drugs or other forbidden items: "They are always listening and watching," officers said.

As an example, officers say, a prisoner might overhear one officer complain to another about debts he owes. The inmate might later approach the officer with an offer to earn some easy money by helping get contraband inside, they said.

None of these various manipulative things have ever happened to us over our twenty years of prison teaching. We were, as teachers, treated well by the prisoners.

PRISONERS COMPLAIN

Prisoners often complain of officers making periodic cell searches or massive prison searches (shakedowns) looking for contraband and destroying it, sometimes apparently at random. Somewhat like school fire drills, unannounced cell searches for contraband happen frequently. Prison guards may descend on an individual cell or several cells at any time, day or night. The prisoner occupant is left to rearrange a cell turned inside-out by prison guards.

As prison college teachers, we would often honor unusual excuses for a student not having homework done—such as a prisoner student excuse for a late paper because, as the student prisoner explained, "The guard searched my cell late last night and I'm still looking for my papers. It took me three hours to clean it up and I couldn't get to bed until 2 a.m."

The 1998 report below, "Michigan Prisoners Lost Major Property Issue," written by Ali Hhalid Abdullah, describes a contraband lawsuit:

Michigan prisoners have been fighting a (class action) lawsuit in the Ingham County Circuit Court under the case title Cain v. MDOC for the past 12 or so years. . . . The case involved prisoners litigating the MDOC regarding the restricting and taking of property from them that the MDOC had initially allowed them to have. [They lost the case].

Several prisons have already begun the massive shakedowns by ordering prisoners to pack all their belongings (including state-issued clothing not allowed to be taken from the prison during transfers, i.e., extra state pants, shirts, and pajamas) into one duffel bag, . . . and all else that does not fit into the duffel bag . . . are considered contraband.

The wardens of various prison completely locked down the entire prisons for this massive shakedown. . . . There is no consistency in the process. (Abdullah 1998)

—⁂—

PRISONER ESSAYS ON CONTRABAND

Below is a (2005) student essay describing his experience and opinion on rules regarding contraband.

Prisoner Essay #76

What Is Really Contraband?

Contraband in prison is a serious problem for the institutional staff who try to do a good job. And half of the time (estimated) it is used as money. It is basically cash. Or some of it, anyway. Ranging from legal contraband like food, cassette tapes to illegal contraband like spud juice (A.K.A. alcohol) and drugs.

What is really contraband? It can mean something that is illegal, damaged, altered, or for having something at the wrong place and/or time. It might even be a single and harmless as an empty pop bottle filled with water and Kool-Aid. Or deadly, like a shank (basically a homemade weapon) designed to be used to either stab or cut someone. The latter being not only dangerous to staff, but also to other inmates.

The legal contraband is still contraband. Which means that: inmates are still not supposed to have it. You might as well say breaking the rules; not the law. Tobacco and food are the most common. And pretty much the best to have. They go for double the price on the yard. But most prisoners refer to it (the yard) as the "streets" for some reason I don't really care to ask about. Cosmetics are another big seller. Mostly soap, toothpaste, and deodorants. These are the most common on the streets of prisons.

Next we come to the dark-side of contraband: liquor and drugs. Spud juice (what we in prison call the homemade orange-flavored alcohol).

That's the most common. They will cost from four to five dollars for a container that holds a least two eight-ounce cups full. I would assume more. But I can't be sure.

And of course nearly over 90 percent of every inmate's most favorite form of contraband: Marijuana. You might come across maybe one for every hundred who have not used weed at one time or another. If you're lucky. And it makes you wonder; if everybody who does it is in prison. Or at least everyone in prison's a user, is it really so harmless? There are other drugs too. But they are once-in-a-blue-moon. Anyway, if you can find weed in here, it will probably not have any stems or seeds in it. You see, people try to get rid of the junk. After all, they want the best of the drug into the package for them to smuggle it into prisons. If you want to know what it costs: It goes for $25 a spoon or $1,000 for an ounce. And the price goes up if you are at a facility that doesn't sell cigarettes. At those facilities, cigarettes cost what weed does.

This is a little off the subject but my own mother was caught trying to smuggle in weed to a guy at Carson City Correctional Facility (Michigan). Now because of what she did they restricted my visits. That means I might never get to hug her again. Or at least, not for the next ten years anyway.

This concludes all of the information I have on legal and illegal contraband items/substances in prison. I caution you to learn from the mistakes of others: drugs aren't cool and stay in school. It might be just weed, but it's against the law. Wanna be cool, stay in school.

POSTSCRIPT

The "prison self" can be a struggle, much as the self in the streets of the home neighborhoods could be a struggle. Yet, as the person entering prison begins to "settle into" the daily activities, prison can become a familiar place. There is some free time. A few prisoners write stories, keep journals, or write poetry. Some classes or workshops are available, taught by prisoners themselves or volunteers, that may contribute to personal growth. There is cell cooking. There are patterns of prison homosexuality. Drugs and contraband exist in prison.

Yet, while prisoners are kept busy, the "prison self" can be a struggle in the sense of tension between the reinforcements of a past life of deviance and the current effort to develop, practice and maintain a "straight life" going into the future. The yard time figures prominently in this struggle. The yard is the "streets." The predominant talk in the yard is about how to do street crimes better "next time." The prisoner struggling to form and maintain a self-concept of not-reoffending, or "not coming back to this place," can benefit from educational programs in the school. Practicing personal "self-talk" and reinforcing the self that talks about going straight *when in the school* (self-improvement programs) can help avoid, later, being "dragged back into the street" when subject to pressures to talk pro-criminality "self talk" conversations in the "yard." For the African American coming from the inner city the tension between the "school" and the "yard" can be especially difficult. One solution from the past, as the expanding prison world enveloped those caught in the incarceration binge, was the ability to "get into the prison college" classes.

V

—⚭—

AFRICAN AMERICANS CAUGHT IN THE EXPANDING PRISON WORLD

INTRODUCTION

In chapter 2, "Premises of the Incarceration Binge," we outlined how it was not just the 1986 drug laws that quadrupled the prison growth, but that there was also a good deal of racism involved. Would white suburbanite parents have stood for their white kids being swept up in frequent—almost constant—crackdowns on drug use and small-time dealing? So much so that the American prison system would grow to the world's largest with *their* kids in there? And for such long sentences? There was a good bit of "them" in the passage and support by the "rational public" for what was, in effect, a war on the jobless ghettos. Up to 80 percent of prisoners come from just a handful of "high impact" jobless ghetto areas. Why not focus on improving conditions in those areas?

TODAY'S AFRICAN AMERICAN PRISONER POPULATION

African Americans are 13 percent of the U.S. population but 48 percent of those incarcerated. How does this happen? There have been historical patterns of discrimination. For instance, more blacks have gone to prison than whites over the last 150 years since Emancipation (1865). For instance, by 1926 black offenders represented 21 percent of those admitted to prison, and, by 1954, African Americans represented 30 percent of those admitted to prison (Mauer 1999:120–21).

Blacks had moved north to New York City in the 1930s during the Harlem Renaissance and there were thriving black communities in many major cities of the United States, with middle-class blacks and working-class blacks as well as the poor (Cruse 1966). A segregated black ghetto with residents who have *jobs* (such as the urban black experience from 1920 to 1960) is a different type of neighborhood than the recent decades of "jobless ghettos" and concentrated poverty (Waquant 2002). Yet there was always a lot of black poverty, and a slightly higher rate of violence on the "black side of town."

African American writer Richard Wright wrote his well-known 1940s novel, *Native Son*, to flesh out the racist context of impoverished black male violence. Bigger Thomas, the protagonist, is defended by an impassioned lawyer who argues the case for the mitigating circumstances of social discrimination (Wright 1966). On black poverty and prison admittance, Mauer notes:

> This figure (30 percent of prisoners) should have been disturbing, since it was substantially higher than the African American share of the national population. But by 1988 this proportion had increased still more dramatically to the point where blacks represented *half* of all prison admissions. (Mauer 1999:121)

By the 1960s, while the unemployment rate for white youth was falling, the "rates of unemployment for nonwhite youth were increasing—as was the proportion of nonwhites not even looking for work" (Mauer 1999:123). Mauer continues:

> These labor market changes alone were sufficient to explain increasing crime rates for youths in the 1960s. Essentially those young people who are so isolated from the mainstream that they are not even looking for work have little incentive to conform to societal norms, since they do not perceive themselves as having an opportunity to share in the rewards of the working world.
>
> Even among those youth that are engaged in the labor market, but largely confined to low-wage jobs, the phenomenon of "relative deprivation" became a contributing factor to crime. It was and is not just a question of whether one has enough to eat and survive, but how one's material standards compare to others' and to perceptions regarding whether hard work results in appropriate rewards. (Mauer 1999:123–24)

Such high rates of unemployment for black youth are an instance of an uneven development process that was exacerbated in the 1950s by Federal Home Mortgage Assistant (FHA) programs and the building of the interstate highway system that, by the late 1950s and 1960s, had resulted in disinvestment from inner cities and a major shift in investment to the suburbs. These policies (FHA and highways) favored the middle class and left a growing "jobless ghetto" in the nation's inner cities (Eitzen & Baca Zinn 2000:ch 6). By 1983 Detroit had become the "number one" city in the disparity of household income with surrounding suburban metropolitan income at $33,241 and inner city income of 21,556—a disparity of $11,685 (Darden et al. 1987:99). Mauer notes: "the ranks of the black middle class expanded (to the suburbs) but for those left behind in inner cities . . . residents inhabited a place isolated from the social and economic changes going on in the wider world . . ." (Mauer 1999:124).

These are not a few isolated people in the inner city but, rather, *concentrated poverty.*

By "the new urban poverty," I mean poor, segregated neighborhoods in which a *substantial majority* of individuals adults are either unemployed or have dropped out of the labor force altogether. For example, in 1990 only one in three adults ages 16 and over in the twelve Chicago community areas with ghetto poverty rates held a job in a typical week of the year (Wilson 1996:19).

Into this context of the festering inner city jobless ghetto came the "war on drugs" which, by late 1986 began police sweeps of drug neighborhoods and street corners.

Increasingly the clutches of the nation's prisons and jails became the temporary or permanent home of the local downtrodden.

By the mid-1990s a study by the Sentencing Project (had) found that in 1989 one in four black males in the age group 20–29 was under some form of criminal justice supervision on any given day—either in prison or jail, or on probation or parole—(and) a follow-up study in 1995 then found that this figure had increased to almost one in three. (Mauer 1999:124–25)

Street drug arrests vastly increased, state legislators made drug laws much harsher with penalties of up to five years for first-offense drug possession and up to ten years for second offense drug possession. All of this "politics of tough," Mauer notes:

was bound to have a disproportionate impact on minority communities . . .

A more profoundly consequential policy change was the shift from indeterminate to determinate sentencing.

(The theory of mandatory sentencing) was dependent on the notion that discretion could somehow be eliminated from the sentencing process. What seems to have been forgotten in this calculation was that the entire criminal justice process is predicated on the use of discretion—where police officers will patrol, whether to arrest kids who are drinking underage or to inform their parents, whether to charge a shoplifting offense as a misdemeanor or a felony, whether to offer a plea or go to trial, and so on. (Mauer 1999:136)

Research from the Federal Judicial Center found that by 1996 blacks and Hispanics were 20 to 30 percent more likely than whites "to receive a mandatory prison term for offense behavior that fell under the mandatory sentencing legislation. . . . Sentencing Commission guidelines, for example, forbid reductions in sentencing for 'lack of guidance as a youth and similar circumstances indicating a disadvantaged upbringing'" (Mauer 1999:136–39).

In summary, the result of uneven development creating concentrated poverty in the "jobless ghettos," the "war on drugs" street-level enforcement approach and the "mandatory-minimums" sentencing philosophy has been that African Americans, 12 percent of the population, are now 48 percent of the prison population. As Tonry observes: "The decision heavily to favor law enforcement over prevention and treatment strategies in the American War on Drugs . . . was pre-ordained to affect young black males especially severely and for that reason alone . . . the 'war' should never have been started" (Tonry 1995:341–45).

Coauthor Marjorie Larmour writes narratives about her young (seventeen-to twenty-five-year old) prisoner/students and their first college speech class in chapter 13, "Michigan Reformatory—Young Blacks Caught in Detroit's Incarceration Binge Drug Sweeps, 1987–1994." Then two more narratives follow by Larmour—"The First Day of Class," and "We Meet the MR Students"—and then two student speeches are presented, including: "Call Me Spank," and "I Grew Up Too Quick on Streets of Detroit."

Chapter 14, "Detroit's Inner City: Critique by Black Youth Prisoners (under twenty-five) at Michigan Reformatory," presents a poignant narrative by Larmour of how Mellons-X and his classmates, later that semester in their MR speech class, have to make research oral presentations on growing up in their inner city neighborhoods.

Chapter 15, "Inner City Experiences—Black Prisoners Over Twenty-five at Jackson Prison, 1990–2000," gives a description of the de-industrialization and rapid population loss of American inner cities and the subsequent concentration of poverty and urban decay, street life and the gangster drug economy, which becomes "the only game in town." Adult (over twenty-five) prisoner essays from Jackson State Prison tell the story: the dare of becoming a gangster and how to become a street culture "player," the frequency of the death of fellow gangsters and players, the code of the streets that was learned "coming up," and how all of this is not something you choose but "just the way it is."

Part of "the way it is" involves the street drugs, crack and powder cocaine. Chapter 16, "Cocaine and Addictive Deadly Crack in Detroit's Inner City," presents a factual description of the drugs: how cocaine is made and how crack, which can be made cheaply from powder cocaine, has a far more powerful "rush" and is highly addictive with days or weeks of the start of use. This chapter presents two revealing prisoner essays—one on powder cocaine and its slow path to destruction, and a second on crack's unexpectedly quick path to addiction. And, as the essays reveal, both drugs can "fast track" your feelings to a mood of "being on top of the world." So much so, that you'd steal from your grandmother; so much so that you'd "wake up in prison."

In American inner cities by the mid-1980s, crack had, thus, become a drug epidemic. The consequence? An increase in drug-related crime from 1986 to 1991 when there were many more home invasions, burglaries, larceny, robbery—due to the money needed for a crack addition—and violence related to gang drug-turf wars, and increases in homicides and assaults, due to the amplification of violence related the drug economy, and to crack-induced "irritability, rage and aggression." Truly, we have spoken with many people who have "woken up in prison" out of a crack-induced haze, not really knowing "what they did" that landed them in prison.

As we have described in chapters 1–3, this historically specific "crack epidemic" resulted in the 1986 mandatory sentence federal drug laws (with long sentences), and a focus in crime policy on enforcement and incarceration of street-level drug dealers. Little, if any, attention was paid in this historical period of 1986 to 1991 on harm reduction, prevention, drug treatment or solving the underlying inner city problems. Instead, the focus was punitive, with the consequent unprecedented quadrupling of the U.S. prison system (Figure 2.2), and the rise of the incarceration binge culture.

Meanwhile, as crack crept up and down every street and alley of Detroit, the guns spread. Chapter 17, "Guns in the Inner City," describes how guns, previously not too prevalent in inner city life, became so prevalent by the late 1980s that "now all the young guys coming in (to the prison) brag about the piece they had out on the street." Prisoner essays are presented, such as "I Had Been Shot," and "I Fell in Love with Guns. . . ."

13

—ɯ—

Michigan Reformatory

*Young Blacks Caught in
Detroit's Incarceration Binge
Drug Sweeps, 1987–1994*

INTRODUCTION

After the build-up of the jobless ghettos, the 1986 "war on drugs" and the mandatory minimum sentencing laws were passed at the federal and state levels, young black men seventeen to twenty-five years old were arrested and convicted of drug felonies in police crackdowns that swept them off Michigan city streets and into the Michigan Reformatory.

Both authors taught for many years (1983–1997) in the Michigan Reformatory (MR), a high-security prison in Ionia for prisoners between the ages of seventeen and twenty-five. We taught in the COPE (College Opportunity Prison Education) program run by Montcalm Community College at the prison. The young prisoners in our classes mainly came from Detroit's inner cities after 1986 as the "war-on-drugs" laws put more and more African Americans in prison.

One of the authors, Marjorie Larmour, who taught many English and Speech classes at the Reformatory, had collected her stories of being a teacher there in an earlier book (Larmour & Tregea 2002). Drawn from that earlier work, her narrative below introduces the prisoner/student speeches given on the first day of a college-level speech class in the Fall term of 1992.

AUTHOR'S REPORT #7

"The First Day of Class"

When my teaching assignment from Montcalm Community College for Fall Term of 1992 at Michigan Reformatory finally arrived in the mail, I was pleased to see that I had finally gotten the Speech class. The Speech class is a good assignment for a prison college teacher because it gives the chance for prisoner/students to get up and give a lot of speeches, which is good for their educational development. The Reformatory, or MR as it is known, is the state's maximum-security prison for young-adult offenders, aged seventeen to twenty-five. It sits, unwelcoming, a century-old out-dated structure, three hours west of Detroit in the small and unlikely town of Ionia hidden deep within mid-Michigan's agricultural heartland.

Of course, as we all remember—oh God, can we remember!—for students, the required Public Speaking class is pure unadulterated hell. It's the class where—if you did it in no other—you fought your best friend to the death for the farthest seat in the corner, away from the teacher's desk.

Thus one o'clock on the afternoon of August 28th found me using all my strength to shove the incredibly bulky old desk in Room 2 forward about ten feet on the scratched linoleum in order to be closer to the students. They, predictably enough, had clustered their chairs solidly around the back of the room, shrinking the occupants as far in physical space from the instructor as absolutely possible.

Before me, a layer of gloom, thick as valley smog, reflected back from the silent rows of unwelcoming faces. There were twenty-five students in class and all but four African American. All were young, many seventeen to twenty, and most looked like a disaster experience about to happen.

Gearing up to punctuate the gloom layer, I walked forward. "Good afternoon, gentlemen. This is Speech 101. Welcome."

Looks appeared, signaling "Oh Boy, here we go!"

"Over the next weeks we will learn a skill many would like to acquire—how to speak on our feet before others." A quiet moan-like hiss of dread traveled around the room.

"In order to perfect this new skill, each of you over the term will be giving eleven speeches."

The hiss stopped, to be replaced with dead silence.

Eleven speeches! Great Holy Mother of Fat Fullbacks! Is the woman crazy?

The room moved into shock.

"And we will start right off today with our first talk—but now . . ."

Start TODAY?! Man, she IS crazy! Horrified whispers circled the room, heads turned to neighbors, unbelieving. Mouths sagged.

"I will hand out the list and dates due later . . ."

The expected hand shot up from the back and waved wildly.

"Uh, Miss Uh —" He was young, black and desperate.

"Larmour, Instructor Larmour. I've written my name on the board. Sorry I don't know all your names yet."

"Uh, Instructor Larmour. Some of us work and also take other classes."

His tone was respectful but apologetic as if to imply "Gosh, Instructor, Your Honor, I'd personally love to give eleven speeches, I really would. Even more—twenty, thirty. Lay them on me. But circumstances, you understand—"

"You work?" The response was bright, caring. "Good. Your work will make a great subject for speeches. Tell us all about it. Tell us exactly what you do on your job." I gazed closely around the room, concentrating on the back row, where faces appeared to be sagging exponentially with the distance from the front. "Give us all the details and you'll have a fine talk."

Desperate Dan cocked an eyebrow at his frowning neighbor across the aisle and tried again. "Uh, what I mean is that we have assignments in other classes too and—well—eleven speeches would seem—uh, well"— he was fading fast—"well, a lot."

The class agreed wholeheartedly. Mutters of "yeah, yeah" rolled up and down the aisles like waves lapping on the shore.

"You are perfectly right, sir." The smile was agreeable. "It is a lot— almost one a week. And, as you also understand, that's the best way to learn to speak on your feet—to actually speak as much as possible."

"But—"

I continued as if unhearing. "However, as you will see on the outline that you will be receiving, you will have four weeks that are entirely speech free." A sarcastic "Thanks a lot" look passed over the faces until I went on to say,

"On two of these weeks we will have a written exam on the text." The look disappeared and another universal groan made the rounds. I could see Desperate Dan being urged to raise his hand again on this one, but he just shrugged. Not only was she crazy, the shrug said, the woman obviously lacked any mercy whatsoever.

At this point through the open door walked two more men in prison blues, grinning cheerfully, text and writing pad in hand.

"Sorry, they broke us late for chow," one smiled over at me. It was the one with the close-cropped near bald haircut.

"It's alright. Just take a seat anywhere."

Immediately picking up on the starkly downbeat tenor of the room, the smiles on the late pair vanished and the men headed toward the last two single seats left in the back. There, each slid noisily into a chair without glancing at neighbors and promptly focused on the desk below his nose, obviously willing himself to become invisible.

I smiled at them. "For those who just came in, I was saying there'd be eleven speeches this term."

A terror-filled glance promptly sailed between the two, each clearly signaling "I warned you not to sign up for this fuckin' thing, asshole!"

"Now, I want each of you to prepare a two-minute speech of introduction about yourself." I reached for the roster sheet. "We'll be starting to present them right after roll is taken."

No one moved. The long somber faces, already seeming to bounce off the old brown linoleum, grew even longer, if possible.

Be aware that the long faces mentioned belonged only to the black class members. Unlike the African Americans, who were mainly dropouts, the four men in the first row, like most whites in the prison college program, were high school graduates, some even with a year of community college behind them. Science, sociology, psychology, speech—these were words they felt comfortable around. Theirs were the only smiles or signs of movement toward making notes on today's two-minute talks in the long, stretched-out but narrow and crowded room, however. The remaining near two dozen, still displaying long faces and deep dismay, sat unmoving, waiting, uncomprehending.

So I went on. "You've received a pad of issue paper and pen. Watch the pens carefully. They do seem to walk away." I smiled, while the tiny joke just lay there and died like everything else. "Just jot a few notes for your own use, a half page is plenty." My smile was more insistent. "Alright, then, let's start."

On cue, the four white students, who were all lined up receptively in the first row, each ruffled promptly for paper and dutifully went to work. Twenty-one black bodies, crowding the room behind them, remained immobile, uncomprehending.

This told you right away who had the diplomas and had taken the speech classes. In fact, easy glances were being exchanged up front. "Hey, this class is gonna be a piece of cake," their looks said.

To prime the pump for the class, I suggested, "Tell us something about yourself. Where you're from. Your background if you wish. Your family—are you married? Children? What do you like to do? Perhaps any goals you'd like to share?"

Stones would have been more receptive to my suggestions.

The black students in the back rows of the class were mainly dropouts. All the years the straight white boys up front had been doing their school thing, the rest of the black young men had been rapping and hustling on street corners. So now that the moment of truth had arrived, well—speeches, panels, brainstorming, group reports? How you do those things, man?

A command was necessary. "Take a piece of scratch paper and write notes to help you remember once you get up front." I smiled. "I'd say five minutes would be long enough to jot something down."

Glancing up automatically to the wall to check the time, I saw the old plastered expanse was bare; no clock hung there. Well, it figured. In this ancient old building wing we were lucky to have one double electrical outlet in each room, one slot for the fan, one for the VCR. And that electrical outlet was invariably situated in the most inaccessible location imaginable, with no extension cords permitted. Oh well, remember. You're in prison now.

So I peered at my own watch and smiled. "I'll tell you when the five minutes is up. OK"—and the tone was final—"Let's go."

The last groan and final defeated frown traveled the rows.

Then, as heads were scratched and pencils noisily borrowed—the pens, it developed, not having yet arrived—twenty reluctant bodies slowly shifted into low gear.

Roll was taken, orchestrated by periodic loud sighs arising from around the room, and revealing five men not present. "He hasn't gotten his detail yet," was called out for each. That meant five more students would show up next week, eager to be seated in an already full class. Now I too sighed loudly.

Suddenly a hand went up.

"Yes—"

"Do we tell about children if we don't be married to the mother?" The speaker, black, around nineteen, was serious. No one seated around him laughed, indeed, others listened for the answer. But a contemptuous sneer appeared on the face of a white student seated up front. Unlike the others, this rough looking white man, longhaired, tattooed, muscular man, seemed out of place in a classroom. Turning to the blond-haired white guy on his left, wearing a red bandana, he mouthed the words, "Fuckin' jeez," but the other was having none of it and ignored him.

"If you wish to tell about your children, that'd be just fine," I said. Seeming satisfied, the man's head bent once more.

Then there was the sound of nothing but pencils scratching, the continued sighs, and an occasional loud cough or nose sniff. Through the big, old door which had been propped open with a chair to try for a little air and ventilation in the always stuffy rooms, I could hear prison noises filtering in—the metallic slam of a gate down the hall, an officer's voice echoing, far-off, the hollow way it does in a jail.

Nearby, if I listened closely, I could hear the low measured words of Nancy Gartner teaching Marketing in the room directly across the hall, her door propped open also. In the room past Nancy's, I knew Don Stall was teaching Humanities—I'd seen him earlier. And in the small computer lab beyond, I knew there was a new man from campus. But I couldn't hear either of them.

A half-hour ago, the guard had unlocked the school gate and I walked through the last of five gates and down the long bare hallway of the small set of ancient rooms called the "college wing" of the prison.

Don't be misled by the term. True, the Reformatory, which sits on a hill overlooking the flood plain of the Grand River, is as old as an ivy-covered Harvard whose wings overlook an historic old quad. Its weathered bricks are equally ancient, its foundations equally cracking. Too, like Harvard, it is a resident institution, its facility housing young men who live, eat and sleep on the premises. Indeed—and it is a fact often pointed out with no little bit of irony—the cost of housing and tuition for these young men is roughly the same for both places—about $30,000 for Harvard or for Michigan Reformatory, a year, per man.

But now the similarity ends. Here at MR, as it is called, we have no institution of higher learning, no carillon bells ringing in stately tower, no likenesses of famed alumnus gilt-framed on library walls. This is a prison, plain, simple, harsh. It started as a harsh place, originally constructed over a century ago (1860) as a county insane asylum with chains on beds to restrict the elderly demented patients and bars on windows. Grim, stark, unyielding. Today it still remains an institution with chains and barred windows. Grim, stark, unyielding.

The only thing live that covers the building walls and towers are not dark green runners of ancient ivy, but bored guards who man its lonely corner lookouts. The only quad its barred windows overlook is a bare patch of well-trod dirt—the yard—almost lost within the enclosing fortress-like walls. And the one and only hall within this college wing dead-ends not into a spacious curved auditorium lecture hall or perhaps a glassed-in faculty lounge but into a tiny, extremely dirty, ancient bathroom with stained urinals and open stalls. There is no door on the entrance to the bathroom either. And no doors on the toilet stalls. This tiny decrepit room also serves as a "smoking room" during a classroom break.

As a student or instructor walks down the narrow barren corridor past all the classroom doors, as I was doing now, this open bathroom awaits you in full view. One is almost led to view the whole prison panorama, dead-ending as it does this way right smack into the toilet, as virtually symbolic of the entire incarceration experience, a stained pot at the end of a rainbow. Anyway, this uninspiring scene is what I had been gazing when I heard a jangle of keys. "Here's the officer," I thought.

Officer Stanton, the patient chubby black guard who continually was around to make things right, had arrived to unlock my classroom door and say, "Hi! Back this semester for more, I see!"

"Yes, guess I'll try it again." My smile this time was sincere, not tenuous like that first "Hello" to him five years ago.

"Well, call if you need anything," he'd said in his laid-back way and we both knew what he meant.

I had then walked into the square, white-washed, ancient old room with the six high-up little pull-out windows that stuck either open or closed and the radiator that, in the winter, ticked and gurgled noisily and once more I knew without a doubt that I was far inside a prison.

I plunked my worn briefcase—crammed, stitching starting to split at the seams—on the same ancient desk and sat in the old, brown teacher's chair.

Stark and miserable and grunchy as it all was, the room abruptly felt as familiar as my own bedroom. "Watch it!"—a cynical smile—"You'll become institutionalized and be wearing prison blues next."

How had one of these young guys felt when he first entered MR, I wondered. Could he possibly have been as scared and anxious as I?

Once again, I recalled entering the prison and this incredibly ugly room that first time, five years ago. Depressed, uncertain, I'd been within seconds of turning and bolting from the whole awful place.

Had it really been five years since Barb had dropped that casual remark? "You might like teaching an extra class at the Reformatory in Ionia," she'd said. I had been teaching prison college at Jackson Prison with calm, older adult prisoners over twenty-five. Did I want to step into the equivalent of an inner city high school class? A fellow instructor in the college program at Jackson State Prison, the big, old state prison south of the state capitol at Lansing, she'd uttered it offhand, almost without thinking. But I recoiled as if she'd suggested I take up heroin.

"What!? Teach at the Reformatory? ME?!" I had reacted in horror. What an unbelievable suggestion!

The Michigan Reformatory was well-known as the prime hard time dumping ground for the ghetto's young and the bad. It was a rare issue of the Detroit News or Detroit Free Press that didn't carry a story of yet one more inner city drive-by shooting, one more gang execution, another crack house bust, another felonious rape or vicious assault, another drug dealer roundup. And it was an even rarer guard working at the Reformatory who didn't read the same story and know that in three months or so he or a fellow guard would be welcoming that young convicted felon into an 8×10 cell down the hall in his block. He could only hope he'd go quietly.

I stared at Barb. It was as if she'd ordered me to teach in the worst blackboard jungle in the world, and I told her so.

"Barb, you're crazy. I'd sooner go teach in an inner city high school in Detroit." I threw up my hands. "Or I could simply commit suicide right off the bat. In fact, come to think of it," I ranted on, "the two would amount to the same thing. I read where even with all those new metal detectors in the high school hallways the inner city students last year still managed to gun down two teachers." Again I stared coldly at this unthinking person." Thanks, but no thanks!"

"Oh, they're not so bad. They're still young, you know."

Not so bad?? I couldn't believe my ears. Barb was forty, a mother, divorced, mature. God, she should know better. But on she went. "Some of the kids used to sit on my desk and tell me their problems." She laughed. "I felt like a mother." she shrugged. "I didn't mind. In fact, I thought some of them were kinda cute."

Cute?!! This woman needs therapy, I thought, and I retorted with some spirit. "Barb, that's all I need. I have thirty-year-old unshaven hunks now at Jackson lounging in the back row with their feet up. I should have eighteen-year-old delinquents at MR sprawled all over my desk? Thanks, no."

So one day I turned reluctantly off the noisy freeway, after traveling an hour west of Lansing, and followed a creeping truck trailer loaded with crates of onions north seven miles on a slow, two-lane road into the farm town of Ionia. There, at the only signal downtown, I made a left at the big old Gen Corp factory, where they made car fenders, which stood alone on the corner—the biggest building in town beside the prisons—and drove a half mile past a few scattered quasi-Victorian houses that sat along the wide flood plain of the Grand River.

At the sign warning "Reformatory, Drive Carefully" I turned up a short hill, pulling up in a cramped sixty-car parking area before a tiny, old, domed building with windows that had bars, surrounded by a twenty-foot century-old wall. Crossing my fingers, I headed inside.

Well, I suspected that things at MR would be different than I was used to, and they certainly were.

In fact, it turned out, these young MR students were pretty motivated. First, once instructed on how class worked, assignments were handed in promptly. The familiar excuse at Jackson that "The guard chewed up my homework" was never heard. Work was neatly done with often an apologetic note to effect that "I am very sorry that my pen has been stolen and I must do this assignment in pencil against your instructions."

All this naturally warmed the cockles of my pedagogic heart. As you might expect, these weren't your ultra-cool freshmen strolling in from the slurbs like you'd get at other regular colleges. Saggy pants, internet savvy, high school diploma in hand with a high SAT, and all. No, these guys were fresh off the street, uncool and no SAT score. They had never had the expectation of dutifully working through the high school to go off to college as God and parents had intended. They had never had the expectation to land that eventual good job in business, or go to law school or grad school.

No, most of our MR African American students had already become businessmen by the age of fourteen or sixteen. Ghetto-hustlers. It was a fast, entrepreneurial, work-a-day business world they'd entered. School had been forgotten. All that hated juvenile "school crap" of days past had become just a long ago dim memory. Replacing it had been the daily corner and alley existence of buying, selling, packaging, survival, clothes, cars, ladies and otherwise pursuing the fast track. In the process they'd become cool, suspicious, savvy, streetwise guys on the outside looking in.

College, of course, had been the remotest thought possible from their minds; usually no one in their family had even finished high school. Once incarcerated, however, the DOC had kicked butt, getting them to enter GED classes with state-paid teachers. Now, a mere two years away from the free-floating street jungle, many having finished the GED at MR, they unexpectedly found themselves actually sitting in—of all fuckin' places, man—a college classroom.

Reactions to this unexpected turn of events ranged from amazed to astounded. Most felt totally out of place. Then had wanted to give it a try—a prison college class was better than being in the yard. But they were uncertain how to behave. It was as if they'd suddenly found themselves attending an opera. With only the old high school mode to call upon, the cocky smart-asses among them picked up where they had left off—as undisciplined, tenth grade, back-row hoodlums. They'd mouth off, stalk in and out of class, and in general use the class period as a vacation from their cell. For them, instructors existed simply to show off just who was in charge. After a couple of sessions of this, however, I kicked them out of class. They learned who was in charge and landed back in their cell.

By far, though, most just sat and listened like they were supposed to, with no trouble. For which I was thankful. But, it was time to stop reminiscing and get down to business.

AUTHOR'S REPORT #8

"We Meet the MR Students"

"Uh, Miss Lamoore—' The tone was patient, waiting. His hand, I knew, had been raised for some time.

"Yes" . . .

The student was seated midway on the left aisle and he was grinning, aware he'd wakened me from my reminiscing trance. I could see he was the one requesting to be first.

"You said, I could I be first?"

"Of course. You're Mr.—?"

"Shade." And Robert Shade, black, cheerful, announced loudly to his neighbor, "I want to get it over with." Hearing this, other hands immediately shot up, "Could I be next after him?"

"Alright. We'll take volunteers first, then I'll just call on people. OK, give me your names—"

A moment later a list of many names was compiled and after my "Alright, here we go," a nervous sigh passed softly around the small crowded room. Eyes looked hastily down at lines written studiously on prison-issue lined paper. You suspected the owners were grabbing at last-minute reminders of who they actually were before the experience of standing up front erased the memory from dead brains.

"Let's go in the order selected then. Mr. Shade, I believe you volunteered to be first."

Shade stood up. Medium build, dressed in ragged denims, worn running shoes and blue sweatshirt emblazoned with the pro-basketball team name "Detroit Pistons," he grinned broadly. "Yeh man, ah figerred I'd go first, get it over with," he repeated to all around him.

Striding briskly to the old desk in front, he reached down to lift an equally old, dark blue, wooden podium which sat on the floor. Next, adjusting it atop the desk, he cleared his throat, grinned again at the audience and announced, "I'm Bobby Shade."

"Yeah Bobbie," came a voice from the rear. "Hey, laid in the shade," rose from a corner.

"Thank you, brothers." The cheerful speaker smiled easily at the owners of these welcome voices.

Then, clearing his throat several times, he stopped smiling abruptly, tried to speak and became frozen in space. The sudden sound of his own voice in the unexpectedly still room had successfully activated the panic button and no words could escape his paralyzed throat.

Hastily glancing around at the faces which now stared patiently up at him, he made contact with several pair of eyes. Becoming terrified at the impact, he next silently raised his gaze to the ceiling. Someone snickered but, with a disapproving punch from a frowning neighbor, the snicker stopped in a swallowed gulp. The room remained deadly still.

For one fast moment, the freeze unthawed. "Uh, I'm twenty-one years old," began the halting voice. "I come from Detroit—West Side."

"Yeah, West Side!" someone called out. Bobby smiled nervously at this second welcome show of humanity and continued, "I been in here . . . here in MR three years uh."

The thaw ended and again he looked silently around for help—at the floor, at his classmates, at the ceiling. Now, his audience was beginning to cough and squirm, not so much in sympathy for the speaker as in terror at clearly visualizing themselves in the same horrible predicament in a matter of moments.

Then, finally remembering the sheet of paper clutched in his right hand, Bobby looked down at it and finished off rapidly.

"I got three brothers and two sisters. I dropped out of school in the tenth grade but I finished a GED in here last year. This is my second term in college."

Frowning, he asked thoughtfully, rhetorically, of the ceiling, "Uh, what do I like to do? I like to watch sports. Especially I like to watch those real winners"—and here came a big grin as he pointed to his chest and concluded with a thankful explosion—"the Dee-troit Pistons." The accent came on the first syllable.

"Yea Pistons!" the class called out in unison.

Exhaling a deep breath, Bobby looked beseechingly at me.

"Thanks Robert," I said, feeling somewhat as a governor granting pardon. "That was fine."

Wiping his forehead in relief, Shade rushed back to his seat to receive an encouraging pat on the shoulder from the man seated behind him and a comment, "You did good Bobbie." From across the aisle came another whispered, "Way to go." Bobbie smiled broadly and, overjoyed, slid lazily far down in his seat on his spine. Now, at last, he could sit back and watch the rest of the class sweat.

The next condemned man, also black, rose and slowly approached the guillotine. His name, I noted, was Larson.

As he dragged forward, trying not to look scared, I watched the eyes of the four white students where they sat bunched in the front row seats. While they followed his reluctant path with sympathy enough to his plight, their looks nonetheless held that superior air of the man who's been there before. Middle class, smart, polite, you knew without asking that each possessed a diploma, each had long since sat similarly initially nervous, through a speech course back somewhere, maybe even later been on a debate team. And each, obviously, couldn't wait for his turn to vault up to the podium and shine.

How different, I thought, were the faces of those twenty-two black students seated in the several rows behind them. No looks of easy confidence here. Only a mirroring of the same stark anxiety now being displayed by the man who'd finally reached the podium.

"My name is Coleman Larson." The voice wavered nervously. From a rear seat the same voice cheered softly, "Atta Boy, Ears."

Larson, a tall skinny kid with sleepy looking eyes and long arms which poked out from the sleeves of a blue regulation shirt, raised a hand to pull at one of his large protruding ears. Self-consciously he smiled in the direction of the voice. "Uh yeah," he acknowledged. You could see beads of sweat above the ear.

"Uh, I been in this place . . . , y'know, two years." His voice was low and slow, indistinct. Almost in pleading fashion, he gazed out toward those rows of dark faces that looked back with stares as nervous as his own. For he'd get no help here. These men had taken no high school speech class, been on no debate teams. They'd spent their time on the street or in one juvenile facility after another until finally, reaching the age of seventeen, they had eventually graduated to a real prison.

Then, after some hesitation, Ears rolled slowly on. "Uh, I'm twenty-two. . . . I'm from, y'know, Southfield—and like that." With each labored breath, his voice was becoming lower and slower, the sweat more pronounced.

You could almost feel the class breathing with him. For, like Coleman, almost to a man out there—back of the front row, that is—each class member was today being faced for the first time in his life with maybe the ultimate terror of any he could remember. It was worse than the time he was shot, worse than sentencing by the judge, worse even than the day he met his sworn enemy in an alley. That terror was giving a speech.

"I got, y'know, one brother and one sister . . . I, uh, like females, y'know, ha ha. . . ." This brought a few understanding guffaws. Then for a contemplative moment he rubbed the other ear before revving up to resume slowly again. "I, uh, y'know, like to watch sports, and like that. Uh, I want to finish school here, y'know, and get a, y'know, Associates Degree."

His gaze then remained fixed trance-like on a spot on the dirty brown linoleum for an uncomfortably long time. Had he died also, like Shade? Everyone began to wonder. No. The audience could tell he was seeking a suitable ending to avoid being condemned to talk himself into eternity. And so they were happy when he finally concluded, if lamely, with a feeble, "and all that kind of thing."

Rubbing an ear, he glanced quickly at the class, down at the podium and then plaintively at me. "Is that enough?" he asked.

I should have let poor Larson die mercifully. But, no, I had to take the occasion do some teaching. "Now Mr. Larson, just stay at the podium for a moment." He promptly looked sick and the class smiled. "Do this," I ordered. "Take a deep breath, drop all the 'y'knows' and 'like that's' and keep both hands on the podium. Now look right over at Mr. Smith there and repeat the whole thing. Relax. Just talk to him as if the two of you were talking in the mall—as if it were no big thing."

The tall kid manfully drew a deep breath, refrained from reaching for an ear, fixed his gaze piercingly on Smith's belt buckle and, the sweat beginning to drop, managed to get through his talk a bit faster.

The men clapped in approval. "Better?" I asked. "Yes," they agreed loudly. Larson flushed. Stalking to his seat, banging the chair clumsily as he sat down, he stared fixedly down at his book with a faint half-smile. He too, thank God, was done for the day.

By now I could sense the students, their big young frames shoehorned into old fashioned wooden armed chairs, beginning to relax a bit, to smile at their neighbors. Most men in this small dingy room tucked far inside the walls of maximum security were doing long sentences on drug charges.

I knew that sentences given our students were fairly typical of the state's recently imposed harsher sentencings.

For instance, a man drew twenty-to-life for cocaine possession of 650 grams or over. And I'd be surprised if at least one lifer wasn't sitting somewhere in the rows right now. For possession of 225 to 650 grams, the time was twenty to thirty years, and for 50 to 225 grams, ten to twenty years. And again I knew that several men with those sentences were scattered around the room. Below 50 grams the sentences varied anywhere from probation to twenty years, depending on priors. Possession "with intent to deliver," or even "conspiracy with intent to deliver" drew stiff sentences. At least half of some home invasions, shoplifting, uttering and publishing (bad checks)—other crimes—were "drug-related addict crime" as well. Men convicted of all of these would also be represented in the room. Then, the turf wars over selling drugs in the streets also meant seventeen-year-olds with guns fighting rival gangs. Thus, there would be "drug-related" crimes such as murder, assault "with intent to do great bodily harm," arson and other violent crimes associated with the drug trade "in the streets." Then there were just plain screw-ups who had done all kinds of things.

Being sentenced to the Reformatory might mean serving the entire period of age from seventeen to twenty-five, eight long years, in the maximum security facility where you passed every hour of your days within a walled, close-security compound. And then, because of the length of the sentences, you might spend even more of your nights dreading the eternity of doing a further two to twelve years of a "ten-to-twenty-year" sentence, the remainder of which is served out at Jackson Prison after age twenty-five. Some drug sentences alone were "twenty to life." Ten or twenty years—or life—spent confined in these horrible places.

That's how my students refer to the prison—as "this place." Slang expressions like "the joint" or "slammer" are not heard. That would somehow make it all seem too casual, too homey. No. They just frown and say "this place." Or, "this rotten place." Or, "this fuckin' rotten place." And if I try to be cute or familiar and refer to their cell as a "house" or "home," as older prisoners at Jackson Prison and elsewhere sometimes do—as for instance, "You may take this material back to read in your house"—I am corrected by these still angry young men with an insistent "You mean my cell," once more frowning.

Close security means never going outside the wall, or even usually seeing outside it. Sometimes when I used to hurry up the front walk, with a lawn, bank of green trees or view of the river behind me, I would look up at twelve windows, each with bars, placed on the prison's very top floor that peeks over the tall wall. With a strange feeling I would realize that only the prisoners in these third-floor cells, two dozen among hundreds, could see me, see the green trees, see the river, see over the wall. Then the main view was only of the tops of tree branches in a scraggly woods located who knows where.

There was another small facility nearby called the "MR dorm," a dormitory for still under-twenty-five that, with shorter sentences, were getting out soon. Since I had taught at the MR dorm located across the street that is at the back of the old walled prison itself, I knew that "MR dorm trustees" walked back and forth across the street between the dorm and the prison. Thus, I knew that right now, as we sit in class, outside on the narrow road that circles the prison, there may be some lucky blue-shirted guy from the minimum security dormitory whistling as he walked the road on some errand. He'll be coming over to rake the leaves, sweep the front steps, raise or lower the flag on the lawn. But the prisoners inside can't do that—can't rake their own leaves, raise their own flag—things that would get them outside where they could see the river, see the nearby town. They can't even see the blue-shirted trustee guy walking out there or even know he was ever there.

Across the river were the medium security facilities called Riverside and Ionia "Temporary Facility" (or ITF) whose outlines on the banks of the hill you could see if you were outside. In the summer visitors at those facilities relax at pleasant outdoor picnic tables. Once in a while they even watch a visiting softball team from town play the prison team. But my students at MR, in class or sitting on a bunk in their cells or area, don't know any of this is going on. They don't even know there's a facility there. Or a hill. They're behind the tall twenty-foot wall. They meet visitors in a crowded stuffy room inside the twenty-foot wall, go to work in the factory inside the twenty-foot wall, play softball in the small dark dirt yard inside the twenty-foot wall.

Many of my MR students, at age twenty-five, will be sent to Jackson's maximum security Central facility to complete the rest of their sentence. There his days will be spent in an even tougher closed security compound, at the largest walled prison in the world, with an even taller wall.

Sometimes as I look around the classroom—as I was doing now—the thought is strong that here, crowded into this tiny cramped room and into tiny cells, are young healthy men who will spend ten years, twenty years, maybe a lifetime, without ever seeing another meadow, a river, a passer-by on a street. The wall is in the way.

And the thought is strong that the use of a prison for nonviolent offenders, which describes many (but not all) drug offenders—possession and drug trafficking as teens on the streets—is probably the world's most expensive waste of young muscles. Twenty-year-old youth, with good backs, strong muscles and lots of energy. What have they done over history? Fought the wars, worked the farms, built the bridges. During the Great Depression (1929–1941), when there was up to 25 percent unemployment, the Civilian Conservation Corps (CCC) built hundreds of roads and small bridges and planted tens of thousands of trees in Michigan. This work was done by eighteen- and twenty-year-olds, poor, jobless, many "at risk" for some type of youth criminality. And, while Michigan built Jackson Prison in the 1920s and during the 1920s and early 1930s had a "war on alcohol," no new prisons were built in the depression years after the 1933 repeal of Prohibition. We didn't handle our "surplus population" during the Great Depression by building prisons.

Recently, due to overcrowding, a new block was annexed to the back of the building. And, because it was beyond the wall, its occupants smiled. "Now I can see a whole tree," one said. Built in a tiny gully, the view from barred window of twenty trees and the dumpster was nonetheless a magnificent view.

So when I see a student stretching his tall body to look out one of the tiny up-high classroom windows, as occasionally does happen, I don't ask what he's looking at for I know the answer would be, "Nothing. I was just wondering if I can see over the wall from here."

"Alright. Who's next?" I asked and consulted the list. "Jones. Martin Jones."

Promptly at hearing his name, a black student, gangly like Larson but much shorter, sprang from his seat. He had a different feel about him. His was the look and charge of a competitor.

Whoops, I thought to myself, here is the exception to the rule. Here comes the possibly one student from the back rows—a person who is not unsure, not nervous. In fact, you could tell by the determined way he moved that here was a man who had sat through the miserable performances of his previous African American brothers long enough. Tired of being patient, paternal, now he would show them. It was as if he were a professional baseball player watching his son's Little League team and the time had come for the beginners to receive a few pointers on the game.

Striding confidently onstage with all the outward self-assurance of the president entering Congress, Jones grasped the podium and looked over the class for a long moment of calm deliberation. One could imagine him waiting for the last strains of "Hail to the Chief" to fade.

He looks somewhat like a chipmunk, I thought. A rather long nose set in a long face, with large teeth protruding slightly, gave a definite rodent effect when he smiled. And he was smiling now. It was a smug smile that announced to all, "Fear not. You've sat through two wimps but now I'm giving you a break."

Finally, with the room hushed, he leaned forward casually and announced that he was twenty-one years old and had been in MR for three years. He was from Detroit, had two sisters and a brother, liked rap, especially liked basketball, was OK at math. Then in conclusion—and obviously saving the most impressive until the last—when he got out of prison he was going into business for himself. This ambitious goal was delivered with quiet conviction and a great amount of self-confidence—perhaps, as it developed, a bit too much.

"What business?" someone called out.

"Probably drugs." Another volunteered. The class laughed.

Jones considered for a long thoughtful minute. "I haven't decided yet." His smile came easily. "Likely be carpet cleaning."

"What you know 'bout the rug cleaning business?" The question boomed out like a trombone call from row three. The voice was big, deep and rough with a drawling sarcastic edge to it and belonged to the big man called Monk sitting across from Desperate Dan.

Involuntarily, Jones flinched at the booming voice. "I done that once for a guy." His answer sounded startled but confident.

"How long you work at this business? This rug cleaning?" Monk persisted gruffly in his near animal-like growl. The voice boomed out deep as an open pit, sounding just as deadly, and caught Jones, about half the man's size, like a boomerang.

The speaker bit his lip and answered rapidly, shakily. "I can't remember. Maybe a week or two weeks in the summer."

Monk wouldn't go away. "You do this work by yoself?" His words sounded even more threatening. Leaning forward abruptly, the big man fixed the now confused speaker with a scowling stare.

'Well, not exactly." Jones' voice had suddenly lost its confidence, now most of its volume as well. "I drove the truck and helped the guy with the equipment, with the solution." The response was offered softly, the feet shifted nervously.

"Hmpf," snorted Monk loudly, the sudden snort issuing like a blast of air from a tuba's spit-valve. Turning to face his neighbors, he grunted in disgust, "He don't know nuthin' about rug cleaning." Monk was a large muscular and very positive type guy. And this was said positively.

Promptly, the man up front backpedaled. "Well, as I said, I haven't decided yet. Maybe I'll open a restaurant. Or a bar."

"Man, you can't get no liquor license," a different voice called out. Several other voices agreed. "Yeah, he can't get no license." And someone else pounded in the final nail. "An ex-felon? No way."

Martin hedged frantically. "Uh, there's ways," he said mysteriously.

"Hm," Monk's neighbor turned toward him and pronounced equally gruffly, equally definitively, "He don't know nuthin' bout runnin'no bar neither."

Monk nodded in emphatic agreement and, swinging around toward the distressed man at the podium, proclaimed loudly. "You don't know nuthin' about running no bar neither." Before the speaker's face had finished falling, the big man was on him again, rearing back to shoot out like a shotgun round, "What you know about restaurants? You ever work in a restaurant?"

Jones hedged again. He was becoming the tired fighter now, ducking and weaving. "Not for sure. But my brother—he running a restaurant right now." Uncomfortable, beginning to sweat, you could tell he was longing for the round to end.

But Monk, hot on the chase, resumed the cross examination. "Your brother—he own the restaurant? He can put you on?"

"Well, no, he just the night manager. But—"

That cross-examination ended for the moment, Monk summarized flatly. "He don't know nuthin' about running no restaurant neither."

Figuring the uneven exchange had gone on long enough, I rose to say, "Let's wait until the speaker finishes before asking questions or making comments," adding, "Then try to make the comments helpful, also remember to raise your hand first."

Before I had returned to the creaking old teacher's wooden swivel armchair, remembering to sit down gingerly lest the ancient arm suddenly spill me backward to the floor—always an entertaining spectacle for the students—a hand waved from across the room.

"I worked in a McDonald's once. Yep. For six months. In East Detroit." He was a lanky kid named Dale Quaid. And he said it like he had a chip on his shoulder.

"Is that right?" his neighbor asked, with an edge of contempt. Others too turned to stare at the man.

Quaid bridled. He knew why they were staring. Hell, he was probably the only black guy in the room who'd worked in a fast food instead of making fast money on the streets. Contempt was, indeed, behind the stares in the room. "The jerk," he could hear them thinking right now, just like his friends used to say about him back in the hood.

There it was again, the note of incredulous contempt from another voice. "No foolin' man! You worked in a McDonald's?"

"Sure did!" Angrily, he almost barked it. He remembered when he'd be walking from high school over to the Jefferson Avenue McDonald's for the late afternoon shift, hauling his book bag and everything, and the guys would cruise by in their new red Grand Am, wearing their new Air Jordans, and stare. What a jerk! the stare said. Still going to school and working at McDonald's Man, I can't believe it! He'd glue his eyes to the sidewalk and walk faster. Well, things were different now.

Defiantly, he stared back and spoke up. "Yeah man, ya gotta know a whole lot in that ole Mickey D. You wouldn't believe all the stuff ya gotta learn." He knew he was sounding defensive but shit—he'd ceased caring. "I finally got to be the French Fry manager."

"For real?" the same guy asked, sounding impressed.

"For sure." Quaid responded, now almost casually. Then he could hear himself even bragging a little. "Ya gotta learn all this technology. Read meters on the machines. It can be dangerous too if you don't know what you're doing."

"No shit?" came again.

"Dangerous eh?" Someone else swung around to ask.

It's funny, Quaid thought, these guys actually seem interested now. He grimaced. They sure weren't then, back in the hood. He remembered when he'd tried to talk his friend Arnold out of the street drug game and into joining him at McDonald's. Arnie had just laughed. Really laughed. And pretty soon Dale had seen why.

"Dale baby," Arnie's voice had been low. "Come in this alley and lemme show you somethin'." And, once out of sight, he'd squinted around and then pulled this roll of green out of a deep pocket—Dale was positive Arnie had a gun in the other pocket—and cupped the money in his hand so no one wandering by could see. And there were fives, tens and twenties along with the ones—a lot of them.

"That there's likely more than you make in a month. Made it yesta-day—weekends are good." He laughed. "Jess look. Don't touch." Hastily, he stuffed the roll back in his pocket. "Ah'm on my way with it to make a car payment. Most dealers stay away from us—y'know, too young, break contracts and all, but Sam down here at Eastside Wheels"—he knows me, ah got mah last new car from him."

"Oh," Dale had said, seeing again the flashy new Grand Am right now waiting back at the curb. Then he remembered his fifteen-year old dented 1980 Olds Cutlass sitting in the backyard needing a new motor. But who had $300 bucks for even a junk-yard motor?

Arnie leaned forward: "Ya gotta understand, Dale, that ah'm a family man now. Got responsibilities and it takes money."

"Oh, didn't realize, man."

"Yeah, my lady just had a little girl. Cute as a button."

"Well now, that's great, man." Dale had smiled. He thought, Arnie's the same age as me, seventeen. Maybe sixteen even. He'd seen Marsonna, Arnie's girlfriend. She was the same age as Dale's sister, fifteen. Dale wondered what he'd do if his own girlfriend announced she was pregnant and a cold lump had suddenly formed in his stomach.

"Man, you wouldn't believe what baby stuff costs. Whooee!"

"No. Guess not."

"We went out all day Saturday. Bought a crib. Little designs on it, y'know. Best one in the place. One of them dressing tables you change diapers with. Two chests. A purty furry carpet, wall to wall, one that look like a bunny y'know. Wallpaper. One of them baby monitors where you can hear 'em at night. Lamps. An' ah don' know what all. 'Bout five hundred bucks worth."

"Whee!" Dale had said, thinking that was over a month's pay at McDonald's. He reminded himself he sure better talk tough to his own lady before she go getting ideas.

"Yeah. They deliverin' it all." Arnie had kind of slapped the other's arm. "So y'see, Dale man, even effen ah wanted to work down there wit you which ah sure as hell don't—ah can no way afford it. Baby. Car. My own clothes"—his hand moved head to foot to indicate, "All brand new threads. Good stuff. You gotta keep up appearances, y'know. Oh, an'ah gotta be helpin' my mom out at home too."

"Yeah. Know what you mean." With his own Dad not around the home, Dale was splitting his pay with him mom at home for food, rent and utilities.

"So y'see, man. My business is too demanding." And he'd climbed back in his new car.

"But you a good man," he had called back, "Effen you ever want to give it a try come see me. Ah got some good accounts. Make yourself some cash." And he'd driven off while Dale walked on, thinking.

"Yep," Quaid now repeated loudly, "you work your tail off alright in a Mickey D. But, man, you learn a lot. Yes sir." And he threw out a brave glance at the staring eyes. "Ah'm glad ah did it."

Well, he was glad. He'd made his point and fuck what they thought. In here, their drug money meant nothing. But he was still proud of his Mickey D stint. It gave him job experience, labeled him somehow as legit, something the hustlers could never claim.

He sighed. If only he'd kept the fuckin' job and not listened to Arnie.

When the black-and-whites finally pulled up to ship five 18-year-olds to county jail and then to the Reformatory—guys that looked just like the Jones, Colemans, Shades, Dansons, Washingtons in this class—a lanky eighteen-year-old guy named Dale Quaid—who had been sucked into the street drug trade—was with them. And almost before the police cars had completed their run to pick up Dale Quaid, six more sixteen-year-olds had arrived to take their places on the drug-selling corners.

"Yep," Dale repeated one last time to his neighbor and the class, "It's a hard job and you gotta learn a bunch of things," and the deprecating glance he threw up at the speaker said it all. "You don't jest walk into a Mickey D' and be a boss, like that man up there given the speech 'spect to do." He motioned towards Jones, who was still standing at the podium and whose confidence was now fast fading. "No sir," Dale emphasized to those seated nearby. "You sure don't."

Dale's classroom neighbors nodded assent and began to glare even more hostilely up at Jones at the podium. It was impossible not to comprehend that they were conveying the general opinion that Jones should pack up and move out. Martin Jones aplomb was vanishing under this barrage, like March snow under the heat of spring, and I decided a rescue was overdue.

"Hey, that was just fine, Mr. Jones," I said, standing up, "Let's give him a hand."

A few in the class reluctantly clapped as Jones stumbled back to his seat, a broken warrior. I followed his sad retreat with my own standard "reminder" speech which went something to effect that we should all remember the difficulty most folks experience in speaking in public and so a modicum of respect and empathy was always in order for whoever was up front.

In a moment, after I had explained what the word "empathy" meant, and then the word "modicum," we proceeded onward. I could hear one man translating my words to his neighbor, "She means don't laugh at the fuckin' dorks like him."

Five more students, all African American, followed. As each did his time up front and then clumped thankfully back to his seat, the class clapped politely.

There was Charles Thompson. He was a really little guy from the West Side. There wasn't much of him, in fact he must have been one of the smallest men I have seen—a bare five feet high—but fast, energetic and smart. Pencil thin, with flashy white-toothed smile, his manner was so quick you'd expect him to break into a tap dance any minute.

"Hey, what's your goal, Sammy?" he was asked. They called him "Sammy," they explained, because he was like Sammy Davis, Jr. Well, Sammy answered unblinking," I want to be a lawyer. I got eighteen credits toward a degree as a Paralegal and want to become independent." He frowned: "But I been back in court five times." He shook his head. "I really need to set goals."

"When you're a lawyer, Sammy, are you going back home to work?" The little man's frown turned to a grimace. "No! I never want to go back to the ghetto"

Another, Carl Washington, a twenty-two-year-old from Detroit, said he'd gotten in trouble eight years ago, been in prison for five years. "I got out once and then came back. I don't want to come back again. That's why I'm in the college program. I'm trying to practice having goals." He laughed wryly. "And the first goal is to stay away from this fu—uh—lousy place." The class laughed and gave him a big hand. "You gonna make it, brother."

And next after them, all also inner city alumni, came Darnell Danson and Eddie Vincent and Tyrone Smith.

"I got in here 'cause I had the wrong role models," explained Darnell seriously. A big, strong-looking kid, Darnell's was an open face, broad, big mouth with wide lips that looked as if they'd break into a smile any time. But he didn't smile today, he wanted to talk.

"When I was a little kid comin' up, eight years old, out the window I'd watch these older kids hangin' in the alley back of my house. They were cool. Had neat clothes, expensive shoes, gold earrings, big new cars, always smilin', havin' a good time. I'd watch people come up to them and I'd see money exchanging. And I thought, that's who I want to be like."

His gaze fixed on the floor for a moment before continuing.

"My mother was alone, she worked all the time, sometimes an extra part-time job too. She wasn't never at home. An' when I asked her for shoes an' clothes like they had she said we couldn't afford it. I never saw my father, he was outta the state somewhere." Darnell turned to me. "Ah guess ah'm talkin' too long."

I nodded an "It's alright."

He picked up his talk thoughtfully: "Anyway, ah was thinking' bout goals just now an' figgering exactly why ah never had any 'cept to have money like the big kids in the alley did."

Looking down once more, his voice becoming softer, almost indistinguishable. "Ah got in trouble an ah'm gonna be in this place here a while." That means a fifteen-to-twenty-year sentence, I noted silently to myself.

For a good bit longer, he stood there, just looking down, thinking, figuring it out, searching for an answer. Then he looked up, but still unsmiling. "Ah think effen ah'd had a father aroun' maybe ah'd had goals." He gazed out over the staring faces, unsure. But that was it. He'd said it all. 'Uh—Thank you," he concluded and headed silently for his seat, head down.

"You gonna be OK, brother," someone called out.

"We all wit' you," came another voice.

You could tell the words helped. Raising his head, the lips now did break into a smile, but it was wan and grim.

"Ah relate to what the brother said." Eddie Vincent was up next. "I had my mom—she worked—an' a sister but she was older an' she had a baby of her own and didn't care 'bout me." He half smiled. "Anyway, mah goals were like his—to get those cars and—ha, ha—the ladies." He laughed. "Cept the first time the police caught me when ah was sixteen mah only goal was to be more clever and not get caught the next time."

Then the laugh faded quickly and he too stared down at the floor and his voice too became rough, grating, almost indistinguishable like Darnall's had been, as he said softly: "Now ah'm lookin' at twenty years."

He paused. "Well—" he shrugged. "Guess that's it." And sat down.

Most of the speakers we'd heard so far, all African American, wore the regulation blue shirt and pajama-style blue pants, although not required to. Jeans or sweats along with a shirt or T-shirt were allowed, and two wore this. Aside from a difference in clothes, however, their stories were remarkably similar. Each was under twenty-three years of age, had been in prison two to five years, had a single parent, had one to four siblings, had left high school in the ninth or tenth grade. All were unmarried but three had one or more children. Other than sports and women, none had a real outside interest or hobby. For all, the trip to prison, some 140 miles, had been the farthest they had traveled outside the Detroit environs. For all also, goals had not been just vague or unstructured, they'd been nonexistent.

I glanced at my watch. Barely forty minutes had passed and so far it had been a litany of remarkably empty backgrounds, barren lives and hopeless futures.

A stranger sitting through this recital, shocked, dismayed, might well ask—How could any man grow to twenty-one or older without doing any of the "normal" things that teenagers do?

So—what were things that normal teenagers did anyway? And he or she might spell out a few right here in Michigan that came to mind.

Like—go places with a parent? Go hiking or camping or fishing or hunting? Go to a zoo or library? Travel someplace—even to the Mackinaw Bridge? Visit Cedar Point amusement park, nearby in Ohio, or even the little White Water slide in Kalamazoo? Build model planes or collect stamps? Have a paper route, work after school or deliver pizzas? Learn about exciting current technologies like computer games or the internet?

You knew right away that the white students in class had done most all these things, and probably more, and would probably mention some in their speeches. And yet with half the class already introduced, the listener would have heard none mentioned from the black speakers. Didn't this seem strange!?

But anyone who's lived or worked in the nation's ghettos or taught in a prison for several years, where today close to 50 percent of prisoners are African American, knows that it's fairly typical for the inner city youth to grow up without doing a single one of these. I'd guess that nearly 70 percent of the students in this room right now, the black students, had grown up the same way—without doing a one of them.

And don't think for a minute that the 70 percent didn't resent white kids who had.

Take that black student scowling fiercely right now in the back row, and right now thinking: "Just look at the fuckin' spoiled white dudes sittin' that way right up front, while we sittin' in the back of the bus."

"Man! An' yawning!" he exclaimed. He'd caught the bored yawn of one of the white students a moment ago and his boiling anger was no secret. " They jess wettin' their pants waiting to get up and brag on how much they know, how much they done."

"Sure," his inner grumbling continues, "that ole Emperor Jones a minute ago, stands up and chooses to make an ass of himself with the braggin'. Well that be alright. But—one of them high and mighty white dudes rubbin' our noses in it? Well—" And you could almost hear the teeth grate.

Yes. As anyone will tell you, in any prison, racial tension is always just under the surface.

And here we had an explosive situation just waiting to explode. Men matching lives and deeds at the podium? It was a black-white scenario hand-tailored for trouble. So as I surveyed the two groups before me, a mixture of apprehension and hope flooded through me.

Inwardly, I could also feel a little inner anxiety stirring. I, too, could sense the white students just itching to get up there. I sighed. Well, it'd be their turn soon.

14

—ᄴ—

Detroit's Inner City

Critique by Black Youth Prisoners (under Twenty-Five) at Michigan Reformatory

INTRODUCTION

L ater that term the speech class at MR prepared talks on "Detroit's Inner City," an area most prisoner-students had grown up in. It was on these Detroit streets that most of the class members had been picked up at as drug dealers and sent off to Michigan Reformatory (MR) for long sentences, Michigan's maximum-security prison for males twenty-five and under.

AUTHOR'S REPORT #6

Speak What You Know

Mellons-X took his big frame up to the old podium on Thursday and cleared his throat.

"My title is 'The Experience of a Dead Man Who is Now Alive.' He looked down at the podium, then up at the ceiling as if counting to four as per instructions, then said, "I will say this quotation, 'Power comes through time just as knowledge comes through being educated.'" Down for another two count, then up and he was confident, ready for the tossup. "Now I will give the body of my speech." With a smile he began and the class smiled back.

"I began my life on the streets of the ghetto world. I was raised in the projects. My mother didn't have much. I never saw my father, and my brothers and sisters were just there as I was . . . pushin' to pay the bills."

As I sat on one side of the classroom chairs in a row with other students, I knew I ought to be moving my chair to one side, an objective impersonal observer, judgmental. But the sigh of the class beguiled and before I realized it, I was drawn into the group and, omniscent clang of a gate down the hall forgotten, I too was running the city streets.

"It was tough to be hard," the big speaker continued. "My life was hard and everything I saw in my life was dealing with the street game. I loved the girls and the dope game. I played school sports, loved ball—played basketball and football—was selling dope at school. I believed there was a God but I needed money to help my family and keep pushin' my habit. I was a living dead."

"I finished school and went to college on a scholarship for basketball. Because of the dope game and staying in trouble I made a mistake and came up here. In prison I've started listening to my mom an' started studying Islam and helping other brothers to the truth. I've changed my life, and keep positive friends in my circle and hope to be a lawyer one day and a great leader for my people. That's the End. Thank you for listening."

And with a great sigh of relief, Mellons-X grinned and half stumbled to retake his seat, long legs sticking across the aisle.

As the clapping and whistles broke out, I gazed for a moment at the filthy curtains hanging beside the barred windows, became aware once more of the dim distant metallic clangs as in a foundry, and returned to cold judgment. Mellons-X's speech was not spectacular as I had known full well it would not be, at least he had not forgotten any of it. Was his story unique? Not at all. Single-parent family. Absent father. Brothers and sisters reared in poverty. On the streets at a young age. Drug selling to raise money. Eventual lock-up. It was the story of two-thirds of the class.

Unlike most, the speaker, as I had learned from his words, had actually stayed in school long enough to graduate. Perhaps it was because he'd been ambitious to pick up a sports scholarship to college, perhaps the school offered a handy market for drug selling. But after a week's parade of soul searchers, I had thought grimly to myself, "Damn, this podium is turning into a confessional booth." So I had ordered the students to the prison library in no uncertain terms: "Bring us research on something outside your personal life."

And what did each student know best? These nineteen- to twenty-two-year-old black kids from Detroit's ghetto? Well, certainly, I knew without saying we wouldn't be analyzing in depth any hot topics on the six o'clock news—partisan wrangling over a Congressional bill, immigration, a hurricane in South Carolina, the latest courtroom drama. These were light years removed from their desperate concerns; they had other things on their minds. I knew, as no stranger could certainly know, that what each student knew best—and really all he knew—was the stark immediacy of his own well-defined street life within the hood. The daily life within those six or eight rundown blocks he called home and within which he had precariously survived for his entire short existence, that's what he would talk about. So just as we had absorbed Islam, the newly adopted faith of so many young black prisoners on our second week—completely, saturatingly—we now reviewed, detailed and fully documented the plight of the inner cities in our third week.

Over the next two hours while a late summer thunderstorm blew past outside unheard, and unnoticed within the concrete mausoleum of the Michigan Reformatory, statistics were now offered in reports on poverty, teenage pregnancy, homicides, crackhouses, drive-by shootings. Articles had been researched from pages of *Time*, *Newsweek*, *Ebony*, the *Detroit News* and *The Wall Street Journal*. More information dug up on topics already so familiar that you'd think additional research was scarcely needed by men who had lived the scene, but still a speech class research report project had been ordered to be done.

But, as one after another student came forward to add his particular findings to the growing shared network, a strange thing happened. Each began to see that his own small hood, the only small square of turf he'd known over his entire brief life and thus had thought so unique, was not unique at all. It was simply a miniscule part of a very large pattern of hoods all over the United States—in Chicago, Philadelphia, Brooklyn, Oakland, Baltimore, in Los Angeles. And that he, John Doe, black, imprisoned in a cell in a reformatory in Michigan, was very much like all the young John Does, black, products of the jobless ghettos of U.S. inner cities who sat within similar prisons—or on parole or probation—throughout the nation. Nearly one in every three black men ages twenty to twenty-nine. His brothers. His homies.

Dimly, he began to see that he had become a statistic, part of a larger social problem that needed solving. And he seemed to realize, although no one had told him, that it could very well be up to him to help solve it. Likely it was the first time this street guy, putting self-pity and rebellion aside for once, had looked at his own private life and times not only as a set of personal troubles, but also as a social issue.

Who would be Master of Ceremonies? Jasper Martin, serious, smart, respected, was selected by his mates for the role. It was his job to appoint a time-keeper to bang his desk after five minutes, to enforce the rules— respect, quiet, no questions until over, and then only hands raised and one at a time—and to lead a brief post-speech discussion.

Lifting the old, brown, wooden podium from the floor where it sat in the corner beside the wastebasket, Martin set it on the heavy ancient desk, and solemnly stood behind it.

"We start by introducing Vernon Thompson——"

"Sorry." We were interrupted by Officer Sanford, poking a head in the door, a paper in hand: "You got a Timothy Ewing in here?" The officer looked around. I answered, "No one in here by that name," and he replied, "OK, sorry," again and moved down to the next room with the question. You could see students glancing briefly at each other with the silent question: "Who was Timothy Ewing and what had he done?" Usually this type of search indicated something disciplinary in the offering. A form not returned properly. A detail not accounted for. Shed a quick tear for Timothy and his probable time in the hole. But we had other things on our minds.

Martin picked up again. "Ok. We gonna start by introducing Vernon Thompson who will talk on 'The Black Family of Today.'" A long lanky guy with a determined look glued to his face walked firmly to the podium and began.

"More and more black children are being raised in single-parent homes, 85 percent of them females. A woman is left to discipline and deal with all the financial responsibilities. The single, poor black woman, usually a teenage pregnancy, tries to raise a child, or two or three, who desires the same luxuries the white family has but she can't come close to providing. So the children turn to the street as a solution and get involved with drugs and crime. They die of unnatural causes or suffer imprisonment."

At conclusion, in the room's quiet, speaker Thompson, serious look still glued on, clumped frowning down from the podium to his seat. You could tell he thought he'd bombed. But immediately hearty clapping, interspersed with approving calls of "Yeah Thompson," followed and the grim façade promptly melted into a wide, bashful grin and proud, embarrassed look.

Martin, the Master of Ceremonies, stepped forward to lead the discussion. "How many of us were raised in a single-parent household?" Fifteen out of twenty-two hands went up, including those of both the speaker and the M.C.

"I raised by my grandma," said one student.

"Yeah, me too," said a second. "They the best people in the world."

"You right, man. Better than my mom, that's for sure. She doped out all the time."

"Ok." Martin continued. "As Mr. Thomson tells us, it's the same all over. Not just in Detroit." He looked down at his shoe tops before continuing. "Now, we know that some single parents do fine, we can't condemn them all." Then he began walking back and forth as he spoke. "But for most of those little ladies like Thompson describes who got pregnant too young and didn't know all that much about raising kids." He raised his hand in a discouraged fashion to encompass the room, the hall with its steel gates, the whole prison—"Well, here we are." He looked around the room. "You, me, all of us—the result."

He waited for the statement to sink in, then staring, first right, then left, quietly asked, "Now, the big question, gentlemen, is what we gonna do about it?"

Silence fell over twenty-two students like a blanket. Confused, they turned to stare quizzically at each other. A few shrugged. Do about it? Them? You could see each thinking abjectly to himself, "Shit, man, Speech classes are to listen, not to think." So it was understandable that responses came hesitantly.

A gruff voice called out, "Government gotta give more AFDC money." Agreement, sagely nodded, followed the suggestion and the long pause continued. Then another voice with a definite accusatory whine to it bolted out—"Women gotta' take better care of their kids, it's their responsibility." Near unanimous approval endorsed this loud proclamation. Another seeming unending pause ensued. There was a cough or two, a clearing of throat, then more silence. The ideas had died out. Martin stalked back and forth, impatient.

From my seat against the back wall, I muttered wryly to myself, "Boy, this is just great." Purposely I had selected as inconspicuous a spot as possible to encourage what I supposed would be a brisk level of free-flowing discussion. I had decided everyone's imagination should remain undampened by my presence. Imagination? Ha. The students might as well be bored animals in a sleepy zoo.

Obviously Martin was thinking the same. Impatiently he stalked back and forth, promptly, "Any ideas at all? Let's just brainstorm." But the silence continued. Hector-Bey, trying to be cooperative, was staring so hard at the ceiling I thought something must burst. Nevertheless, no energetic sparks from the storm outside made its way into his, or any other brain, in the room. The silence thickened.

Martin tried another tack. "Her responsibility? You say? Ok. Let me ask you a second question: How many in here are fathers? I'll start by raising my own hand." Eight other hands went up; over one-third of the class. "And anyone married to the lady?" He asked, but no one responded in the affirmative.

Once more he gazed calmly around the room and this time the slow look was cynical. "How many of you supporting your child?" The question caught them off guard, and the silence was broken by laughs. "Support her from in here? You got to be kiddin' brother." And a wise crack floated from a back corner, "Least ways while I'm in here, she ain't gonna get pregnant again." Nervous laughs followed, and a response, "Don't be too sure, brother."

Martin backtracked. "Or ever supported that child, even when you were on the outside?" The room was still again as eyes dropped. "Not a one, I bet." Two raised their hands, hesitatingly.

Then in the quiet came the same accusatory voice, speaking angrily, defensively, "Listen man, that's for her to worry about, she's the one got herself pregnant." The agreeing murmurs were loud, supportive, final, as if to indicate that this definitive statement should end the discussion once and for all.

Well, this is really great, I decided, feeling my temperature rising. What insensitive clods! I could sense myself edging forward on the seat, ready to jump into the fray—rather, into the dismal lack of fray. Once or twice in the past I have found myself forcing other predominately black classes to sit squirming though an extemporaneous lecture I entitle "Today's Great Cop-out of the Arrogant Black Male." This chewing-out would begin with the subject of the role of the vanished black father in teenage pregnancy, and proceed apace through a host of other gender negligence's. It had in the past always been given with a fair amount of feminist fervor, took the unwary students completely by surprise, and usually earned me all the instant and fearful respect of an old-time hellfire and damnation minister.

At this point, one more laconic voice re-echoed the general buck-passing theme, "Yeah, man, it's her fault." At this final straw, I braced myself for the stern and dramatic rush toward the podium I could feel would happen in about thirty seconds, give or take a few, when Martin looked up. "Her fault? You say." Then he plowed on like an unexpected hero.

"Yeah, that's what I always thought," he said. "It was her fault. It was up to her to do something about it." He looked around the room. "Like you guys, I was the big stud. An' I never thought about my lady till I got in here and she wrote me letters. Said she'd always dreamed of going to college, maybe even be a doctor—a baby doctor."

His voice suddenly filled with wonder and pride. "Imagine that, a real doctor. And she coulda done it too. She's smart. A lot smarter than me." He sighed. "Sure, she says she's happy and she loves our little boy." Then his voice turned grim and harsh. "But she's living alone and on food stamps. An' I saw that if I was all that big a man I shoulda kept her from having that baby till later when we could share it. It was my responsibility, not hers." He paused.

The voice from the back came again. "Hey, man, we're sorry. But I sure can't agree with you."

Martin stared at the speaker. "That's your son, man. Yours. What kinda life he having right now? How long you in for, man?"

"Ten to fifteen. Possession with Intent to Deliver."

Martin glared angrily out at his adversary. "You're lucky. I'm here for fifteen to twenty. I ain't never gonna know my son an' be able to help raise him right." And his voice sunk even lower. "And before long I know our kid's gonna be right in this place too. An' there' not a dam thing I can do to keep it from happening." And he looked up. "But I could have."

The quiet lay thick. Eyes dropped and feet shuffled guiltily. The whiny voice from the back had stopped. In the silence you could hear the wheels churning as thoughts turned to other ladies and children out there, alone. The churning was saying to each person, maybe things should have gone down differently. Maybe brother Martin is right after all.

Relieved, I slid back in the chair, whispering to myself, "Thank you, Jasper, you saved us all from a boring lecture." Mine would have ended with that Jesse Jackson remark that "Any man can make a baby; it takes a real man to raise one" but—and I gazed around, noting the student's strong personal reactions—Martin, old man, I liked yours better.

Next up was Leeland Lanton, a thin, quiet guy who worked the kitchen and always had to leave early.

Leeland began his speech, "Murder Rate with Guns" with a dramatic flare. "Gentlemen, take a look at your watches and start counting. You're lucky that this isn't nuthin' but a speech and not a 9mm. I could kill all of you in a minute if this was the real thing. The nation's body count keeps mounting as reckless gunplay continues at an alarming rate. In inner cities, 84 percent of the violence results from guns. Fifty-one percent worry about being a victim. And 27 percent say they were threatened by someone with a gun. *The Detroit News* yesterday told of a 14-year-old young guy shooting this lady to grab her purse. An' two weeks ago a twelve-year-old on the East Side was deliberately killed in a drive-by shooting."

And, following the talk, Master of Ceremonies Martin once again stepped forward.

"How many of us in here owned guns on the street?" Ten hands hesitantly went up. Martin looked over the class and said, "I think maybe it was more. Like maybe everybody." Then he asked, "How many were afraid of people with guns?" Promptly fourteen hands went up. Then he paused and asked, "What if nobody carried guns—would you be afraid then?"

Loud laughter rang out at the absurd question. "No, course not," was the unanimous response. "Only if the police didn't carry no guns neither," called out one student and the response came, "Yeah. You right there, brother."

But Martin, always the intellectual, pursued it. "An like our speaker said, the worst is the inner city." He frowned. "When I was comin' up, just a little fella, I never saw guns. At school, on the street—no guns. Why they all over now?"

It came back to me forcibly that there existed so much wasted talent in prisons. Young men with strong backs who could be out there building bridges. Young men with strong minds who could be designing them. Martin was one of the latter, someone who, given advanced education, could be making change. Here he was, putting his finger on the heart of the matter.

Mellons-X raised his hand. "We all know why, brother. It's the drug game. That's the truth." He glanced around at this classmates, friendly, unworried. "I finally had to carry one too. But ah never shot a man, thassa fact. An ahm glad for that."

"Drugs, eh? Well, we have a speaker on drugs right now." And he introduced Winton Sommers who had researched the topic, "Drugs in the Ghetto." As the speaker reported, African Americans are 13 percent of the population and 13 percent of the drug users, but are 48 percent of the prison population. And that was because it was the blacks who sold their drugs on the street who were easily caught. And got into gangs to control their drug sales territory.

And, then, finally, in a room where over two-thirds were in for drug possession or drug sales, or drug-related crimes, the discussion suddenly became hot and heavy.

"The police going after us. It not right."

"How come they come down so bad on us for crack; and not on the white guys? They all over our neighborhood."

"The police, they crooked. Take payoffs from the big guys."

"The police, they jess wantta beat somebody up."

And channeling the anger into anything constructive was hard.

"But what if we cleaned up the drugs?" Martin asked.

"Us? By ourselves?" The students laughed, and someone imitated a bigtime gang member going ra-ta-ta-tat with an Uzzi.

"I mean it." Martin said. "Since we been in here, most, we seen the light."

Mellons-X jumped up. "You right, brother Martin. How many of us Muslims in here? Most of us. And we give up drugs. Right?"

The class nodded solemnly. "I don't want to end up no crack-head," one muttered.

Fired up, Mellons-X went on, "An' we can clean up the crack houses, we surely can."

And so it went. Lewis Paul, one of our two white students, spoke on "Child Abuse," quoting statistics that over 80 percent of state prisoners have a history of child abuse and neglect, like himself, but "just didn't like to talk about it." Bill James spoke on "AIDS in the Ghetto," someone else on "Prostitution" and another on "Poverty."

And always there sounded the recurrent theme of self-destruction. The 1965 riots in Watts, 1967 Riots in Detroit. The recent 1992 burning of South Central L.A. All the destructions showcased on television simply symbolized the smaller-scale destruction that was occurring daily, hourly, in the neighborhoods.

"We have been caught into material items, drugs and selfishness," said Lawrence Simon in the final speech titled: "Death of the Black Race." Simon was big, deep-voiced, and into sports, playing left tackle for the defense team of one of the prison football teams. His T-shirt bore the logo "Football MR." His voice now boomed out, dead serious:

"Statistics show that rates of homicide, suicide, drug overdose, disease deaths and incarceration among inner city residences are by far the highest in the nation." Then he looked around at his brothers. "How could our race fall to undermining its own self? Slavery had broken up the unity in the family. Isolation has caused the black race to distance ourselves from parents, kin and our community."

"But the most disastrous part is that we as blacks are hurting, stealing and killing each other mentally and physically." Solemnly his gaze moved slowly around the room, his last line a dramatic undertone.

"What we need to do is stop killing ourselves."

Simon back from the podium amidst clapping and whistles that raised the roof. No discussion was needed.

"That's the truth, Larry, man." Mellons-X had jumped to his feet to lead an enthusiastic response for this other big guy who had made this impassioned speech, a fellow in sports. "The truth for sure," he kept hollering. "We gotta help change things. We gonna do it."

The class was over. The podium was moved back in the corner and two students had pushed the heavy ancient desk to one side so the next class could see the small old blackboard which extended only part way across the back wall. Scraping their worn chairs back noisily on the old brown linoleum, each student grabbed his small blue Speech book, tablet of prison-issue blue-lined paper and joined the crowd filtering through the door.

Back slaps and inept congratulations could be heard. "Good talk, Thompson-Bey, way to go." "Thanks, man, you done purty good yourself, man." "Yeah, ya think so? Well, man, ah was a little nervous, ya understand, didn't do as good as ah sounded when ah practiced." "Well, fuck, man, done none of that showed." "For sure? Well, shit, man, that make me feel better." "Yeah, ah think the speeches were purty good, didn't you?" "Yeah man, real good."

Slowly gathering the speech outlines handed-in in a scattered pile on the desk top, I stood looking around at the crowded stuffy room, emptying now of rough, young men in prison blues.

I reviewed the day's speeches which had addressed themselves to the city's troubles—drugs, guns, violence, dysfunctional families, the flight of the middle-class, the human dregs left behind in a decaying city. And as I watched the inmates filing out, it all seemed appropriate. They were the city's discarded human dregs, to be swept up and warehoused out of sight in a decaying old prison.

I sighed. And all those problems so eagerly attacked this afternoon by the students as if newly discovered had been well-documented for more decades than any harried, big-city council member cared to remember. One could not really say that anything new had been added today. In fact, as I zipped up my briefcase, I thought, no, just the opposite. Something has been left out.

"Mellons-X," I said. "Answer me something." He and Patterson-El were drifting out of class, bringing up the rear.

"Sure. What's that?" He swung around to face me and threw the old cheery smile my way. "You like my speech?" He asked in his husky voice. Putting his book down, he lowered his six-foot-four clumsily into one of the too-small chairs for a moment to await my question. Patterson-El, almost as tall, slid into the next chair. "And I rehearsed." Another big Mellons-X smile.

"I noticed. The students could tell the difference too,"

"That good. I practice on the next one too."

Then I looked down at the two sitting there slouched to overflowing in the two old brown chairs. "But tell me this. We had so many speeches on problems of the inner city."

"Yes ma'am, we surely have got 'em." Heads nodded in sorry agreement.

"But," I asked quickly. "Don't you think that in many ways *you* are the problem? You and all the guys in this room?"

I thought the question would confuse and insult them—return them to the same old self pity and accusations against society. But instead the two broke into broad grins.

"That's it," said Mellons-X. "You exactly right." And his grin got even broader and he kind of slapped his knee. "That's jess what we wanta tell our young brothers out there. That's why we want them to join the Muslims like us an' be proud of their selves *before* they get in trouble."

"Yeah," added Patterson-El. "We wanta tell 'em all about how bad it is in here. They should stay in school an' make somethin' of themselves an' improve their neighborhood."

"Yeah," said Mellons-X, frowning. "We wanta change from being a problem. An' be a solution, you might say."

"Well," I said, approvingly. "Your leaders like Jesse Jackson will be proud of you."

Mellons-x shrugged politely. "Well, we Muslim men don't much go along with Jesse Jackson." Then his teeth shone in a big smile. "But we go to school anyway. Jess for ourselves."

"But will they listen to you?"

Abruptly he looked down at the floor, quiet. "I dunno but I'll tell them anyway." Then the big dark eyes with the long lashes appeared troubled again and he said softly, almost resignedly, "Don't know what else to do."

I figured these long faces wouldn't do and said heartily, "Well, sure they'll listen, you will do just great."

"I'm glad you understand," Patterson-El said. They grinned their old cheerful grins again and each lumbered out of his chair. "We gonna do it. You see."

I could hear them disappearing down the hall to the gate. They had picked up enroute singing an old Motown tune. With Patterson carrying the melody in his off-the-rafters soul tenor and Mellons-X adding the da-dums in his deep bass and snapping his fingers, it all sounded great, especially bouncing off the echoing concrete walls of the prison hall that way. I smiled and shook my head. They were twenty-one-year-olds again. We'll change the world for sure, they were saying. But we'll do it a little later.

15

—ᴍ—

Inner City Experiences

Black Prisoners over Twenty-Five
at Jackson State Prison, 1990–2000

INTRODUCTION

Each of the young African American prisoners with long sentences under twenty-five years of age we met at Michigan Reformatory (see chapters 13 and 14) grew up in Detroit's inner city. At twenty-five, if still in prison, he will be transferred to Jackson State Prison, or other Michigan prisons to serve out his sentence. Other prisoners aged twenty-five and older when arrested and convicted in Detroit go directly to Jackson Prison, about eighty miles away, or to other state prisons.

When his prison time is completed, each will be released back to Detroit, or other Michigan cities—whatever the site was of where he was convicted, to complete his parole. Most will return to their homes and former neighborhoods in the inner city, now populated largely by African Americans and often called the "ghetto." A description of Detroit's inner city, more accurately a "jobless ghetto," as viewed by the authors, on some driving explorations through northeast Detroit neighborhoods, follows.

A large rundown area of approximately some ten square miles or more, Detroit's near northeast (Gratiot Street north from Greek Town) sits as a large blemish on the east side of the state's largest city, Detroit, a commercial hub of Southeastern Michigan. An otherwise modern city of downtown freeways and tall office buildings, the "Motor City" is famed for its lovely old residential areas, prime convention headquarters, GM Headquarters, UAW Solidarity House, revitalized restaurant district of "Greek Town," casino gambling, proximity to Windsor, Canada, and views of the Detroit River.

Today, Detroit has high unemployment rates in jobless-ghetto districts, and a lot of homicides. In 2006 Detroit was listed as "second" in violence and homicides, ranking only after St. Louis as the most dangerous city in the United States. This city has a thirty-year history of drugs and record numbers of drug-turf battles between fifteen-year-olds with guns, and consequent homicides and assaults "with Intent to Do Great Bodily Harm." Detroit's high rate of drug sales, and violence, results in many felony convictions.

To simply drive through its dozens and dozens of dilapidated city blocks, each block seemingly more spotted with old, wooden-frame houses, mostly abandoned, and vacant, weed-covered lots of burned-down houses, and still-open liquor stores, is a completely depressing experience that leaves a long-lasting impression. Another reason for violence, thus, is the pervasive aura of poverty and hopelessness that afflicts the inner city, begetting unrest.

Some areas of the section approximate normality. Lining the cracked asphalt streets, occasionally interspersed with streets of gravel where asphalt pavement has run out, are blocks of occupied older wooden-frame houses, a sagging porch, a touch of lawn, a struggling tree or two. Neighbors talk on the unpainted front steps, men repair an old car in the driveway, kids play on the cracked sidewalk. Then come perhaps two more blocks of abandoned houses. Then maybe a large once-operating, but now closed, manufacturing building or wholesale warehouse—abandoned, with a rusted spur train track running to it—all of it enclosed within a cluttered cyclone fence holding wind-blown tumbleweed and paper trash. In an adjoining vacant lot next to a closed restaurant, a drunk sleeps on the sidewalk outside a still-open liquor store next door. Empty liquor bottles scatter the curbs nearby. Periodically a youth speeds by in his car on the now-vacant street, boom box pounding.

The inner city "business strips" sprawl for blocks, encompassing a mishmash of small rundown stores, many of them vacant—Mom and Pop groceries, small variety stores, Dollar Stores, check cashing or "cash advance" outlets, appliance repair, food bank, Salvation Army, two laundromats, two pawn shops, three liquor stores, small restaurants, several vacant and boarded-up store fronts, a tire shop, three thrift shops and so on.

Then the so-called residential section of the inner city continues on. Dozens of burned-out houses are scattered along many of the grubby streets and garbage-strewn alleys. In fact, until a few years ago when the police cracked down, Halloween in Detroit was called "Devil's Night," with gangs of youth running through streets of the inner city torching long-empty houses. Houses and other buildings burn for other reasons. Frustrated owners or landlords—unable to rent or sell their house, commercial building or rental property—hire arsonists to set it afire. If they cannot, thereby, collect insurance, at least they will not need to pay taxes or have to respond to code enforcement. With the city too poor to remove the charred hulks, they remain as bitter reminders of a once-proud residential section.

Once in a while, almost standing out in contrast to its dirt-poor surroundings, a shiny new car carrying well-dressed passengers drives by. It does not seem out of place to posit that they are gang members, with undoubtedly late-model pistols tucked into their belt or under the seat.

Black and white police cars slowly cruise the neighborhoods, siren at the ready, alert for possible drug deals underway, or gang fights or drug-dealing "crew" turf wars, that can lead to later grudge drive-by shootings. Or, the police may simply follow that shiny car doing a Law Enforcement Information Network (LEIN) check for "warrants outstanding," or otherwise patrol, waiting for a call.

This is Detroit's inner city. Some residents growing up on its mean streets tolerate it. On the other hand, most growing up here have seen all they want of crime and poverty and do everything they can to move out of the area.

In their book *Burglars on the Job*, Wright and Decker (1994) describe the locale of their study on home invasion (breaking and entering, or burglary). Their words capture the home-boy streets of many of our young MR drug sellers we have already encountered and the home of the over-twenty-five-year-old Jackson Prison student essays that follow.

> The study of residential burglary on which this book is based was conducted on the streets of St. Louis, Missouri, a declining "rust belt" city. St. Louis has fallen victim to some of the same problems that have plagued other American cities in the post-World War II era, namely deindustrialization followed by rapid population loss and the concentration of poverty. However, these problems have been writ large in St. Louis owing to its limited size relative to the surrounding metropolitan area. As urban decay took hold, residents with the financial ability to do so—both black and white—moved out of the city and into one of the more desirable communities on its borders, taking much of the tax base with them. Left behind in this process were "the truly disadvantaged" (Wilson, 1987), people with few resources and a consequent need for social services that have become impossible to maintain in the face of decreasing revenues. The crime rate in St. Louis consistently outpaces that for most other cities in the United States; for instance, its 1988 burglary rate, at 2,950 per 100,000 population, more than doubled the national rate. (Wright & Decker 2004:7)

Many, many U.S. cities have their "jobless ghetto" districts or "throw-away cities." Wright and Decker continue:

> St. Louis is a city made up of 79 neighborhoods with well-defined and well-known boundaries. As might be expected, some of these neighborhoods

have suffered the consequences of economic decline much more severely than others. Unemployment rates, poverty, and female-headed households all display their highest levels in a handful of neighborhoods clustered in the northern part of St. Louis. These areas, which are predominantly black, possess many of the physical signs commonly associated with urban decay: abandoned, boarded-up buildings, litter-strewn vacant lots, and gang graffiti sprayed on every available wall. There is also a visible street life, epitomized by the groups of young to middle-aged men who congregate on the corner, drinking, using drugs and, in their words, "kickin' it up." (Wright & Decker 2004:8)

The prison's current parole policy is to release the prisoner to the jurisdiction of his arrest. Is this policy of returning the prisoner to his home area, to his former hang-outs, or essentially back to the scene of his crime, the best for the prisoner and for the community? Is he more likely to go back to his old friends and old habits and soon return to prison?

Or perhaps the real question concerns the inner city itself. Is simply growing up in these squalid violent surroundings a contributing cause of delinquency and eventual prison in itself? Some European countries do not let "inner cities" develop because they have social policies of higher wage, adequate unemployment benefits, and more social services, such as municipal child care or day care, universal health care, apprenticeships for good jobs and other social support services. Crime-ridden "inner cities" are not due to fate but rather to the existence of, or lack of, social policy decisions (Eitzen & Baca Zinn 2000; Williamson et al. 2003).

AUTHOR'S REPORT #10

Gangs, Players and Street Code: Death Becomes a Way of Life in Detroit

In U.S. inner cities nationwide, with their lack of jobs for youth, sale of illegal drugs is, of course, the one big moneymaking enterprise for the young job seekers. It is literally "the only game in town." Just as filmmaking is known as "The Industry" in Hollywood, the drug business—buying, selling, promoting, marketing, distributing, handling of all aspects of drugs in Detroit's "inner city"—is known as "the game," that is, "the drug game." A top profiteer in "the game," that is, a drug dealer with many clients, territories and top sales who has accumulated ostentatious riches—cars, women, jewelry, especially women—is known as "a player" (a major player in the drug game). Often there are urban gangs that control inner city drug-selling locations.

While we have previously heard from the young men at MR on growing up in the jobless ghetto, our older men (over tewnty-five) at Jackson Prison have written descriptions of gangs, becoming a player, and the jobless ghetto street code. Here are some prisoner/student comments:

> One summer my cousin showed up from the South Side of Chicago in Michigan to stay. At that time I had turned fifteen years and wanted to hang out with him along with his crew to party for my fifteenth birthday. But for some reason "Shorty" just wasn't buying me hanging out with him and his crew.
>
> So the next day when he came to my mother's house to pick me up, I asked him: "Why can't I hang out with you when your crew is around?" He told me, "You have to be a gangster to hang around me and my crew." I responded, "I could be a gangster too just like you." He just laughed and walked away.

After our prisoner/student had begun to hang out and party with his older cousin Shorty's crew for a while, and had assaulted a gang rival's girlfriend on command—completing the "dare of blood"—his older cousin said he wanted the younger cousin to be "part of our crew as a gangster."

> But one of the members stood up and asked me what made me worthy to be a part of their crew. So I told him that I could do anything they could do, and he said, "Oh yeah then if that is the case then I dare you to drink a whole fifth of Wild Irish Rose to get my vote." So I did it to the point where I was staggering drunk.
>
> Then my cousin stood up a second time, and called his crew to attention again to where everybody was listening and told them that I had completed the dare of blood, but there was one more dare I had to fulfill before I could really become a full-fledged member of the gangster world.
>
> And my cousin had all of his crew form a line on my right and left hand sides to the point where there was six to seven members on each side of me.
>
> Then he said to me: "I dare you to walk through the middle of my crew on both sides of you, if you make it through to the end, you, my cousin, will become a full-fledged Gangster."

School is a place where gangs can recruit and dominate. In some of the rougher inner city jobless ghetto schools this gang pressure can become oppressive in middle school. A prisoner/student comments:

> As I passed the sixth grade I knew when I started the seventh grade I'd catch hell because every year when newcomers come to a new school the gangs pick them out for punks to turn on. You are either with them or against them, these gangs always mess with you.

Well anyway, it was June of 1983, our last day in elementary school. I dreaded that day cause I knew I was going to IS 10, one of the baddest schools in New York where kids get stabbed and shot and raped.

On our first day (the writer and his two friends) went to the bathroom together with a Mexican guy I knew, Jose, from 125th Street. While we were in the bathroom, some guys came in—my face got pushed in the toilet, one guy had an automatic. Suddenly, I knew I had gotten shot.

Later in that episode, our prisoner/student writes, the three victims of the gang were dragged down to the Bronx River behind the school:

They made us watch Jose as they slit his throat and shot him in the groin by the fence behind the school. We couldn't save him as he fell in the river like a sack of grain. They left us alive. They knew we wouldn't snitch. It's like this on your coming to a new school. Most schools are dangerous in New York City, do or be did.

—ᴍ—

Along with gangs, the jobless inner city bring forth desires to "excel" through winning respect as a "player," a man who can string several women along. A prisoner/student proudly recalls his prowess and gives advice on how to be a player:

Being involved with several women at the same time may lead to some very sticky situations. Because of this a player must be a quick thinker with the gift of gab.

A player's appearance is very important. You must be well-groomed and your attire has to be immaculate. A player sees himself as the manufacturer of a product that every woman wants (himself) and is willing to pay for or spend money on himself.

So he takes pride in self-maintenance very much like women do. He gets manicures; pedicures; he goes to the gym; and some even get facials and perms. You also have to be extremely intellectual and financially stable.

—ᴍ—

Still, while "being a player" may sound attractive (in a juvenile sort of way), the part about being "financially stable" in the inner city is "iffy." The loss of jobs and increasing economic insecurity in the U.S. central cities, with up to 50 percent unemployment in some areas, led to the rise of the central city as a "retail sales" site for the illegal drug economy. In turn, drugs and violence go together in the inner city "dealing" context. One prisoner/student writes:

After the riot (1967 Detroit) everything had changed. Most of my friends moved away. After the riot, there was not much to do on Baldwin or Kerchvel Streets. The little part of Detroit I knew all went to hell.

After a time, drug houses began to appear everywhere. If not down the street it was around the corner from wherever one may live, no matter who.

I was about to enter a part of my life I knew nothing about. As I got older, death, drugs and money were becoming a way of life whether I wanted it to be or not.

I was out everyday selling weed. Money was the only thing on my mind. Detroit by the early 1980s became a big dope house to me.

My friends were killing themselves with the hard drugs, and that is one reason why I did not do the hard drugs. If a person did not O.D., someone was getting shot. One way or another death came a-knocking. I had to keep a black funeral suit in the closet, ready to wear when going to say goodbye to the next friend. There were a lot of friends I said goodbye to.

—⚏—

Consider this: if you grew up in these big inner city neighborhoods—it would seem natural, "the way it is," to you. One of Tregea's main campus students who did grow up in Detroit's inner city writes:

I don't disagree that there are gangs and drugs and killing because I am eighteen years old and I have witnessed many things. I do disagree with the picture that the media has painted about inner city youth, the so-called, "products of the ghetto."

I spent most of my life in the city of Detroit, on the East Side of town. I lived exactly two doors down from a crack house. It seemed like it belonged there, the drug dealers who owned it were always around. During the summer months they would play basketball in the street and when the ice cream man came by they would buy ice cream for all of the kids. We would sit on the curb eating our ice cream watching them play. They were good neighbors—some would say even hardworking. They were active in our community even though they sold drugs. The neighbors were never afraid of them and neither were the children. Most of their customers were white people who had migrated on the other side of Eight-Mile-Road, and come into our neighborhood to buy their drugs.

I understand Elijah Anderson's theory on the "decent families" and the "street families." It was almost as if we had worked out a system. Our parents—a "decent family"—sent us to the neighborhood school that was very dangerous and full of gangs and violence. So it was simple, the deal was clear. We let them "roll" on our street—the drug gangs and "street families"—and they kept us safe. We had to adapt to each other's lives accordingly.

When I think about it now, I feel bad. There were so many lives wasted, many of them were extremely intelligent men who if given the chance could have become anything, from doctors to accountants.

This 100-level "Sociology and Social Problems" main-campus student emphasizes that "Most of the kids lived in single-parent homes. The boys started to glorify the drug dealers, admiring the fast money, and the flashy cars and jewelry." She also notes that the young boys most admired the respect that they could get as drug dealers. Then, she notes: "Greed soon took over the dealers' hearts and they quickly began to recruit young boys." She continues:

I don't know what it is, but to them—the young boys—having a gun made them men. Then they lost control; kids shot kids, people were dying everywhere, all the time. Mothers were losing sons left and right. It became a game then, someone would get killed for whatever reason and his or her friends would then retaliate, seeking revenge.

The police were no help. It wasn't until one of their men was killed in the area that they decided to start "patrolling." In my eyes this is what began everything, the lack of support from our system. This sort of thing would never have gone that far in the white neighborhoods of our white working-class districts or white suburban counterparts.

16

—ᗰ—

Cocaine and Addictive Deadly Crack in Detroit's Inner City

INTRODUCTION

In the United States from the 1930s to the 1960s, there was little demand for cocaine and so little supply. Cocaine was associated with those at the fringes of society—jazz musicians and members of the criminal underworld. What is cocaine?

COCAINE

The prime growing area for cocaine is in the northern mountains of South America—in Peru and Colombia, particularly the latter.

Coca is a flowering bush or shrub that stands five to six feet high, and yields at most four ounces of waxy elliptical leaves, per bush, that are about 1 percent cocaine by weight. Many fields of coca plants must be grown for any large output of processed cocaine.

Conversion into cocaine hydrochloride—powdered cocaine—is done in the field and requires several steps using different chemicals—alcohol and benzene, sulfuric or hydrochloric acid, and sodium carbonate, leaving behind crystals of crude coca cocaine known as coca paste. This is allowed to dry, treated with more chemicals and finally emerges as cocaine hydrochloride—a white crystalline powder that is about 95-percent pure.

In the United States cocaine hydrochloride is cut (diluted) for street sale by adding sugars (lactose) or talcum, borax or other neutral substances and is finally sold as a white powder that is sniffed.

291

During the late 1960s and the 1970s there came to be a good deal of experimentation with drugs, and especially the wide acceptance of marijuana. Cocaine was no longer associated with the less desirable fringes. The media helped shape the new demand (glamorizing the lifestyle of affluent, upper-class drug dealers and use of cocaine by celebrities and athletes) (Wesson & Smith 1985 in Abadinsky 2001:41). The increasing demand was enough to generate new drug sources and cocaine flowed heavily into the inner cities to be circulated by an army of new young drug sellers on street corners.

Cocaine or "coke" was king. Ever-increasing domestic demand for the drug triggered more drug-supplier-network organized crime "wars" between foreign drug cartels. At the same time, concern was growing at home about its pervasive use in the United States.

Crack

All this was overshadowed, however, by the sudden drug epidemic in 1986 of a cocaine derivative—rock cocaine. Known as "the fast food of drugs," "crack," as it was called, could be made cheaply at home in small rocks from cocaine and other ingredients. "Crack" cost much less on the street to buy as a single small rock than powdered coke, had a far more powerful "rush"—and even just initial use led far more quickly into addiction.

While the end product of cocaine was a white powder (coke) that was sniffed, the product of the additional crack cocaine process was a solid opaque slab that was broken into approximate inch-square or smaller cubes or pieces known as "rocks," that would be smoked in small special pipes. The drug crosses the blood-brain barrier quickly, producing an intense high, similar to—but more powerful than—sexual orgasm. The crack cocaine rush lasts a few seconds and is followed by a euphoria for several minutes, which, in turn, is followed by a less pleasurable hyper-excitability. This is followed by a real low. Smoking crack repeatedly develops an intense craving for more, and within days to weeks, the user progresses from recreational use to compulsive use.

Abadinsky reports on interviews with crack users that revealed: "Despite the many years of using other drugs, the experience with Crack was quite different. The experiences with Crack was very much a jolt, with feelings and behaviors . . . they had never experienced before—the irritability, rage, and aggression." The clients he interviewed who, at the time, were in drug treatment, had held jobs, valued their paycheck, but the loss of so much money spent on crack was "incomprehensive to them." (Abadinsky 2005:119–20).

Abadinsky emphasizes, also, that, in the context of the inner city drug economy, drug sales and the street drug-culture, crack "constitutes the first psychoactive drug experience of many young abusers, who try it even before alcohol and marijuana" (Abadinsky 2008:135).

The *epidemic* of the drug "crack," in the period 1986–1993, was so pervasive it resulted, as we outlined in chapters 2–3, in moral panics and associated politically motivated toughening of sentencing laws (Chiricos 1995/2002; Blumstein 2002; Kraska 2004; Musto 1991). Crack helped to bring along increases in drug-related crimes (e.g., home invasion, burglary, larceny, robbery, violence related to gang drug-turf wars)—but also increases in homicide and assaults due to crack-induced "irritability, rage and aggression." Consequently, the vast increase in incarceration, already started, accelerated.

Prisoner Essay #77

The Path to Destruction

"Arena, look you have to give up the cocaine because I can't take this any longer," I said. Arena being my blond-haired, blue-eyed, bombshell of a girlfriend for the past three years. We had a little two-year-old boy named Dee.

It was November, 1989, and we had been doing coke (sniffing powdered cocaine) for about a year at this time.

I had just gotten off work and we were standing in our living room, right in front of the fireplace. I stood there holding her hand while looking down into the fireplace at the cold ashes of a fire from the previous night. The cold ashes reminded me of what a cold world we live in.

I was feeling nothing but despair and helplessness for the both of us. I was becoming desperate because I didn't know how to make her understand that we were both out of control. We were doing $1,400 of cocaine a week and it was wrecking our lives.

As I looked up from the fireplace, I noticed she was smiling. This made me furious.

"You either give up the coke, or you can kiss me and Dee good bye!" I stated hotly.

She walked over to the bay window and stood there leaning on the loveseat out over our yard where our son was playing with his toys.

So I asked her again "What's it going to be, us or the coke?"

She refused to look at me and just kept staring out the window.

I decided I needed a beer. Walking into the kitchen I could not believe my eyes. All I saw was destruction. The dishes from breakfast were still in the sink, Dee's cereal was spilt on the floor and the table was covered with dishes from lunch. I thought: "Here I was working twelve hours a day, six days a week, making good money just to put coke up her nose and she couldn't even clean the house."

I walked over to the refrigerator and opened the door and all I saw in the near empty refrigerator was a gallon of milk, Kool-Aid, and some leftovers. No beer! I yelled to her, "Arena, come here a minute."

As she stepped around the corner I noticed she had something in her hand but paid no attention to it.

"Where did my beer go that was in here last night?" I asked, pointing at the fridge.

"Mike drank it." She replied. Mike was our dope dealer who usually stopped over every other day because we were doing about an 8-ball a day. An 8-ball being 1/8 of an ounce of powdered cocaine, and runs about $175.00 to $250.00.

"Please tell me no!"

"No what?" she replied.

"That you didn't buy an 8." I said sadly.

At this time I was looking at what she had in her left hand and knew it was too late.

"How could you?" I yelled, knowing deep down inside me in a few minutes we would both be sitting down in front of the TV with the coke out, doing it. "Arena, Christmas is less than a month away and we haven't even started doing our shopping yet."

It wasn't the money that was bothering me the most; it was the fact coke was coming before everything else. We were getting to where we were so scared; we wouldn't answer the door when somebody knocked because we thought it was the cops coming to bust us. We were living in fear, which is not the way to be living.

Our relationship was doing good so far. We had a strong relationship and were doing financially well but were starting to feel effects of what the coke was doing to us. We were spending money we didn't have to spare with Christmas so near.

One month later, with Christmas behind us, things were getting worse. I had found out right after Christmas that Arena had pulled all of her money out of her checking account and was going around town buying Christmas gifts with bad checks. She wasn't just buying Christmas gifts, she was buying TVs, house stereos, VCRs. She would then take the items back and get cash refunds.

Things were out of control. I didn't know what to do. I had never had to face a problem like this before. I did the only thing I could think of: I went to the bank where we had a joint checking account with both our names on the account. I asked to see the balance. There was no balance.

I went home, and later that night I waited for her to fall asleep, I got out of bed and got into her purse for her checkbook. I got it out and wrote VOID on every check and put it back in her purse. I didn't know how long it would take before she tried to write one but I found out real quick.

By mid-afternoon she came flying in the driveway like a bat out of hell, in her 1980 Ford Mustang. She was pissed off.

"What the hell do you think you were doing?" she screamed.

"Saving your life." I replied.

She turned around and stormed right back out the door and got into her car and left. I didn't see her for a couple days of days after that. When she finally did come home we had a long talk and decided to get away for a while and try to get off the dope. We knew we couldn't get off it if we stayed around home because everybody we knew was on coke or something else.

We had to make some arrangements before we could just up and take off. Like who would take care of Dee, who would stop over and feed my dog without stealing him. I wasn't about to turn my house keys over to a dope head and say "See ya!" So my family took care of Dee and my dog for me—only after I told them why I was leaving. They wished us good luck and we were off.

We returned six months later and we were both clean of dope with Arena three months pregnant for our second child.

She had already agreed that after the baby was born, she would go on a diet rather than use dope because neither one of us wanted to go through this again.

It has been four years and we are both still clean of dope.

To sum it up for you, cocaine is one of the most addictive drugs out there. You get hooked on it without even realizing it and by the time you do, it's too late to just stop. It tears households, friendships and families apart and you don't even see it happening. You become a liar, a cheat and a thief and don't see that happening either. You become somebody you don't want to be and you have very little say so in the matter. So your best bet is not to go down this path to destruction, just say "No!"

Prisoner Essay #78

Rock Star—Freebasing in Detroit

The most memorable experience in my life was also the most devastating.

It all began when I moved back to Michigan after being locked up for five years in Mississippi. For the first year after I got out, everything in my life was lovely. With assistance and support of my family, I was able to establish myself back into society, by obtaining two jobs and going to school at night.

But the most significant event to take place in my life was the rekindling relationship of my first love, Gloria. That act alone made me the happiest man alive. We had even planned on getting married.

But, all that joy began to deteriorate the moment I started smoking crack cocaine. In my blind ignorance, I tricked myself into believing that I was competent and strong enough to smoke "rock cocaine," or "crack," and not get hooked. After all, I told myself, I used to snort powdered cocaine for quite a while and I could handle that. So, I felt smoking crack shouldn't be a problem.

That was the worse presumption anyone should ever make, to compare rock cocaine to the powder form. Because, once you cook powder cocaine to the rock form, you intensify the compound and by heating it up it and inhaling it, it goes quicker through your lungs to your brain, whereas sniffing the powder goes slower through your nose into your blood stream.

Initially, no one starts out with the intention of having a drug become the focus of their life. But, when you smoke crack cocaine, ultimately it will take total control of your life.

Freebasing, which is smoking crack cocaine through a pipe, induces a strong feeling of being on top of the world. This feeling of exhilaration, experienced while under influence of the drug, is quickly followed by depression when you run out.

This addiction also has an enormous impact on family members. When a person is addicted to cocaine, the time and money that you would ordinarily have spent on your family is, instead, spent on obtaining and using drugs. And it will continue to get worse as cocaine assumes more and more importance in your life.

Eventually, everything you hold dear in your life is completely disrupted by the desire and need for cocaine.

17

—ɱ—

Guns in the Inner City

INTRODUCTION

Our twenty years of prison college teaching (1981–2000) in eleven Michigan prisons required us to teach simultaneously in two or more prisons to make a living. However, this allowed us to observe two types of prisoners—older prisoners (over twenty-five) and the younger prisoners (seventeen to twenty-five). And, we observed these two types of prisoners before, during and after the crack epidemic (1986–1993) and the start of the "war on drugs." We noticed a difference in the prisoner experiences with guns.

By 1986, with the entrance of crack to the drug scene and its immediate rise to the top as the low-cost "drug of choice," the number of gang-related drug sales "turf battles" in the cities increased drastically. So did the number of guns. And, while some older men stayed in the gangs longer because of the drug money, most of the gang members got younger. Juvenile homicides skyrocketed. Describing this new trend of kids killing kids, Zimring & Hawkins note: "African-Americans are no more than twice as likely as whites to become victims of property crimes; (but) they are more than five times as likely to be killed" (1997:87).

Earlier, guns had seldom been seen in inner-city neighborhoods. Even up to the 1970s, guns were simply not around—anywhere. As older prisoners (over twenty-five) at Jackson State Prison told us, "Before I went to prison I never saw a gun. Now all the young guys coming in brag about the piece they had out on the street."

And that statement was true. As the young prisoners (under twenty-five) we taught at MR (especially during the 1986–1997 period) often solemnly proclaimed, "You had to have a gun, it was like something you put on in the morning; you didn't go out without it."

As the older prisoners recalled, the younger inmates did brag about their "pieces" and how they had competed to own the latest model and style. Later when we taught former MR students, who were now over twenty-five years of age and had moved to Jackson prison, we might overhear two or more students reminiscing about life on the streets and bragging about the exact gun(s) or pistol they had carried.

Soon, even more powerful handguns—357 magnums, 9 millimeter "glocks"—and larger, multi-firing guns like the "uzi" and "AK-47s" were being routinely carried by street sellers.

Whereas, formerly, individuals or gangs had long fought with time-honored weapons such as fists, knives, brass knuckles, saps, chains, bats, now guns were used almost routinely by young blacks instead of fists or knives to settle every score. Whether it was to defend a drug location, to claim a woman or protect her, to rob or steal from someone, or mug them, or to use in drive-by shootings—and very often just to avenge a real or imagined insult or disrespect—the gun was always available at the ready, waiting to be used.

The presence of guns inordinately increased the risk of violence with its attendant lengthy sentence. Many a young prisoner involved in what would formerly have been just a fight, even a drug-related fight, could well have gotten off with a relatively light sentence of assault and battery and perhaps drug possession. Instead, in the heat of anger and youthful emotion, he pulls a gun, shoots and kills someone, and ends with a life sentence. In Michigan, the parole board, since shifting in composition to political appointees in 1992, has very seldom granted parole for "life with the possibility of parole" cases. Even if the judge says "twenty to life," the Michigan parole board seldom paroles such prisoners, saying, instead, "life means life" and, in effect, "resentencing" for the original offense (CAPPS 2008). So these emotion-driven youth crimes keep prisoners, who have matured in prison by their thirties, for an additional forty years beyond that, or until they die in prison, even though there is little risk of recidivism.

Prisoner Essay #79

I Had Been Shot

On November 20, 1984, my day started as normal. It was kind of cold outside and the night before it had rained quite a bit. I decided to stay around the house to do some odds-and-ends repairs that were badly needed. Everything was going fine until all of a sudden my girlfriend and I started arguing. This startled me because everything was fine between us only minutes ago.

The argument went on for quite a while and became very intense. I decided it would be best if I left the house in order to avoid any further confrontation.

I returned home the following day and learned that my girlfriend had also left the previous day. My sister was home; however she did not know where my girlfriend had gone. I didn't worry much because I knew that she would eventually come home. Then she phoned me to request that I bring some diapers and powder over to her sister's house for the baby. Our conversation continued and it ended on a peaceful note.

After a while, I walked to the corner store. As I approached the store, I observed three or four guys loitering by the entrance. I didn't pay much attention to them because this was normal in my neighborhood. I purchased my things and while leaving the store, two of the men approached me demanding money. I informed them that all I had was what was in the bag.

Everything was going fast; my mind was racing because I didn't know what was going to happen next. The men did not appear to possess weapons.

Therefore I believed my chance of escaping or defending myself was fair. Before I knew it I had knocked one of them down.

All of a sudden I heard a loud bang. For about a minute or less I didn't feel or hear anything, I was knocked unconscious, I saw a guy standing over me with a gun.

The guy turned to aid his friend, allowing a small opportunity in which I was able to get up and run.

My left side was numb of all feeling, and my adrenaline was pumping. I couldn't believe it! I had been shot.

I made it home to find my sister there. I told her that I had been shot, I opened my jacket and blood was gushing out of my chest; my sister was hysterical.

She finally calmed down enough to drive me to the hospital. I underwent thirteen hours of surgery to repair the nerves, arteries and broken bones that made up my rib cage.

I was able to leave the hospital five days later, on Thanksgiving Day. I was truly thankful and blessed just to be alive.

Sometime later on Thanksgiving Day I went to visit my girlfriend; she was no longer staying at my house, she had moved out and had her own place. As I entered her house to my amazement, the guy who had shot me was there.

I thought this was a random act of robbery. I couldn't believe it—my girlfriend had set me up! I stayed for only a few minutes because all sorts of things were going through my mind.

I didn't want to alert them that I knew what was going on so I left the house, and never returned.

Today, I live with the painful memories of this event, both physically and mentally. I've asked my ex-girlfriend why did she have this done and she denies any involvement. Nevertheless, her actions show that she orchestrated the entire ordeal. I live my life now with a great distrust of people and not letting women get too close or personal.

—m—

Prisoner Essay #80

I Fell in Love with Guns: Twenty to Forty Years for Murder

Junior high school was a hard process of getting used to at first, but once I got used to my schedule it was easier. I made a transition from being dependant at home to being more independent—and I started to do robberies.

In junior high I was to see my first bag of drugs. By the grace of God, I only smoked weed once while there and weed was only the one drug I used ever. Junior high was also the year I saw my first real gun. A black pistol, with a brown handle. It was a .25 automatic. At first glance I fell in love with guns and continue to be in love with guns til this day.

In high school I was the guy all the girls liked but were scared to ask to go out with. Nice, handsome, smart, well-dressed and popular. No one would think I would be imprisoned for a violent crime. But the gods had a different fate for me.

In 1991 I was arrested for murder and it being my first arrest, I was scared as hell. It was bad enough being arrested but murder made it a devastating experience for me and my mother. In 1993 I was sentenced to twenty to forty years in prison.

—m—

PRISONER SURVEY #1

Should handguns be banned, or require a strict registration law? (A small, in-prison, post-GED workshop Class Survey 2004)

Prisoner #1: Yes, because when weak-minded people can easily get them, they use guns to kill people.

Prisoner #2: Handguns should not be banned because every man has the right to protect himself and his home

Prisoner #3: If you have handguns they turn into paraphernalia similar to drugs and the fact of the matter is that handguns may be made illegal, but there is no possible way to take all handguns off the street.

Prisoner #4: No.

Prisoner #5: Yes. Handguns should be banned. They serve no purpose but to kill. Furthermore they make it too easy for someone to take a life.

Prisoner #6: No, handguns should not be banned, because it's a persons right to own a firearm, and to violate that right is like spitting on the Constitution and what it stands for. Also people use them for sport and recreation. If a criminal wants to kill or rob someone he or she will do it with or without a gun or handgun. GUNS DON'T MAKE PEOPLE COMMIT CRIMES *PERIOD*.

Prisoner #7: No. Because we as Americans have "The right to bear arms." (U.S. Constitution).

—⚬⚬⚬—

POSTSCRIPT

The young seventeen- to twenty-five-year-old men who made their way from big-city streets to the Michigan Reformatory (MR) came out of inner city backgrounds. As teachers we meet them at MR. We've asked these young prisoners to tell their stories for you of life in the inner city. The under-twenty-five prisoners prepared talks on "Detroit's Inner City." They are asked to "speak what you know."

Other prisoners we taught at the over-twenty-five Jackson Prison were also asked to tell stories of their inner city experiences. They talk of becoming a gangster. Many prisoners have become involved with cocaine and addictive deadly crack. These drugs become their path to destruction. Guns have figured prominently in inner city life since the rise of the illegal drug economy. We get reports of how "I had been shot."

In all of this, we get very little indication of leading a good life, or a fun life. For instance, typical fun or educational things that suburban or small-town kids do are seldom mentioned in the lives of inner city youth. Instead, there is chronic exposure to poverty and violence (Green 1993). Loic Wacquant suggests American prisons act as a "surrogate welfare system" for the inner city male (Wacquant 2002). Many prisoners do mature, or "age out," in prison. Yet, at $32,000 per year, per prisoner, this seems to be a pretty expensive "social service" system. Could the prisoners and taxpayers, as "citizens" of our prison system and our society, look forward to a different, and a better, future?

VI

—⚉—

THE FUTURE OF THE
PRISONERS' WORLD

INTRODUCTION

In the traditions of prisoner voices there have been philosophic works
such as Jean Paul Sartre's *Saint Genet* (1952) exploring the existential
choice of criminality, literary works such as Eldridge Cleaver's *Soul on Ice*
(1968) reflecting on African American life, and various social movement
books such as George Jackson's *Soledad Brother* (1970) about prison conditions in the late 1960s and early 1970s, during a time of prisoner push
for rights—an extension of the civil rights and protest movements of the
1960s—that turned "deviants" into citizen-spokespersons (Trout & Tregea 1971; Jacobs 1977). These movements included a demand for the right
of prisoners for access to accredited prison post-secondary education.

We have described the rise, since 1972, of the Pell grant eligibility for
prisoners and how that supported over 770 prison college programs in
the United States until 1995 when, with a turn toward a punitive mood,
the U.S. Congress terminated the prison college programs.

Our experience with prisoner voices comes from the prison college
classrooms between 1981 and 1995, and in teaching certain court-ordered
prison college programs in Michigan from 1995 to 2000, and in offering
volunteer post-GED workshops from 2003 to 2008. We entered prison college teaching without any preconceived ideas about "prisoners voices."
Rather, we came to the realization through prison teaching that not only
were prisoners articulate human beings, but that they were also becoming
enabled through prison college experience to "find their voice."

Coauthor Bill Tregea recalls a "Business Communications" class he taught in 1983 in the maximum-security central complex at Jackson Prison where, to fulfill the assignments for the course, the students gave written and oral reports on the current issues in the Warden's Council. There were reports from the Prisoner Store Committee, the Prison NAACP, the Prisoner Inmate Benefit Fund, and several other "citizen" issues which, to some extent, were empowering the average prisoner.

Prison college classes themselves also gave the opportunity to raise issues, such as coauthor Marjorie Larmour's account of the seventeen- to twenty-five-year-old Michigan Reformatory students in her Speech class who researched the personal troubles of the inner city and found their separate troubles were also part of a larger social problem of the continuing "jobless ghetto."

Once you are educated you never go back to being the same. Chapter 18, "Prisoners' Views on the System and Reentry," presents prisoner insights on why it's hard to make it once released, why so many blacks were swept into the prison in the first place and some criticisms of the prison system itself.

What is the future of the prison world? Chapter 19, "The End of the Incarceration Binge?" asks: Will the prison system grow or downsize? What is the future of the jobless inner city from where the vast majority of prisoners come from? Will it continue to fester or will it change, due to new investment—perhaps "green jobs" investment?

A key pragmatic question is: Can state budgets support a continuously expanding prison apparatus? Through what policies can we cap prison growth? If we can save money this way, can there be a "holistic" approach which shifts *some* of the money saved to evidence-based crime prevention?

Another key question of both pragmatism and justice is: How can we help prisoners make in during reentry?

Finally, can we move from a punitive "war," (with its implicit racism), to a more even-handed, British or European model policy of harm reduction? Why is crime and punishment so salient in the United States, skewing our policies toward punishment? These large questions will be answered briefly in our concluding chapter 19.

18

—∭—

Prisoners' Views on System and Reentry

INTRODUCTION

Over the years of teaching college courses in prisons the coauthors have listened to many prisoners give their views: prisoner views on too much time spent in prison, prisoner views on how the guards are interested in keeping the prisoners coming back, prisoner views on getting another "flop," prisoner views on the causes of the massive growth in the prison system. As teachers, during the years of coming into and out of prisons, we were mostly trying to keep a focus on the teaching and learning assignments. We had a tendency to ignore a great deal of the comments prisoners made about "prisoner issues." Things prisoners said may not have "made a connection" in our busy, real world, busy teacher, straight way of thinking. Or, if we did begin to understand, this understanding could only be restricted to the car during commute time in our shared rides to and from prisons—in our busy adjunct lives.

But as the years went by Marjorie Larmour began collecting essays and writing our first coauthored book, *The Great American Drug Bust*, in the mid-1990s. The coauthors became more reflective about the actual prisoner stories and the lives behind them. Then the coauthors founded Michigan STEPP Coalition in 1996, and in 1998–2000 put out newsletters around the effort to reinstate prison college. Bill Tregea got the job directing the bachelor criminal justice program at Adrian College and began focusing on prisons and prevention. He worked in 1998 with the Chair of the Michigan House Corrections Committee on issues of prisoner education. He finished a grant report for the Soros Foundation on prisoner post-secondary education and began working in professional ways in this academic area. Tregea became a founding member and continuing board member of the newly forming Citizens Alliance on Prisons and Public Spending in 1998. Meanwhile, the "convict criminology" movement was taking hold at the criminal justice professional meetings. Tregea, in participating each year in professional conferences, met up with those critiquing the incarceration binge.

Both coauthors, therefore, began reflecting on our teaching, our writing, and began learning about our students' lives in a deeper way—we learned to respect the prisoner view. Several of these prisoner views critical of America's incarceration world are presented below.

A. The Convict Hypothesis

Many prisoners believe that they should be in prison, but that their sentence is too long. After already serving many years in prison they have changed, but they're still inside. They see the world passing them by. They are losing touch with their family, technology changes, the job market gets tougher, they are increasingly behind in their education. And, they have picked up a near-inevitable "used to" feeling about prison—it is a place where the longer they stay in, the more familiar to them it becomes as their lifestyle. They begin to suffer from "prisonization," a lowered self-concept that has adjusted to prison life (Terry 2003). Therefore, the "convict hypothesis" is this: *the longer they are in, the harder time they have in "making good" in society once released,* for the reasons listed above. This is an important *prisoner* critique of excessively long sentences, for example, the excessively long "mandatory minimum" drug laws (FAMM 2008)

B. The Perpetual Revolving Door

Many prisoners interact with guards that may not have much more education than the prisoners. The guards have good jobs, with benefits. Prisoners often say that the guards want the prisoners to fail, once released, so that the prisoners will return to prison (recidivism) and continue to make good jobs for guards. This links into some concerns that academic researchers also have. For instance, Joan Petersilia (former director of RAND's criminal justice division), worries that the California Correctional Peace Officers Association (CCPOA) may be interested in sending people back to prison precisely because a constant revolving door links into the union interest in maintaining a high level of parole officer job security. The CCPOA also represents the prison guards. Both guards and parole agents are in the same union. So the correctional officer (in prison) and the parole officer (on the outside) may have a mutual interest to keep their employment. It is easy enough to "justify" sending an ex-con on parole back to prison. The prisoners can see this from an *economic* perspective: they are captives of a prison industrial growth complex where they are the "raw material."

A sub-thesis of this view is that there are so many impediments to "beating the perpetual incarceration machine" that prisoners *ought* to have good access to job training, education and other programs that can help them make it on the outside. Ex-con academics Richards and Jones (1996) note:

> Historically, the legal status of prisoners has been defined by civil death statutes . . . (which) implies that their worldly legacy is claimed or inherited by others; a prisoner's property is confiscated in the name of the state (a common practice of the federal government); a man's wife is declared a widow and is free to remarry; and a 'dead' person is disqualified from signing contracts or conducting business affairs.
>
> Many prisoners leave prison with barely enough money to survive a few days. According to Lenihan (1974:4–6): "Most State governments give each releasee clothing, transportation, and 'gate money,' ranging from $10 to $200—the median is $28. Fifteen states do not provide transportation; six do not provide clothing; three give neither; and two give no money." Today, in Iowa and many other states, prisoners are issued $50 gate money and a bus ticket.
>
> Convicts are released from prison with considerable debts and financial liabilities . . . and (are) typically hit with delinquent bills that have built up for years, including court costs and fees, fines, restitution, tax deficiencies, child support and domestic family bills.
>
> Considering the research on parolees securing employment, it is no surprise that many persons return to prison . . . recent studies . . . suggest that unemployment contributes to community programme failure and recommend priority be given to job development assistance. (Richards & Jones 1996:205–6)

Prisoners often believe that the guards, wardens and Departments of Corrections don't want them to get prepared, in order to keep the revolving door going and thus keep the "bloated bureaucracy" or prison growth complex going. Often prisoners will miss the political dimension of this. We, as prison college instructors, might point out to prisoners (in our classroom discussions) that it is the *legislature* that tells the Department of Corrections what to do. However, some of the African American prisoners do have a political view, and it tends to be more sharp-edged.

C. Sweeping the Blacks into Prison

Some of the African American prisoners feel there is something of a conspiracy going on in a *political* sense. They believe that the power elites or some kind of oligarchy has decided to contain the nascent political revolt of inner city blacks by passing laws that put them all (or many of them, especially the males) in prison, in probation or on parole.

In fact, as we've reported, by 1995 one in three African American males (ages twenty to twenty-nine) have had some experience with either probation or prison and parole (Mauer 1999). There are 7.2 million people in the U.S. corrections system (2.2 million in prison and 4.9 million on probation or parole, and a *lot* of them are African American).

"Why is this happening to our people?" the black prisoners ask. They answer that there is some purposiveness to this. That the inner city problems—poverty, jobs, homeless, drugs—are being swept under the carpet through massive incarceration. That it is a political decision to achieve this result—to avoid solving the problems of the jobless ghetto and contain a potential for black revolt.

D. A Conspiracy Introduced Drugs to Inner City

It has been a fairly common view in U.S. prisons for African American prisoners (12 percent of U.S. population, 48 percent of prisoners) to believe that crack, especially, was *introduced* to South Central Los Angeles and other inner cities in 1984–1986 period by the CIA as a purposeful effort to undermine the black family and lead the black males into prison. This is more than rumor. In August of 1996 Gary Webb, reporter for the *San Jose Mercury*, did a three-part investigation into the U.S. government links to the trade in crack cocaine in South Central Los Angeles. The story uncovered links between the Central Intelligence Agency covert war against Nicaragua and cocaine trafficking in Los Angeles. Gary Webb subsequently published a book entitle *Dark Alliance* and there have been some Congressional investigations (Webb 1999).

There is a long history in the United States revealing that the politically powerful have created drug laws precisely aimed against competing ethnic groups, or "minorities." Thus, through the political use of drug laws, dominant groups oppress or beat back competing ethnic groups, ultimately through use of imprisonment (Musto 1991).

E. Economic Free Labor, "Phone Fees" and Decimating the Inmate Benefit Fund

A narrower set of critiques or complaints by state prisoners is that the state economy they are imprisoned by benefits from their free (or extremely low-paid) labor. Prisoners often make furniture used in legislative and state administrative offices, as well as license plates, grow food for the kitchen and in other ways produce goods and services without significant pay.

Also, prisoners' relatives (often poor) must pay exorbitant telephone fees for phone calls that are required to be "collect" calls that the prisoners make from the pay phone in the prison yard. This "phone money" (fees) goes to the Department of Corrections budget, and not to prisoner rehabilitative services, although some of the money might go to mandatory prison legal services, e.g., to support a law library and legal advocate.

A third complaint is that, over the recent years of a punitive approach to prisoners, the Inmate Benefit Fund has been emasculated. For instance, prisoners used to run the commissary and their "wages" and a "slice" of the profit went to the Inmate Benefit Fund. But, in Michigan, the MDOC replaced the prisoner store clerks with guards and these correctional officers now run the store. Again, in Michigan, prisoners used to be able to organize concerts in the prison (e.g., by a benefit concert by, say, Johnny Cash or BB King) and place the money raised (from prisoners to pay to go to the concert) into the Inmate Benefit Fund to pay for rehabilitative prisoner services. There have been no such concerts in Michigan in recent years.

After the elimination of Pell grant eligibility for prisoners (1994) and the subsequent collapse of all of the prison college programs, the coauthors (still teaching under a court-order prison college program at two prisons in Michigan from 1995 to 2000) had informal talks with prisoners who served on the Inmate Benefit Fund Council at Jackson Prison. In these talks the prisoner-representatives suggested that they would be willing to vote for some of any money raised by an enhanced benefit fund to go into funding a start-up of accredited skills training and education (prison college) that had been terminated. For instance, there could be fifteen credit skill sets and thirty credit certificates through starting up, in Michigan and other states, community college offerings. The State of Ohio does this. So far the Michigan Department of Corrections is not interested, arguing that reentering prisoners "need ID cards and other basics," not accredited skill sets or job skill certificates and general education (*Blade* 2005).

Regarding prisoner ID—this issue had *still* not been effectively resolved by the MDOC as of the Summer of 2008 in Michigan, even after the prisoner need for basic ID (birth certificate, driver's license, Social Security card) had been identified as a priority by MPRI in 2005. How revealing of the MDOC basic bureaucratic lethargy and willingness to let legal tangles result in taking so long for something so simple, especially when what is really needed is a lot of social support for reentry, delivered at a much faster pace—and for one reason, to save the budget crisis state of Michigan some money. Thankfully, by the Summer of 2008 *all* of Michigan counties had MPRI Steering Committees and Community Coordinators, and were well on their way to solving several of these issues, and customizing, or "wrapping services" around the reentering prisoners.

While better reentry services does not solve the problem of sentencing reforms for shorter sentences, or the problems of the jobless ghetto, it can reduce the effect of the perpetual revolving door. Yet the larger question still looms: what is the future of the incarceration binge culture?

19

—٭—

The End of the
Incarceration Binge?

INTRODUCTION

The prison world expanded, massively, during a specific historical context—a power world, partly driven by a rational public prison build-up movement responding to the 1986–1993 crack epidemic and increase in crime rates from 1986 to 1991, partly driven by politicians' strategies "tough on crime" and a media hype, and partly driven by a deeper function for the prison as an institutional racism response controlling the festering jobless ghettos of America. In these jobless ghetto streets a substitute drug economy had grown, leading street youth—vulnerable to an enforcement tactic of arrest and incarceration of lower-level drug dealers—straight into prisons. Underneath all this was the power world of money and power—the dynamics of investment in suburbs and disinvestment in inner cities, and the political powerlessness of African Americans to focus any large-scale federal solution to the criminogenic uneven development in America's urban process that resulted. It was that criminogenic set of conditions in the inner cities that led to the epidemic of youth violence in the period 1986 to 1991.

As a mature Jackson Prison convict observed in a prison college essay:

> I don't know what it is, but to them—the young boys—having a gun made them men. Then they lost control; kids shot kids, people were dying everywhere, all the time. Mothers were losing sons left and right. It became a game then, someone would get killed for whatever reason and his or her friends would then retaliate, seeking revenge.

The police were no help. It wasn't until one of their own men was killed in the area that they decided to start "patrolling." In my eyes this is what began everything, the lack of support from our system. This sort of thing would never have gone that far in the white neighborhoods of our white working class district or white suburban counterparts.

Yes, there should have been more police support from "the system," but the writer's main point is that the white suburbs would demand an entirely different approach if all this economic devastation—and substitute drug economy—hit them and affected their kids. As we've noted, regarding the different approach taken by the British:

> In the harm reduction approach the use of drugs is accepted as a fact. Instead of a "warrior" approach of an aggressive law enforcement, the focus is placed on reducing harm while use continues. . . . The British do not tackle the problems of economic decline and "inner city" drug-related crime with a massive incarceration binge. Instead, they offer a comprehensive harm reduction program. For instance, in a severely disadvantaged region of unemployed dock workers replaced by containerization called Merseyside that includes Liverpool, England, the British criminal justice system (Home Office) supports a program that:
>
> > . . . involves needle exchange, counseling, prescription of drugs including heroin, and employment and housing services . . . services are integrated to provide drug users with help when they need it. Pharmacists . . . fill prescriptions for smokeable drugs . . . the police sit on health advisory committees . . . the overall effect of this policy is to steer users away from crime and possible imprisonment. (Abadinsky 2008:412)

Beyond harm-reduction programs as a drug abuse policy lies the underlying problem of uneven development that leads to the inner city itself. Alternative accounts explaining the massive prison expansion in the United States were laid out in chapters 2 and 3, but it is clear that long-festering devastated communities such as American "jobless ghettos" breed crime. Certainly we need a criminal justice system to respond to the resulting crime. However, with the *balance* of values in the United States toward narrow crime control, instead of solving the underlying problems, a long run of politics, media, myth and a growing, bloated prison bureaucracy is what results. In America's past, powerful ethnic groups have made laws and taken approaches that have imprisoned less powerful "minorities." It's hard not to conclude, again, that massive U.S. prison expansion serves the interests of the powerful.

Clarence Page, writing an opinion column about comments made by the script-writers David Simon and Ed Burns of *The Wire*, a well-scripted HBO crime show series, notes that Simon and Burns said: "If asked to serve on a jury deliberating a violation of state or federal drug laws, we will vote to acquit, regardless of the evidence presented." These comments were in a *Time* magazine essay. Opinion writer Page says:

> Although I have some reservations, I've learned enough as an urban-affairs journalist to know that they make a powerful and persuasive argument. The war on drugs too often has become a war against poor people.
>
> That theme is driven home with bracing clarity and authenticity on *The Wire*, which is more than a cop show. It's really about the two Americas left behind to coexist unreality in the social rubble that departing factory jobs left behind.
>
> Kids get killed, addicted, or jailed, Politicians get elected. Lawyers get rich. Jails get filled. The drug war goes on. Drug arrests soar without a noticeable decline in drugs.
>
> In Baltimore, Mr. Simon and company note, arrests for drugs have soared over the past three decades while arrest rates for murders have dropped in half. In other words, serious crimes against lives and property are going unsolved in a system that encourages police to spend time snatching cheap drug arrests off the nearest corner.
>
> With lawmakers unwilling or unable to repair the drug war's damage, Mr. Simon and Company invite juries to look the other way by exercising their right to nullify a law they see as unjust or unwise. (Page 2008)

Our prisoner essays often reveal a single-parent home life and a syndrome of child abuse and neglect, domestic violence, alcohol and drug abuse by parents and the children learning drugs—and drug-related crimes—from the neighborhood or school peers. Single-parent home life is part of the consequence of the jobless ghetto where men cannot have access to a job to "carry their own weight" and be good fathers.

The men who were our prisoner students dropped out of high school, learning life in the street drug trade. The inner city school dropout rate is 50 percent. They were arrested and convicted as easy prey "in a system that encourages police to spend time snatching cheap drug arrests off the nearest corner." They entered prison—and as they entered they found that "the prisoners' world" requires you to be "in your own mind at least, ready." As a prisoner student reflected:

> This is real life on the inside, and you must be in your own mind at least, ready. If you're not, you might lose it—your mind that is. The shock of the first night hearing grown men cry, knowing this is your home for the next nine years. And you know without a doubt, who you really are.

THE FUTURE OF THE INNER CITY

America's inner cities, beginning to decline by 1958, have been neglected for fifty years. President Johnson declared a "war on poverty" in the mid-1960s, but his programs remained under-funded as the United States fought the Vietnam War (1963–1974). And then we turned from a war on poverty to a "war on crime" (1968–present) and a "war on drugs" (1968–present). Politically the Republican Party captured the historically Democratic, white, Southern, male vote in 1968 in a "Southern Strategy." As the nation "moved to the suburbs" (and to the West Coast, to the South, and to the Southwest), the urban north experienced a political weakening. The nation's big-city mayors have spent decade after decade in a frustrated effort to regain a national focus on the cities.

Since the Democrat's Congressional victory in the election of 2006, and with the 2008 Democratic Presidential candidate from a big-city urban area with a community organizing background—combined with a shift in the U.S. Senate toward the Democrats in the 2008 election—a new historical power world may bring the inner cities back into focus for new ideas, especially if the Democrats are pushed by urban social movements.

One suggestion is that, with the new urgency to slow global warming and achieve a measure of energy independence, biomass electrical power plants (very large pellet boilers) could be built in the inner cities with hot-houses connected to them, running on their heat, to develop year-round, commercial, urban hot-house gardens in Midwestern, Middle Atlantic, and East Coast northern cities as a new source of inner city jobs. Fish farms could be connected to such biomass power plants, again, for inner city jobs. The power plants themselves would burn corn, or pelletized switch grass, wood or other biomass that grows within fifty miles of the inner city.

Recycling plants, wind turbine and solar panel manufacturing firms, and other new "green business" could locate in the inner city through federal tax incentives and green industry subsidies.

An active coalition is currently working on such a proposal, advocating that $300 billion in federal program money be spent to do this (Apollo Alliance 2008). Presidential candidate Obama supports slowing global warming by cutting carbon emissions 80 percent by 2050, and 25 percent by 2025, and has made a pledge of $150 billion to be spent over the next ten years on alternative energy (Blade 2008). And, the U.S. House of Representatives is listening and considering such programs (U.S. House of Representatives 2008). The technology is there both to solve global warming and to revitalize the inner cities. All that is needed is some concerted effort and political will.

With a shift toward harm reduction as a drug-abuse policy to replace the "war" on drugs, and the kind of federal and private investment in green business described for the inner city, a forty-year-old dynamic "crime control" could change toward a "needs-based" economic development and a public health model and crime prevention model for fighting crime.

Governors could commute some sentences and push for shorter sentences through sentencing reform and parole guidelines. Additionally, prisoners could be declared eligible again for Pell grants, and undergo "the prison as surrogate welfare agency" for urban black males through a revitalized prison college movement that would provide quality accredited skills training and education for prisoners reentering, and needing skills training and education for, such "green business" revitalized inner cities.

STATE BUDGET CRISIS

While the federal-level budget could afford $300 billion for an "Apollo Project" to fix the inner cities and build a green economy—as we wind down the Iraq war—many of the nation's states are themselves broke. States are finding they can no longer afford to sustain the type of massive prison build-up that has occurred over the last twenty-five years. Corrections budgets are now directly competing with other state priorities, such as public higher education—pitting the hope of parents for their children's future against a falling crime rate and potentially lessening of the "fear of crime."

An editorial, reprinted in Lenawee County's *The Daily Telegram*, appeared in the Sunday, July 6, 2008, *Grand Rapids Press* that suggests a broad bi-partisan coalition, pushed by Governor Granholm, that can make realistic structural changes to the state's budget, must emerge in Michigan. To do this legislation must downsize the state's prison system.

> . . . the new budget, for the fiscal year beginning October 1, continues a familiar pattern: tinkering with the externals of state government without delving in to its broken machinery.
> . . . not enough of the hard work was done.
>   Ms. Granholm last year proposed saving prison costs by reforming sentencing guidelines. The idea has gone nowhere. Ms. Granholm should be pushing the Legislature to get off the dime. Corrections took a $39 million cut this year, but that doesn't begin to trim the $2 billion total that is spent on prisons—20 percent of Michigan's general fund. Michigan continues to incarcerate more people than other Midwestern states, primarily because if keeps them longer behind bars.
>   Dealing in a serious way with that issue will require courage that is evidently lacking. No lawmaker wants to appear soft on crime. But this isn't about releasing hardened felons like to assault, murder or rape again. Locking bad actors behind bars must remain a priority for the community and the budget, and a core function of state government. Continuing to imprison people who pose no real threat to society, however, makes no sense. If lawmakers are serious about trying to avoid the yearly spending squeeze, this is one area of savings they must attack, and soon (*The Daily Telegram* 2008).

Power constituencies of voters and interest groups are beginning to line up in critical resistance to the expansion and unnecessary overuse of confinement. In California the "Little Hoover Commission" report of 2004 highlighted the overuse of confinement as it relates to the state budget, and a social movement to cap prison growth and shift to community justice issues is afoot (Critical Resistance 2004). In Michigan the Citizens Alliance on Prisons and Public Spending has been working for ten years to craft rational legislation that can safely downsize Michigan's prisons and free up some resources to shift to evidence-based crime prevention (CAPPS 2008).

States are also moving away from the federalization-of-drug-laws model—challenging federal law around medical marijuana and instituting, through referendums, their own state-level harm-reduction approaches.

The public may be tiring of the "tough" political rhetoric. Often polls show citizens want their tax dollars to go for *both* punishment and treatment. A new pragmatic concern for better crime prevention in the community (front end), and improved success in prisoner reentry (back end) policies, is emerging to push for a better balance in the use of tax payers investment in public safety.

CAP PRISON GROWTH, CAP PRISON COSTS, SHIFT RESOURCES TO PREVENTION

In Michigan, in 1998, leaders from several statewide organizations met and formed the Citizens Alliance on Prisons and Public Spending (CAPPS). The then–Republican Governor, John Engler, had just called for the building of seven to eight more new prisons. Michigan had already had a build-up from eight prisons in 1983 to thirty-four prisons in 1998, in just fifteen short years, one prison after another being built, and the prison system analysts and crime prevention network came together to say "no more," and formed CAPPS to explore ways to seek consensus on safe public policies that could cap prison growth. It was clear that more emphasis needed to be put on crime prevention.

Prison growth was being driven by policies, not the crime rate. In fact, as we've repeatedly emphasized, the crime rate had been going down since 1991. Prison growth was being driven by policies such as "mandatory minimums," "truth in sentencing," long drug sentences and fewer paroles. CAPPS pounded out, among diverse board members representing a wide coalition in the policy community, a consensus view that was critical of the politically appointed parole board that had reduced paroles at "earliest parole date" from 63 percent to 51 percent. Over 22,000 prisoners were backed up, past their earliest parole date (ERD). Half of those backed up in prison each year were kept another two years with a "flop"—the other half were paroled. CAPPS's position was that the sentencing guideline legislation had set minimum sentences, and the judges had sentenced the prisoner to a minimum sentence with the expectation that, with good behavior in prison, there would be release on parole when the prisoner had served his or her minimum sentence. Instead of a lot of parole denials, there should be a policy of presumption of parole after serving the minimum, since this is what the judge and legislature had intended. This view was researched by profiling all 51,000 Michigan prisoners and drafting legislation for "parole guidelines."

By 2007, CAPPS draft legislation to move toward parole guidelines had reached the Michigan legislature and had bi-partisan support. Other draft legislation is in the wings (CAPPS 2008). Through these prison reform policies, Michigan can downsize its prison population and save money. For pragmatic reasons during the current Michigan budget crisis, these CAPPS reform policies have found agreement from the governor's office and the legislature. Michigan's Governor Granholm is also preparing a commutation of about 2,500 prisoners (the older, the sick and the non-violent past parole date), and reducing sentencing from felony to misdemeanor for several crime categories. All of this was needed, in a pragmatic effort, to meet a $1.8 billion dollar deficit in the 2007–2008 state budget. Now the 2008–2009 state budget faces another large deficit and the corrections budget is squarely on target for cuts.

One problem for a state holistic approach to crime prevention will be, as cutting the corrections budget saves money, can *some* of that money be *shifted* to effective, evidence-based crime prevention? For instance, early child development programs are currently underfunded. So are after-school programs. These are two proven programs. And more revenue-sharing to county and city jurisdictions for currently unfunded police and sheriff's deputy positions is needed. There is a need to ramp up resources for prisoner reentry. Or will *all* the savings go back into the general fund to balance the budget and beef up the important priority, and politically more popular needs of higher education?

MICHIGAN PRISONER REENTRY INITIATIVE (MPRI)

Under the advice of analysts who could see that the huge national prison build-up would mean 600,000 prisoners reentering society each year, and as part of his "compassionate conservatism" program (before he became, after 9/11, in his own eyes a "war" President), in early 2001, then-President Bush authorized about $1 million per state to launch new prison reentry initiative programs.

In Michigan this new prisoner reentry initiative took the form of a committee of 140 meeting from 2003 through 2004 to develop a better prison reentry program. Starting in 2005, and with a budget of $13 million, the first pilot projects began to form local county steering committees that assessed the resources for prisoner reentry, such as housing, jobs, transportation, drug treatment, clothes, skills training and education. Also assessed were the gaps in these services, followed by an effort to line up the necessary resources.

Then transition teams were formed by volunteers and some paid services that would interview reentering prisoners the last two months of their sentence before release, getting to know the prisoners' needs for successful reentry, and then helping them on the outside as they try to go about "making good" (Maruna 2001).

By late 2007 all eighty-three counties in the state of Michigan had come on board with steering committees and transition teams and the MPRI program has now, as of the Summer of 2008, moved beyond the pilot program phase into county sustainable prisoner reentry programs, currently budgeted at a modest $34 million. Michigan is the only state that has an MPRI program in every county. We've mentioned that the shift of emphasis in the MDOC to prisoner reentry, and the prospect—indeed, the mandate to the MDOC—to cap prison growth and reduce the prisoner population (in order to free up needed state resources), has begun to change the organizational culture within the MDOC Field Operations (Parole) division.

Whereas, in the past, parole agents did all case management for their parole clients, now, the MPRI Steering Committee and Transition Teams, guided by the community coordinator, work in collaboration with the parole agents, doing some or even most of the case management for reentering MPRI parolees. This is forcing an adjustment: before, the parole agent's primary duty was control and enforcement, sending many parolees back to prison. Recall, the largest source of prison admittance in the past has been from parole revocation. Now the parole agents work much more closely with community services to create success in reentry and *not* send reentering prisoners back to prison—as often.

Other states are also working away at such programs to keep ex-cons from returning to prison, and many are trying to downsize prisons as well.

In Michigan parole failure has been the source of more prison admittance than all new or first crime convictions. So a new focus on "criminology of reentry" is needed with resources to do the back-end crime prevention. As the states lower prison admittance from parole violations and downsize prisons through parole guidelines, sentencing changes, commutations, can *some* of the money saved be shifted into doubling and tripling the budget for successful prisoner reentry?

Recall the "convict hypothesis" mentioned in chapter 18. This was the hypothesis that the longer the time in prison the harder it is to make it on the outside. Because of the long sentences of the "war" approach to drug-related crime we have put millions of people behind prison bars for long enough to make it very difficult for them to now make it after release.

WHY THE INCARCERATION BINGE MAY NOT END

We've made the case for optimism that the prison binge growth era will end, that the incarceration binge culture will be replaced with sentencing reform, prison reform and commutations, prisoner post-secondary opportunity, parole guidelines, reentry concern and a needs-based, restorative justice "reconceptualizing of the corrections project" through a new set of community justice institutions, and a commitment of resources to "green jobs" inner city development. But for the last forty years there has been little reason for hope.

Despite the opening citizens in some states have, due to budget problems or budget crises, such as in Michigan, to downsize the prison system—and despite the likely shift in the U.S. Congress in the 2008 election to Democrats representing "Blue States," or urban voters—the incarceration binge may not end, and the inner cities may not get their underlying problems solved.

Regarding prison downsizing in the context of budget crises, there remains conservative reactions. In Michigan, the July and early August 2007 announcements by the governor, Jennifer Granholm, of intentions to support parole guidelines releasing more prisoners on parole, to commute the sentences of 5,000 prisoners and to change sentencing guidelines to make some felonies into misdemeanors (thus sending those convicted to the county jail instead of state prison), brought forth a conservative reaction. Extreme comments appeared in the press in the late Summer of 2007 about the dire consequences of increasing paroles and adjusting sentencing guidelines. The Michigan Senate, controlled by the Republicans, had Republican members saying more paroles would cause panic in the streets. Oakland County Executive and former prosecutor L. Brooks Patterson suggested that people respond to sentencing changes by purchasing an Uzi, or at least two guard dogs (Levine 2007).

In an opinion guest editorial in the *Lansing State Journal*, the former Director of Corrections, 1984 to 1991, and CAPPS board member Robert Brown responded:

> The current debate over prison spending misses a fundamental point. Crime prevention is the best protection for public safety!
>
> Prevention includes pre- and post-natal care, early childhood education, after-school programs, mental health and substance abuse treatment.

. . . Many people who repeatedly commit property or public order offenses have substance abuse or mental health problems—or simply lack the skills to find employment. More punishment will not enable them to function as law-abiding citizens. Addressing their problems before they offend is a much better investment.

Sixty percent of annual prison commitments are probation or parole violators.

To reduce these numbers, the Michigan Department of Corrections is moving away from sheer surveillance of people under community supervision. It is marshalling community resources through the Michigan Prisoner ReEntry Initiative to improve parolees' chances of success.

Many prisoners serving long sentences for crimes against people are in prison for the first time and are unlikely to re-offend. They receive no credit for good behavior and are often denied parole.

. . . Imprisoning fewer people who commit property crimes and other non-assaultive offenses will not threaten public safety. Nor will paroling more people who have finished their minimum terms.

Of people paroled in Michigan in 2000, 16.3 percent were returned to prison for new crimes. Only 2.8 percent were convicted of crimes against persons. Of the 11,000 people paroled in 2003, 70 percent had not returned to prison within two years for any reason.

If we really care about crime prevention, we will stop paying for more prisons than we need. We will invest instead in the universities that make our state great, the services that vulnerable citizens need badly and, above all, the children we can keep from becoming the next generation of prisoners. (Brown 2007)

The *Bay City Times* editorial, "Out-of-Control Prison Spending Is the Real Injustice," responded to those who were sowing fear in the Summer of 2007 over the governor's proposals as follows:

With one of every 200 residents in prison, Michigan has one of the highest rates of incarceration in the nation—twice that of Iowa, for example, and 40 percent higher than that of several other Great Lakes states.

Michigan will spend $1.9 billion this year operating 49 prisons and camps. That's $4.9 million per day—more than we spend for K-16 education and libraries combined.

That flies in the face of public priorities. In a 2004 poll, Michiganders ranked corrections lowest among spending priorities, listing education, juvenile-offender programs and treatment for the mentally ill as preferred fronts in the fight against crime.

Robert Brown, Jr., who directed Michigan prisons from 1984 to 1992, said it best:

"We need to reserve prison space for criminals we're afraid of and use more conducive and less costly alternatives to rehabilitate offenders we are simply mad at." (Bay City Times 2007)

Despite the level-headed analysis of former MDOC Director, Bob Brown, there is still an unreasoning general public "fear of crime." University of California Professor, Frank Zimring (2006), reminds us that we have excessive punishment because the public resents and fears criminals and believes that punishments are not hard enough. Because criminals are seen as domestic enemies the U.S. Congress, when under control by either the Republicans or the Democrats, has appealed to this fear to apply extreme federal crime-control measures.

What is worse is that this is *not* an example of American exceptionalism. All democratic governments, including Europe, carry a danger of "democratic punishment." This "vulnerability to punishment" is an aspect of the relationship of government and its enemies.

Yet Europe *has not had* the massive incarceration binge witnessed in the United States. If both continents of democratic government have a "structural vulnerability" to overuse of confinement, why has there been no incarceration binge in Europe? Zimring believes "two factors pulled the trigger on the carceral explosion" in the United States.

The first factor is the "increased exposure of crime" in the United States. In Europe the population is more interested in unemployment or soccer, and this is reflected in the European media. But in the United States "that larger salience of crime in the late 1960s and 1970s resulted in an enormous focus on lurid crime. For instance, the rate of child sexual murders has gone down, but it's a wonderful political issue for you if even *one* occurs." That is to say that, in the U.S. context, there is a "*high salience* of crime even when the rates go down." A high salience of crime means that crime is a concern to a population that is highly politicized around crime. It is this politicization that brings forth repeated calls for an increase in punishment.

The second factor is that the Europeans generally trust government, but people in the United States generally *distrust government*. For instance, citizens don't trust judges—they push legislatures to make mandatory sentences rather than entrust more power in the discretion of government and judges. "The less trust we give government the more we want to specify in a fixed punishment" which undergirded the repeated push for long mandatory-minimum sentences (Zimring 2006).

A third factor, argued by Michael Tonry, comes at this from a different view: in the United States local county judges (District and Circuit Courts) are often elected, putting them in a position to have to bend to public fear of crime, and this makes for a trend of more punitive sentences. In Europe, judges are most often appointed—they more often can "hold out" against the public's tendency for "democratic punishment."

It may seem strange that a *distrust* of government would lead to the world's largest prison system in the first nation to make a revolution to establish modern democracy—but that is what we have done with the philosophy of mandatory minimums. On the other hand, we paint our elected judges into a corner where they have to sentence "within the grid" and be "tough" on crime to get reelected.

Perhaps in our experiments with prisoner reentry as we try to downsize the prisons due to *pragmatic* budgeting concerns, and the growing need to meet our *other priorities*—such as education, health, energy independence and slowing global warming, and family and community-level crime prevention—we might become more trusting of self-governance. We might rediscover the active process of governing, instead of retreating behind a distrust of our democratic heritage. Are we to be known as a people of "the prison state?"

POSTSCRIPT

We hope the prisoner voices in this book can help readers think not only about issues of "the prisoners' world," but also about how the "incarceration binge culture" has painted the United States into the corner of a "prison state." We hope to inspire readers to join with others who want to see America move in a more democratic direction in which we reduce harm, fix the inner cities (Wilson 1996; Williamson et al., 2003), lessen poverty and move away from cycling blacks, and other "minorities," from inner city high-input neighborhoods to prison and back again in a "backfire" policy that worsens the life chances of those in the inner city further and chews up our state resources that could be directed toward education and prevention (Lynch and Sabol 2001; Clear 2007).

We need more sensible sentencing, parole and reentry policies (Austin & Irwin 1997/2001; Tonry 2007; CAPPS 2008).

Truly, to be a criminal justice practitioner, a criminologist, or a criminal justice student today is to learn to be a social reformer. This is what our main campus criminal justice students will learn from our prisoner student voices from "the prisoners' world," and from their continuing encounter with today's power world.

Websites and Organizations

BOP. Federal Bureau of Prisons. www.bop.gov

The Federal Bureau of Prisons protects society by confining offenders in the controlled environments of prisons and community-based facilities that are safe, humane, cost-efficient and appropriately secure, and that provide work and other self-improvement opportunities to assist offenders in becoming law-abiding citizens.

CAPPS. Citizens Alliance on Prisons and Public Spending. www.capps-mi.org

A non-profit public policy organization that is concerned about Michigan's excessive use of punitive strategies rather than preventive ones to deal with crime and its impact on our quality of life. Because policy choices, not crime rates, have caused our prison population to explode, CAPPS advocates re-examining those policies and shifting our resources to services that prevent crime, rehabilitate offenders and address the needs of all our citizens in a cost-effective manner.

To achieve these goals, CAPPS develops data-driven proposals for reducing the prison population while ensuring public safety. It informs policymakers, advocacy groups, affected communities and the general public about these issues through numerous means, including a website, a newsletter, research reports, legislative testimony, speaking appearances and the distribution of information kits to policymakers and the media. Barbara R. Levine, Executive Director, 403 Seymour Avenue, Suite 200, Lansing, MI 48933. 517-482-7753, blevine@capps-mi.org.

CEA. National Correctional Education Association. www.ceanational.org

The Correctional Education Association (CEA), founded in 1945, is a non-profit, professional association serving educators and administrators who provide services to students in correctional settings. The CEA is the largest affiliate of the American Correctional Association. CEA is the leading professional association in correctional education, both nationally and internationally, providing leadership, direction and services to correctional educators and programs, and representing correctional education to broader educational, political and social agencies. Correctional education is an effective rehabilitative program enabling detained and adjudicated adult and juvenile students to reassess their values, goals and priorities in life in a positive way, while acquiring the personal, social and technical skills necessary for a successful and permanent reentry into society as productive citizens, parents and coworkers.

Convict Criminology. www.convictcriminology.org

Excellent site, includes: Definition of Convict Criminology, Organization of Convict Criminology Group, Books, Relevant Articles and Chapters, Mentoring, Convicts Going to College, Contacts, and Links.

CRC. Citizens Research Council. www.crcmich.org

For over ninety years, the objective of the Citizens Research Council of Michigan has been to provide factual, unbiased independent information on significant issues concerning state and local government organization and finance. CRC believes that the use of this information by policymakers will lead to sound, rational public policy in Michigan.

Critical Resistance. www.criticalresistance.org

Critical Resistance seeks to build an international movement to end the Prison Industrial Complex (PIC) by challenging the belief that caging and controlling people makes us safe. We believe that basic necessities such as food, shelter and freedom are what really make our communities secure. As such, our work is part of global struggles against inequality and powerlessness. The success of the movement requires that it reflect communities most affected by the PIC. Because we seek to abolish the PIC, we cannot support any work that extends its life or scope.

Prisons and policing are destroying us. In the past two decades, the number of people in prison in the United States has risen 400 percent. The system is filled with 68 percent people of color. One in three black males born today will end up in a cage. And an additional 4 million former prisoners in the United States are left without hope or resources—barred employment opportunities, disenfranchised and often prohibited from getting federal loans, applying for public housing or getting services.

CSG. Council of State Governments. www.csg.org

To assist states with multi-state and regional solutions, CSG maintains offices throughout the country that staff regional associations of legislative and executive elected officials.

CSG helps states increase efficiency by identifying the best new and creative approaches to significant state problems in our Innovations Awards. Our information products are full of useful and practical policy solutions. In addition, CSG draws upon experts in the states, and marshals them as consultants to help sister states in need of services. And CSG's leadership training helps state officials enhance their skills in managing strategic change.

We at the Council of State Governments are proud of our long history of support to the states. Please feel free to call us at (859) 244-8000 should your state need more information about our services or products.

FAMM. Families against Mandatory Minimums. www.famm.org

Families against Mandatory Minimums is the national voice for fair and proportionate sentencing laws. We **shine a light** on the human face of sentencing, **advocate** for state and federal sentencing reform and **mobilize** thousands of individuals and families whose lives are adversely affected by unjust sentences.

Our Vision

FAMM's vision is a nation in which sentencing is individualized, humane, and sufficient but not greater than necessary to impose just punishment, secure public safety and support successful rehabilitation and reentry.

FAMM's national membership includes prisoners and their families, attorneys, judges, criminal justice experts and concerned citizens.

John Jay College of Criminal Justice, City University of New York. www.jjay.cuny.edu/general_info/about.html

The College serves as major research center for criminal justice.

MDOC. Michigan Department of Corrections.
www.michigan.gov/corrections

The goal of the Michigan Department of Corrections is to provide the greatest amount of public protection while making the most efficient use of the state's resources. It meets its goal by ensuring that the state's judges and other criminal justice administrators have the broadest possible array of viable sentencing and sanctioning options, and by ensuring that appropriate supervision is maintained so that Michigan's neighborhoods, families and citizens can be protected.

Michigan STEPP Coalition. www.socialflag.org

Founded in 1998, this non-profit organization works to achieve accredited post-secondary skills training and education for Michigan prisoners. Approaches have included national research, national grant-funded reports, Michigan-focused newsletters, legislative testimony, information kits for legislators, research seminars and workshops, news articles and op eds and meetings of community colleges and universities as a Michigan STEPP Consortium. Contact Bill Tregea at wtregea@adrian.edu; 517-264-3965; P.O. Box 181, Adrian, MI 49221.

MPRI. Michigan Prisoner Reentry Initiative. www.michpri.com/

Organizes through county-level Steering Committee led by Community Coordinator to assemble services for reentering Michigan prisoners. Then Transition Teams do "in-reach" to prisoners in nearby prisons who will reenter the community and wraps services around them, especially for the first few days and first several months.

The primary goal of the Michigan Prisoner Reentry Initiative (MPRI) is to promote public safety by increasing the success rates of prisoners transitioning from prison to the community. The vision of the MPRI is that every prisoner released from prison will have the tools needed to succeed in the community.

- MPRI is a statewide strategic approach to create safer neighborhoods and better citizens.
- MPRI delivers a seamless plan of services, support and supervision from the time a prisoner enters prison through their return to a community.

National Clearinghouse for Drug and Alcohol Information. www.health.org/

Research information and links to federal, state and local anti-drug and alcohol-abuse-related resources.

Urban Institute. www.urban.org/

The Urban Institute gathers data, conducts research, evaluates programs, offers technical assistance and educates Americans on social and economic issues—to foster sound public policy and effective government

USDOJ. Department of Justice. www.usdoj.gov/

Site links to major DOJ agencies, the best "one-stop shop" for finding U.S. Federal Government criminal justice data NCJRS (National Criminal Justice Reference Service). Broad-based criminal justice research resource. Online reports can be downloaded. www.ncjr.org.

U.S. House Select Committee on Energy Independence and Global Warming. http://globalwarming.house.gov/

This unique committee was established by Speaker Nancy Pelosi in early 2007 to add urgency and resources to the commitment of this Congress to address the challenges of America's oil dependence and the threat of global warming. Use this website to learn about how these issues are impacting America and the world, and what you can do to help solve these twin challenges.

The Select Committee will be working every day to make a difference, but it will also take concerned citizens to enact the significant changes we need to effectively address two of the most important issues of our time: global warming and energy security. Edward Markey is chairman.

References

Abadinsky, Howard. 2006. *Parole and Probation: Theory and Practice.* Upper Saddle River, NJ: Pearson/Prentice Hall.

———. 2008. *Drug Use and Abuse: A Comprehensive Introduction,* Belmont, CA: Thomson/Wadsworth.

Abdullah, Ali Hhalid. 1998. "Michigan Prisoners Lost Major Property Issue," (October) at www.infoshop.org/blackflag/216/216mich.htm.

Advisory Council in Misuse of Drugs. 1998. *Drug Misuse and the Environment.* London, England: Home Office.

Agnew, Robert. 1999. "A General Strain Theory of Criminality Differences in Crime Rates." *Journal of Research in Crime and Delinquency* 36:2 (May). In Henry J. Pontell. 2005. *Social Deviance: Readings, Theory and Research,* 5th ed. Upper Saddle River, NJ: Pearson/Prentice Hall.

American Heart Association. 2008. "Cigarette Smoking Statistics." www.americanheart.org/presenter.jhtml?identifier=4559.

Apollo Alliance. 2008. "Green Jobs for Inner City." www.appolloalliance.org.

Archambeault, William G. 2003. "Soar Like an Eagle, Dive Like a Loon: Human Diversity and Social Justice in the Native American Prisoner Experience." In Jeffrey Ian Ross and Stephen C. Richards, Eds. *Convict Criminology,* pp. 267–86. Belmont, CA: Wadsworth/Thomson Learning.

Austin, James. 2003. "The Use of Science to Justify the Imprisonment Binge." In Jeffrey Ian Ross and Stephen C. Richards, Eds. *Convict Criminology,* pp. 17–58. Belmont, CA: Thomson/Wadsworth.

Austin, James, and John Irwin. 1997/2001. *It's About Time: America's Imprisonment Binge,* 3rd ed. Belmont, CA: Wadsworth.

Avalon Project at Yale Law School. 1996. www.yale.edu/lawweb/avalon/fugitive.htm.

Bagley, C., and P. S. Tremblay. 1997. "Suicidal Behaviors in Homosexual and Bisexual Males." *International Journal of Suicide and Crisis Studies* 18:1, pp. 24–34 (see www.pubmed abstract link).

Baltimore Sun. 2005. "Contraband Floods Maryland Prisons." July 6.

Bauman, Zygmut. 2000. "Social Issues of Law and Order." *British Journal of Criminology* 40, pp. 205–21.

Bay City Times. 2007. "Out-of-Control Prison Spending is the Real Injustice." August 12. Editorial.

Beal, Calvin. 1998. "New Prisons in Rural and Small-town Areas." In CFECP 1998 Conference Materials.

Beccaria, Cesare. 1764/2004. "Of Crimes and Punishments." In Peter B. Kraska. *Theorizing Criminal Justice: Eight Essential Orientations.* Long Grove, IL: Waveland Press, pp. 23–28.

Becker, Eddie. 1999. "Chronicle of the History of Slavery and Racism 1790–1824." www.innercity.org/holt/chron_1790_1829.html.

Beckett, Katherine, and Theodore Sasson. 2000. *The Politics of Injustice: Crime and Punishment in America.* Thousand Oaks, CA: Pine Forge Press.

Berger, Ronald J. 1985. "Organizing the Community for Delinquency Prevention." *Journal of Sociology and Social Welfare* 12:1, pp. 129–53. In Ronald J. Berger, Ed. *The Sociology of Juvenile Delinquency,* 2nd ed. Chicago, IL: Nelson-Hall, pp. 261–81.

Best, Joel, and David F. Luckenbill. 1994. *Organizing Deviance,* 2nd ed. Englewood Cliffs, NJ: Prentice Hall.

Blade, The Toledo. 2005a. "Prison Education Puts Inmates on the Right Path, Advocates Argue." Kim Bates. November 27, A1.

Blade, The Toledo. 2005b. "Education and Rehabilitation." December 4, B4. Editorial.

Blade, The Toledo. 2008. "Oil Threatens U.S. Security, Obama Says: Illinois Senator Wants to Spend 150B to Develop Renewable Energy." July 12, A3.

Blumstein, Alfred. 2002. "Prisons: A Policy Challenge." In James Q. Wilson and Joan Petersilia, Eds. *Crime*: Public Policies for Crime Control, Oakland, CA: ICS Press, pp. 451–82.

Blumstein, Alfred, and Jacqueline Cohen. 1987. "Characterizing Criminal Careers." *Science,* 237 (August), pp. 985–91. In Richard C. Monk. *Taking Sides: Clashing Views on Controversial Issues in Crime and Criminology,* 4th ed. Guilford, CT: Dushkin.

Blumstein, Alfred, and Joel Wallman, Eds. 2000. *The Crime Drop in America.* New York: Cambridge University Press.

Bradsher, Keith. 1995a. "Gap in Wealth in U.S. Called Widest in West." *New York Times.* August 14, 7.

———. 1995b. "Widest Gap in Incomes? Research Points to U.S." *New York Times.* October 27, C2.

Braithwaite, John. 1989. *Crime, Shame and Reintegration.* Cambridge University Press.

Brennan, Tim. 1998. "Classification for Control in Jails and Prisons." In Timothy J. Flanagan, James W. Marquart, and Kenneth G. Adams, Eds. *Incarcerating Criminals: Prisons and Jails in Social and Cultural Context.* Oxford University Press, pp. 168–73.

Bright, Charles. 1996. *The Powers that Punish: Prison and Politics in the Era of the Big House, 1920–1955.* Ann Arbor: The University of Michigan Press.

Brown, Robert. 2007. "Prevention, Not Prisons, Best Serves Public Safety: Behind Bars, No One Gets Rehabilitated; Costs Unsustainable." *Lansing State Journal,* August 12, 9A.

Castells, Manuel. 1996. *The Rise of Network Society.* Malden, MA: Blackwell Publishers.

CEA. 2005. Correctional Education Association. "Reentry in Ohio Corrections: A Catalyst for Change." In Wilkinson, Rhine and Henderson-Hurley. *The Journal of Correctional Education.* 56:2 (June). Ashland University Department of Outreach Programs. pp. 158–73.

CFECP. 1998. Campaign for Effective Crime Policy. "Crime and Politics in the 21st Century: Public Safety and the Quality of Justice." Conference materials, November 12–14, Bethesda, MD.

Chambliss, William J., and Robert B. Seidman. 1971/2004. "Poverty and the Criminal Process." In Peter B. Kraska. *Theorizing Criminal Justice: Eight Essential Orientations.* Long Grove, IL: Waveland Press, pp. 257–60.

Chiricos, Ted. 1995/2002. "The Media, Moral Panics and the Politics of Crime Control." In George F. Cole, Mark G. Gertz, and Amy Bunger, Eds. *The Criminal Justice System: Politics and Policies.* Belmont, CA: Wadsworth/Thomson Learning. CRC 2008. Citizens Research Council. www.crc.org

Clear, Todd. 2007. *Imprisoning Communities: How Mass Incarceration Makes Disadvantaged Neighborhoods Worse.* New York: Oxford University Press.

Clear, Todd, and Eric Cadora. 2003. *Community Justice.* Belmont, CA: Wadsworth.

Cleaver, Eldridge. 1968. *Soul On Ice.* New York: Delta Books.

Cloward, Richard, and Lloyd Ohlin. 1960. "Illegitimate Means and Delinquent Subcultures." In Henry Pontell, Ed. *Social Deviance: Readings in Theory & Research,* 5th ed. Upper Saddle River, NJ: Pearson/Prentice Hall, pp. 45–49.

Cohen, Stan. 1972. *Folk Devils and Moral Panics: The Creation of the Mods and Rockers.* Oxford: Blackwell.

Cole, George, and Todd Clear. 2000. *American Corrections,* 5th ed. Belmont, CA: Wadsworth Publishing Company.

Cole, George, and Christopher Smith. 2005. *Criminal Justice in America,* 4th ed. Belmont, CA: Wadsworth Thomson Learning.

Conklin, John E. 2003. *Why Crime Rates Fell.* Boston, MA: Allyn & Bacon.

Conley, Peter, David Hewitt, Wayne Mitic, Christiane Poulin, Diane Riley, Robin Room, Ed Sawka, Eric Single, and John Topp. n.d. "Harm Reduction: Concepts and Practice: A Policy Discussion Paper." Canadian Centre on Substance Abuse (CCSA) National Working Group on Policy.

Convict Criminology. 2008. www.convictcriminology.org

Council of State Governments. 2008. "Corrections Budgets." www.csg.org

Cox, Steven M., and John E. Wade. 2002. *The Criminal Justice Network,* 4th ed. "U.S. Constitution," pp. 335–56, Boston: McGraw-Hill.

Critical Resistance. 2004. Personal communication. www.criticalresistance.org.

Cromwell, Paul, Ed. 1999. *In Their Own Words: Criminals on Crime,* 2nd ed. Los Angeles: Roxbury Publishing Company.

Cruse, Harold. 1966. *The Crisis of the Negro Intellectual.* New York: Basic Books.

Currie, Elliot. 1993. *Reckoning: Drugs, the Cities, and the American Future*. New York: Hill and Wang.

The Daily Telegram. 2008. "State Ignoring Long-Term Structural Budget Issues." Guest Editorial. July 6, 2008, A6. From *Grand Rapids Press*.

Darden, Joe T., Richard Child Hill, June Thomas, and Richard Thomas. 1987. *Detroit: Race and Uneven Development*. Philadelphia, PA: Temple University Press.

DeRose, Julie. 2006. Director of Correctional Education, Michigan Department of Corrections. Personal communication.

Diulio, John J., Steven K. Smith, and Aaron J. Saiger. 1995. "The Federal Role in Crime Control." In James Q. Wilson and Joan Petersilia, Eds. *Crime: Twenty-Eight Leading Experts Look at the Most Pressing Problems of Our Time*. San Francisco, CA: ICS Press (Institute for Contemporary Studies).

Duguid, Stephen. 1992. "Becoming Interested in Other Things: The Impact of Education in Prison." *Journal of Correctional Education* 47:2, pp. 74–85.

Duguid, Stephen, Colleen Hawley, and Wayne Knights. 1998. "Measuring the Impact of Post-Secondary Education in Prison: A Report from British Columbia." *Journal of Offender Rehabilitation*, 27:1/2, pp. 87–106.

Duguid, Stephen, and Ray Pawson. 1998. "Education, Change, and Transformation: The Prison Experience." *Evaluation Review*, 22:4, pp. 470–95.

Duneier, Mitchell. 1999. *Sidewalk*. New York: Farrar, Strauss and Giroux.

Durkheim, Emile. 1995. "Social Solidarity Defines Society." In Lynn Barteck and Karen Mullin, Eds. *Enduring Issues in Sociology: Opposing Viewpoints*. San Diego, CA: Greenhaven Press, Inc.

Eitzen, D. Stanley, and Maxine Baca Zinn. 2000. *Social Problems*, 8th ed. Boston: Allyn and Bacon.

FAMM. 2008. Families against Mandatory Minimums. "FAMMGram Archives." www.famm.org/Resources/BrochuresandPublications/FAMMGramarchives.aspx.

Farrington, David, Doris Layton, Lawrence Sherman, and Brandon C. Welsh. 2006. *Evidence-Based Crime Prevention*. London: Routledge.

Farrington, David, and Brandon C. Welsh. 2006. *Saving Children from a Life of Crime: Early Risk Factors and Effective Interventions*. New York: Oxford University Press.

Feeley, Malcolm M., and Jonathan Simon. 1992. "The New Penology: Notes on the Emerging Strategy of Corrections and its Implications." *Criminology* 30:4 (November), pp. 449–74.

Garland, David. 2001. *The Culture of Control: Crime and Social Order in Contemporary Society*. Chicago: The University of Chicago Press.

Garland, David. 2001/2004. "Crime Control and Social Order." In Peter B. Kraska. *Theorizing Criminal Justice: Eight Essential Orientations*. Long Grove, IL: Waveland Press, pp. 286–301.

Garreau, Joel. 1991. *Edge City: Life on the New Frontier*. New York: Anchor Books/Doubleday.

Gerstein, Dean R., and Henrick J. Harwood, Eds. 1990. *Treating Drug Problems, Vol. I: A Study of the Evolution, Effectiveness and Financing of Public and Private Drug Treatment Systems*. Washington, DC: National Academy Press.

Gido, Rosemary, and Ted Alleman. 1998/2002. *Turnstile Justice: Issues in American Justice,* 2nd ed. Upper Saddle River, NJ: Prentice Hall.

"Granholm Pushing to Change Sentencing Laws." 2007. *The Daily Telegram,* Adrian. July 16, A1.

Gray, Tara. 2002. *Exploring Corrections: A Book of Readings.* Boston: Allyn & Bacon.

Green, Michael. 1993. "Chronic Exposure to Violence and Poverty: Interventions that Work for Youth." *Crime & Delinquency* 39:1 (January), pp. 106–24.

Griffin, Marie. 2007. "Prison Gang Policy and Recidivism: Short-Term Management Benefits, Long-Term Consequences." *Criminology & Public Policy* 6:2 (May), pp. 223–30.

Grinstead, O., B. Faigeles, and B. Zack. 1997. "The Effectiveness of Peer HIV Education for Male Inmates Entering State Prison." *Journal of Health and Education* 28, pp. 531–37.

Gusfield, Joseph P. 1967. "Moral Passage: The Symbolic Process in Public Designations of Deviance." In Henry N. Pontell, Ed. *Social Deviance: Readings in Theory and Research,* 5th ed. Upper Saddle River, NJ: Prentice Hall, pp. 228–37.

Hall, Stuart, Chas Critcher, Tony Jeffers, John Clarke, and Brian Roberts. 1978. *Policing the Crisis: Mugging, the State and Law and Order.* London: MacMillan.

Haley, Alex, and Malcolm X. 1964. *The Autobiography of Malcolm X.* New York: Grove Press, Inc.

Harvey, David. 2000. "Time-Space Compression and the Rise of Modernism as a Cultural Force." In Frank Lechner and John Boli, Eds. *The Globalization Reader.* Malden, MA: Blackwell Publishers, pp. 134–44.

Hassine, Victor. 1996. *Life without Parole: Living in Prison Today.* Los Angeles: Roxbury Publishing Company.

Hayner, Norman S., and Ellis Ash. 1939. "The Prisoner Community as a Social Group." *American Sociological Review* 4 (June), pp. 362–70.

Hernandez, Raymond. 1996. "Give Them the Maximum: Small Towns Clamor for the Boon a Big Prison Could Bring." *New York Times.* February 26. In CFECP 1998 Conference Materials.

Heyman, Phillip B., and Mark H. Moore. 1996. "The Federal Role in Dealing with Violent Street Crime: Principles, Questions, and Cautions." *Annals of the American Academy of Political and Social Sciences.* In CFECP January 1998 Conference materials.

Higgins, Gina O'Connell. 1994. *Resilient Adults: Overcoming a Cruel Past.* San Francisco, CA: Jossey-Bass Publishers.

Huebner, Beth, Sean Varano, and Timothy Bynum. 2007. "Guns, Gangs, and Drugs: Recidivism among Serious, Young Offenders." *Criminology & Public Policy* 6:2. May.

Irwin, John. 1970. *The Felon.* Englewood Cliffs, NJ: Prentice Hall.

———. 1980. *Prisons in Turmoil.* Boston: Little, Brown.

———. 1985. *The Jail.* Berkeley: University of California Press.

———. 1985. "The Return of the Bogeyman." Keynote Address at American Society of Criminology, San Diego.

———. 2005. *The Warehouse Prison: Disposal of the New Dangerous Class.* Los Angeles: Roxbury Publishing Company.

———. 2006. "Prisons in Turmoil." In Edward J. Latessa and Alexander M. Holsinger. *Correctional Contexts: Contemporary and Classical Readings*. Los Angeles, CA: Roxbury Publishing Company, pp. 112–37.

Irwin, John, and James Austin. 1997. "It's About Time: America's Imprisonment Binge." In Edward J. Latessa and Alexander M. Holsinger. *Correctional Contexts: Contemporary and Classical Readings*, 3rd. ed. Los Angeles, CA: Roxbury Publishing Company, 2006.

Irwin, John, Vincent Schiraldi, and Jason Ziedenberg. 2000. "America's One Million Nonviolent Prisoners." *Social Justice* 27:2, pp. 135–47.

Jackson, George. 1970. *Soledad Brother: The Prison Letters of George Jackson*. New York: Bantam Books.

Jacobs, James B. 1977. *Stateville: The Penitentiary in Mass Society*. Chicago: The University of Chicago Press.

Jacobson, Michael. 2005. *Downsizing Prisons: How to Reduce Crime*. New York University Press.

Johnson, Robert. 1987/1996. *Hard Time: Understanding and Reforming the Prison*, 2nd ed. Belmont, CA: Wadsworth Publishing Company.

Johnson, Robert, and Hans Toch. 2000. *Crime and Punishment: Inside Views*. Los Angeles: Roxbury Publishing Company.

Kalinich, Davis. 1980. *The Inmate Economy*. Lexington, MA: D.C. Heath.

Kappeler, Victor E. 2004. "Inventing Criminal Justice: Myth and Social Construction." In Peter B. Kraska. *Theorizing Criminal Justice: Eight Essential Orientations*. Long Grove, IL: Waveland Press, pp. 167–76.

Kraska, Peter B. 2004. *Theorizing Criminal Justice: Eight Essential Orientations*. Long Grove, IL: Waveland Press.

Lansing State Journal. 2007. "Brown: Prevention, Not Prisons, Best Serves Public Safety." August 12. Op Ed.

Larmour, Marjorie S., and William S. Tregea. 2002. *The Imprisonment Binge: Or, The Great American Drug Bust* (unpublished).

Lawson, Jessica. 2005. "Lock Up a Corrections Career." *Decision Times*. February 15. At www.armytimes.com/story.php_F=1-292313-599975.php.

Levine, Barbara. 2007. Executive Director, Citizens Alliance on Prisons and Public Spending. August 13, personal communication.

Li, Guoha, Gordon S. Smith, and Susan P. Baker. 1994. "Drinking Behavior in Relation to Cause of Death Among U.S. Adults." *American Journal of Public Health* 84:9, pp. 1402–6.

Lipsky, Michael. 1980. *Street-Level Bureaucracy: Dilemmas of the Individual in Public Services*. New York: Russell Sage Foundation.

Lynch, James P., and William J. Sabol. 2001. "Prisoner Reentry in Perspective." *Prisoner Reentry and Community Justice*, National Institute of Justice Data Resources Program Workshop, ICPSR. Ann Arbor, MI, June 18–22.

Mannheim, Karl. 1938. *Ideology and Utopia*. New York: Harcourt, Brace & World/ Harvest Book.

Marlatt, G. Alan, Julian M. Somers, and Susan F. Tapert. 1993. "Harm Reduction: Application to Alcohol Abuse Problems." In Lisa Simon Onken, John D. Blaine, and John J. Boren, Eds. *Behavioral Treatments for Drug Abuse and Dependence*. Rockville, MD: National Institute on Drug Abuse, pp. 147–66.

Maruna, Shadd. 2001. *Making Good: How Ex-Convicts Reform and Rebuild Their Lives*. Washington, DC: American Psychological Association.

Marx, Karl. 1995. "Class Conflict Defines Society." In Lynn Barteck and Karen Mullin, Eds. *Enduring Issues in Sociology: Opposing Viewpoints*. San Diego, CA: Greenhaven Press, Inc.

Mauer, Marc. 1999. *Race to Incarcerate*, New York: The New Press.

Mauer, Marc, and Meda Chesney-Lind, Eds. 2002. *Invisible Punishment: The Collateral Consequences of Mass Imprisonment*. New York: The New Press.

MDOC. 1996. "Characteristics of Michigan Prisoners." Michigan Department of Corrections publication.

Miller, David. 1976/1989. *Social Justice*. Claredon Press: Oxford.

Miller, Gerald G. 1996. *Search and Destroy*. New York: Cambridge University Press.

Miller, Walter B. 1973/2004. "Ideology and Criminal Justice Policy: Some Current Issues." In Peter B. Kraska. *Theorizing Criminal Justice: Eight Essential Orientations*. Long Grove, IL: Waveland Press, pp. 110–20.

Mobley, Alan. 2003. "Convict Criminology: The Two-Legged Data Dilemma." In Jeffrey Ian Ross and Stephen C. Richards, Eds. *Convict Criminology*. Belmont, CA: Thomson/Wadsworth, pp. 209–25.

Moffit, Terrie F. 1997. "Adolescent-Limited and Life-Course Persistent Offending: A Complementary Pair of Developmental Theories." In Terence P. Thornberry Ed. *Developmental Theories of Crime and Delinquency*. New Brunswick, NJ: Transaction, pp. 11–54.

Morris, Norval, and Michael Tonry. 1990. *Between Prison and Probation: Intermediate Punishments in a Rational Sentencing System*. New York: Oxford University Press.

Musto, David F. 1991. "Opium, Cocaine and Marijuana in American History." *Scientific American* (July), pp. 40–47.

National Geographic. 1996. "Drugs in New York City." August.

National Institute of Justice (NIJ). 2001. "Prisoner Reentry and Community Justice." NIJ Data Resources Program Workshop, June 18–22. Ann Arbor, MI. Inter-University Consortium for Political and Social Research. (workshop working materials).

Newbold, Greg. 2003. "Rehabilitating Criminals: It Ain't That Easy." In Jeffrey Ian Ross and Stephen C. Richards, Eds. *Convict Criminology*. Belmont, CA: Thomson/Wadsworth, pp. 150–69.

Newman, Annabel. 1993. "Prison Literacy: Implications for Program and Assessment Policy." Technical Report TR-93-1. Philadelphia: National Center on Adult Literacy.

Obermaier, Otto G. 1996. "Crime Isn't Always a Federal Case." *The National Law Journal*. September 23. In CFECP 1998 Conference materials.

Owen, Barbara. 1998. *In The Mix: Struggle and Survival in a Woman's Prison*. Albany: State University of New York Press.

Packer, Herbert. 1968/2004. "Two Models of the Criminal Justice Process." In Peter B. Kraska. *Theorizing Criminal Justice: Eight Essential Orientations*. Long Grove, IL: Waveland Press, pp. 85–100.

Page, Clarence. 2008. "A *Wire* War vs. The Drug War." Daryl Cagle's *The Cagle Post Cartoons and Commentaries*, March: search www.caglepost.com.

Parenti, Christian. 1999/2004. "Crisis and Control." In Peter B. Kraska. *Theorizing Criminal Justice: Eight Essential Orientations*. Long Grove, IL: Waveland Press, pp. 271–75.

Patterson, Gerald, and Marion Forgatch. 1987. *Parents and Adolescents: Living Together, Part I: The Basics*. Eugene, OR: Castalia Publishing Company.

Perrone, Dina, and Travis C. Pratt. 2006. "Comparing the Quality of Confinement and Cost-Effectiveness of Public versus Private Prisons: What We Know, Why We Do Not Know More, and Where to Go From Here." In Edward J. Latessa and Alexander M. Holsinger. *Correctional Contexts: Contemporary and Classical Readings*. Los Angeles, CA: Roxbury Publishing Company, pp. 474–86.

Petersilia, Joan. 2003. *When Prisoners Come Home: Parole and Prisoner Reentry*. New York: Oxford University Press.

Pollock, Jocelyn, Ed. 1997. *Prison: Today and Tomorrow*. Gaithersburg, MD: Aspen Publishers, Inc.

Pratt, John, David Brown, Mark Brown, Simon Hallsworth, and Wayne Morrison. 2005. *The New Punitiveness: Trends, Theories, Perspectives*. Portland, OR: Willan Publishing.

Radelet, Louis A., and David L. Carter. 1994. *The Police and the Community*, 5th ed. Englewood Cliffs, NJ: Prentice Hall.

Reiman, Jeffrey. 2004. *The Rich Get Richer and the Poor Get Prison: Ideology, Class and Criminal Justice*, Boston: Pearson/Allyn and Bacon.

Reisig, Michael. 1998. Professor Criminal Justice, Florida State University. Personal communication.

Richards, Stephen C. 2003. "My Journey through the Federal Bureau of Prisons." In Jeffrey Ian Ross and Stephen C. Richards, Eds. *Convict Criminology*. Belmont, CA: Wadsworth/Thomson, pp. 120–49.

Richards, Stephen C., and Richard S. Jones. 1996. "Beating the Perpetual Incarceration Machine: Overcoming Structural Impediments to Re-entry." In Shadd Maruna and Russ Immarigeon, Eds. *After Crime and Punishment: Pathways to Offender Reintegration*. Portland, OR: Willan Publishing, pp. 201–32.

Rifkin, Jeremy. 2006. *The European Dream*. New York: Basic Books.

Riley, Diane. n.d. "The Harm Reduction Model: Pragmatic Approaches to Drug Use from the Area between Intolerance and Neglect." Canadian Center on Substance Abuse. www.ccsa.ca/eng/pages/home.aspx.

Robbins, Ira. 1997. "The Case against the Prison-Industrial Complex." *Public Interest Law Review* (Winter). In CFECP 1998 Conference materials.

Rosenbaum, Dennis P., Arthur J. Lurigio, and Robert C. Davis. 1998. *The Prevention of Crime: Social and Situational Strategies*. Belmont, CA: West/Wadsworth.

Ross, Jeffrey Ian, and Stephen C. Richards. 2002. *Behind Bars: Surviving Prison*. Belmont, CA: Alpha.

———. 2003. *Convict Criminology*. Belmont, CA: Wadsworth/Thomson.

Russell, Kathryn K. 1998. "Affirmative Race Law." In Peter B. Kraska. *Theorizing Criminal Justice: Eight Essential Orientations*. Long Grove, IL: Waveland Press, pp. 245–56.

Santos, Michael G. 2007. *Inside: Life Behind Bars in America*. Gordonsville, VA: St. Martin's Griffin.

Sartre, Jean Paul. 1952. *St. Genet*. Paris: Gallimard.

Scheingold, Stuart A. 1982/2004. "Crime, Culture, and Political Conflict." In Peter B. Kraska. *Theorizing Criminal Justice: Eight Essential Orientations.* Long Grove, IL: Waveland Press, pp. 126–36.

Schmalleger, Frank. 2001. *Criminal Justice Today: An Introductory Text for the 21st Century,* 6th ed. Upper Saddle River, NJ: Prentice Hall.

Scott, Richard W. 1992. *Organizations: Rational, Natural, and Open Systems.* 3rd ed. Englewood Cliffs, NJ: Prentice Hall.

Segre, Sandro. 2003. *Controlling Illegal Drugs: A Comparative Study.* Trans. Nora Stern. New York: Aldine de Gruyter.

Selke, William. 1993. *Prisons in Crisis.* Bloomington: Indiana University Press.

Shaw, Clifford. 1930/1996. *The Jackroller: A Delinquent Boy's Own Story.* Chicago: University of Chicago Press.

Sheehey, Gail. 1976. *Passages: Predictable Crises in Adult Life.* New York: E. P. Dutton.

Shelden, Randall G. 2008. *Controlling the Dangerous Classes: A History of Criminal Justice in America,* 2nd ed. Boston: Pearson/A&B.

Shubinski, Robert. 2006. "Smoking Statistics." www.unr.edu/homepage/shubinsk/whosmok1.html.

Simon, David, and Edward Burns. 1997. *The Corner: A Year in the Life of an Inner City Neighborhood.* New York: Broadway Books.

Simon, Jonathan. 2007. *Governing through Crime: How the War on Crime Transformed American Democracy and Created a Culture of Fear.* New York: Oxford University Press.

Spergel, Irving A. 1995. *The Youth Gang Problem: A Community Approach.* New York: Oxford University Press.

Stenson, Kevin. 1991. "Making Sense of Crime Control." In Kevin Stenson and David Crowell, Eds. *The Politics of Crime.* London: Sage, pp. 1–32.

Sullivan, Dennis, and Larry Tifft. 2001. *Restorative Justice: Healing the Foundations of Our Everyday Lives.* Monsey, NY: Willow Tree Press.

———. 2005. *Handbook of Restorative Justice.* Routledge: Taylor and Francis Group.

Sutherland, Edwin. 1947. "Differential Association." In Henry Pontell, Ed. *Social Deviance: Readings in Theory & Research,* 5th ed. Upper Saddle River, NJ: Pearson/Prentice Hall, pp. 139–41.

Sykes, Gresham. 1958. *The Society of Captives: A Study of a Maximum Security Prison.* Princeton, NJ: Princeton University Press.

Terry, Charles M. 2003. *The Fellas: Overcoming Prison and Addiction.* Belmont, CA: Wadsworth/Thomson Learning.

Thomas, Paulette. 1994. "Rural Regions Look to Prisons for Prosperity." *The Wall Street Journal.* July 11. In CFECP 1998 Conference Materials.

Tonry, Michael. 1994. "Racial Disproportions in U.S. Prisons." *British Journal of Criminology* 34, pp. 97–155. In Geroge F. Cole, Marc G. Gertz, and Amy Bunger. *The Criminal Justice System: Politics and Policies,* 9th ed. Belmont, CA: Wadsworth/Thomson Learning, pp. 328–48.

———. 1995. *Malign Neglect: Race, Crime, and Punishment in America.* New York: Oxford University Press.

———. 1999. "Why Are U.S. Incarcerations Rates So High?" In *Crime and Delinquency* 45:4 (October), pp. 419–37.

————. 2008. "Crime and Human Rights—How Political Paranoia, Protestant Fundamentalism, and Constitutional Obsolescence Combined to Devastate Black America: The American Society of Criminology 2007 Presidential Address." *Criminology* 46:1 (February).

Travis, Jeremy. 2002. "Invisible Punishment: An Instrument of Social Exclusion." In Marc Mauer and Meda Chesney-Lind, Eds. *Invisible Punishment: The Collateral Consequences of Mass Imprisonment.* New York: The New Press, pp. 15–36.

Tregea, William S. 1998. "Prison Post-Secondary, Recidivism, and the Current Political Climate." Research report for Center on Crime, Communities, and Culture, Open Society Institute (Soros Foundation) (unpublished).

————. 2001. "Prison Education and Skills Training in the Transition to Community." A presentation in collaboration with John Linton, U.S. Department of Education, at the "Prisoner Reentry and Community Justice" National Institute of Justice (NIJ) and ICPSR Data Resources Program Summer Program Workshop, June 18–22, 2001. Institute for Social Research. Ann Arbor, MI.

————. 2002. "State Must Cut Prison Costs: Granholm Can Lead the Way to a Better Corrections Policy." *Lansing State Journal.* December 15, 15A.

————. 2003. "Twenty Years Teaching College in Prison." In Jeffrey Ian Ross and Stephen C. Richards, Eds. *Convict Criminology.* Belmont, CA: Wadsworth/Thomson, pp. 309–32.

Tregea, William S., and Marjorie S. Larmour. 2005. *The Deviant World: Prison Life Stories and Criminology* (unpublished).

————. 2005c. *The Real World: Prisoner Views on Reentry, Job Training and Education* (unpublished).

Trout, Grafton, William S. Tregea, and Geoffry Simmons. 1968. "Youth Makes Itself Heard: Changing Participational Contexts." *AAUW Journal* (May).

Trout, Grafton, and William S. Tregea. 1971. "The Social Problem Tradition: Crisis or Impasse?" Paper delivered at the Society of the Study of Social Problems. Denver, CO. August.

Tunnel, Kenneth D. 2000. *Living Off Crime.* Chicago: Burnham Publishers.

U.S. Census Bureau. 2000. "2000 Census of Population and Housing: Profile of General Demographic Characterization."

U.S. House of Representatives. 2008. "House Select Committee on Energy Independence and Global Warming." www.house.globalwarming.gov.

Useem, Bert, and Peter Kimball. 1991. *States of Seige: U.S. Prison Riots 1971–1986.* New York: Oxford University Press.

Useem, Bert, Raymond V. Liedka, and Anne Morrison Piehl. 2003. "Popular Support for the Prison Build-up." *Punishment & Society* 5:1 (January), pp. 5–32.

Useem, Bert, and Anne Morrison Piehl. 2008. *The Prison State: The Challenge of Mass Incarceration.* New York: Cambridge University Press.

Vera Institute of Justice. 2006. "Dollars and Sentences: Legislators' Views on Prisons, Punishments, and the Budget Crisis." In Edward J. Latessa and Alexander M. Holsinger. *Correctional Contexts: Contemporary and Classical Readings.* Los Angeles, CA: Roxbury Publishing Company, pp. 474–86.

von Solinge, Tim Boekhout. 2004. *Dealing with Drugs in Europe: An Investigation of European Drug Control Experience: France, The Netherlands, and Sweden.* The Hague: Bju Legal Publishers.

Wacquant, Loic. 2002. "Deadly Symbiosis: Rethinking Race and Imprisonment in Twenty-first Century America." *Boston Review*. April/May. Internet.

———. 2006. "Hyperghetto and Hyperincarceration." Presentation, American Society of Criminology annual meetings. November 14, 2006., Cambridge: Los Angeles, CA.

———. 2008. *Deadly Symbiosis: Race and the Rise of the Penal State*. Polity Press.

Walker, Samuel. 1992/2004. "Origins of the Contemporary Criminal Justice Paradigm: The American Bar Foundation Survey, 1953–1969." In Peter B. Kraska. *Theorizing Criminal Justice: Eight Essential Orientations*. Long Grove, IL: Waveland Press, pp. 46–68.

Walsh, Edward. 1994. "Strapped Small Towns Try to Lock Up Prisons." *New York Times*. December 24. In CFECP 1998 Conference materials.

Wanberg, Kenneth, and Harvey Milkman. 1998. *Criminal Conduct and Substance Abuse Treatment: Strategies for Self-Improvement and Change—The Participants Workbook*. Thousand Oaks, CA: Sage Publishers.

Webb, Gary. 1999. *Dark Alliance*. New York: Seven Stories Press.

Wenda, Walter. 1997. "The Relationship between Life-Skills Literacy and Vocational Education and Self-Perception of Eleven Domains and Global Self-Worth of Adult Incarcerated Males." *Journal of Correctional Education* 47:2, pp. 74–85.

Wesson, Donal R., and David E. Smith. 1985. "Cocaine: Treatment Perspectives." In Nicholas J. Kozel and Edgar H. Adams, Eds. *Cocaine Use in America: Epidemiological and Clinical Perspectives*. Rockville, MD; National Institutes on Drug Abuse.

Western, Bruce. 2006. *Punishment and Inequality in America*. New York: Russell Sage Foundation.

Wicker, Tom. 1987. "Drugs and Alcohol." *New York Times*. May 13, 27.

Williamson, Thad, David Imbroscio, and Gar Alperovitz. 2003. *Making a Place for Community*. New York: Routledge.

Wilson, William Julius. 1996. *When Work Disappears: The World of the New Urban Poor*. New York: Vintage Books.

Wright, Kevin N. 1981/2004. "The Desirability of Goal Conflict within the Criminal Justice System." In Peter B. Kraska. *Theorizing Criminal Justice: Eight Essential Orientations*. Long Grove, IL: Waveland Press, pp. 121–25.

Wright, Richard. 1966. *Native Son*. New York: Harper & Row.

Wright, Richard T., and Scott Decker. 1994. *Burglars on the Job: Streetlife and Residential Break-ins*. Boston: Northeastern University Press.

Zatz, Marjorie S. 1987/2004. "Chicano Youth Gangs and Crime: The Creation of a Moral Panic." In Peter B. Kraska. *Theorizing Criminal Justice: Eight Essential Orientations*. Long Grove, IL: Waveland Press, pp. 156–66.

Zimring, Frank. 2006. "Why the Incarceration Boom May Not End." Plenary Session, American Society of Criminology. November 3. Los Angeles, CA.

———. 2007. *The Great American Crime Decline*. New York: Oxford University Press.

Zimring, Frank E., and Gordon Hawkins. 1997. *Crime is Not The Problem: Lethal Violence in America*. New York: Oxford University Press.

Zinberg, Norman. 1984. *Drug, Set, and Setting: The Basis for Controlled Intoxicant Use*. New Haven, CT: Yale University Press.

Index

About the Authors

William S. Tregea taught prison college classes from 1981 to 2000 in eleven prisons in Michigan and California, writing "Twenty Years Teaching Prison College" for *Convict Criminology*, by Ross & Richards (2003 Wadsworth). He has continued to teach volunteer prison classes (2001–present). From these prison-teaching experiences he has gathered, with his coauthor, Marjorie Larmour, graphic prisoner essays. Tregea wrote a timely report on "Prison Postsecondary Education" (OSI 1998), led a prison post-secondary education state-of-the-art research session (ACJS 1999), and presented a workshop on prison college effect on lowering recidivism at the June, 2001, NIJ-sponsored "Prisoner Reentry and Community Justice" workshop (ISR–Ann Arbor). Bill Tregea helped to found the Michigan STEPP Coalition (1998), putting out a newsletter and holding meetings in 2002 and 2003 to push Michigan toward renewed opportunity for accredited post-secondary education in Michigan prisons. He is a founding member and continuing board member of the Citizens Alliance on Prisons and Public Spending (www.capps-mi.org), and he serves on the Michigan Prisoner Reentry Initiative (MPRI) Steering Committee for Lenawee County

William Tregea is professor and chair of the Department of Sociology, Social Work, and Criminal Justice at Adrian College, MI, and is the director of the Bachelor of Criminal Justice program there. In 2006 he was awarded the Ross Newsom Award for Outstanding Teaching. He has used the *The Prisoners' World* in earlier drafts successfully in his criminal justice classes where he also takes his students into the prison as part of his volunteer classes. Tregea has a Ph.D. (1993) in sociology, a M.S. (1999)

in criminal justice and an M.A. (1968) in sociology, all from Michigan State University. He has taught with Jackson, Lansing and Montcalm community colleges, and Kings College (PA), Central Michigan University and Michigan State University.

The late **Marjorie S. Larmour** (1920–2007) was a teacher and a writer, worked as a copywriter, story writer, advertising copywriter, newspaper and TV columnist, information specialist and publications editor. She also taught prison college classes for twenty years (1980–1999) in twelve Michigan prisons and at San Quentin, CA. She earned an M.A. in journalism from University of California–Berkeley, and had completed sixty credits of Ph.D. work at Michigan State University. She authored general audience books on travel and the health care of the aging, as well as drafts of four books on "the prison campus."